D0083267

THE COLLECTED WORKS OF
SAMUEL TAYLOR COLERIDGE · 10

ON THE CONSTITUTION OF THE CHURCH AND STATE

General Editor: KATHLEEN COBURN
Associate Editor: BART WINER

THE COLLECTED WORKS

1. LECTURES 1795: ON POLITICS AND RELIGION

2. THE WATCHMAN

3. ESSAYS ON HIS TIMES

4. THE FRIEND

5. LECTURES 1808–1819: ON LITERATURE

6. LAY SERMONS

7. BIOGRAPHIA LITERARIA

8. LECTURES 1818–1819: ON THE HISTORY OF PHILOSOPHY

9. AIDS TO REFLECTION

10. ON THE CONSTITUTION OF THE CHURCH AND STATE

11. SHORTER WORKS AND FRAGMENTS

12. MARGINALIA

13. LOGIC

14. TABLE TALK

15. OPUS MAXIMUM

16. POETICAL WORKS

GENERAL INDEX

SAMUEL TAYLOR COLERIDGE

from a portrait painted by Moses Haughton, 1832

Christ's Hospital; reproduced by kind permission

THE COLLECTED WORKS OF

Samuel Taylor Coleridge

On the Constitution of the Church and State

EDITED BY

John Colmer

ROUTLEDGE & KEGAN PAUL

BOLLINGEN SERIES LXXV
PRINCETON UNIVERSITY PRESS

The Collected Works, sponsored by Bollingen Foundation,
is published in Great Britain
by Routledge & Kegan Paul Ltd
Broadway House, 68–74 Carter Lane, London EC4V 5EL
ISBN 0-7100-8107-3
and in the United States of America
by Princeton University Press, Princeton, New Jersey
ISBN 0-691-09877-8
LCC 74-32569
The Collected Works constitutes
the seventy-fifth publication in Bollingen Series

The present work is number 10 of the Collected Works

Designed by Richard Garnett
Printed in the United States of America
by Princeton University Press

THIS EDITION
OF THE WORKS OF
SAMUEL TAYLOR COLERIDGE
IS DEDICATED
IN GRATITUDE TO
THE FAMILY EDITORS
IN EACH GENERATION

CONTENTS

LIST OF ILLUSTRATIONS

ACKNOWLEDGMENTS

I OWE a special debt of gratitude to Miss Kathleen Coburn, whose kindness and understanding have sustained me in my long editorial labours and whose immense scholarship has been a constant inspiration and always so generously put at my disposal. To Mr Bart Winer too I owe a great debt.

My task has been lightened as a result of the editions that have already appeared in this series, and I should like to thank Barbara Rooke, Lewis Patton, and Peter Mann for all the invaluable help they have provided. The works published on Coleridge's later political writings by David P. Calleo, William F. Kennedy, R. J. White, Basil Willey, Raymond Williams, and Carl R. Woodring have also influenced me in ways that will be obvious to the reader from my Introduction and notes. For the solution of a particularly elusive source in St Augustine I am grateful to Mr Gerald Bonner of the University of Durham; for comment on the historical and political background I owe a special debt to Professor Austin Gough, who kindly read a draft of my Introduction and drew attention to interesting Continental parallels; for information about Coleridge's political journalism and for transcripts of passages in Egerton 2801 I am grateful to Professor David V. Erdman; for the solution of several problems I owe a debt to Dr John Barrell, whose edition of *Church and State* appeared in 1972; for tracing classical sources and for supplying translations I am indebted to the following: Mr A. French, Mr R. F. Newbold, Mr R. F. Willetts, but especially to Mrs G. J. R. Arnold. And for help with Biblical allusions to Mr Michael J. Tolley, and for legal allusions to Dr John Finnis.

Many libraries and their staffs have been exceptionally co-operative. It is impossible to thank them all, but I should like to record my gratitude to the British Museum and its staff, to Victoria College Library and its staff, to Mr I. D. Raymond and the staff of the Barr Smith Library, Adelaide, and to Mr Peter Pagan for providing special research facilities in the Public Library at Bath in 1967.

At an early stage in my editorial work, the award of a Senior Research Fellowship at the University of Birmingham gave me time to explore some of the relevant background to Coleridge's ideas on Church and State. I am particularly grateful to Professor T. J. B. Spencer for his kindness and hospitality during this period. A generous grant from the Bollingen Foundation enabled me to examine printed and manuscript holdings in American and Canadian libraries, and I am grateful to the following libraries for allowing me to publish material gathered then: Berg Collection, The New York Public Library; Pierpont Morgan Library, and the University Libraries of Harvard, Yale, and Victoria College, Toronto. A later grant from the Princeton University Press allowed me to visit the British Museum at a time when I urgently needed to carry out final checking of manuscripts. I should also like to thank the University of Adelaide for granting me study leave in 1966–7 and 1973–4, and for support from its research funds.

For the skilful typing I should like to thank Mrs W. Reeves, Mrs Christine Pullen, and Mrs Joan Craik, and for assistance in assembling research materials, Miss Helen Brown and Miss Robin Eaden.

From time to time my wife has given very substantial help, often on occasions when her own work was making severe demands on her precious time. For this and her constant encouragement I am deeply grateful.

Adelaide, S. Australia JOHN COLMER

EDITORIAL PRACTICE, SYMBOLS, AND ABBREVIATIONS

THE text of the present edition follows Coleridge's second edition of 1830, except for the correction of obvious printer's errors. Corrections given in Coleridge's annotated copies are reproduced in the textual notes. Two editions were published in Coleridge's lifetime, both dated 1830, although the first edition actually appeared in December 1829. Since Coleridge himself revised the text of the second edition, expanding it in the process, this forms the basis of the copy text. Henry Nelson Coleridge edited a third edition, which was published, together with a second edition of the *Lay Sermons*, five years after Coleridge's death, in 1839. The phrase on the title-page, "Edited from the Author's Corrected Copies with Notes", would seem to apply only to the *Lay Sermons*. Since the revisions of *Church and State* cannot be traced back to copies marked by the author and consist mainly of corrections of syntax, idiom, and punctuation, they seem to have no special authority and are not therefore included in the textual apparatus. However, H. N. Coleridge's corrections of Coleridge's Greek quotations have been silently adopted where appropriate. His excellent notes have also been used occasionally, with due acknowledgment. All significant variants between first and second editions are recorded in the textual notes, together with variants in copies annotated by the author.

There are fragments of original manuscripts in the British Museum (Add MS 34225 ff 115–27^{v} and Egerton 2001 ff 204–7^{v}) for two small sections of the text (pp 53–75 and 139–44). In Editor's Appendix C, these fragments are printed literatim, including Coleridge's cancellations, for the light they may throw on his process of composition.

The two following copies contain revisions in Coleridge's hand:

Copy G. A copy of the second edition, inscribed to the Rev James Gillman, now in the Yale University Library.

Copy W. A copy of the second edition, inscribed to W. Wordsworth, now in the Harvard University Library.

Variants are recorded in the textual notes. Further details of these and other presentation copies appear in Appendix F.

Coleridge's footnotes are indicated by symbols (*, †, etc) and are printed full measure. Editor's footnotes are numbered and (when not too brief) printed in double columns. The order of the editor's footnotes follows (perhaps Coleridgian) logic; i.e. it is assumed that when the text contains an asterisk or a dagger the reader then turns from text to note and then goes back again. The editor's footnotes, which are sometimes notes on Coleridge's footnotes, follow that order. Thus the footnote indicators within the text may leap from 1 to 5, notes 2–4 being notes on Coleridge's footnotes.

Textual notes ($^{a-b}$, etc) at the foot of the page, preceding the editor's notes, give the earlier wording in the first edition and manuscripts, and revised wording in annotated copies.

The editions referred to in the editor's footnotes are, when they are known, those Coleridge used; "see" before the edition indicates that it is not necessarily the edition Coleridge cites or quotes (though it may be an edition he is known to have used).

The text of all quotations from Coleridge's marginal comments in books has been made to conform to the reading adopted in the manuscript of the *Marginalia* in the *Collected Works*, even where, for the reader's convenience, a reference is supplied to another source—for example, *Coleridge on the Seventeenth Century* ed R. F. Brinkley (Durham, N.C. 1955).

The following symbols are used in quoting from manuscript (with "wild") as an example):

[wild]	A reading supplied by the editor.
[?wild]	An uncertain reading.
[?wild/world]	Possible alternative readings.
⌈wild⌉	A tentative reading (owing to obliterations, torn paper, etc).
[. . .]	An illegible word or phrase.
⟨wild⟩	A later interpolation by Coleridge.

ABBREVIATIONS

(In the works listed, place of publication is London unless otherwise noted)

AR (1825)	S. T. Coleridge *Aids to Reflection* (1825).
BE	*Biographia Epistolaris* ed A. Turnbull (2 vols 1911).
BL (1817)	S. T. Coleridge *Biographia Literaria* (2 vols 1817).
BL (1907)	S. T. Coleridge *Biographia Literaria* ed John Shawcross (2 vols Oxford 1907).
BL (1956)	S. T. Coleridge *Biographia Literaria* ed G. Watson (1956).
B Mag	*Blackwood's Magazine* (Edinburgh and London 1817–).
BM	British Museum
C	Samuel Taylor Coleridge

C&S (1st ed)	S. T. Coleridge *On the Constitution of the Church and State, According to the Idea of Each* (1830 but appeared Dec 1829).
C&S (2nd ed)	S. T. Coleridge *On the Constitution of the Church and State, According to the Idea of Each* (1830).
C&S (3rd ed)	S. T. Coleridge *On the Constitution of the Church and State, According to the Idea of Each* ed H. N. Coleridge (1839).
C&S (Ev ed)	S. T. Coleridge *On the Constitution of the Church and State, According to the Idea of Each* ed John Barrell (1972).
C at H	L. E. (G.) Watson *Coleridge at Highgate* (1925).
CC	*The Collected Works of Samuel Taylor Coleridge* (London and New York 1969–).
CIS (1840)	S. T. Coleridge *Confessions of an Inquiring Spirit* ed H. N. Coleridge (1840).
CL	*Collected Letters of Samuel Taylor Coleridge* ed Earl Leslie Griggs (6 vols Oxford and New York 1956–71).
C Life (G)	James Gillman *The Life of Samuel Taylor Coleridge* (1838).
C Life (H)	Lawrence Hanson *The Life of Samuel Taylor Coleridge, the Early Years* (1938).
C Life (JDC)	James Dykes Campbell *Samuel Taylor Coleridge* (1894).
CM	S. T. Coleridge *Marginalia* ed George Whalley (in ms). *The Collected Works of Samuel Taylor Coleridge* XII.
CN	*The Notebooks of Samuel Taylor Coleridge* ed Kathleen Coburn (New York, Princeton, N. J. and London 1957–).
Conciones	S. T. Coleridge *Conciones ad Populum. Or Addresses to the People* (Bristol 1795).
Copy G	*On the Constitution of the Church and State* (2nd ed 1830), inscribed to the Rev James Gillman and annotated by Coleridge.
Copy W	*On the Constitution of the Church and State* (2nd ed 1830), inscribed to William Wordsworth and annotated by Coleridge.
C Talker	R. W. Armour and R. F. Howes *Coleridge the Talker* (1949).
C 17th C	*Coleridge on the Seventeenth Century* ed R. F. Brinkley (Durham, N. C. 1955).
DC	Derwent Coleridge
DNB	*Dictionary of National Biography* (1885–).
DW	Dorothy Wordsworth

Ed Rev	*The Edinburgh Review* (Edinburgh and London 1802–1929).
EHC	Ernest Hartley Coleridge
EOT	S. T. Coleridge *Essays on His Own Times, Forming a Second Series of "The Friend"* ed Sara Coleridge (3 vols 1850).
EOT (*CC*)	S. T. Coleridge *Essays on His Times* ed David Erdman (3 vols London and Princeton, N. J. 1976). *The Collected Works of Samuel Taylor Coleridge* III.
Friend (1809–10)	S. T. Coleridge *The Friend* ([Penrith] 1809–10).
Friend (1818)	S. T. Coleridge *The Friend* (3 vols 1818).
Friend (*CC*)	S. T. Coleridge *The Friend* ed Barbara E. Rooke (2 vols London and Princeton, N. J. 1969). *The Collected Works of Samuel Taylor Coleridge* IV.
Hansard	*The Parliamentary Debates*. T. C. Hansard. New Series; commencing with the accession of George IV.
HC	Hartley Coleridge
HCR	Henry Crabb Robinson
HEHL	Henry E. Huntington Library and Art Gallery, San Marino, Cal.
HNC	Henry Nelson Coleridge
H Works	*The Complete Works of William Hazlitt* ed P. P. Howe (21 vols 1930–4).
House	Humphry House *Coleridge* (1953).
IS	*Inquiring Spirit, a New Presentation of Coleridge from His Published and Unpublished Prose Writings* ed Kathleen Coburn (1951).
JDC	James Dykes Campbell
L	*Letters of Samuel Taylor Coleridge* ed E. H. Coleridge (2 vols 1895).
L&L	*Coleridge on Logic and Learning* ed Alice D. Snyder (1929).
LCL	Loeb Classical Library
Lects 1795 (*CC*)	S. T. Coleridge *Lectures 1795: On Politics and Religion* ed Lewis Patton and Peter Mann (London and Princeton, N. J. 1971). *The Collected Works of Samuel Taylor Coleridge* I.
LL	*The Letters of Charles Lamb to Which Are Added Those of His Sister Mary Lamb* ed E. V. Lucas (3 vols 1935).
LR	*The Literary Remains of Samuel Taylor Coleridge* ed H. N. Coleridge (4 vols 1836–9).
LRR	S. T. Coleridge Six Lectures on Revealed Religion,

	Its Corruptions and Political Views. Ms transcript by E. H. Coleridge.
LS	S. T. Coleridge *A Lay Sermon, Addressed to the Higher and Middle Classes, on the Existing Distresses and Discontents* (1817).
LS (*CC*)	S. T. Coleridge *A Lay Sermon* ed R. J. White (London and Princeton, N. J. 1972). In *Lay Sermons: The Collected Works of Samuel Taylor Coleridge* VI.
MC	*Coleridge's Miscellaneous Criticism* ed T. M. Raysor (Cambridge, Mass. 1936).
Method	*S. T. Coleridge's Treatise on Method as Published in the Encyclopaedia Metropolitana* ed Alice D. Snyder (1934).
Migne *PG*	*Patriologiae cursus completus...Series Graeca* ed J. P. Migne (162 vols Paris 1857–1912).
Migne *PL*	*Patriologiae cursus completus...Series Latina* ed J. P. Migne (221 vols Paris 1844–64).
Misc	S. T. Coleridge *Miscellanies, Aesthetic and Literary; to Which Is Added "The Theory of Life"* ed T. Ashe (1885).
MPL	S. T. Coleridge *A Moral and Political Lecture* (Bristol [1795]).
M Post	*The Morning Post* (1772–1937).
Mrs C	Sara (Fricker) Coleridge
N	Notebook (numbered or lettered) of S. T. Coleridge
NED	S. T. Coleridge *Notes on English Divines* ed Derwent Coleridge (2 vols 1853).
N F°	Coleridge's folio notebook, now in the Henry E. Huntington Library
N Q	Coleridge's notebook, now in the Berg Collection, New York Public Library.
NTP	S. T. Coleridge *Notes, Theological, Political and Miscellaneous* ed Derwent Coleridge (1853).
NYPL	New York Public Library
OED	*Oxford English Dictionary* (13 vols Oxford 1933).
Omniana	*Omniana, or Horae Otiosiores* ed Robert Southey with articles by S. T. Coleridge (2 vols 1812).
PD	S. T. Coleridge *The Plot Discovered; or, An Address to the People Against Ministerial Treason* (Bristol 1795).
Phil Trans	*Philosophical Transactions of the Royal Society* (1665–1886).

P Lects (1949)	*The Philosophical Lectures of Samuel Taylor Coleridge* ed Kathleen Coburn (London and New York 1949).
PML	Pierpont Morgan Library
Poole	M. E. Sandford *Thomas Poole and His Friends* (2 vols 1888).
P Speeches	*The Speeches of the Late Right Honourable Sir Robert Peel, delivered in the House of Commons* (4 vols 1853).
PW (EHC)	*The Complete Poetical Works of Samuel Taylor Coleridge* ed E. H. Coleridge (2 vols Oxford 1912).
PW (JDC)	*The Poetical Works of Samuel Taylor Coleridge* ed J. D. Campbell (1893).
QR	*The Quarterly Review* (London and Edinburgh 1809–).
Remarks...Peel's Bill	S. T. Coleridge *Remarks on the Objections which have been urged against the Principle of Sir Robert Peel's Bill* [1818].
RS	Robert Southey
SC	Sara Coleridge
SH	Sara Hutchinson
SM (1816)	S. T. Coleridge *The Statesman's Manual; or, the Bible, the Best Guide to Political Skill and Foresight. A Lay-Sermon Addressed to the Higher Classes of Society* (1816).
SM (*CC*)	S. T. Coleridge *The Stateman's Manual* ed R. J. White (London and Princeton, N. J. 1972). In *Lay Sermons: The Collected Works of Samuel Taylor Coleridge* VI.
TL (1848)	S. T. Coleridge *Hints Towards the Formation of a More Comprehensive Theory of Life* ed Seth B. Watson (1848).
TT	*Specimens of Table Talk of the Late Samuel Taylor Coleridge* ed H. N. Coleridge (2nd ed 1836).
V&A	Victoria and Albert Museum, London
VCL	Victoria College Library, University of Toronto
VS	*Victorian Studies* (Indiana 1957–).
WL (*L*)	*Letters of William and Dorothy Wordsworth; the Later Years* ed Ernest de Selincourt (3 vols Oxford 1939).
WL (*M* rev)	*Letters of William and Dorothy Wordsworth; the Middle Years* ed Ernest de Selincourt, revised Mary Moorman and A. G. Hill (2 vols Oxford 1969–71).
WPW	*The Poetical Works of William Wordsworth* ed Ernest de Selincourt and Helen Darbishire (5 vols Oxford 1940–9).
WW	William Wordsworth

CHRONOLOGICAL TABLE
1772–1834

(public events to the final publication of *On the Constitution of the Church and State*)

1772	(21 Oct) C b at Ottery St Mary, Devonshire, to the Rev John and Ann (Bowdon) Coleridge, youngest of their 10 children	George III king (1760–1820) Wordsworth 2 years old Scott 1 year old *M Post* began
1774		Southey b
1775		American War of Independence C. Lamb b
1776		Adam Smith *Wealth of Nations* Gibbon *Decline and Fall*
1778		Hazlitt b Rousseau and Voltaire d
1780		(Jun) Gordon Riots
1781	(Oct) Death of C's father	Kant *Kritik der reinen Vernunft* Schiller *Die Räuber*
1782	(Jul) Enrolled at Christ's Hospital preparatory school for girls and boys, Hertford (Sept) Christ's Hospital School, London, with C. Lamb, G. Dyer, T. F. Middleton, Robert Allen, J. M. Gutch, Le Grice brothers; met Evans family	Priestley *Corruptions of Christianity* Rousseau *Confessions*
1783		Pitt's first ministry (–1801)
1784		Samuel Johnson d
1785		De Quincey b Paley *Principles of Moral and Political Philosophy*
1789		(14 Jul) French Revolution Blake *Songs of Innocence* Bowles *Sonnets*
1790		Burke *Reflections on the Revolution in France*
1791	(Sept) Jesus College, Cambridge, Exhibitioner, Sizar, Rustat Scholar; met S. Butler, Frend, Porson, C. Wordsworth, Wrangham	(Mar) John Wesley d Paine *Rights of Man* pt I (pt II 1792) Boswell *Life of Johnson* Anti-Jacobin riots at Birmingham

1792	(3 Jul) Encaenia, C's prize-winning Greek Sapphic *Ode on the Slave-Trade*	Pitt's attack on the slave-trade Fox's Libel Bill
1793	(May) Attended Cambridge trial of Frend (7 Nov) First poem in *Morning Chronicle* (2 Dec) Enlisted in 15th Light Dragoons as Silas Tomkyn Comberbache	(21 Jan) Louis XVI executed (1 Feb) France declared war on England and Holland (Mar–Dec) Revolt of La Vendée (16 Oct) Marie Antoinette executed (16 Oct) John Hunter d Irish Act to admit RC's to commissions up to rank of colonel Godwin *Political Justice* Wordsworth *An Evening Walk* and *Descriptive Sketches*
1794	(7–10 Apr) Back at Cambridge (Jun) Poems in *Cambridge Intelligencer*; set out with Joseph Hucks to Oxford (met Southey); planned pantisocracy with Southey; Welsh tour (Aug–Sept) Met Thomas Poole; engaged to Sara Fricker (Sept) With RS published *The Fall of Robespierre* (Cambridge); *Monody on Chatterton* published with *Rowley Poems* (Cambridge) (Dec) Left Cambridge; sonnets in *M Chron* (24 Dec) Began *Religious Musings*	(23 May) Suspension of Habeas Corpus (28 Jul) Robespierre executed; end of the Terror (Oct–Dec) State Trials: Hardy, Tooke, and Thelwall acquitted of charge of treason (–1795) Paine *Age of Reason* Paley *Evidences of Christianity*
1795	(Jan) Bristol lodgings with George Burnett, RS (Feb) Political lectures (late Feb/early May) *MPL* published (May–Jun) Lectures on Revealed Religion (16 Jun) Lecture on the Slave-Trade (Aug–Sept) Quarrel with RS; pantisocracy abandoned (4 Oct) Married Sara Fricker (26 Nov) Lecture on the Two Bills (3 Dec) *Conciones ad Populum* published (c 10–18 Dec) *An Answer to "A Letter to Edward Long Fox"*; and *Plot Discovered* published; *Watchman* planned	(Jun–Jul) Quiberon expedition (26 Sept) WW and DW at Racedown (Nov) Directory began (3 Nov) Treason and Convention Bills introduced (18 Dec) Two Acts put into effect Lewis *Ambrosio, or the Monk*
1796	(9 Jan–13 Feb) Tour to Midlands to sell *The Watchman*; met Erasmus Darwin, Joseph Wright (painter) (1 Mar–13 May) *The Watchman* in ten numbers (16 Apr) *Poems on Various Subjects* (19 Sept) Hartley b; reconciliation with RS	(Jul) Robert Burns d (Sept) Mary Lamb's violent illness (Nov) Catherine of Russia d England treating for peace with France Threats of invasion of England Jenner performs first smallpox vaccination

	(31 Dec) *Ode to the Departing Year* in *Cambridge Intelligencer*; move to Nether Stowey	
1797	(Mar) WW at Stowey (5 Jun) At Racedown (Jul) DW, WW, and Lamb at Stowey; DW and WW in Alfoxden House (16 Oct) *Osorio* finished; *Poems, to Which Are Now Added, Poems by Charles Lamb and Charles Lloyd* (13–16 Nov) C's and WW's walk to Lynton and *Ancient Mariner* begun	(Feb) Bank of England suspended cash payments (Apr–Jun) Mutinies in the British Navy (9 Jul) Burke d (17 Oct) France and Austria sign peace treaty (Nov) Frederick William II of Prussia d (Nov) *Anti-Jacobin* (to 8 Jul 1978)
1798	(Jan) C's Unitarian sermons at Shrewsbury; Hazlitt heard C preach on Church and State; Wedgwood annuity £150 accepted (Mar) *Ancient Mariner* completed (Apr) *Fears in Solitude* (18 Sept) *Lyrical Ballads* published; WW, DW, and C to Hamburg; met Klopstock (Oct) C to Ratzeburg	(Feb–Oct) Irish rebellion (Apr) Helvetic Republic (12 Jun) Malta taken by French (Jul) Bonaparte invaded Egypt (1–2 Aug) Nelson's victory in Battle of the Nile Lloyd *Edmund Oliver* Bell introduced Madras system of education in England
1799	(Apr) C had news of death of Berkeley; C at University of Göttingen (May) Ascent of Brocken (29 Jul) In Stowey again (Sept–Oct) Devon walking tour with RS; met Humphry Davy in Bristol; experiments with nitrous oxide (Oct–Nov) First Lakes tour, with WW (26 Oct) Met Sara Hutchinson (27 Nov) Arrived in London to accept *M Post* offer (Dec) DW and WW at Town End (later Dove Cottage)	(Nov) Directory overthrown (Dec) Constitution of Year VIII; Bonaparte First Consul Schiller *Die Piccolomini* and *Wallensteins Tod* published Royal Institution founded
1800	(Jan–27 Mar) *M Post* reporter and leader-writer; wrote (13, 15, 27 Jan) on union with Ireland and on Catholic Question; translating *Wallenstein* at Lamb's (Apr) To Grasmere and WW (May–Jun) In Stowey and Bristol (24 Jul) Move to Greta Hall, Keswick (Sept–Oct) Superintended printing of *Lyrical Ballads* (2nd ed)	(Mar–Apr) Pius VII Pope (25 Apr) Cowper d (14 Jun) Battle of Marengo Burns *Works* ed Currie (Aug) Union of Great Britain and Ireland (5 Sept) Malta after long siege fell to English

1801	(Jan) *Lyrical Ballads* (1800) published; prolonged illnesses (Jul–Aug) With SH at Stockton (15 Nov) In London writing for *M Post* Christmas at Stowey	(Mar) Pitt resigned over Emancipation Addington ministry (–1804) (Jul) Bonaparte signed Concordat with Pope Davy lecturer at Royal Institution RS *Thalaba*
1802	(Jan) In London: attended Davy's lectures at Royal Institution; writing for *M Post* (Mar–Nov) In Lakes, severe domestic discord (Apr) *Dejection* (Aug) Scafell climb; visit of the Lambs (Sept–Oct) Writing for *M Post* (Nov) Tour of S Wales with Tom and Sally Wedgwood (23 Dec) Sara C b	(25 Mar) Peace of Amiens (18 Apr) Erasmus Darwin d (8 May) Bonaparte Consul for Life (2 Oct) WW married Mary Hutchinson (Oct) French army entered Switzerland *Edinburgh Review* founded Cobbett's *Weekly Political Register* founded Paley *Natural Theology* Spinoza *Opera* ed Paulus (1802–3)
1803	(Jan–Feb) In Somerset with Wedgwoods, Poole; with Lamb in London; made his will (Jun) *Poems* (1803) (summer) Visits by Hazlitt, Beaumonts, and S. Rogers to Lakes; Hazlitt's portrait of C (15–29 Aug) Scottish tour with DW and WW (30 Aug–15 Sept) Continued tour alone	(Feb) Act of Mediation in Switzerland (30 Apr) Louisiana bought by U.S. from France (18 May) England declared war on France (25 May) Emerson b (Sept) Emmet's execution in Ireland Cobbett *Parliamentary Debates* (later Hansard) Hayley *Life and Posthumous Writings of Cowper* Chatterton *Works* ed RS and Cottle Malthus *Principles of Population* (2nd ed)
1804	(Jan) Ill at Grasmere, then to London; portrait by Northcote (9 Apr) In convoy to Malta (Aug–Nov) Sicily, two ascents of Etna; stayed with G. F. Leckie; private secretary to Alexander Ball, British High Commissioner at Malta	(12 Feb) Kant d (Mar) Code Napoléon (Apr) 2nd Pitt ministry (–1806) (18 May) Napoleon made Emperor (12 Dec) Spain declared war on Britain Blake *Jerusalem*
1805	(Jan) Appointed Acting Public Secretary in Malta; news of loss of John Wordsworth on *Abergavenny* (Sept–Dec) In Sicily (Dec) To Naples and Rome	(Apr) Third Coalition against France (9 May) Schiller d (26 May) Napoleon King of Italy (17 Oct) Napoleon's victory at Ulm (21 Oct) Nelson's victory at Trafalgar (2 Dec) Austerlitz Hazlitt *Principles of Human Action*

		Knight *Principles of Taste* Scott *Lay of the Last Minstrel* RS *Madoc*
1806	(Jan) In Rome, met Washington Allston, the Humboldts, L. Tieck, and Schlegel; to Florence, Pisa (23 Jun) Sailed from Leghorn (17 Aug) Landed in England; London, job-hunting, Parndon with the Clarksons and to Cambridge (26 Oct) In Kendal (Nov) Keswick, determined on separation from Mrs C (Dec) At Coleorton with WW and SH, crisis of jealous disillusionment with them	(Jan) Pitt d, "Ministry of all the Talents" under Grenville, who resigned (Mar 1807) after rejection of Bill to open all commissions to RC's (6 Aug) Holy Roman Empire ended (26 Aug) Palm executed (13 Sept) Fox d British blockade (Oct) Jena (Nov) Berlin Decree and Continental System Arndt *Geist der Zeit* (–1818)
1807	Coleorton; heard WW read *Prelude* and wrote *Lines to William Wordsworth* (Jun) With C family at Stowey (Aug) Met De Quincey; in Bristol (Nov) In London	(Mar) Portland ministry (–1809) (25 Mar) Abolition of slave-trade (Jul) Peace of Tilsit (2 Sept) Bombardment of Copenhagen by British fleet (Dec) Peninsular War began Davy and oxymuriatic acid WW *Poems in Two Volumes* RS *Letters from England by Don Espriella; Specimens of the Later English Poets* C. and M. Lamb *Tales from Shakespeare* *Letters of Peter Plymley* Parnell *An Historical Apology for the Irish Catholics*
1808	(15 Jan–Jun) In rooms at *Courier* office, Strand; lectures at Royal Institution on Poetry and Principles of Taste; illnesses, Bury St Edmunds (Jun) Miniature painted by M. Betham (Jun–Aug) Bristol, Leeds, Keswick (Jul) Review of Clarkson's *History of the Abolition of the Slave-Trade* (1 Sept) Arrived Allan Bank, Grasmere (Nov) First Prospectus of *The Friend;* Kendal	Bell–Lancaster controversy Sir Arthur Wellesley to Portugal Crabb Robinson *Times* correspondent in Peninsula (1 May) Hazlitt married Sarah Stoddart (30 Aug) Convention of Cintra signed (Dec) Dr T. Beddoes d Dalton *New System of Chemical Philosophy* and pub of atomic theory Lamb *Specimens of English Dramatic Poets* Scott *Marmion* John and Leigh Hunt's *Examiner* began Goethe *Faust* pt I Croker *A Sketch of the State of Ireland*

1809	(1 Jun–15 Mar 1810) *The Friend*, 27 numbers plus supernumerary (7 Dec–20 Jan 1810) "Letters on the Spaniards" in *Courier*	(Feb) *Quarterly Review* founded (9 Mar) Byron *English Bards and Scotch Reviewers* (May) Napoleon's capture of Vienna and his excommunication; Pius VII imprisoned WW *Convention of Cintra* pamphlet (21 Sept) Canning–Castlereagh duel Perceval ministry (–1812)
1810	(Mar) SH left for Wales; last number of *Friend* (Oct) To London; Montagu precipitated WW–C quarrel; with Morgans in Hammersmith (Nov) Personal association with HCR began	(Mar) Battle over admission of press to House of Commons (May) First Reform Bill since 1797 introduced (Jul) Napoleon annexed Holland George III recognised as insane WW *Guide to the Lakes* Mme de Staël *De l'Allemagne* Scott *Lady of the Lake* RS *Curse of Kehama*
1811	(Mar) Met Grattan (20 Apr) First table-talk recorded by John Taylor Coleridge (Apr–Sept) Contributions to *Courier*, including 3 letters on the Catholic Petition; J. Payne Collier met C (18 Nov–27 Jan 1811) Lectures on Shakespeare and Milton at Scot's Corporation Hall, Collier, Byron, Rogers, HCR attending (Dec) George Dawe bust of C	(5 Feb) Prince of Wales made Regent Scheme to set up representative assembly in Dublin (Nov to 1815) Luddite uprisings Shelley *Necessity of Atheism*
1812	(Feb–Mar) Last journey to the Lakes to collect copies of *Friend* (Apr) With the Morgans, Berners Street, Soho (May–Aug) Lectures on drama in Willis's Rooms; portrait by Dawe (May) Lamb and HCR patch WW quarrel (Jun) Catherine Wordsworth d (Jun) *The Friend* reissued (3 Nov–26 Jan 1813) Shakespeare lectures in Surrey Institution (Nov) Half Wedgwood annuity withdrawn; RS and C *Omniana* (Dec) Thomas Wordsworth d	(11 May) Perceval shot; Liverpool PM, resigned but resumed after Canning (pro-Catholic) declined to serve with Wellesley (18 Jun) U.S. declared war on Great Britain (22 Jun) Napoleon opened war on Russia (Oct–Dec) The retreat from Moscow Combe *Tour of Dr Syntax in Search of the Picturesque*
1813	(23 Jan) *Remorse* opened at Drury Lane (2 Sept) Met Mme de Staël (Oct–Nov) Bristol lectures on Shakespeare and education; with Morgans at Ashley	(May) Grattan's Bill for Relief of Roman Catholics abandoned (Jul–Aug) Peace Congress at Prague failure (10 Aug) Austria declared war on Napoleon

		(Sept) RS Poet Laureate (Autumn) Wellington successful in Peninsula; Switzerland, Holland, Italy, Rhineland, Spain, Trieste, Dalmatia freed of French rule RS *Life of Nelson* Northcote *Memoirs of Reynolds* Leigh Hunt imprisoned for libel (1813–15)
1814	(5 Apr) Lectures at Bristol on Milton, Cervantes, Taste; lecture on French Revolution and Napoleon; under medical care of Dr Daniel for addiction and suicidal depression (3 May) Charles Danvers d (1 Aug) *Remorse* performed in Bristol (Aug–Sept) Allston portrait of C; Allston's exhibition of paintings; essays "On the Principles of Genial Criticism" published in *Felix Farley's Bristol Journal* (Sept) At Ashley with the Morgans (20 Sept–10 Dec) "Letters to Mr. Justice Fletcher" in *Courier* anticipate arguments in *Church and State*	(Jan) Invasion of France by Allies (Mar) Castlereagh's treaty with Austria, Prussia, and Russia against Napoleon (6 Apr) Napoleon's abdication (May) First Treaty of Paris; Napoleon exiled to Elba; Restoration of the Bourbons (8–9 Jun) Cochrane perjury trial (Sept–Jun 1815) Congress of Vienna (24 Dec) Peace of Ghent signed by Britain and U.S. Inquisition re-established in Spain WW *Excursion* Scott *Waverley* Cary's *Dante* completed
1815	(Mar) At Calne with the Morgans (Jun) *Remorse* performed at Calne (Jul–Sept) Dictating *Biographia Literaria* (Aug–Sept) *Sibylline Leaves* and *Biographia Literaria* sent for publication in Bristol	(Mar–Jun) The Hundred Days: Napoleon escaped Elba, returned to France (6 Apr) Allies mobilise vs Napoleon (18 Jun) Waterloo Restoration of Louis XVIII Napoleon from Plymouth to St Helena (20 Nov) Second Treaty of Paris WW *Poems* of 1815; *The White Doe of Rylstone* Scott *Guy Mannering*
1816	(Feb) Grant from Literary Fund, also from Byron (Mar) London: illness (10 Apr) Sent *Zapolya* to Byron (15 Apr) Accepted as patient and house-mate by Dr Gillman, Moreton House, Highgate (May–Jun) *Christabel* published (three editions); renewed acquaintance with Hookham Frere; offered Stuart tract or essays on Catholic Question	(24 Apr) Byron's departure from England (21 Jun) Motion for relief of Roman Catholics rejected in the Lords (7 Jul) Sheridan d Parliamentary Committee on Education of the Poor (Nov) *Cobbett's Political Register* reduced price to 2d (2 Dec) Spa Fields Riot Shelley *Alastor and Other Poems* Peacock *Headlong Hall*

	(Dec) *Statesman's Manual* published Hazlitt's antagonistic reviews in *Examiner* (Jun, Sept, Dec) and *Edinburgh Review* (Dec)	Maturin *Bertram* J. H. Frere ms tr of Aristophanes
1817	(Apr) Second *Lay Sermon* published (14 Apr) *Remorse* revived (Jul) *Biographia Literaria*, *Sibylline Leaves* published (summer) Met J. H. Green (Sept) Met Henry Cary (Nov) *Zapolya* published; C's tr of Hurwitz's *Hebrew Dirge* for Princess Charlotte; Tieck visited C	(13 Feb) RS *Wat Tyler* (4 Mar) Habeas Corpus suspended (27 Mar) Sidmouth Circular on libels (Apr) *Blackwood's Magazine* founded as *Edinburgh Monthly Magazine* (May) Motion for relief of Roman Catholics rejected in the Lords (6 Nov) Death of Princess Charlotte Elgin Marbles purchased by government and put in BM Keats *Poems* Hazlitt *The Characters of Shakespeare's Plays* Moore *Lalla Rookh* Ricardo *Principles of Political Economy* Cuvier *Le Règne animal*
1818	(Jan) "Treatise on Method" in *Encyclopaedia Metropolitana* published (Jan–Mar) Lectures on poetry and drama (Jan) Met T. Allsop Annotated 1817 Catholic Emancipation Debate in copy of Hansard (Apr) Two pamphlets supporting Peel's Bill against exploitation of child-labour (Nov) *The Friend* (3-vol edition) (Dec) Lectures on the History of Philosophy (–Mar 1819); literary lectures (–Mar 1819)	(28 Jan) Habeas Corpus restored and never again suspended (1 Jun) Parliamentary motion for universal suffrage and annual parliaments defeated (Jun) Westmorland election Keats *Endymion* (Aug) *Blackwood's* and *Quarterly* attacks on Keats Hallam *Middle Ages* Hazlitt *Lectures on the English Poets* Lamb *Collected Works* (dedicated to C) Peacock *Nightmare Abbey*
1819	(Mar) Financial losses in bankruptcy of publisher Rest Fenner (29 Mar) Lectures end (11 Apr) Met Keats in Millfield Lane; HC elected Fellow of Oriel; revived interest in chemistry; occasional contributions to *Blackwood's* (to 1822)	(May) Grattan's Motion for Relief of Roman Catholics defeated (Jun) Grey's Bill to abolish Declaration against Transubstantiation defeated
1820	(May) HC deprived of Oriel Fellowship (Aug) Green began to act as weekly amanuensis to record C's work on Books of O and N Testament (Oct) DC to St John's, Cambridge	(29 Jan) George III d Accession of George IV Cato Street Conspiracy (Feb) Parliament dissolved (Jun) Grattan d. Plunkett became main Irish spokesman

	(Dec) Recommended writings of friend Hyman Hurwitz	Revolution in Spain and Portugal (Aug–Nov) Trial of Queen Caroline Crawfurd *History of the Indian Archipelago* Godwin *Of Population, in Answer to Mr Malthus* Keats *Lamia and other Poems* Lamb *Essays of Elia* Shelley *Prometheus Unbound* RS *Life of Wesley* WW *The River Duddon*
1821	(Apr) Ms notes on Grenville's speech supporting anti-vetoists (Apr–May) Projected 3 Letters to C. A. Tulk, MP, on Catholic Question (Jul) Reunion with brother George (autumn) Invitation to lecture in Dublin refused	(Feb) Plunkett's Motion for Relief of Roman Catholics with 2 Securities (ban on foreign correspondence and veto on appointments) passed by majority of 6 in Commons, rejected by 39 in Lords after intervention of Grenville (Apr) (Feb) Keats d (Aug–Sept) King visited Ireland Napoleon d Greek War of Liberation De Quincey *Confessions of an English Opium Eater* Hazlitt *Lectures on Elizabethan Drama* Mill *Elements of Political Economy* RS *Vision of Judgment*
1822	(spring) C's "Thursday-evening class" began; SC's tr of Martin Dobrizhoffer *An Account of Albipones, an Equestrian People of Paraguay* (Nov) Meeting with Liverpool and Canning at Ramsgate (Nov–Feb 1823) Wife and daughter visit C at Highgate (29 Dec) HNC began recording his *Table Talk*	(30 Apr) Canning's Catholic Peers Bill carried by 5 in Commons, rejected by 42 in Lords (Jul) Shelley d (Aug) Castlereagh d and Canning became Foreign Secretary (Nov–Dec) Faction-fights between Orangemen and Catholics in Ireland Byron *Vision of Judgment* Grattan *Speeches* Shelley *Hellas* Blanco White *Letters from Spain* [Doblado] WW *Ecclesiastical Sketches*
1823	(Jun–Jul) Heard Edward Irving preach (Sept) *Youth and Age* begun (Sept) Sought admission to BM through Sir Humphry Davy (Dec) Gillmans and C moved to 3, the Grove	Foundation of Catholic Association by O'Connell and R. L. Sheil (Apr) Plunkett's Motion for Relief of Roman Catholics abandoned for lack of support (May) First meeting of Catholic Association in Dublin

		(Jun) First meeting of Catholic Association in London War between France and Spain (Aug) Death of Pius VII Hazlitt *Liber Amoris* RS *History of the Peninsular War*
1824	(Mar) Elected FRSL, annuity of £100 (Jun) Carlyle and Gabriele Rossetti called at Highgate DC B.A. Cambridge J. T. Coleridge became Editor of *Quarterly*	(Apr) Byron d (May) Lansdowne's Bills to allow English Catholics the vote and to act as JP's defeated Foundation of London Mechanics' Institution Cary tr *The Birds* of Aristophanes Godwin *History of the Commonwealth of England* RS *The Book of the Church*
1825	(May) *Aids to Reflection* published (18 May) Royal Society of Literature essay "On the *Prometheus* of Aeschylus" (May) 6 essays, including 1 on Church and State, promised to publisher (J. A. Hessey) (Jun) Partnership of C's publishers (Hessey & Taylor) dissolved (Jul) Blanco White visited C at Highgate; C received copy of *Evidences*, informed White he was about to put to the press "a small work on the Church" (Nov) Corrected proofs of Hurwitz's *Hebrew Tales*; proposed three lectures on projected London University (Dec) Received Blanco White's *Letters from Spain* and *Poor Man's Preservative* Marginal notes on subject of Church and State in Hooker and other 17th century writers; DC ordained	(Feb–May) Burdett's Motion for the Relief of Roman Catholics, with 2 "wings" for Veto and State payment of Clergy passed in Commons, but defeated in Lords after intervention of Dukes of York and Liverpool (May) Liverpool's speech on Coronation Oath; quoted with approval by Canning (Aug) Frere arrived in England Brougham *Practical Observations upon the Education of the People* Butler *The Book of the Roman Catholic Church* Hazlitt *Spirit of the Age* Lawless *An Address to the Catholics of Ireland* Mill *Essays on Government; Poor Man's Preservation against Popery* Blanco White *Practical and Internal Evidences against Catholicism*
1826	(spring) Intensive work on Daniel and the Apocalypse (summer) Frere spent long periods with C (Jul) Letter to Edward Coleridge on Mysticism, later incorporated in *Church and State* (Sept) Frere obtained promise of sinecure of £200 from Liverpool for C	General Election with Corn Laws and Catholic Emancipation as main issues England sends troops to Portugal HNC *Six Months in the West Indies* Irving *Babylon and Infidelity Foredoomed of God* Turner *History of Henry VIII* RS *Vindiciae Ecclesiae Anglicanae* Blanco White *A Letter to Charles Butler*

1827	(Feb) Lord Dudley Ward intended to speak to Liverpool on C's behalf (10 May) Thomas Chalmers called at Highgate; C's serious illness DC married Mary Pridham Sir George Beaumont d, leaving £100 to Mrs C Poole visited C at Highgate	(Feb) Liverpool seized with paralytic stroke (Mar) Burdett's Bill, which dispensed with 2 "wings", rejected in Commons by 4 votes (Mar) Canning PM (8 Aug) Canning d (Aug) Goderich Ministry University of London founded Blake d Hallam *Constitutional History* Hare *Guesses at Truth* Irving tr of *The Coming of Messiah* Keble *Christian Year* Phillpotts *Letter to Canning on the Bill of 1825* Tennyson *Poems by Two Brothers*
1828	(Feb) Marginal notes on Brougham *A Speech* (Land as a Trust) (22 Apr) Fennimore Cooper met C (21 Jun–7 Aug) Netherlands and Rhine Tour with Dora and WW (Aug) *Poetical Works* (3 vols); John Sterling called at Highgate	(Jan) Wellington Ministry (Feb) Brougham's speech on Law of the Country (Apr) Repeal of Test and Corporation Acts (May) Burdett's Bill for Relief of Roman Catholics passed in Commons, rejected in Lords (Jun) (Jul) O'Connell elected at Clare (Aug) Peel and Wellington in correspondence over the Catholic Question (Dec) Lord Liverpool d Russia goes to war with Turkey The Greek Question Brougham *A Speech on the Present State of the Law of the Country* Hazlitt *Life of Napoleon* vols I, II Phillpotts *A Letter on the Coronation Oath*
1829	(Jan–Feb) Refused to sign Petition against Catholic Emancipation (spring) Illness delayed writing on Church and State *Poetical Works* (2nd ed) *Poetical Works of Coleridge, Shelley, and Keats* (Galignani, Paris) (Sept) SC married cousin HNC; Lady Beaumont left C £50; Poole visited Highgate (Sept) Working on proofs of *On the Constitution of the Church and State* (Dec) *Church and State* published	Meetings held throughout the country to petition against Catholic Emancipation (Jan) King agrees to discussion of Catholic Emancipation in Cabinet (Feb–Mar) Bill passed to suppress Catholic Association Act passed to raise franchise in Ireland from 40s to £10 (10 Mar) 1st Reading in the Commons of Catholic Relief Bill (30 Mar) 3rd Reading passed by 178 votes (31 Mar) 1st Reading in Lords (10 Apr) 3rd Reading passed by 104 (13 Apr) George IV gave reluctant assent

		(May) Sir Humphry Davy d Arnold *Sermons* Hurwitz *The Elements of the Hebrew Language* RS *Sir Thomas More* [Isaac Taylor] *Natural History of Enthusiasm* (May)
1830	(Jan) Revision of *C&S* into chapters *On the Constitution of the Church and State* (2nd ed) (Jun) HNC and SC settled in Highgate (Jul) C made his will Republication of *The Devil's Walk* "by Professor Porson" (Sept) Detailed marginal notes in Blomfield's *Charge*	Reform Agitation (Jun) Death of George IV (Jun) Accession of William IV (Nov) Grey Ministry Greece independent Bishop Blomfield *Charge* to Clergy of London Diocese Comte *Cours de philosophie positive* Lyell *Principles of Geology* Miller *Sermons* Tennyson *Poems Chiefly Lyrical*
1831	Royal Society of Literature grant withdrawn; refused personal grant from Grey; Frere made up loss Last meeting with WW; *Aids to Reflection* (2nd ed) Active interest in Parliamentary Reform, reflected in *Table Talk* and marginalia	(Mar) Lord John Russell introduced Reform Bill in Commons Dissolution of Parliament Second Reform Bill rejected by Lords Final Reform Bill introduced British Association founded Hegel d J. S. Mill *The Spirit of the Age* in *Examiner* Peacock *Crotchet Castle* Review of *C&S* in *Eclectic Review* (Jul) Walsh *Popular Opinions on Parliamentary Reform*
1832	Legacy of £300 from Steinmetz	Grey resigned; Wellington failed to form Ministry; Grey recalled (May) Reform Bill passed Scott d Green *Address Delivered in King's College* Martineau *Illustrations of Political Economy* Park *The Dogmas of the Constitution* RS *Essays, Moral and Political*
1833	HC's *Poems* dedicated to C (24–9 Jun) To Cambridge for meetings of British Association (Jul) Harriet Martineau visited C (5 Aug) Emerson called at Highgate	Arnold *Principles of Church Reform* Carlyle *Sartor Resartus* Keble Sermon on "National Apostacy" begins Oxford Movement

	HC's *Biographia Borealis* published	Lamb *Last Essays of Elia* Mill "Corporation and Church Property" Smith *Seven Letters on National Religion* *Tracts for the Times* (Newman et al)
1834	(Apr) Instructed Hurst to dispose of his share in the editions of *AR* and *C&S* (Jul) Proofs of *Poetical Works* (3rd ed) (25 Jul) Death at Highgate	New Poor Law Augustus Hare d (Feb) Malthus d (Dec) Lamb d (Dec) Bentham *Deontology*

EDITOR'S INTRODUCTION

THE HISTORICAL BACKGROUND

It is fitting that Coleridge's last published prose work should have been *On the Constitution of the Church and State* (1830), for it is a brief but brilliant synthesis of the political and theological thinking of a lifetime. In it he writes as a great lover of the English Church, as a marginal note in a book of sermons makes clear:

God knows my heart! there may be & I trust are, many among our Clergy who love, prize, and venerate our Church as earnestly and as disinterestedly as I do! But that any man, "on this side idolatry" can love & prize it more, or more sincerely, it is not in my power to believe.[1]

He also writes as someone thoroughly aware of the magnitude of his great theme. This he had defined nearly twenty years earlier in the *Courier*:

Church and State—civil and religious rights—to hold these essential powers of civilized society in due relation to each other, so as to prevent them from becoming its burthens instead of its supports; this is perhaps the most difficult problem in the whole science of politics, which the efforts of centuries have not succeeded in solving theoretically, though in one or two countries the differences may have been happily compromised in practice. From the first ages of Christianity to the present period, the two relations of a rational being, to his present and to his future state, have been abstracted and framed into moral personages, Church and State: and to each has been assigned its own domain and its especial rights.[2]

This was a theme that, as Coleridge saw, had attracted the greatest minds in Europe.

For St Augustine, for Dante, and for England's "judicious Hooker", Church and State were ideally one; belief in a single universal order embracing both was common to Western Christendom.[3] Any conflict, therefore, was not between two distinct societies, but

[1] Marginal note written by C on 12 Sept 1830 in BM copy of John Miller *Sermons Intended to Show a Sober Application of Spiritual Principles to the Realities of Life* (Oxford 1830) 34–5.

[2] "Letter III. On the Catholic Petition" *Courier* 26 Sept 1811: *EOT* (*CC*) II 308.

[3] In *De civitate Dei* (written 413–26), *De monarchia* (c 1313), *Of the Laws of Ecclesiastical Polity* (4 books 1594, 5th 1597, 6th and 8th 1648, 7th 1661).

between two sets of officials within a single society.[1] All this changed with the growth of the secular national state. Even at the end of the sixteenth century, when Hooker published his *Laws of Ecclesiastical Polity*, the idea of a single society embracing all believers no longer corresponded with the facts. Indeed, the identification of Church and State, as Sir Ernest Barker has remarked, "was rather the vision of Hooker and Laud than the actual and established fact of daily life".[2] The ideal of unity was embodied in the Acts of Supremacy and Uniformity: the first of these declared the King to be the supreme head of the Church of England and made it treasonable to deny this; the second forbade the use of any form of public prayer other than the second prayer-book of Edward VI.[3] The unity that this legislation sought to enforce was immediately open to challenge both from the growing strength of Dissent and from the universality claimed by the Roman Catholic Church. By the beginning of the eighteenth century, unity had been replaced by the notion of a political alliance between Church and State. Warburton's *Alliance Between Church and State* of 1736 provided a common-sense explanation of the interdependence of the two, satisfying alike to statesmen and Anglican clergy. It epitomised the spirit of bland eighteenth-century equipoise and enabled the Church to retain its popularity as a compromise between the two extremes of Popery and Puritanism.[4] So mechanical and utilitarian a concept of the constitutional balance made little appeal to Coleridge. Unlike Dr Arnold, who returned to an anachronistic unitary concept of Church and State in the *Principles of Church Reform* (1833), Coleridge accepted their necessary separation both as the expression of a philosophical

1 "The medieval mind, whether clerical or anti-clerical, envisaged the struggle as one between different officers of the same society, never between two separate bodies; this is as true of Dante and Marsilius as it is of Boniface and Augustinus [author of *Summa de ecclesiastica potestate*]." J. N. Figgis *Studies of Political Thought from Gerson to Grotius: 1414–1625* (Cambridge 1907) 49.

2 *Church, State and Study* (1930) 139; see also Figgis *Churches in the Modern State* (1913) and recent criticism of Figgis by John Kent "The Victorian Resistance: Comments on Religious Life and Culture" *VS* XII 2 (Dec 1968) 154.

3 The first Act of Supremacy (1534) declared the King to be supreme head on earth of the Church of England. By the second Act (1559), passed in Elizabeth's reign, the title was abandoned, but an oath was imposed on all officeholders acknowledging the Queen to be the supreme governor of the realm in spiritual and ecclesiastical matters. The Act of Uniformity (1559) forbade the use of any form of public prayer but one; the Act of 1662 required clergymen and schoolmasters to accept this form.

4 W. L. Mathieson *English Church Reform: 1815–1840* (1923) 16.

principle and as an historical fact. By reference to the principle of polarity, he was able to demonstrate that the opposition of Church and State was not incompatible with their necessary interdependence. By reference to historical change and by means of a profound insight into the actual forces at work in society, especially into the nature of consensus, he was able to combine contemporary relevance and universality in his analysis. The central problem for Coleridge, as it is for us today, is: What is the Church's rôle in a pluralist society? His answer, *On the Constitution of the Church and State*, takes its place as one of the great works of constitutional theory, while his vision of the cultural rôle of the National Church, or the Clerisy, inspired countless nineteenth-century thinkers and still retains the power to inspire and to provoke radical discussion.[1]

The issue that raised the question of Church and State in so acute a form during Coleridge's lifetime was Catholic Emancipation, itself a part of a larger problem, the Irish Question. These twin issues dominated English politics for over a century, stirring fierce passions, arousing false hopes, dividing parties, and destroying ministries. The Catholic Question, Lord Stanhope asserted, was the rock on which one ministry after another foundered. Coleridge comes near to stating the essence of this complicated problem towards the end of *Church and State*:

> But why do I waste words? There is and can be but one question: and there is and can be but one way of stating it...three-fourths of the sum total of His Majesty's Irish subjects are Roman Catholics, with a papal priesthood, while three-fourths of the sum total of his Majesty's subjects are Protestants.[2]

[1] C was disappointed at the reception of *C&S* and complained that it had been ignored by the main journals. In fact, a long review appeared in the *Eclectic Review* VI (July 1831) 1–28, reprinted J. R. de J. Jackson (ed) *Coleridge: the Critical Heritage* (1970) 562–84. It was probably written by Isaac Taylor, whose *Natural History of Enthusiasm* (1829) C had commented on in the final pages of *C&S;* see below, p 166. The writer of an essay on C (nominally a review of *Table Talk*) in the *Dublin University Magazine* (July 1835) praised *C&S* highly and said it should be reprinted; it was probably written by John Anster, who had written to C on 25 May 1825 saying that he wished Parliament would take the risk and pass Burdett's Bill of 1825; letter in VCL S/MS/F 8.43. For general influence of *C&S*, see last section of this Introduction, pp lxi–lxviii.

[2] See below, p 150. In a ms paragraph in the BM on the "Catholic Question", C says that the ratio of Protestants to Catholics in Ireland "is asserted to be, by some as 1 in 5, by others and with more confidence as 1 in 6". He there suggests that if the question had been stated properly as "What obstacle to plenary Electiveness and Eligibility is there in Non-protestant *Irishism*, under the existing state and circumstances of the British Empire collectively we should not, I

For Coleridge, as for the majority of Englishmen, the question was: could Roman Catholic subjects be allowed full civil and political rights without grave danger to the Protestant Constitution, a constitution that each King promised to uphold in his solemn Coronation Oath.[1] From our present vantage point, the question may seem to answer itself, but at the time the danger to the constitution seemed real enough.[2] The very means proposed by some for keeping the Roman Catholic Church subordinate to the State—the payment of its clergy by the State—was seen as a double attack on the Protestant Constitution, double since it would involve not only the misappropriation of national wealth entrusted to the English Church, but also the degrading of that Church to the status of one sect among many. Other grave sources of anxiety were the allegiance of Roman Catholic subjects to an extra-national sovereign, the Pope; their dual standard of keeping faith; and their duty to proselytise. Many of those who opposed Catholic Emancipation were neither illiberal reactionaries

---

think, have heard so much declamation about theological tenets" nor listened "to a British Senate quarreling, like girls, about what the Roman Catholics" would or would not do if the Bill passed. MS Egerton 2800 ff 109–9ᵛ, printed as App D 1, below, pp 227–8. Owen Chadwick states that the population of Ireland was 7 million, 5½ being Roman Catholic. The population of England and Wales was 14 million. *The Victorian Church* (1966) 8–9.

[1] The crucial section of the Coronation Oath prescribed by 1 William and Mary c 6, as given by Henry Phillpotts in *A Letter to an English Layman on the Coronation Oath* (1828) 21–2, runs: "Will you, to the utmost of your power, maintain the laws of God, the true profession of the Gospel, and the Protestant reformed religion established by law? And will you prescribe unto the Bishops and Clergy of this realm, and to the Churches committed to their charge, all such rights and privileges as by law do or shall appertain unto them, or any of them?" The issue of the Coronation Oath produced numerous pamphlets, many of which were prompted by Canning's statements on 26 May 1825 and 6 Mar 1826 that the oath was not a barrier to Catholic Emancipation. Henry Phillpotts, later bp of Exeter, was the chief defender of the oath; in 1827 he published *A Letter* to Canning on Burdett's Bill of 1825 and on Canning's speech in support of that Bill. For C's reference to Canning's view of the oath, see below, p 106.

[2] "The core of the Protestant Tory idea of the Constitution was that it had attained its peculiar excellence only after a long, painful struggle with Popery, not concluded until 1689; that both religious and secular advantages (so far as they could be distinguished, which ideally they could not) were secured to Britons by this constitution, and in particular by its religious establishment; and that while the established Church remained materially subject to Parliament, it was a self-evident absurdity to allow Roman Catholics any share in legislating for it." G. F. A. Best "The Protestant Constitution and Its Supporters, 1800–1829" *Transactions of the Royal Historical Society* 5th ser VIII (1958) 109; hereafter cited as Best.

nor rabid extremists, but sincere defenders of the principles of tolerance and constitutional freedom. These they thought had been embodied in the Revolutionary Settlement of 1689.[1] The issues were highly complex; there were men of high principle and good conscience on both sides. Partly in recognition of this, and partly because no Ministry was strong enough to resolve the issue, it remained an "open" question throughout the 1820's, but far from speeding the cause of Emancipation the "open" system led to indecision and stalemate.[2]

The main motive for introducing penal statutes against Roman Catholics in the sixteenth and seventeenth centuries had been fear of foreign aggression, not religious intolerance; and although, after this fear abated, relief measures in the 1770's reduced the severities of the Penal Code, the Test Acts of 1673 and 1678 still called on all officeholders and Members of Parliament to take an oath against transubstantiation. However, after the repeal of the Test and Corporation Acts in 1828, a repeal that finally legalised the participation of Dissenters in municipal and political life, the case for Catholic Emancipation was enormously strengthened. Nevertheless, even when Peel and Wellington had come to accept its inevitability, a severe practical difficulty lay in drafting an oath that would not be repugnant to the Catholic conscience (as the oath against transubstantiation had been), but that would at the same time provide satisfactory proof of loyalty to the principles of the Protestant Constitution. A further difficulty lay in convincing the Anti-Emancipationists that the Bill included adequate "securities" for both Church and State.[3] With a characteristic grasp of essentials, Cole-

[1] "The opponents of Emancipation proposed to retain limitations on civil liberty, and legal superiorities for the established churches, only because they doubted whether religious liberty could otherwise be secured." Best 122. For a selection of documents, see E. R. Norman (ed) *Anti-Catholicism in Victorian England* (1968); the Introduction provides a valuable perspective.

[2] G. I. T. Machin *The Catholic Question in English Politics 1820 to 1830* (Oxford 1964) 3–5, to which I am indebted for much essential information; hereafter cited as Machin.

[3] Best summarises the most important securities demanded by the defenders of the Protestant Constitution as: "a royal veto over episcopal elections, and a power to examine incoming briefs and bulls known as the *Placet* or *Exsequatur*; payment of the Roman Catholic hierarchy and priesthood by the state; licences for priests which could be revoked in case of disloyal conduct; a concordat with the Pope; permission for Roman Catholics to sit in the legislature only at Protestant pleasure, by annual suspension of the tests; and statutory limitations whether of the number of Roman Catholics in either House or of the subjects within

ridge cut through the tangled threads of the nineteenth-century parliamentary debate on securities by insisting that the enunciation of a constitutional principle was more important than the drafting of specific "securities". For Southey, by contrast, the only satisfactory security would be a change in doctrine, "an authentic disclaimer of whatever is unchristian or pernicious...by a council, and confirmed by the Pope".[1] Coleridge rested his argument on constitutional principles; Southey on an uncompromising hostility to Catholic doctrine.

For most people the term "Established Church" is a highly misleading one. It means, as J. N. Figgis has pointed out, that form of service, among many others, which was established by law through the Act of Uniformity. It does not refer to the founding of a state church.[2] Although this explanation is sufficiently accurate historically, the questions of church discipline and state legislation have necessarily been closely connected. Thomas Arnold, for one, thought that such interaction was desirable in as much as church discipline humanised and spiritualised the state. Coleridge, on the other hand, considered that the objection that bore hardest on the Church Establishment was the impossibility of reconciling "Christian discipline with a Church established by Law, and all the permitted acts of which have the force of penal or compulsory Laws".[3]

Even if the Established Church was not, in fact, a Church founded by the State, it enjoyed national endowment, its two archbishops and its bishops sat in the House of Lords, appointments to high ecclesiastical office were made on the advice of the sovereign, and the Coronation Oath bound the King to uphold and defend

---

their legislative purview." Best 105–27. Wellington favoured elaborate securities, but Peel persuaded him to give full concession with the minimum of securities, thus facilitating the rapid passage of the 1829 Bill. Earlier discussions had been bedevilled by talk of "securities". Norman Gash *Mr. Secretary Peel: The Life of Sir Robert Peel to 1830* (1961) 585.

1 *QR* XXXVIII (1828) 597; see also Scott Bennett "Catholic Emancipation, the 'Quarterly Review' and Britain's Constitutional Revolution" *VS* XII (Mar 1969) 285–304.

2 *Churches in the Modern State* (1913) 9–11.

3 Annotation on Richard Baxter *Reliquiae Baxterianae* (1696) 271, in *C 17th C* 324; cf *Friend* (*CC*) I 94–5 and ms comment in *Encyclopaedia Londinensis:* "Not the practice of *Virtue*, but the peace of Society and the *Legality* of Individuals, are the objects of Law; these secured, it trusts and may safely trust to Religion, Education, [and] Civilisation for the rest." *NTP* 220 (corrected from *CM* ms).

it.[1] But what was to be the future of the Church of England in a pluralist democratic society? That was the question that had to be answered by the Church in an Age of Revolution.[2] The rising tide of democracy served gradually to erode some of the Church's traditional privileges. The continuous and insistent demand for Catholic Emancipation raised basic principles about the relationship between Church and State. And the forces of Dissent, together with the growth of the secular liberal state in the nineteenth century, acted as a further challenge to the Church. The "great question" of the relations of Church and State was not an academic constitutional issue. As Owen Chadwick has remarked, it

> affected every town and village in the country, embittered relations, bred enmity between church and chapel, governed the utterance aud programme of political candidates, entered class-room and guild hall. Except in Ireland and Wales and among Independents and Quakers, the question was not usually framed, ought there to be an established church? England continued to believe in a church as by law established, which in many eyes was part of Englishness as well as wise Christianity. The question was framed, how is an established church compatible with equality before the law? Or, does equality before law include religious equality?[3]

Coleridge saw clearly the interconnexions of Revolution, Emancipation, and Parliamentary Reform; and although some of his later pronouncements recorded in *Table Talk* are alarmist and reactionary,[4] no such fear of rapid change distorts his argument in *Church and State*.

The Church of England at the beginning of the nineteenth century was certainly in need of urgent reform. As Norman Gash has remarked, it was "politically unpopular, socially exclusive, and administratively corrupt".[5] Its parish divisions, like those of the unreformed constituencies, no longer corresponded with the distribution of population, and its clergy were for the most part worldly

[1] For useful 'summary see David Nicholls *Church and State in Britain since 1820* (1967) 2.

[2] The phrase is taken from Alec R. Vidler *The Church in an Age of Revolution: 1789 to the Present Day* (1961) (*Pelican History of the Church* v).

[3] *The Victorian Church* 3.

[4] For example, the entry for 14 Jun 1834. A barely decipherable passage written at the end of Feb 1832 declares that "the wrath of Heaven is on the Land", states that "the Catholic Bill" was "passed without principle by the D. of Wellington", condemns the Reform Bill, and ends with a prayer to God to "have mercy on this poor Country". N F° f 78.

[5] *Reaction and Reconstruction in English Politics 1832–1852* (Oxford 1965) 61.

and materialistic, both in their attitude to their pastoral duties and in their theological assumptions. For the few who cared about theology, Paley's *Evidences* provided an undemanding utilitarian approach. But few cared. Economic interest and a strongly entrenched Toryism bound Church to State, thus inhibiting any radical enquiry into the Church's rôle in society. All this was gradually to change. And that it did so was mainly owing to large-scale economic and political forces. But it was also owing to the influence of such men as Coleridge, who referred the whole question of the Church's rôle in society back to first principles, to the "idea" of Church and State; and to men like F. D. Maurice, who searched for some alternative to what he called the "dreariness of political Anglicanism",[1] a dreariness that was a characteristic product of the preceding age of easy compromise. In setting his back against all that that age stood for in the way of intellectual and spiritual compromise, Coleridge pointed the way to the future for his contemporaries and his successors.

COLERIDGE'S LIFELONG INTEREST IN CHURCH AND STATE

When Hazlitt heard Coleridge preach as a young man in 1798, the sermon at Shrewsbury was "upon church and state—not their alliance, but their separation—on the spirit of the world and the spirit of Christianity, not as the same, but as opposed to one another".[2] Over thirty years later, the thesis of his last published prose work, *On the Constitution of the Church and State*, was the necessary interdependence of Church and State. A typical Coleridgian reversal, it might be suggested; but the truth is more complex, for there was continuity as well as change. In 1830, he still rejected any idea of a formal alliance on Warburtonian lines. He also continued to contrast the "spirit of the world" and the "spirit of Christianity", but he now recognised the important part a National Church should play in the life of the nation, and distinguished between the informing idea of such a church and its temporary and necessarily imperfect embodiment in the nineteenth-century Church of England.

In his youth, as an opponent of Pitt's Ministry, with its rallying cry of Church and King, it was natural for Coleridge to attack the

[1] *The Kingdom of Christ; or, Hints to a Quaker Respecting the Principles, Constitution, & Ordinances of the Catholic Church* ed A. R. Vidler (1958) II 319 (first published 3 vols 1838).

[2] "My First Acquaintance with Poets", first published in the *Liberal* Apr 1823: *H Works* XVII 108.

English Church as "the Religion of Mitres and Mysteries, the Religion of Pluralities and Persecution, the Eighteen-Thousand-Pound-a-Year Religion of Episcopacy",[1] but in later life a clearer insight into the nature of institutions led him to explore the "Idea", or ultimate end, for which a National Church existed. From his boyhood days in a Devonshire vicarage to his last years at Highgate, Coleridge was concerned with the Church's rôle in society. It may not be entirely fanciful to trace the original idea of the educational and cultural rôle of the National Church or Clerisy back to his father's dual rôle as clergyman and schoolmaster at Ottery St Mary. Coleridge was justly proud of his lifelong devotion to the cause of the Church and is recorded as saying near the end of his life: "If an inscription be put upon my tomb, it may be that I was an enthusiastic lover of the Church; and as enthusiastic a hater of those who have betrayed it, be they who they may."[2]

Coleridge's youthful opposition to any close alliance between Church and State was both religious and political in origin. At Cambridge and later in Bristol, where he delivered lectures on politics and revealed religion in 1795, he had first-hand experience of the "Church and King" mobs that were used to suppress reform and to rally support for the Pitt Ministry in its war with France.[3] In the lecture he delivered in Bristol "On the Present War", he represented the Established Church as the willing tool of a repressive government. Indeed, in his early poems and political works, Coleridge consistently referred to the English Church as the source of superstition, corruption, and repression.

The theological, as opposed to the political, objections to the alliance of Church and State arose largely from the Unitarian connexions Coleridge formed at Cambridge and in Bristol. The chief attraction of Unitarianism, apart from its close connexion with revolution and reform societies, lay in its luminous rationalism, its freedom from superstition and mystery, its humanistic message, and its absence of traditional dogma. As the poem *Religious Musings* makes clear, it was a religion ideally suited to anyone who wished to combine the social message of Jesus with a purely rational theology. Years later, however, Unitarianism appeared to Coleridge nothing better than the "Sans cullotterie of Religion".[4]

[1] "On the Present War" *Conciones: Lects 1795* (*CC*) 66–7.

[2] *TT* 3 May 1830.

[3] "Mobs and Mayors, Blockheads and Brickbats, Placards and Press gangs have leagued in horrible Conspiracy against me—"Letter to G. Dyer [late Feb 1795]: *CL* I 152.

[4] At the end of an imaginary dialogue between S. T. C. and B. A. on the

Two events between 1800 and 1802 forced Coleridge to reconsider drastically his whole conception of the relations of Church and State. The first of these was the Union with Ireland, while the second was the Concordat that Napoleon signed with the Roman Church in France. In order to secure the support of the Catholic majority in Ireland, Pitt let it be known that Union would be followed by Catholic Emancipation. Even at the time, he must have been aware that the promise was unlikely to be fulfilled because of the King's opposition. Having secured the Union, Pitt was obliged to resign when George III would not accede to Catholic Emancipation, on the grounds that it would be a violation of his Coronation Oath. At the time Coleridge was writing leaders for the *Morning Post*. In these early essays,[1] as in his later writings on the same issue, he recognised that the question of the Union and of the Irish members in the imperial legislature was part of a much more complicated problem, to understand which a sense of history and grasp of first principles were absolutely necessary. It is clear that Coleridge came to recognise that neither Union nor Emancipation would solve Ireland's complex problems and that he also saw with extraordinary clarity the challenge the Union offered to the existing constitution of Church and State.[2] What he feared most in later life in this context was that once Ireland attained Emancipation, it would sever all connexion with England and constitute a perpetual threat to English security.

The second event that led Coleridge to re-examine his ideas on Church and State at this early stage in his life was Napoleon's Concordat of 1801. By the Concordat, Napoleon restored the Catholic religion on condition that his government should choose the bishops, and, through them, control the education of the priests and the instruction of the faithful. It was the Concordat, so Coleridge

different meanings of the term "Catholic Church", written after 30 Aug 1829, C summarises the main stages of his religious life and speaks of the time when he "became unsatisfied with my Unitarian Scheme, as a Creed of Negatives". N Q ff 46–8^{v}; see below, p 135 n 3. See also *BL* (1907) I 114, 136–7, and Basil Willey "Coleridge and Religion" *S. T. Coleridge* ed R. L. Brett (1971) 223–30.

[1] 15, 27 Jan 1800: *EOT* (*CC*) I 105–8, 133–4.

[2] "Mr Pitt has received great credit for effecting the Union; but I believe it will sooner or later be discovered that the manner in which, and the terms upon which, he effected it, made it the most fatal blow that ever was levelled against the peace and prosperity of England. From it came the Catholic Bill. From the Catholic Bill has come this Reform Bill! And what next?" *TT* 17 Dec 1831. Cf ibid 5 Feb 1833: "I am deliberately of opinion, that England, in all its institutions, has received injury from its union with Ireland."

told his clergyman brother George, that made him for the first time "think accurately & with consecutive Logic on the force & meaning of the word *Established* Church".[1] In correspondence, apparently both he and his brother had expressed doubts "as to the effects & scriptural propriety of this (supposed) alliance of Church & State". Confronted with the new French alliance, based on sheer political expedience, Coleridge found that his previous objections to the established church in England "were wholly removed", presumably because its relations with the State seemed innocent beside those of the French Church. Contrasting the situation in England and France, he remarked to his brother in the same letter that "the Church of France at present ought to be called—a *standing* church—in the same sense as we say a *standing* army". Ironically, France, the country that had once symbolised freedom for Coleridge, had now concluded an alliance that appeared far more dangerous and disreputable than the English alliance that he had attacked in his sermon at Shrewsbury in 1798. Unfortunately, the poet's offer to give his opinions on the Concordat in full was not taken up by his brother. Nevertheless, Coleridge speaks so confidently of his being able to give "an historical account...of the Warburtonian System of defence," and told Southey, a month later, on 29 July, that he planned to publish a Book "Concerning Tythes & Church Establishment",[2] that it seems likely that he had given much thought to the whole subject and had already begun to relate the new French Concordat to English constitutional theory and practice.

The next opportunity Coleridge had to address newspaper readers on Catholic Emancipation, after the *Morning Post* essays on Ireland of 1800, was in 1811, when he was working as sub-editor on the *Courier*. He then wrote three letters on the Catholic Petition[3] and several shorter related pieces. The *Courier*, as an organ of the Tory party, could be expected to oppose the Catholic Petition and to attack its rival, the Whig *Morning Chronicle*, which supported the

[1] 3 Jun 1802: *CL* II 803.

[2] 29 Jul 1802: *CL* II 829. An entry in N F° f 8 states that "The Error, which 20 years ago I noted in Warburton's Alliance of Church & State, prevails generally in theological reasoning of that & the preceding Age—"; on 9 Feb 1805 C suggested that the "Germ" of the "Conspiracy" to make bargains between the religious conscience and the law was to be found in Warburton (*CN* II 2440); and HNC and the writer of the *DNB* article on Warburton are mistaken in suggesting that Warburton's *Alliance* had some affinity with *C&S*. A note to *CN* II 2440 rightly finds the seeds of all C's later thoughts on Church and State in his radical opposition to Warburton's dualistic compromise.

[3] 13, 21 and 26 Sept 1811: *EOT* (*CC*) II 279–82, 305–13.

cause of Emancipation. Without actually reversing his paper's policy, Coleridge argued in favour of a gradual settlement and thus raised the debate above narrow party lines. Grattan, the chief publicist for the Catholic cause, whom Coleridge probably met at Godwin's and whose "love of Liberty" and "*moral* dignity" he praised, may have influenced his views.[1] More important, however, was his recourse to philosophical ideas and to historical documents for a broader perspective of the complex issues. It was characteristic of Coleridge's historical approach to political questions that, in preparing articles for the *Courier*, he should have spent several days in the Westminster Library, reading the "best documents" he could find on the "Debates of the Irish Parliament from the earlier period of the American War to the Union".[2] In spite of some research the essays are somewhat disappointing. Although they contain passages of acute analysis, the argument is never fully developed; the tone is cautious, tentative, and evasive; and the third essay, which optimistically promises a "Critique on the Systems of Toleration and Religious Rights, of Hobbes, Locke, and Warburton", ends abruptly and inconclusively; moreover, the manuscript draft in the British Museum[3] does not enable one to complete the argument. Another manuscript note, however, indicates that Coleridge thought that

> Toleration tho' from motives of expedience it may be wisely practised, can never be logically proved either a right on the part of a Sect, or a Duty on the part of a Government, if under the term, Religion, we are compelled to admit whatever hideous doctrine & practise any man or number of Men assert to be their Religion, & an article of their faith.[4]

Coleridge's humane statesmanship emerges most clearly in the first letter on the Catholic Petition, in which he argued that the whole safety of the British Empire is bound up with the future of Ireland, and acknowledged England's responsibility for Ireland's sad history.

> Meantime, all agree in the one fact, that, like a fort detached, yet included in the same plan of fortification, Ireland must either remain part of the common defence, or become the most perilous and commanding counterwork for our annoyance. . . . It is fatal to this branch of the British Empire,

[1] C thanked Godwin for an invitation to meet Henry Grattan (1746–1820), the Irish statesman, saying "To sit at the same table with GRATTAN—who would not think it a memorable Honor, a red letter day in the Almanach of his Life?" [18 Mar 1811]: *CL* III 312. For C's tribute to O'Connell's high principles, see *TT* 5 Feb 1833.

[2] Letter to Godwin 5 Oct 1811: *CL* III 335.

[3] BM MS Egerton 2800 f 115^{v}.

[4] BM MS Egerton 2801 f 225.

that it cannot be severed from the tree but to furnish the handle for the axe employed to fell it.[1]

Far from being opposed to Emancipation in 1811, Coleridge accepted it in principle, but pointed out the grave dangers of granting it at the wrong moment and for the wrong reasons. He therefore argued that everything must be done "to conciliate the heart, for the purpose and with the earnest intent of gradually conceding the whole claim".[2]

Weak as the general impact of these essays must have been, especially the inconclusive "Critique", which was reminiscent of the critique of Hobbes that had appeared two years earlier in *The Friend*,[3] they do contain ideas that are of special interest to the reader of the later work, *Church and State*. They show clearly that in 1811, as in 1829 and later, what Coleridge most feared was that Emancipation would be regarded in Ireland as "the stepping-stone to separation, as an engine to a repeal of the Union".[4] There was, too, at both periods of his life a similar concern with "securities", especially security against foreign allegiance, although in *Church and State* the whole question of specific securities is subordinated to the clear enunciation of a constitutional principle. In the *Courier*, on 5 August 1811, he stressed that Catholics were

excluded from some offices of State and from the Legislature, not on account of their religious tenets, but because they involve in their religion a numerous and most powerful magistracy, whose *spiritual* authority intermixes itself with almost every point that nearly affects the temporal interests and conduct of their subjects, which magistracy will not suffer itself to be placed under either the control or the superintendence of the Sovereign, while they swear allegiance to a foreign Sovereign.[5]

Undoubtedly Coleridge's fear of an *imperium in imperio*[6] was exaggerated at all times and his naïve trust in securities in 1811 was in striking contrast with his profound understanding of political

[1] 13 Sept 1811: *EOT* (*CC*) II 280.

[2] Ibid II 282.

[3] *Friend* (*CC*) II 98 (I 166–7).

[4] *Courier* 5 Aug 1811: *EOT* (*CC*) II 243. A modern historian confirms C's fears and notes that Emancipation "came too late to save the Union. For nearly a century the main object of Irish elected representatives was to be the repeal of the Act of the Union, and little by little the Protestant Ascendancy was thrown off, the Church of Ireland disestablished in 1869, and an Irish Nationalist Party emerged at Westminster to keep the Irish question in the forefront of British politics." Douglas Woodruff *Church and State in History* (1961) 69.

[5] *EOT* (*CC*) II 243.

[6] Crane Brinton has pointed out that Coleridge's fears of any *imperium in imperio* led him to underestimate the valuable function of corporate bodies within the state. *Political Ideas of the English Romanticists* (1926) 82.

consensus in *Church and State*, but it is nevertheless clear that many of the main lines of Coleridge's approach were first laid down in these early *Courier* essays. The three chief essays as a whole leave one with the impression that Coleridge would have preferred writing a treatise on the subject rather than brief newspaper articles. Such a treatise was not to appear, however, until nearly twenty years later in *Church and State*.

The next occasion on which Coleridge wrote on Irish affairs was in 1814, when he contributed a series of six letters "To Mr Justice Fletcher" to the *Courier*, under the signature "An Irish Protestant".[1] The letters, which are solemn warnings against the re-emergence of Jacobinism, touch on a number of issues that are taken up again much later in *Church and State*. For example, the severe condemnation of all secret oaths and secret societies, mainly directed at Catholic associations, is in line with his condemnation of any *imperium in imperio* in *Church and State*.[2] Moreover, the ecstatic praise of Lessing's "exquisite Dialogues on Free-masonry, entitled *Falk and Ernest*" anticipates a similar tribute to Lessing in *Church and State*.[3] Also interesting in relation to his later ideas is Coleridge's appearance as "an earnest advocate for national education" in the letters "To Mr Justice Fletcher".[4] Turning to the question of the Union in one of the later letters, he points out the consequence of separation—"separation of Ireland from Great Britain. . .is impracticable; and, were it not so, yet the success of the undertaking would be an event to be deprecated, as but another name for war, intestine discord, insignificance and slavery".[5] Finally, he castigates the false patriotism of the United Irishmen, who confuse the part with the whole. Once

[1] *EOT* (*CC*) II 373–417. On 20 Jan 1832 C re-read these letters "To Mr Justice Fletcher" with pride, saying that "no good man would read them without interest". In retrospect, his only regret related to the style, "a work of Reason and Reflection translated into the language of Dreamland". In a transcript by an unknown scribe of the *Courier* Fletcher essays, with corrections and notes in C's hand, made 1832, now in the Berg Collection, NYPL.

[2] Cf "If there be indeed such a thing as an axiom in politics, a truth involved in the very definition and idea of a state, it is this, that no government can consistently tolerate any organized powers not subordinated to itself" (Letter II to Mr Justice Fletcher: *EOT*—*CC*—II 381) with "If I met a man, who should deny that an imperium in imperio was in itself an evil, I would not attempt to reason with him: he is too ignorant. Or if, conceding this, he should deny that the Romish Priesthood in Ireland does in fact constitute an *imperium in imperio*, I yet would not argue the matter with him: for he must be a Bigot" (*C&S*, below, p 149).

[3] In Letter II 29 Sept 1814: *EOT* (*CC*) II 382; cf *C&S*, below, p 114n.

[4] Letter IV 2 Nov 1814: *EOT* (*CC*) II 397.

[5] Letter VI 9 Dec 1814: *EOT* (*CC*) II 411.

again, he claims that the foreign education and foreign connexions of the Catholic gentry might endanger security, a very different attitude from Sydney Smith's, who wrote, "My cry is, no Popery; therefore emancipate the Catholics, that they may not join with foreign papists in time of war."[1]

Coleridge's next projected contributions to the issue were never published. On 8 May 1816, he wrote to Daniel Stuart saying that if he were to write on the Catholic Question, he must be allowed "to express the Truth & the whole Truth concerning the impudent avowal of Lord Castlereagh that it was not to be a *Government Question*"; he then went on to promise to write "a Tract on the Question, which to the best of my knowlege will be about from 120 to 140 Octavo Pages; but so contrived that Mr Street may find no difficulty in dividing it into 10 or 20 Essays or Leading Paragraphs".[2] To reassure Stuart and Street, the latter now Editor of the *Courier*,[3] he claimed that he had excluded metaphysical reasoning and brought the problem under three heads: "1. Plain evident Sense.—2. Historical documental Facts.—3. Existing circumstances, character, &c of Ireland in relation to G. Britain, and to its own Interests & those of its various classes of Proprietors." Five days later, he asked Stuart what would be the best form—"simply, Essays—or Letters, addressed to Lord Liverpool, for instance".[4] On 24 June he complained to J. J. Morgan that Street would never let his "Essays" be published, and two and a half years later, in January 1819, said that he would have to apply to Street for their return.[5] Although no Letters appeared in the *Courier*, on 24 September 1816 he wrote confidentially to J. H. B. Williams, Gillman's assistant, to ask him to send "the Letter to Lord Liverpool (Letter the third, *I believe*) on the Catholic Emancipation", and told him which drawer to look in.[6] A week earlier, he had assured Hugh J. Rose in a letter that "there will soon appear in the Courier some *Anti Emancipation* Essays".[7]

In May 1817, when Grattan moved for a committee to consider the laws relating to Roman Catholics, Coleridge was too busy seeing

[1] Sydney Smith *Works* (1850) 579, quoted by Machin 19.

[2] *CL* IV 640.

[3] Stuart claimed that after 1810 or 1811 he found it better "to leave Street entirely to his own course" (*CL* IV 640n), but C clearly assumed that Stuart still influenced Street's editorial policy.

[4] *CL* IV 643.

[5] 24 Jun 1816: *CL* VI 1041 and letter to William Mudford 19 Jan 1819: *CL* VI 1046.

[6] [24] Sept 1816: *CL* IV 683.

[7] [17] Sept 1816: *CL* IV 671.

Biographia Literaria and the three volumes of *The Friend* through the press to record his views in print, but he did record them in the margins of a copy of the *Parliamentary Debates* for 1817, which is now in the Berg Collection in the New York Public Library. These notes, apart from proving how closely Coleridge followed the Emancipation debates in Parliament, suggest that he was almost as critical of the opposers of Emancipation as of its supporters, although of course it is dangerous to read too much into such brief notes, since a chance phrase may prompt hostile comment on a speech otherwise perfectly acceptable to the writer of the note. To the part of the speech in which Lord Castlereagh said that he could never "believe that any existing danger could be aggravated by the introduction into parliament of a few noble Catholic peers or of a few generous Catholic commoners", Coleridge added the marginal note:

> Who rests the Objection on this basis? Who fears the danger from this quarter? The Obj. is—You will yourself establish an irresistible *Right* to be the Established Church in Ireland for the Catholic Hierarchy—and increase the Zeal for Proselytism a 100 fold.—"[1]

And he seized on Grattan's claim that the constitution was not a Protestant but originally a Catholic one as "the ground-error, of the Philo-Romanists".[2] While one might have expected Coleridge to praise Peel's speech, described by his modern biographer as "one of his most outstanding parliamentary achievements",[3] in fact he described it as a perfect example of the way "the most zealous defenders of Protestantism betray the strongholds of their cause in their anxiety" to prove "their own Liberality and *Gentlemanly* Feelings".[4] However, Coleridge's main criticism was reserved for the speech of the anti-Emancipationist, Dr Marsh, Bishop of Llandaff, a genuine "Flower of the indigenous growth of Marsh-land!" The extensive notes on the flyleaves of the *Parliamentary Debates* of 1817 reveal Coleridge's contempt for Marsh's futile attempt to argue the question of the Catholic franchise on the basis of the "*comparative* worth" of individuals, instead of on the "eligibility of Classes of Men" as defined by the Legislature, yet a further example of Coleridge's wish to relate the question to constitutional principles and not to irrelevant details of persons and hypothetical individual action.

[1] Hansard xxvi (1817) 399–400. NYPL.

[2] Ibid xxvi 427–8.

[3] To support this judgment, Norman Gash assembles an impressive series of tributes from comtemporaries and notes that the speech was said to have influenced the voting of thirteen members, *Mr. Secretary Peel* 209–10.

[4] Hansard xxvi 419.

But he makes it clear that he would have voted with Marsh, yet on different grounds. "But this is not *my* ground of Objection. Not the Bill, but the principles set forth in the Preamble of the Bill, and the (ως εμοι δοκεῖ) inevitable Consequences of the legislative solemn Sanction of these Principles—these are *my* terror!—"[1] It was the threat to the constitution rather than the particular consequences of "permitting Romanist Men of Property to sit in both Houses" that Coleridge feared. It was on this ground that he would have voted against the 1817 movement for Catholic relief.

By 1821, when Coleridge once again recorded his reactions to parliamentary debates on Emancipation, several important events had occurred. George III, the inveterate opponent of Emancipation, and Grattan, its chief advocate, were no longer alive. An Irish lawyer, Plunkett, now took over Grattan's role. On 28 February 1821, he introduced a motion, based on two securities; one ensuring that the State had knowledge of all correspondence between Catholics at home and abroad, the other providing a veto on ecclesiastical appointments. The second security aroused violent opposition among the Irish, and by the time the Bill was debated in the Lords, even Lord Grenville, who had previously insisted on firm securities, was obliged to compromise and throw in his weight with the anti-vetoists. Coleridge wrote a long note on Grenville's speech of 17 April 1821. In form, it suggests preliminary jottings for a newspaper article. If so, this never appeared.[2] To Coleridge, Grenville's speech seemed to be:

> A Declamation of Combustibles and Common-places, and Confusions of accidents with Principles, without an approach to a senatorial or even a dialectic statement of the true *Question*. He keeps out of sight the points adhuc sub lite, and spouts away, like a Lead-gutter in a ~~Rain-storm~~ Thaw, on the points admitted on all sides; ~~and~~ or rather like a kennel in White Chapel or Newgate Market, in a Rain-storm, swells and sweeps onward the bloody offal, filth, guts and garbage which the very Shambles and Butchers' Dogs had long disowned.—

The note ends with praise of Lord Liverpool's reply to the debate, "like all his other Speeches, sensible and Statesmanlike, but even he does not strike *into*, tho' here & there he appears to strike *at*, the root of the Cause", adding "If for *foreign* he had said *alien* Influence, he would have hit the Eye of the Target". Apparently Coleridge planned to remedy the central deficiency of Liverpool's speech by writing three letters on "The (so called) Catholic Question re-considered in its relations to the ~~social~~ Duties and correlative Rights of the Subject, and the Constitutional Interests of the State". These

1 Ms note on Hansard XXVI 615–18. 2 N 20 ff 8^{v}–9.

three letters were to be addressed to his Swedenborgian friend, C. A. Tulk, recently elected to Parliament. They were to be concerned with (1) "Preliminary Facts"; (2) "removal of certain errors and Misstatements respecting Facts of high importance in the solution of the Problem"; and (3) "The ⟨true⟩ *Root* of the ~~Cause~~ Question: i.e. the actual Ground of the Danger on each side".[1] But if they were written, they were never published.

Although the pro-Catholic campaign in 1821 failed, it was a landmark in the history of the question. G. I. T. Machin writes:

> It was the last occasion when quarrels over the Veto played a prominent part in the struggle, and it was the first time that several recurring features of the question appeared. It set the pattern for the 1820's of a small pro-catholic majority in the Commons whose wishes were rejected by a large anti-catholic majority in the Lords. The pro-catholics might persuade themselves that their majority in the Commons made eventual triumph inevitable, but the Lords continued to reject relief by consistently large majorities until 1829.[2]

If the pattern with the two Houses remained fairly static, the same cannot be said about the situation in Ireland. Dramatic changes took place during the 1820's. In 1823, O'Connell and R. L. Sheil founded the Catholic Association. In the same year the English Catholics, with the approval of the Whigs, formed a similar association. From now on Tory supporters of Emancipation insisted that the Catholic associations should first be suppressed before the granting of any relief. In 1824 Goulburn introduced a Bill to repress all societies, but even his supporters recognised the impossibility of enforcement; and, a year later, the Catholic Association found loopholes in the Act. O'Connell, on a visit to London, indicated that he was ready to accept two securities: the payment of the Roman Catholic clergy out of State funds, thus ensuring their loyalty; and the disfranchisement of the Irish forty-shilling freeholders, a concession to those who feared what would happen if the Catholic peasantry were given the vote and who wished the franchise qualification to be raised to £10. When Sir Francis Burdett introduced his Bill for Emancipation in 1825, it passed the first reading with a majority of 13. For its second reading, the two "Wings", or securities along the lines suggested by O'Connell, were omitted and introduced separately. It passed second and third readings with a small majority. Before

[1] N 20 f 9^v. There is a rough draft of an essay offering a definition of the essential question, which may have been intended for the second letter, in BM MS Egerton 2800 ff 109–9^v. See above, p xxxv n 2.

[2] Machin 31; the account of Ireland in the 1820's that follows draws on this work.

it went to the Lords, the Duke of York, a rabid anti-Catholic, threw his weight behind the Tory opposition, claiming that the Coronation Oath forbade the Royal Assent being given. The defeat of Burdett's Bill now became certain, especially when Liverpool, who had previously wavered, spoke out strongly against it in the Lords. The consequent defeat of the motion carried with it an obvious lesson; from now on the Irish Catholics must find a stronger means of enforcing their cause. And this they did, among other means, by securing the election of O'Connell at Clare in 1828. Had they not done so, some relief might have been conceded in time,

> but it would have been conceded as a boon granted by a superior to an inferior class, and it would have been accompanied and qualified by the veto. It was the glory of O'Connell that his Church entered the Constitution triumphant and unshackled—an object of fear and not of contempt, a power that could visibly affect the policy of the empire.[1]

Wellington sent the King a long memorandum on Catholic Emancipation in the middle of November 1828. With the conversion of both Wellington and Peel to the cause of Emancipation, steps were taken swiftly but secretly to lay a government Bill before the two Houses:[2] a Bill that was accompanied by Bills to suppress the Catholic Association and to disfranchise the forty-shilling freeholders; and though the King's assent remained in doubt almost until the last moment, eventually he gave his reluctant assent to the Bill for Catholic Emancipation on 13 April 1829.

THE GENESIS OF COLERIDGE'S *ON THE CONSTITUTION OF THE CHURCH AND STATE*

In view of the vigorous campaign for Catholic Emancipation in 1825, it is not surprising to find that Coleridge began to write an essay on Church and State in that year, although it is uncertain how much he wrote at the time and what relation this projected essay bore to the completed *On the Constitution of the Church and State*. But it was not only the public controversy aroused by Burdett's Bill of

[1] W. E. H. Lecky *The Leaders of Public Opinion in Ireland* (rev ed 1871) 249, quoted P. Hughes *The Catholic Question 1688–1829* (1929).

[2] Norman Gash traces the complicated manoeuvres in *Mr. Secretary Peel* 545–98. It was Peel who persuaded Wellington to abandon the demand for "securities" and thus secured the passing of the Bill. Gash 586. According to Owen Chadwick: "The bill passed, not because a majority of Englishmen wanted it, but because the government expected civil war in Ireland if it refused to concede the Roman Catholic claims. Wellington afterwards confessed that his only reason for granting emancipation was that he could not help it." *The Victorian Church* 8.

1825 and the publication of Southey's *Book of the Church* in 1824, but also his own work on *Aids to Reflection*, that led him to work out the all-important distinction between the Church of Christ and the National Church. On 7 May 1825, in a letter to J. A. Hessey, a partner in the firm that published *Aids to Reflection*, he included as number 5 in a list of six works ready for the press, the whole of which ran to between 200 and 250 pages, the following: "5. On the Church—& the true Character of the Romish Church."[1] A day later, it appears in a slightly different form in a letter to John Taylor Coleridge as: "5. On the Church + Establishment, and Dissent—and the true character & danger of the Romish Church."[2] On 16 May Coleridge wrote to Hessey saying that he had been encouraged by a friend (probably Hyman Hurwitz) to ask whether Hessey and Taylor thought it "expedient to put to the Press immediately" the various essays he had recently listed in his letters.[3] This time he referred to number 5 on the list as "the church as an institution of Christ and as a Constituent Estate of the State, *Ec*clesia ⨯ *En*clesia", phrasing similar to that in a footnote in *Aids to Reflection*,[4] a marginal note in a copy of Hooker's *Works*,[5] and another marginal note, this time on the Rev Philip Skelton's *Works*, which specifically refers to "my essay on Establishment & Dissent" and also contrasts Ecclesia and Enclesia.[6] All these notes, written about 1825, anticipate the crucial distinction in *Church and State* between the Church of Christ and the National Church and suggest a close connexion between the projected "Essay" of 1825 and the later published work. Moreover, on 20 July 1825, Coleridge wrote to Blanco White:

> I am on the point of putting to the Press a small Work on the Church, in its twofold sense—viz. as an Institution of Christ, and as a State Institution—in the latter part of which I come on the same ground with you, and tho' I cannot ascribe to the perusal of your work what had been written before its publication, I shall feel myself induced by prudence as well as constrained by Justice, to express my sense of its worth & value. . . .[7]

[1] *CL* v 434–5.

[2] *CL* v 444.

[3] *CL* v 455. The dissolution of the partnership between Hessey and Taylor on 30 Jun 1825 made it unlikely that the essays would be published as a supplement to *AR;* see *CL* v 465 n 1.

[4] *AR* (1825) 166n.

[5] Note in C's copy of Hooker's *Works* (1682) 56, in *C 17th C* 144–5.

[6] Note on *Complete Works* (6 vols 1824) III 394–9, made in 1825, in *LR* IV 278; see J. R. Barth *Coleridge and Christian Doctrine* (1969) 160n.

[7] *CL* v 485; C also writes that he would like to show White a "series of Letters, which have for more than a year been in my Publisher's Hands, on the right & superstitious Use & Veneration of the Sacred Scriptures". Ibid v 486. J. Blanco White (1775–1841), an anti-Catholic propagandist, visited C in Jul 1825, and presented him with a copy of his *Practical and Internal Evidence Against Catholicism*

The reference is sufficiently circumstantial to make it likely that the essay had been sketched out in part and did not exist only as a project in Coleridge's mind. When *Church and State* appeared, in 1829, it duly contained a warm tribute to Blanco White along the lines of the 1825 letter.[1] Yet another link between Coleridge's writings in 1825 and the published treatise on *Church and State* in 1829 appears in *Aids to Reflection* (1825), in which he writes that he will quote

> a sentence or two from a Dialogue which, had my prescribed limits permitted, I should have attached to the present Work; but which with an Essay on the Church, as instituted by Christ, and as an Establishment of the State, and a series of Letters on the right and the superstitious use and estimation of the Bible, will appear in a small volume by themselves, should the reception given to the present volume encourage or permit the publication.[2]

The passage that then follows, headed "Mystics and Mysticism", covers much the same ground as the dialogue tacked onto the end of *Church and State*. From all this, it seems that, however little Coleridge actually wrote of his "Essay on the Church" in 1825 and however prone he was to confuse works merely projected with those actually written, he had already laid down some of the main lines of his later thought in 1825. It also seems likely that some of the material written or sketched in 1825 may have been incorporated with little change into *Church and State* in 1829.

Of the six works listed as ready for the press in the letter to J. A. Hessey on 7 May 1825 only the sixth, "On the right and the superstitious Use of the Sacred Scriptures", is known to have been completed in 1825. It was sent to the publishers of *Aids to Reflection* and was originally intended to be part of that work but was omitted on the grounds of length and returned to Coleridge in 1826.[3] It was posthumously published by Henry Nelson Coleridge in 1840 as *Confessions of an Inquiring Spirit*. Had the manuscript of the "Essay on the Church" been submitted to the publisher in 1825 or 1826, one would have expected it to have been returned with the manuscript of *Confessions*. It seems likely, therefore, that it was never sent.

A further reason for believing that the Essay was not completed and submitted at this time is Coleridge's own statement at the beginning of *Church and State* that had the text of his early draft been ready before John Hookham Frere left England, it was Frere's intention to lay it before the Prime Minister, Lord Liverpool. Frere, who

---

(1825) and, later (Dec), with copies of other works. For further details of White, see below p 122 and n 3.

[1] See below, p 80 and n 1.

[2] *AR* (1825) 381.

[3] *CL* v 434n–5.

was in England for a year from September 1825, did in fact forward a copy of *Aids to Reflection* to Liverpool, who promised to "endeavor to do something" for Coleridge.[1] And before he left England in September 1826, Frere had obtained from Liverpool a "positive Promise" of a sinecure for Coleridge of £200 a year.[2] As Coleridge himself acknowledged in a letter of 19 January 1826, he had "strong motives" for "sending to the press *immediately* the supplementary disquisitions".[3] These were, of course, to obtain state patronage. He also thought of sending them to the Whig Marquis of Lansdowne, a strong advocate of Catholic Emancipation, and to the Tory Lord Chancellor, Lyndhurst, but did not do so, saying that he shrank from anything that "would be interpreted as a sort of advance towards connecting myself with the [Whig] Party".[4] By the time the published work on *Church and State* appeared in December 1829, the Catholic Bill had already become law. Its arguments could be of service to neither party. But, in any case, all chance of state preferment had vanished earlier with Liverpool's retirement and Canning's death on 8 August 1827, which gave "the settling Blow" to Coleridge's hopes. That the book appeared too late to affect the issue of Catholic Emancipation mattered little as far as the work itself was concerned, since Coleridge was more concerned with exploring fundamental ideas of Church and State than with offering specific solutions to the problem of Catholic Emancipation. It is clear that he was not altogether opposed to Emancipation but that he wished to relate the issue to fundamental principles and to see the current cry for securities grounded on something more substantial than

[1] When Liverpool returned the copy of *AR* to Frere he wrote: "When I have the Means, I will certainly endeavor to do something for him—but I will be obliged to you not to commit me." *CL* VI 539n. See also note below, p 11.

[2] Ibid; cf *CL* VI 671n.

[3] To Edward Coleridge: *CL* VI 542.

[4] Letter to Stuart 8 Oct 1827: *CL* VI 702. After stating that he had written a "sketch of a Memorial" on "the Catholic Question" before Canning's death, C wrote: "I have thought repeatedly of correcting the one Memorial on the only plan, on which the (so called) Emancipation of the Catholics could be either desirable for Ireland, or palatable to the Country at large—and of sending it to the Marquis of Lansdown." He did not, but he did send a copy of *C&S* to Lord Lyndhurst (now in HEHL; see below, p 237): "Lord Lyndhurst's letter was a kind one—I shall send him my Book on the Constitution with a letter". Marginal note 20 Nov 1829 in H. Hurwitz *The Elements of the Hebrew Language* (1829), now in VCL. In the Preface to *TT*, HNC states that as far as he sided with any party C sided with the Tory party, because the National Church was "the ark of the covenant" and because "the Whigs [were] about to coalesce with those whose avowed principles lead them to lay the hand of spoliation upon it". But HC and HCR said that HNC made C too Tory. See also below p 63 and n 8.

political expedience. Although it may have been unrealistic of him to expect the drafters of the Bill to spell out the full constitutional implications of the securities, Coleridge believed that the Church would be in danger if this were not done by someone and so he sought to do it himself.

Even if it is difficult to establish how much of the 1825 "Essay on the Church" was written and what its precise relation to the published treatise was, it is relatively easy to follow the later stages of composition of *Church and State*. On 23 February 1829 we can observe Coleridge, in a notebook entry, bracing himself for his difficult task:

> Alas! I have to address Men who have never distinctly or consciously referred their opinions to Principles, much less traced the several steps of the ascent; and yet in order to produce any *effect*, to make any immediate and general impression, I must state such positions only and urge only such arguments, as the Reader (or Hearer) will immediately see the full force of, and recognize as a previous Judgement of his own. In short, I dare not pretend to inform, instruct, or guide.[1]

The following month he wrote to Henry Nelson Coleridge that but for illness he would have had "a few printed Sheets to send [him] on the ideas of the Constitution & the Church" and that he had only half a dozen pages to compose in order to finish but, not being in a fit state, had been writing and rewriting without satisfying himself.[2] On 15 July 1829 Mrs Coleridge asked Poole if "it was *printing*".[3] There seems to have been considerable delay up to the last minute, for in September Coleridge was still correcting proofs and sending the publisher the final instalment of the manuscript, the Appendix.[4] An earlier part of the text already in proof had referred to a further discussion of the phrase "another world that now is" in "Appendix A".[5] To supply the necessary Appendix, Coleridge used the long dialogue on mysticism that he had sent Edward Coleridge in a letter in 1826.[6] He also used some marginal comments he had recently made on Isaac Taylor's *Natural History of Enthusiasm*, a volume that had appeared anonymously in May 1829. For the dialogue he drew up a glossary of key terms, and the Appendix was finally rather loosely drawn together with additional commentary. Coleridge was aware that the work was "patchy" and drafted an "advertise-

[1] N 38 f 25.

[2] 23 Mar 1829: *CL* VI 787–8.

[3] *Minnow Among Tritons: Mrs S. T. Coleridge's Letters to Thomas Poole, 1799–1834* ed Stephen Potter (1934) 148. Mrs C reports that WW and RS are strongly against the measure for Catholic Emancipation, C's daughter silently for it.

[4] Letter to Thomas Hurst: *CL* VI 818.

[5] Below, p 117.

[6] 27 Jul 1826: *CL* VI 593–601.

ment" to disarm criticism, but it was never incorporated in the volume and exists only as a scrap of paper in the British Museum. It reads: "The Volume might have been entitled Epistolary Disquisitions, or Extracts from a series of Letters on the word, ⟨Idea; and on the⟩ Constitution, the State, the Church, ~~and~~ according to the Idea. . . . To say, it is *patchy*. . . is but another less courteous way of conveying the same description. For the Work purports to be a Pasticcio."[1] He was also aware, as most readers have been, of the scrappy inconclusive ending. He therefore promised his publisher, Thomas Hurst, a brief conclusion:

> I have before me & needing little more than transcription, a Chapter that would amount to half a sheet, or more—with the title—What is to be done now?—addressed principally to the Clergy of the Establishment—and which would certainly prove an interesting addition to the Volume and give an air of completeness to it. But whether the Volume will not be larger, than you & Mr E. Chance would have recommended, even without this Chapter, I am doubtful—If your judgement is in favor of its being added, it shall be sent with the next proofs.[2]

The publisher, who had already been kept waiting for copy and the return of proof sheets, evidently ignored the suggestion. The following month, on 20 October, Coleridge looked forward optimistically to its immediate appearance and drew the attention of the Editor of *Blackwood's Magazine* to a flattering reference to his journal in *Church and State*:

> In a small volume on the right *Idea* of the Constitution in Church and State, which you will receive I think within a fortnight, and which but for severe sickness you would have received many months ago, you will find how highly I estimate the favour.[3]

However, the work did not appear until December 1829.[4]

[1] BM MS Egerton 2801 f 259.

[2] Letter to Thomas Hurst Sept 1829: *CL* VI 819.

[3] *CL* VI 820. In the letter to William Blackwood C alludes to his note in *C&S* praising John Wilson and *B Mag* for their services to translation (below, p 114). The note was an indirect acknowledgment of *Blackwood's* eulogy of C's own translation of *Wallenstein* (*B Mag* XIV—Oct 1823—378–96). Blackwood did not take the hint to review *C&S* in his magazine. In May 1830 a long article by J. F. Dalton on "The Influence of the Church of England in Society" appeared, but it made no reference to *C&S* and showed no knowledge of it. On 26 May 1832, C told Blackwood that he regretted that no notice had been taken of either first or second edition: *CL* VI 912.

[4] Although the date of publication on the title-page is 1830, it was included in a list of new books published in Dec 1829 in *Bent's Monthly Literary Advertiser;* see also *CL* VI 824n.

Early in January 1830, Coleridge agreed with his nephew Henry Nelson Coleridge that half a guinea was "a *choking* price" and explained that his publishers had defended the price on the grounds that his "many corrections" had "increased the expence" and that only a limited number of copies had been printed, "I believe, not 300". Having complained that this seemed like "levying an *impost*" on the author's friends, he nevertheless went on to look forward to the success of a second edition:

> I have already prepared a Copy for the Press, in which I have reduced the Work into CHAPTERS, with a *Head* to each, stating the Contents—with a small number of insertions, and not a small number of emendations.[1]

This rearrangement of the material improved the lucidity and coherence of the argument; and it is the second edition, revised by the author, that forms the copy text of this edition. But the rearrangement of the material into chapters with appropriate headings was restricted to the first half; the original division of the second into the "Idea of the Christian Church" and "On the Third Possible Church, or the Church of Antichrist" remained the same; and nothing was done to tidy up the last thirty pages, perhaps because in his satisfaction with the balanced division between the Christian Church and the Church of Antichrist, the author had forgotten how disjointed the final pages that followed were, or perhaps because he still planned to add a completely new last section. Certainly, the problem of whether to include a third part, "*What is to be done now?*" still exercised his mind. He even contemplated asking the publishers to print extra copies of a third part to be issued to buyers of the first edition,[2] but nothing came of this complicated manoeuvre, presumably because the part was never completed. And so the second edition, enormously improved as it was, still contained the disastrously ragged ending of the first edition.

[1] [6] Jan 1830: *CL* VI 825–6.

[2] In the letter to HNC on 6 Jan 1830; cf below, p 83 and n 2.

THE INFLUENCE OF *ON THE CONSTITUTION OF THE CHURCH AND STATE*

Coleridge's innate modesty did not prevent him from recognising the seminal qualities of his own works. A note by Henry Nelson Coleridge records Coleridge's own estimate of *Church and State*. It also contains an ironic recipe for the survival of its ideas:

> Mr Coleridge himself prized this little work highly, although he admitted its incompleteness as a composition:—"But I don't care a rush about it," he said to me, "as an author. The saving distinctions are plainly stated in it, and I am sure nothing is wanted to make them *tell*, but that some kind friend should steal them from their obscure hiding-place, and just tumble them down before the public as *his own*."[1]

Many nineteenth-century thinkers were glad to borrow from its pages, some openly like F. D. Maurice;[2] others, associated with the Oxford Movement, more secretly to avoid the taint of theological unorthodoxy; yet others to "just tumble down" the thoughts, careless of their origin. Although *Church and State* had no actual effect on the issue of Catholic Emancipation, it did exert a profound influence on nineteenth-century thought; and many of its leading ideas, especially those relating to culture and society, have been taken up and developed more recently by writers as varied as William Temple, T. S. Eliot, Middleton Murry, and Raymond Williams.[3] Inevitably, the chief interest for Coleridge's contemporaries and immediate successors lay in its vision of a revitalised Church and its philosophical defence of the English constitution. The two were related; and it was Coleridge's distinctive contribution to the issue of Church reform that he provided a definition of the idea for which a National Church existed, together with important distinctions between the idea of such a church and the actual established Church of England, and between both these and the Church of Christ, that universal fellowship of all true believers, united in

[1] *TT* 1 Jan 1823, n on "permanency and progression".

[2] Mainly in *The Kingdom of Christ* (1838); see Pt III of C. R. Sanders *Coleridge and the Broad Church Movement* (1942) 179–262 and A. R. Vidler *F. D. Maurice and Company* (1966) 205–20, which makes a clearer distinction than Sanders' between C's early and late influence on Maurice.

[3] For example, in William Temple *Christianity and the Social Order* (1942), T. S. Eliot *The Idea of a Christian Society* (1939), J. Middleton Murry *The Price of Leadership* (1939)—with its passionate commitment to the ideas of a National Church found in C and Dr Arnold—and Raymond Williams *Culture and Society 1780–1950* (1958).

Christ, timeless, and never to be institutionalised in any estate of the realm. These distinctions may have proved difficult to understand and apply even for his admirers,[1] as we can see from Charles Smith's muddled attempt to apply them in *Seven Letters on National Religion* of 1833 and from Coleridge's irritation at Smith's blurring of his original distinctions.[2] Nevertheless, they provided a new model for discussions on ecclesiastical reform, a model of the Church as both spiritual and natural society.

Even if it were desirable to summarise the complex arguments of *Church and State*, it would be difficult to do so, since they are so rich and diverse and represent in a compressed form the essence of Coleridge's mature thought on a great variety of subjects. His first editor, Henry Nelson Coleridge, in his edition of 1839, the third edition of *Church and State*, provided a useful summary of at least the main lines of the argument, and readers coming to this work for the first time are advised to consult his Preface, printed in the present edition as the editor's Appendix A, before beginning to read Coleridge's text.

For a full understanding of Coleridge's views, the argument in *Church and State* needs to be expanded and clarified by reference to other passages scattered throughout his published works, notebooks, and marginalia, especially *Aids to Reflection* and *Table Talk*. The notes in this edition draw attention to these passages. But Coleridge's widely spread comments on two related themes deserve special comment. Nowhere in *Church and State* does Coleridge work out in any detail the different basis on which membership of the National Church and of the State rests, and nowhere does he state explicitly what the qualities are in Protestantism, as opposed to Roman Catholicism, that make it especially conducive to the creation of representative government and a National State. Two passages are of particular interest. The first is from an entry in *Table Talk* for 19 September 1830:

[1] To H. F. Cary, who had complained of obscurity in *C&S*, C wrote: "One cause of this defect I suppose to be the contrast between the continuous and systematic character of my Principles, and the occasional & fragmentary way, in which they have hitherto been brought before the Public." [29 Nov 1830]: *CL* VI 847–8.

[2] In Letter II Smith recommends his readers to read *C&S* especially for its account of "a national clerisy"; he appears at first to have grasped C's distinctions, only to blur them later by equating the "Church of Christ" and "the National Church": 219–22. C's criticism of Smith are made in the margins of the copy of *Seven Letters* (1833) in VCL, in which he accuses Smith of "*confounding*" what he "had labored to *distinguish* . . . the *En*clesia and the *Ec*clesia".

A state, in idea, is the opposite of a church. A state regards classes, and not individuals; and it estimates classes not by internal merit, but external accidents, as property, birth, &c. But a church does the reverse of this, and disregards all external accidents, and looks at men as individual persons, allowing no gradation of ranks, but such as greater or less wisdom, learning, and holiness ought to confer. A church is, therefore, in idea, the only pure democracy. The church, so considered, and the state, exclusively of the church, constitute together the idea of a state in its largest sense.

The second is from Notebook 44.[1] There Coleridge suggests that it is in the "nature of progressive Civilization" that the State "should display a transition into the character of a Church", a transition already in progress in the United States of America.

The proper object of a State is *Things*, the permanent *interests* that continue in the flux of its component Citizens, hence a distinction & if I might say so, a polarisation of ranks and orders is the very condition of its existence—while the proper Object of a Church is Persons, and no other than personal difference, intellectual and moral. The aim of the first, i.e. of a State is to preserve and defend the ~~grounds~~ difference between the integral parts of its total Body, by establishing and watching over the differential grounds, & causes, and exponents of the difference—the aim of a Church utterly to do away even those personal differences, which it acknowledges and of which it makes use—the comparatively wise to equalise wisdom, the comparatively Good to diffuse the Good. In the United States of America I see an evident, tho' unconscious, experiment to become a Church of this World—a Church temporal.

There are a considerable number of related passages in the notebooks and in marginal comments on the seventeenth-century theologians in which Coleridge speculates on the special appropriateness of the Protestant religion to foster democratic government. The longest and most elaborate, written on 7 May 1826, is in Notebook 26.[2] In it, he argues that Protestantism counteracts the tendency of Christianity "to destroy Nationality". As it is partly an expression of the Understanding, "the faculty of selecting and adapting means to proximate ends", Protestantism stresses the individual, is "instinctively *legislative*", and creates representative bodies to reconcile the clash of individual minds and interests. It is, therefore, concludes Coleridge, "essentially favorable to representative Governments",

[1] N 44 ff 75–6, c 1830.

[2] N 26 f 9 onwards. Professor Austin Gough has pointed out to me that C's remarks on the political tendency of Protestantism might almost be part of the Continental debate at the same time, and anticipate some of the important arguments against which Taparelli, Balmès, and Donoso Cortès wrote in the 1840's. It would be interesting to know whether C had read Lamennais *Des progrès de la révolution* (1829) and *Essai sur l'indifférence* (vol I 1817, vol II 1820).

not only "national, but municipal, not only temporal but spiritual". Passages such as these help to elucidate the central argument of *Church and State*.

It is, however, as a source-book of seminal ideas rather than as a treatise on a single subject that *Church and State* has proved influential in English thought. For the statesman and political philosopher it contained the germs of an idealist theory of the state, free from the absolutism of Hegel; it also contained suggestive remarks on the dynamic relationship between the forces of permanence and progression in society; an original distinction between two forms of energy in the state, the "free and permeative life and energy of the Nation to the organized powers brought within containing channels";[1] and an interesting recognition of the largely unconscious ideas that "possess"[2] ordinary men and that partly account for consensus, social cohesion, and the continuous life of institutions. For the theologian and churchman it provided both a defence of the place in society of the Church of England and, by implication at least, a programme for its reform and development. For the historian and sociologist, as John Stuart Mill testified,[3] Coleridge offered a philosophy of history and a philosophy of society. For the educational theorist and critic of culture and society, *Church and State* offered important distinctions between "civilisation" and "culture", "education" and "instruction", and a rational defence of a permanently endowed learned class, the clerisy, an elitist theory certainly, but one that specifically allowed for the entry of all classes, including the very poor. Most interesting perhaps, because little known, is the immediate practical influence that *Church and State* probably had on the education of a whole generation of lawyers and doctors at King's College, London, through the lectures of Professor Park on the English Constitution and through J. H. Green's *Address* at the opening of the medical session in 1832.[4] The Preface of the *Address* stated that the author had adopted for the groundwork of his reasoning "the ideas of the National Church, or Clerisy" in Coleridge's essay; and, as a whole, it outlined what Green called the "daylight freemasonry" that came into existence when the three professions formed the creative collegiate life of a great Metropolitan University. In view

[1] Below, p 85.

[2] Below, p 13.

[3] In his essay on C (1840) in the *Westminster Review*, reprinted in *Mill on Bentham and Coleridge* ed F. R. Leavis (1950).

[4] John James Park (1795–1833) was Professor of Law and Jurisprudence at King's College; his four lectures *The Dogmas of the Constitution* appeared in 1832; for reference to *C&S* see 130; for C's criticism of the lectures see

of all this, it is hardly surprising that *Church and State*, together with the *Lay Sermons* and *Aids to Reflection*, provided such varied inspiration for so many different schools of thought in the nineteenth century.

The three nineteenth-century writers who drew most heavily on the ideas in *Church and State* were Thomas Arnold,[1] W. E. Gladstone,[2] and F. D. Maurice.[3] But strong traces of Coleridge's thought appear in a host of other writers: in John Sterling,[4] Julius and Augustus Hare, J. S. Mill, F. J. A. Hort,[5] and Matthew Arnold,

---

NTP 223. J. H. Green (1791–1863) was Professor of Surgery at King's and C's close friend, philosophical collaborator, and literary executor. A copy of his *Address* (1832) is in BM; his *Spiritual Philosophy, Founded on the Teaching of the Late S. T. Coleridge* ed J. Simon (2 vols 1865) reflects C's more general influence.

[1] *Principles of Church Reform* (1833) and *Fragment on the Church* (1844; 2nd ed 1845).

[2] *The State in Its Relations with the Church* (1838).

[3] A. R. Vidler *F. D. Maurice and Company* (1966) 215 lists the four main passages that reveal Maurice's debt to C: dedicatory letter to DC in *The Kingdom of Christ* (2nd ed); letter written to his son in 1870 (reference in *The Life of Frederick Denison Maurice* ch 12 ed F. Maurice—3rd ed 1884—I 176–8; final pages of *Moral and Metaphysical Philosophy* (2 vols 1871–2); and 73 pages contributed anonymously to Julius Hare *Charges* (1856), prefixed to Hare *The Victory of Faith* (1874). John Kent accuses both C and Maurice of encouraging "the Anglican clergy to believe that they could recover a position in English society which they probably never held in the past" and of wishing to slip back into a non-existent "tribal paradise". "The Victorian Resistance: Comments on Religious Life and Culture 1840–80" *VS* XII 2 (Dec 1968) 145–54.

[4] John Sterling (1806–44) first visited C in 1828, brought Maurice glowing accounts of C's conversation, and later struggled between the rival influences of C and Carlyle, who later wrote his life. In 1836, Sterling wrote to J. C. Hare: "To Coleridge I owe *education*. He taught me to believe that an empirical philosophy is none, that Faith is the highest Reason, that all criticism, whether of literature, laws, or manners, is blind, without the power of discerning the organic unity of the object." "Sketch of the Author's Life" by J. C. Hare in Sterling *Essays and Tales* (2 vols 1848) xv.

[5] C's influence on the Hares is reflected in *Guesses at Truth by Two Brothers*, compiled in 1827 before *C&S* was published, but amplified in later editions. It was J. C. Hare who was most strongly influenced; see *The Better Prospects of the Church: a Charge to the Clergy of the Archdeaconry of Lewes* (1840), with its statement that the National Church "she, and she alone, can truly educate the people"; see also *Privileges Imply Duties: a Charge to the Clergy of the Archdeaconry of Lewes* (1841); but esp *The Mission of the Comforter* (1848) and *The Contest with Rome* (1851), in which Hare notes (p 345) that C was derided for making a mountain out of a molehill, but was justified in fearing a Papal Bull appointing a Roman hierarchy in England when twenty years later "the Papacy attacks England on this very point" . . . "Thus, among the freaks of Time, it now and then comes out, that the unpractical philosopher, looking into the heart of things, sees far beyond the vision of all his practical contemporaries." See also "Papal Aggression" in E. R. Norman *Anti-Catholicism in Victorian England* (1968) 52–79; also Sanders *Coleridge and the Broad Church Movement*

especially in his ideal of "the general harmonious expansion of those gifts of thought and feeling which make the peculiar dignity, wealth, and happiness of human nature", in *Culture and Anarchy* (1869).[1] Indicative of the breadth of Coleridge's influence is the fact that his ideas permeated no less than three distinct movements of nineteenth-century religious thought: the Broad Church Movement, the Oxford Movement, and Christian Socialism.[2] And partly through John Stuart Mill,[3] his ideas on property as a sacred trust, and on the clerisy and the national endowment of education, although they were transformed almost beyond recognition as they passed through the mechanical utilitarian mind, provided the philosophical radicals[4] with ammunition from an unexpected source to fire at the defenders of the established order.

Both Gladstone and F. D. Maurice formally acknowledge their great debt to Coleridge's *Church and State*, Gladstone calling it a

---

(Durham, N. C. 1942) 123–46, Vidler *F. D. Maurice and Company* 221–41.

It was Mill's lifetime ambition to unite the thought of Bentham and C in a single philosophy; not surprisingly, he failed.

F. J. A. Hort gave one of the most sympathetic nineteenth-century general accounts of C in *Cambridge Essays* (1856). He describes *C&S* as C's "most important work" (p 348) and stated that "the problem of the nineteenth century" was to apply C's distinction between morality and religion "to all the changing conditions of human life" (p 349).

[1] *Culture and Anarchy* ed J. Dover Wilson (paperback ed 1960) 47.

[2] For C's influence on the Broad Church Movement see Sanders *Coleridge and the Broad Church Movement*; for his influence on the Oxford Movement see R. W. Church *The Oxford Movement 1833–1845* (1891) 129, S. C. Carpenter *Church and People 1789–1889* (1959 ed) I 23–4, and J. Coulson *Newman and the Common Tradition: a Study in the Language of Church and Society* (1970). Coulson stresses the connexion between C's and Newman's thought through C's insight into the language of symbols and through his vision of the dialectical relationship between the "idea" of the Church and its social context and physical embodiment, "between its sacramental origin . . . and its empirical reality" (p 40). This was to be Newman's central preoccupation. For C's influence on Christian Socialism (that nebulous term for a line of thinkers from C and Maurice to Bishop Westcott, Hensley Henson, and William Temple, who all stressed the Church's social responsibility), see C. K. Gloyn *The Church in the Social Order: a Study of Anglican Social Theory from Coleridge to Maurice* (Oregon 1942) and C. E. Raven *Christian Socialism 1848–54* (1920).

[3] In the essay "Corporation and Church Property" Mill argued that since the Church was not fulfilling its rôle of educating the people in the highest form of spiritual culture, the State was free to "withdraw the endowment from its existing possessors", and he taunted the defenders of the Church of England who had "taken their weapons chiefly from" C's "storehouse". *Collected Works* ed J. M. Robson (Toronto 1967) IV 221.

[4] See E. Halévy *The Growth of Philosophical Radicalism* (1928) passim.

"masterly sketch",[1] Maurice placing it above all Coleridge's other works. Addressing Derwent Coleridge, in the Dedication to *The Kingdom of Christ*, Maurice wrote:

> The little book upon Church and State you will suppose, from the title and character of these volumes, that I am likely to have studied still more attentively. And indeed, if you watch me closely, you will discover, I doubt not, many more thoughts which I have stolen from it than I am at all aware of, though I think I am conscious of superabundant obligations. It seems to me that the doctrine that I have endeavoured to bring out in what I have said respecting the relations between Church and State, is nothing but an expansion of Mr Coleridge's remarks respecting the opposition and necessary harmony of Law and Religion, though in this, as in many other cases, I have departed from his phraseology, and have even adopted one which he might not be inclined to sanction.[2]

In seeking to define the rôle of the Church in a pluralist society, Gladstone and Maurice both followed Coleridge in rejecting any idea of a formal "alliance" between Church and State, since this suggested some external legal agreement. Instead they preferred to think of relationship and union, "a union which has cemented itself by no human contrivances, and which exists in the very nature of things", according to Maurice.[3] However, whereas Gladstone argued that the moral nature of the State demanded that it should establish and maintain the one true Church,[4] Maurice was more intent on affirming the reality of a universal Church that was truly catholic.[5] And, as he himself realised, he was most Coleridgian when

[1] *The State in Its Relations with the Church* (1838) 17; Gladstone also calls C's argument in *C&S* "beautiful and profound".

[2] *The Kingdom of Christ* ed A. R. Vidler II 357–8; the Dedication to DC was added in the 2nd ed, 1842. In the *Life* ed F. Maurice I 178, the impact of *C&S* on Maurice and the Debating Society, of which Mill and Roebuck were members, is recorded. Maurice wrote: "I was still under the influence of Coleridge's writings—himself I never saw. His book on the 'Ideas of the State,' which appeared at this time, impressed me very much. I accepted to a great degree the principle of it, though not all the conclusions." The influence of C's ideas on education is clear in *Has the Church, or the State, the Power to Educate the Nation? A Course of Lectures* (1839). Comparing the English and Prussian systems, Maurice praises the English, whereby "a student acquires the habit of understanding himself, and the laws of his own mind" (p 102) and stresses in Coleridgian fashion that education "has for its object the cultivation of that essential humanity which constitutes the same under all varieties of costume".

[3] *The Kingdom of Christ* II 312.

[4] *The State in Its Relations with the Church* ch 2 (1838); see also Vidler *The Orb and the Cross: a Normative Study in the Relations of Church and State with Reference to Gladstone's Early Writings* (1945).

[5] After describing his general debt to C, Maurice wrote: "In this way there rose up before me the idea of a Church Universal, not built upon human inventions or human faith, but upon

he insisted on the distinction between law and religion,[1] between what he called the effects of the "righteous principle" on human conduct and the effects of the "spiritual principle" on individual human will. Gladstone drew no such fine distinctions. Yet the charge of unintelligibility was brought against both. Macaulay had great fun at Gladstone's expense in the *Edinburgh Review*[2] and even Maurice's warmest admirers complained that it was not only difficult to understand his ideas but impossible to see how they were to be implemented.[3]

No such complaint could be brought against Thomas Arnold. In Arnold, as Basil Willey has remarked, Coleridgian ideas became "a programme of action".[4] His aims were to construct "a truly national and Christian Church, and a truly national and Christian education";[5] and to this task he brought a forceful prose style, a magnificent grasp of administrative problems, and a hostile but intuitive awareness of the strength of the nineteenth-century utilitarian tradition. The latter enabled him, as it enabled Bishop Blomfield,[6] with his "ungovernable passion for business", to lay down severely practical schemes of reform, schemes especially conducive to the practical spirit of the age; but just as Coleridge had objected to Blomfield's plans for introducing "a Scotch Eldership in disguise"[7]

---

the very nature of God himself, and upon the union which he has formed with his creatures: a Church revealed to man as a fixed and eternal reality by means which infinite wisdom had itself devised." *The Kingdom of Christ* II 363.

[1] Ibid II 357–8.

[2] *Ed Rev* Apr 1839, reprinted in *Critical and Historical Essays* (1870) 468–502.

[3] Benjamin Jowett, for example, recognised his greatness, but complained that he was "misty and confused". *Life and Letters* ed E. Abbott and L. Campbell (1897) I 350. And a twentieth-century admirer, C. F. G. Masterman, complained that his work was "often obscure, not carefully studied, with no particular charm of style", yet claimed that he was "the greatest thinker of the English Church in the nineteenth century". *Frederick Denison Maurice* (1907) 6.

[4] *Nineteenth Century Studies: Coleridge to Arnold* (1949) 53.

[5] A. P. Stanley *Life of Thomas Arnold* (1898 ed) II 12.

[6] Charles James Blomfield was bp of London from 1828 until 1856. With Peel he was instrumental in creating the Ecclesiastical Commission that was responsible for much necessary Church reform. His activities in educational and religious reform are described in detail in Olive J. Brose *Church and Parliament: the Reshaping of the Church of England 1828–1860* (1959). In *Tancred*, Disraeli gave a vivid description of his "bustling, energetic, versatile" energies and limited powers of thought.

[7] C's phrase in a copy of Blomfield's *Charge* (1830) 24. In extensive marginal comments, C approved Blomfield's remarks on the religious education of the poor and the educational and moral fitness of the clergy, but was critical of Blomfield's failure to distinguish between the Church of Christ and the National Church, his views on parochial assistance, and week-day services. The copy is in BM. When

and to his defence of mid-week services, so no doubt he would have objected to Arnold's schemes for reviving the order of deacons and encouraging week-day public worship. In spite of such obvious differences in approach, Arnold's defence of Church property as "something saved out of the scramble, which no covetousness can appropriate, and no folly waste",[1] was clearly based on Coleridge's idea of the "nationalty", a national wealth inalienably apportioned to the Church, and would therefore almost certainly have enjoyed his full approval. Moreover, Arnold's definition of the rôle of the clergy was almost a rewording of Coleridge's idea of the clerisy: "to secure for every parish the greatest blessing of human society, that is, the constant residence of one individual, who has no other business than to do good of every kind";[2] although it must be admitted that in the rewording the original precision of function has been swallowed up in vague piety—"to do good of every kind". In his conception of the rôle of the Church in the parishes and in his solution to the problem of Dissent, Arnold went further than Coleridge, inspired by his own ideal of comprehensiveness. The Church, he insisted, "should be rendered thoroughly comprehensive in doctrine, in government and in ritual".[3] In working out this ideal, he obliterated Coleridge's all-important distinction between the National Church and the Universal Church of Christ, but he did so in order to stress the potential spiritual influence of the Church on the whole nation and was prepared to compromise with the dominant utilitarian spirit in order to defeat the grosser materialism of the "godless party". Anything, Arnold believed, would be better than "a national society, formed for no higher than physical ends; to enable men to eat, drink, and live luxuriously".[4] Thus, if from one point of view, Arnold appears to lose sight of some of Coleridge's most vital distinctions in *Church and State* (what Coleridge

---

Blomfield consecrated St Michael's, Highgate (Nov 1832), he said: "You must have perceived, Mr Coleridge, that the substance of my Sermon was taken from your Work on Church & State." *CL* VI 995n.

[1] *Principles of Church Reform* (1833), printed in *Miscellaneous Works* (1845) 265; ed cited hereafter is *Principles* (1962) ed M. J. Jackson and J. Rogan 93–4.

[2] *Principles* 94; cf C's definition below, pp 43–4.

[3] Arnold states the problem as "to constitute a Church thoroughly national, thoroughly united, thoroughly Christian, which should allow great varieties of opinion, and of ceremonies, and of forms of worship, according to various knowledge, and habits, and tempers of its members, while it truly held one common faith, and trusted in one common Saviour, and worshipped one common God". *Principles* 107–8.

[4] Ibid 142.

called its "saving distinctions"), from another point of view he may be seen carrying on the great tradition of Burke and Coleridge, by restating the higher end for which the State exists.

In the present century the influence of *Church and State* has continued to be felt in writings on religion, politics, and education. The ideas that inspired Maurice's Christian Socialism permeate William Temple's popular writings on the social responsibility of the Church, although he makes no formal acknowledgment of the debt.[1] The one modern work that is most clearly indebted to *Church and State* is T. S. Eliot's *The Idea of a Christian Society* (1939). The very title takes its origin from Coleridge, and Eliot includes a note in which he states explicitly that his definition of the word "Idea" comes from *Church and State*.[2] Moreover, his triple distinctions of the Christian State, the Christian Community, and the Community of Christians owes much to Coleridge, especially the Community of Christians, which is simply a newly defined clerisy, an order that would not be exactly synonymous with the National Church but that would be much more of an intellectual aristocracy than Coleridge's clerisy. In addition, Eliot quotes Coleridge's crucial distinction between "education" and "instruction" with approval[3] and constantly keeps in mind the basic distinction between the spirit of Christianity and the spirit of the world in society. For all its close debt to *Church and State*, *The Idea of a Christian Society* makes embarrassing reading for an admirer of the original work. It ignores the deep social insight that produced Coleridge's distinction between the forces of permanence and progression and the consequent difference in his attitude towards policies designed for agriculture and industry; it both widens and yet paradoxically restricts Coleridge's meaning, so that the Christian State becomes an impossibly wide ideal and the Community of Christians an exclusive aristocracy of intellect; and, strangely enough, its language and tone appear more nostalgic, more feudal and reactionary today than Coleridge's in *Church and State*, for all Coleridge's use of such terms as nationalty and clerisy.[4]

[1] See *Essays in Christian Politics and Kindred Subjects* (1927), *Citizen and Churchman* (1941), and *Christianity and the Social Order* (1942).

[2] *The Idea of a Christian Society* (1939) 18, 67. Eliot's *Notes Towards a Definition of Culture* (1949) also draws deeply on Coleridgian distinctions, but without appropriate acknowledgment and in general either weakening or muddling C's ideas.

[3] *The Idea of a Christian Society* 41.

[4] D. L. Munby *The Idea of a Secular Society* (Oxford 1963) distinguishes clearly between C's dynamic view of society and Eliot's conservative, more

Fortunately, there has been no lack of scholars interested in Coleridge's political works, including *Church and State*, and they have helped to correct these and similar distortions. In describing *Church and State* as "a case study of the application of the ideas of reason to social and economic problems", William F. Kennedy has usefully drawn attention to aspects that Eliot overlooked.[1] And more recently, David P. Calleo has demonstrated the "fascinating combination of philosophical generality and concrete analysis" the work contains, "not dissimilar in its method to Aristotle's *Politics*".[2] What it offers essentially is a "model" for thinking about the permanent relations of Church and State, and the place of religion, education, and culture in the life of any civilised community. Coleridge himself uses the word "model", and in this, as in so many other instances, he anticipates the language and methods of modern sociology and linguistics. What appears so startlingly modern in Coleridge's political thought is his idea of the open dynamic society. He sees the continuous but ever-changing tensions in society as necessary to its freely developing life, not to be arbitrarily controlled or suppressed, but held in perpetual adjustment. His vision is of a society always in the making. A "masterly sketch" rather than "a treatise", *On the Constitution of the Church and State* is Coleridge's greatest single political work. As Julius Hare remarked: "It was his last work, written in the fullest maturity of his judgment, the result of observation and meditation of his whole life."[3]

---

static view; see also Terry Eagleton "Eliot and a Common Culture" *Eliot in Perspective* ed G. Martin (1970) 279–95.

[1] *Humanist Versus Economist: the Economic Thought of Samuel Taylor Coleridge* (Berkeley 1958) 11. See also the section on *C&S* in Colmer *Coleridge: Critic of Society* (Oxford 1959) 153–66.

[2] *Coleridge and the Idea of the Modern State* (1966) 105–6.

[3] *The Contest with Rome* (1851) 246, quoted in Sanders *Coleridge and The Broad Church Movement* (1942) 138.

ON THE CONSTITUTION OF THE CHURCH AND STATE

ON THE CONSTITUTION OF

THE CHURCH AND STATE

ACCORDING TO THE IDEA OF EACH
WITH AIDS TOWARD
A RIGHT JUDGMENT ON
THE LATE CATHOLIC BILL

BY S. T. COLERIDGE, ESQ., R.A., R.S.L.[1]

[1] In 1824 C was nominated for one of the ten Royal Associateships of the newly chartered Royal Society of Literature and duly elected; he read a paper on Aeschylus' *Prometheus* on 18 May 1825. For the 1st ed of *AR*, C had questioned his publisher, J. A. Hessey, whether he "*ought*. . . to attach ROYAL ASSOCIATE of the R. S. L.?—I have no fondness for this Bashaship with *one Tail*—(My Brother-in-law has, at least a dozen queues)" and decided not to use the title then. *CL* v 435.

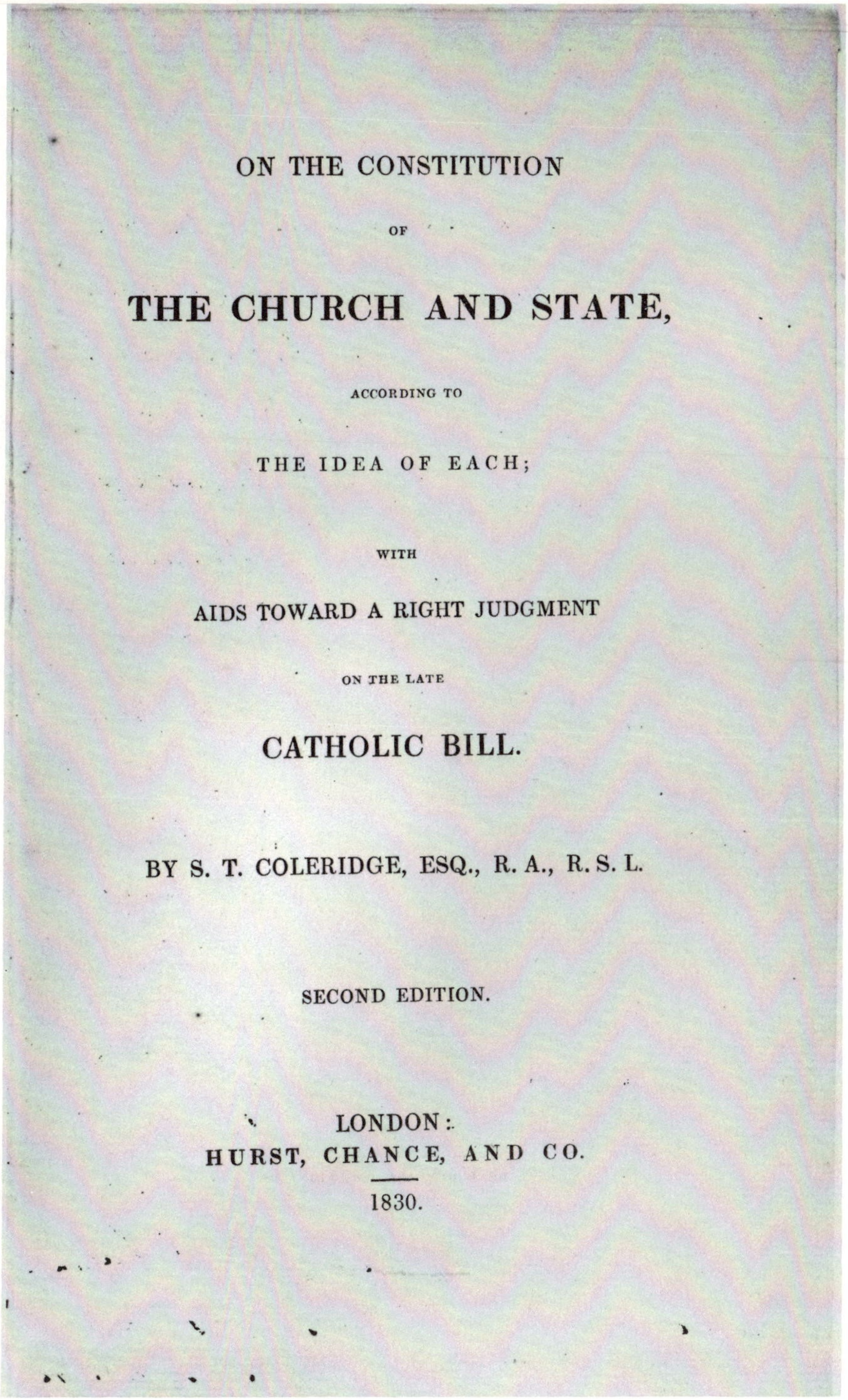

ON THE CONSTITUTION

OF

THE CHURCH AND STATE,

ACCORDING TO

THE IDEA OF EACH;

WITH

AIDS TOWARD A RIGHT JUDGMENT

ON THE LATE

CATHOLIC BILL.

BY S. T. COLERIDGE, ESQ., R. A., R. S. L.

SECOND EDITION.

LONDON:
HURST, CHANCE, AND CO.

1830.

2. *On the Constitution of the Church and State* (2nd ed 1830)

ADVERTISEMENT

THE occasion of this [a]small volume[b] will be sufficiently explained, by an extract from a letter to a friend:—[1] "You express your wonder that I, who have so often avowed my dislike to the introduction even of the word, Religion, in any special sense, in Parliament, or from the mouth of Lawyer or Statesman, speaking as such; who have so earnestly contended, that Religion cannot take on itself the character of Law, without ipso facto ceasing to be Religion, and that Law could neither recognise the obligations of Religion for its principles, nor become the pretended Guardian and Protector of the Faith, without degenerating into inquisitorial tyranny[2]—that I, who have avowed my belief, that if Sir Matthew Hale's doctrine, that the Bible was a part of the Law of the Land,[3] had been uttered by a Puritan Divine instead of a Puritan Judge, it would have been quoted at this day, as a specimen of puritanical nonsense and bigotry—you express your wonder, that I, with all these heresies on[c] my head, should yet withstand the measure of Catholic *Emancipation*, and join in opposing Sir Francis Burdett's intended Bill,[4] for the repeal

[a-b] 1st ed: pamphlet [c] 1st ed: in

[1] The friend may be Dr Gillman: note the example of the physician "called in to a consultation", below. Or the "letter" may be a device like the "letter from a friend" written by C himself in *BL* ch 13 (1817) I 291–5.

[2] Cf *Friend* (*CC*) I 94–5, which includes the distinction between polar opposites and the phrase "inquisitorial tyranny"; cf a similar passage in "To Mr Justice Fletcher" III (21 Oct 1814) in the *Courier: EOT* (*CC*) II 386, and a letter to Daniel Stuart 29 Oct 1814: *CL* III 537–8.

[3] Sir Matthew Hale (1609–76), in giving judgment in a case of blasphemy, Rex v Taylor, declared that "Christianity is parcel of the laws of England; and therefore to reproach the Christian religion is to speak in subversion of the law". HNC, in *C&S* (1839) 2n, noted that Sir Edward Coke (1552–1634) had earlier said that Christianity was "part and parcel of the Common Law". M. T. Sadler, in an impassioned and widely reported speech on 17 Mar 1829 opposing the second reading of the Catholic Emancipation Bill, quoted the phrase. Hansard NS XX (Feb–Mar 1829) 1155 and *Speech* (2nd ed 1829) 17. Cf C's annotation on John Bunyan *Pilgrim's Progress* (1830) lxiv: "Wretched Coward! I never did like that Sir M. H. It was he who fathered the jargon of the Bible being part of the Law of England."

[4] Sir Francis Burdett (1770–1844) introduced Bills for Catholic Emancipation at frequent intervals. His Bill of 1825, which passed the Commons and was defeated in the Lords only after the Duke of York's intervention, was one of the factors that prompted C to project an "Essay on the Church" in that year (see Introduction, above,

of the disqualifying statutes! And you conclude by asking: but is this true?

"My answer is: Here are two questions. To the first, viz., is it true that I am unfriendly to (what is called) Catholic Emancipation? I reply: No! the contrary is the truth. There is no inconsistency, however, in approving the *thing*, and yet having my doubts respecting the manner; in desiring the same end, and yet scrupling the means proposed for its attainment. When you are called in to a consultation, you may perfectly agree with another physician, respecting the existence of the malady and the expedience of its removal, and yet differ, respecting the medicines and the method of cure. To your second question (viz., am I unfriendly to the present measure?) I shall return an answer no less explicit. Why I cannot return as brief a one, you will learn from the following pages, transcribed, for the greater part, from a paper drawn up by me some years ago, at the request of a gentleman (that I have been permitted to call him my friend,[1] I place among the highest honours of my life), an old and intimate friend of the late Mr. Canning's; and which paper, had it been finished before he left England, it was his intention to have laid before the late Lord Liverpool.[2]

"From the period of the Union to the present hour, I have neglected no opportunity of obtaining correct information from books and from men, respecting the facts that bear on the question, whether they regard the existing state of things, or the causes and occasions of it; nor, during this time, has there been a single speech

pp l–li), but the reference here is to Burdett's motion introduced on 8 May 1828: Hansard NS XIX (1828) 375–419. The motion for Committee was carried by 272 to 266 in the Commons (ibid 679); on 10 Jun it was negatived in the Lords 181 to 137 (ibid 1294).

[1] John Hookham Frere (1769–1846), diplomatist and translator of Aristophanes. Frere was at Caius College, Cambridge 1787–92 (*CN* I 1656), and C refers to their meeting as "among the most memorable Red Letter Days of my Literary Life" (to John Murray 8 May 1816: *CL* IV 637). By 1816, C knew him well enough to send him the proof sheets of *BL* to read. In a letter to Edward Coleridge on 13 Jun 1826, he referred to him as "the polished Gentleman, the exquisite Scholar, the man of Genius—but the Good Man the CHRISTIAN shining out among all & beyond all". *CL* VI 585. As friend and patron, Frere contributed to DC's education, helped to nominate C for a Royal Society of Literature annuity, and, when that ceased after the accession of William IV, paid it himself. See Introduction, above, p liv.

[2] Robert Banks Jenkinson, 2nd Earl of Liverpool (1770–1828), was stricken with a paralytic stroke on 17 Feb 1827 and resigned office. George Canning (1770–1827) succeeded him as Prime Minister, but died 8 Aug 1827. For C's disappointed hopes of patronage, see Introduction, above, p liv.

of any note, on either side, delivered, or reported as delivered, in either House of Parliament, which I have not heedfully and thoughtfully perused, abstracting and noting down every argument that was not already on my[a] list, which, I need not say, has for many years past few accessions to boast of. Lastly, my conclusion I have subjected, year after year, to a fresh revisal, conscious but of one influence likely to warp my judgment: and this is the pain, I might with truth add, the humiliation of differing from men, whom I loved and revered, and whose superior competence to judge aright[b] in this momentous cause, I knew and delighted to know; and this aggravated by the reflection, that in receding from Burkes, Cannings, and Lansdownes,[1] I did not move a step nearer to the feelings and opinions of their antagonists. With this exception, it is scarcely possible, I think, to conceive an individual less under the influences of the ordinary disturbing forces of the judgment than your poor friend; or from situation, pursuits and habits of thinking, from age, state of health and temperament, less likely to be drawn out of his course by the under-currents of Hope, or Fear, of expectation or wish. But least of all, by predilection for any particular sect or party: for wherever I look, in religion or in politics, I seem to see a world of power and talent wasted on the support of half truths, too often the most mischievous, because least suspected of errors.[2] This may result from the spirit and habit of partizanship, the supposed inseparable accompaniment of a free state, which pervades all ranks, and is carried into all subjects. But whatever may be its origin, one consequence seems to be, that every man is in a bustle,[3] and except under the sting of excited or alarmed self-interest, scarce any one in earnest."

I had written a third part under the title of "What is to be done now?"[4] consisting of illustrations from the History of the English

[a] 1st ed: the [b] 1st ed: right

[1] Edmund Burke (1729–97), to whose political wisdom C pays tribute in *BL* ch 10, George Canning, and Henry Petty, 3rd Marquis of Lansdowne (1780–1863), all supported Catholic Emancipation. At one time C planned to send Lansdowne a copy of *C&S*; see *CL* VI 702, and Introduction, above, p liv.

[2] Cf a similar passage in *LS* (*CC*) 228. In *The Friend* C wrote: "the whole truth is the best antidote to falsehoods which are dangerous chiefly because they are half-truths". *Friend* (*CC*) I 189. He also spoke of half-truths in relation to his philosophical "system". *TT* 12 Sept 1831. See also below, p 128.

[3] C had a special dislike for bustle; cf "All is in a bustle/ and I do not greatly like Bustle . . .". *CN* I 1682; cf III 3569 and 3754.

[4] HNC prints in *C&S* (1839) 5: "had collected materials for a third part", which suggests that C never completed this section in spite of his

and Scottish Churches, of the consequences of the ignorance or contravention of the principles, which I have attempted to establish in the first part: and of practical deductions from these principles, addressed chiefly to the English clergy. But I felt the embers glowing under the white ashes;[1] and on reflection, I have considered it more expedient that the contents of this small volume should be altogether in strict conformity with the title; that they should be, and profess to be, no more and no other than *Ideas* of the Constitution in Church and State. And thus I may without inconsistency entreat the friendly reader to bear in mind the distinction I have*[a] enforced, between the exhibition of an idea, and the way of acting on the same; and that the scheme or diagram best suited to make the idea clearly understood, may be very different from the form in which it is or may be most adequately *realized.* And if the reasonings of this work should lead him to think, that a strenuous Opponent of the former attempts in Parliament may have given his support to the Bill lately passed without inconsistency, and without[b] meriting the name of APOSTATE, it may be to the improvement of his charity and good-temper, and not detract a tittle from his good sense or political penetration.[2]

S. T. C.

* p. 20.

[a] Footnote added in 2nd ed [b] 1st ed: without either being or

elaborate plans to issue it as a supplement to the already printed 1st ed. See Introduction, above, p lvi, also below, p 83.

[1] Cf "But we hasten to disengage ourselves from personal and temporary facts. . . . We are well aware, that we tread on dangerous ground: and that the live embers still glow beneath the White ashes, that cover them." C's suppressed article of 1811 on the Duke of York: *EOT* (*CC*) III 228. Cf the quotation from Horace *Odes* 2.1.7–8 in *Friend* (*CC*) II 21.

[2] Here C seeks to forestall the charge of apostasy by suggesting that it is not inconsistent for him to favour the present Bill, even though he had been a "strenuous opponent" of earlier bills, e.g. Burdett's of 1825.

ON THE CONSTITUTION OF

THE CHURCH AND STATE

ACCORDING TO THE IDEA OF EACH[a]

[a] Half-title added in 2nd ed

THERE IS A MYSTERY IN THE SOUL OF STATE,
WHICH HATH AN OPERATION MORE DIVINE
THAN OUR MERE CHRONICLERS DARE MEDDLE WITH.

Shakespear [a] [1]

[a] Motto added in 2nd ed

[1] Adapted from *Troilus and Cressida* III iii 202–5:

There is a mystery—with whom relation
Durst never meddle—in the soul of State,
Which hath an operation more divine
Than breath or pen can give expressure to.

C's introduction of the phrase "mere chroniclers" is an expression of his contempt for the historians of his day and earlier (e.g. Hume), because they did not see history from a philosophical point of view; cf *TT* 13 Jul 1832. See also below, p 32 and n 1.

[a]CHAPTER I

Prefatory Remarks on the true import of the word, IDEA; *and what the author means by "according to the Idea"*[b]

THE Bill[1] lately [c]passed for the admission of Roman Catholics into the Legislature[d] comes so near the mark to which my convictions and wishes have through my whole life, since earliest manhood, unwaveringly pointed, and has so agreeably disappointed my fears, that my first impulse was to suppress the pages, which[e] I had written while the particulars of the Bill were yet [f]unknown, in compliance with the request of an absent friend,[2] who had expressed an anxiety "to learn from myself[g] the nature and grounds of my[h] apprehension, that the measure would fail to effect the object immediately intended by its authors."

In answer to this, I reply, that the main ground of that apprehension is certainly much narrowed; but as certainly not altogether removed. I refer to the securities.[3] And, let it be understood, that in calling a certain provision hereafter specified, a *security*, I use the word *comparatively*, and mean no more, than that it has at least an equal claim to be so called, as any of those that have been hitherto proposed as such. Whether either one or the other deserve the name;

[a–b] 1st ed: PREFATORY REMARKS. DEAR SIR, [c–d] 1st ed: passed
[e] 1st ed: which, in compliance with your request
[f–g] 1st ed: unknown. "I am anxious," you say, "to learn from yourself [h] 1st ed: your

[1] In the King's Speech on 5 Feb 1829, the Government announced its intention to introduce the Bill. William Page Wood, later Baron Hatherley (1801–81), who attended C's famous Thursday evenings, recorded that on 5 Feb 1829 they discussed the speech "and agreed as to the gross absurdity of the insertion of the bishops and clergy as detached from the Church, in the recommendation for Catholic emancipation. The event, however, forms an epoch in our history." *C Talker* 240. The Bill for the Relief of His Majesty's Roman Catholic Subjects was introduced in the Commons by Peel on 5 Mar 1829 and in the Lords by Wellington on 31 Mar 1829; it passed both Houses and George IV gave his reluctant assent on 13 Apr 1829: 10 Geo IV cap 7. For further details see Introduction, above, p li, and App B, below, pp 203–9, where the Act is reproduced in full.

[2] John Hookham Frere, who lived in Malta but who visited England in Sept 1825 and stayed for a little over a year; see above, p 6 n 1.

[3] For the much discussed question of securities see Introduction, above, pp xlix–l.

whether the thing itself is possible; I leave undetermined. This premised, I resume my subject, and repeat, that the main objection, from which my fears as to the practical results of the supposed Bill were derived, applies with nearly the same force to the actual Bill; though the fears themselves have, by the spirit and general character of the clauses, been considerably mitigated. The principle,[1] the solemn recognition of which I deemed indispensable as a security, and should be willing to receive as the only security—superseding the necessity, though possibly not the expediency of any other, but itself by no other superseded—this principle is not formally recognized. It may perhaps be *implied* in one of the clauses (that which forbids the assumption of local titles by the Romish bishops); but this implication, even if really contained in the clause, and actually intended by its framers, is not calculated to answer the ends, and utterly inadequate to supply the place, of the solemn and formal declaration which I had required, and which, with my motives and reasons for the same, it will be the object of the following pages to set forth.

But to enable you fully to understand, and fairly to appreciate, my arguments, I must previously state (what I at least judge to be) the true Idea of A CONSTITUTION; and, likewise, of a NATIONAL CHURCH. And in giving the essential character of the latter, I shall briefly specify its distinction from the Church of Christ, and its contra-distinction from a third form, which is neither national nor Christian, but irreconcileable with, and subversive of, both. By an *idea*, I mean, (in this instance) that conception of a thing, which is not abstracted from any particular state, form, or mode, in which the thing may happen to exist at this or at[a] that time; nor yet generalized from any number or succession of such forms or modes; but which is given by the knowledge of *its ultimate aim*.[2]

Only one observation I must be allowed to add, that this knowledge, or sense, may very well exist, aye, and powerfully influence a man's thoughts and actions, without his being distinctly conscious of the same, much more without his being competent to express it in definite words. This, indeed, is one of the points which distinguish *ideas* from *conceptions*, both terms being used in their strict and proper

[a] Added in 2nd ed

[1] The principle, which is stated more clearly later, is that the Catholic Church should not enjoy any part of the national wealth set aside for the National Church; see below, pp 154–7.

[2] T. S. Eliot quoted this sentence with approval in *The Idea of a Christian Society* (1939) 67. Cf the account of the term "Idea" in *SM* App E (*CC*) 100–14.

significations.[1] The latter, *i.e.* a conception, *consists* in a conscious act of the understanding, bringing any given object or impression into the same class with any number of other objects, or impressions, by means of some character or characters common to them all. *Concipimus*, id est, capimus hoc *cum* illo,[2]—we take hold of both at once, we *comprehend* a thing, when we have learnt to comprise it in a known *class*. On the other hand, it is the privilege of the few to possess an idea: of the generality of men, it might be more truly affirmed, that they are possessed by it.

What is here said, will, I hope, suffice as a popular explanation. For some of my readers, however, the following definition may not, perhaps, be useless or unacceptable. That which, contemplated *objectively* (*i.e.* as existing *externally* to the mind), we call a LAW; the same contemplated *subjectively* (*i.e.* as existing in a subject or mind), is an idea. Hence Plato often names ideas laws; and Lord Bacon, the British Plato, describes the Laws of the material universe as the Ideas in nature. Quod in naturâ *naturatâ* LEX, in naturâ *naturante* IDEA dicitur.[3] By way of illustration take the following.

[1] A distinction of fundamental importance to C. In a note (1826?) on "An Appendix to the Life of Mr Richard Hooker" *Works* (1682) 27, C provides a concise definition: "Every Conception has its sole reality in its being referable to a Thing or Class of Things, of which or of the common characters of which it is a *reflection*. An Idea is a POWER (δυνάμις νοερα) that constitutes its own Reality—and is in order of Thought, necessarily antecedent to the *Things*, in which it is, more or less adequately, realized—while a Conception is as necessarily posterior." *C 17th C* 142–3. This marginal note and others suggest that the reading of *Ecclesiastical Polity* inspired C to redefine distinctions that he had drawn earlier and that played a major part in his constitutional theory in *C&S;* cf the distinction between enclesia and ecclesia, below, p 45 and n 1.

[2] C is reminding the reader of the basic meaning of the verb *concipio* (*cum*, "with"; *capio*, "I take"), from which *conception* is derived. Tr: "We *conceive*, that is, we take this *with* that". C frequently makes a point by looking at the primary meaning of words—see below, pp 20 ("majesty"), 24n, 78 ("liege"), 84 ("maxim"), 113 ("chaos"), 117 ("rivals"), 125 ("church"), 165 ("mystic"), 180 ("self-finding"), and nn—and in *AR* stresses the importance of so doing. *AR* (1825) 6n. He often also directs attention to the importance of other aspects of the science of words; see below, pp 108n, 120n, 165–6, and 167 n 1.

[3] Cf *Friend* (*CC*) I 491–2, and for a more comprehensive attempt to reconcile the systems of Plato and Bacon see "Essays on the Principles of Method" ibid I 482–524 and *Method* 37–47. A note in *The Friend* dated 23 Jun 1829 suggests that an idea and a law are "Subjective and Objective *Poles* of the same Magnet....What is an Idea in the Subject, i.e. in the Mind, is a Law in the Object, i.e. in Nature." *Friend* (*CC*) I 497n. "Quod...dicitur" ("what is called LAW in *created* nature is called IDEA in *creative* nature") is not in Bacon. HNC here quotes in *C&S* (1839) Bacon *Novum Organum* I CXXIV: "Sciant itaque homines...quantum intersit inter humanae mentis *idola* et divinae mentis ideas. Illa enim nihil

Every reader of Rousseau, or of Hume's Essays, will understand me when I refer to the Original Social Contract, assumed by Rousseau, and by other and wiser men before him, as the basis of all legitimate government.[1] Now, if this be taken as the assertion of an historical fact, or as the application of a conception, generalized from ordinary compacts between man and man, or nation and nation, to an actual occurrence in the first ages of the world; namely, the formation of the first contract, in which men covenanted with each other to associate, or in which a multitude entered into a compact with a few, the one to be governed and the other to govern, under certain declared conditions; I shall run little hazard at this time of day, in declaring the pretended fact a pure fiction, and the conception of such a fact an idle fancy. It is at once false and foolish.* For what if an original contract had actually been entered into, and formally recorded? Still I cannot see what addition of moral force would be gained by the fact. The same sense of moral obligation which binds us to keep it, must have pre-existed in the same force and in relation to the same duties, impelling our ancestors to make it.[4] For what could

* I am not indeed certain, that some operatical farce, under the name of a Social Contract or Compact, might not have been acted by the Illuminati and Constitution-manufacturers, at the close of the eighteenth century;[2] a period which how far it deserved the name, so complacently affixed to it by the contemporaries of "this *enlightened* age," may be doubted. That it was an age of *Enlighteners*, no man will deny.[3]

aliud sunt quam abstractiones ad placitum: hae autem sunt vera signacula Creatoris super creaturas, prout in materia per lineas veras et exquisitas imprimuntur et terminantur." "Let men learn...the difference that exists between the idols of the human mind and the ideas of the divine mind. The former are mere arbitrary abstractions: the latter the true marks of the Creator on his creatures, as they are imprinted on, and defined in matter, by true and exquisite touches." Tr W. P. Wood. See also *P Lects* Lect XI (1949) 331–3, and, for much the same thoughts, ascribed to Pythagoras, Lect II pp 107–8.

[1] Cf *Friend* (*CC*) I 186–202.

[2] Adam Weishaupt (1748–1830), a German mystic, founded the Order of the Illuminated (May 1776), or, as the members called themselves, the Perfectibilists, a short-lived movement of republican free-thought that aimed to replace Christianity with a religion of reason and that attacked property; many of its ideas survived to influence the leaders of the French Revolution. Joseph Emmanuel Sieyès (1748–1836) was one of the chief "Constitution-manufacturers" at the end of the eighteenth century. At the fall of the Directory in 1799, he had the chance to produce a perfect constitution, but Bonaparte completely remodelled it; for C's analysis, see *M Post* essays 7, 26, 27, and 31 Dec 1799: *EOT* (*CC*) I 31–6, 46–57.

[3] C drew the same distinction in 1814 in "To Mr Justice Fletcher" III: *EOT* (*CC*) II 388.

[4] The sentence occurs (var) in *Friend* (*CC*) I 173.

it do more than bind the contracting parties to act for the general good, according to their best lights and opportunities? It is evident, that no specific scheme or constitution can derive any other claim to our reverence, than [a]that which[b] the presumption of its necessity or fitness for the general good shall give it; and which claim of course ceases, or rather is reversed, as soon as[c] this general presumption of its utility has given place to as general a conviction of the contrary. [d]It is true, indeed, that from[e] duties anterior to the formation of the contract, because they arise out of the very constitution of our humanity, which supposes the social [f]state—it is true, that[g] in order to a rightful removal of the institution, or law, thus agreed on, it is required that the conviction of its inexpediency shall be as general, as the presumption of its fitness was at the time of its establishment. This, the first of the two great paramount interests of the social state demands,[h] namely, that of [i]permanence; but[j] to attribute more than this to any fundamental articles, passed into law by any assemblage of individuals, is an injustice to their successors, and a high offence against the other great interest of the social state, namely,—its progressive improvement.[1] The conception, therefore, of an original contract, is, we repeat, incapable of historic proof as a fact, and it is senseless as a theory.

But if instead of the *conception* or *theory* of an original social contract, you say the *idea* of an ever-originating social contract, this is so certain and so indispensable, that it constitutes the whole ground of the difference between subject and serf, between a commonwealth and a slave-plantation. And this, again, is evolved out of the yet higher idea of *person*, in contra-distinction from *thing*—all social law and justice being grounded on the principle, that a person can never, but by his own fault, become a thing, or, without grievous wrong, be treated as such: and the distinction consisting in this, that a thing may be used altogether and merely as the *means* to an end; but the person must always be included in the *end:* his interest must form a part of the object,[k] a *means* to which, he, by consent, *i.e.* by his own act, makes himself. We plant a tree, and we fell it; we breed the sheep, and we shear or we kill it; in both cases wholly as means to *our* ends. For trees and animals are *things*. The wood-cutter and the hind are likewise employed as *means*, but on agreement, and that too an agreement of reciprocal advantage, which includes them

[a–b] Added in 2nd ed [c] Added in 2nd ed [d–e] 1st ed: From [f–g] 1st ed: state, [h] 1st ed: demand, [i–j] 1st ed: permanence: and [k] 1st ed: objects,

[1] For further discussion, see below, p 24, and *Friend* (*CC*) I 416.

as well as their employer in the *end*. For they are *persons*.[1] And the government, under which the contrary takes place, is not worthy to be called a STATE, if, as in the kingdom of Dahomy,[2] it be unprogressive; or only by anticipation, where, as in Russia, it is in advance to a better and more *man-worthy* order of things.[3] Now, notwithstanding the late wonderful spread of learning through the community, and though the schoolmaster and the lecturer are abroad, the hind and the woodman may, very conceivably, pass from cradle to coffin, without having once contemplated this idea, so as to be conscious of the same. And there would be even[a] an improbability in the supposition that they possessed the power of presenting [b]this Idea[c] to the minds of others, or even to their own thoughts, verbally as a distinct proposition. But no man, who has ever listened to laborers of this rank, in any alehouse, over the Saturday night's jug of beer, discussing the injustice of the present rate of wages, and the iniquity of their being paid in part out of the parish poor-rates,[4] will doubt for a moment that they are fully possessed by the idea.

[a] Added in 2nd ed [b–c] 1st ed: it

[1] The discussion of persons and things appears (var) in *Friend* (*CC*) I 189–90; cf *TT* 18 Dec 1831 and Kant's "Act in such a way that you always treat humanity...never simply as a means, but always at the same time as an end." *The Moral Law, or Kant's Groundwork of the Metaphysics of Morals* tr H. J. Paton (1948) 96.

[2] C knew that slavery was the basis of society in the black kingdom of Dahomy or Dahomey; it was also notorious for human sacrifices. He speaks of a travel book on the Dahomese, which may have been Archibald Dalzel *History of Dahomy* (1793), in a marginal note on a copy of Richard Payne Knight *Analytical Inquiry into the Principles of Taste* (3rd ed 1806), reproduced *Friend* (*CC*) I 11–12 n 5.

[3] C may be thinking of Tsar Alexander's order to his ministers in 1818 to prepare a scheme for the gradual emancipation of the serfs that would not be burdensome to the landowners. Nicholas I, who succeeded to the throne in 1825, although he recognised the evil of serfdom, thought it more dangerous to change it. The absence of slavery is a main principle in C's definition of a state. Cf *OED* "man" 19d for C's "man-worthy", citing *Webster's Dictionary* for C but not *C&S*.

[4] The growth of large estates and the spread of enclosure made many villagers dependent on parish poor rates. The notorious Speenhamland system came into existence in 1795, as the result of a decision by the local magistrates at Speenhamland, Berkshire, not to try to adjust local wages to rising costs, but to supplement agricultural wages with Poor Law allowances, related to the price of bread and the size of the labourer's family. The problem was too complex to be solved in this way and the system came in for sharp attack because it made the labourer dependent on the parish, encouraged large families, and restricted mobility of labour. Arthur Young (1741–1820), noted agricultural writer, attributes a speech to one of the poor that partly parallels C's remarks: "You offer no motives, you have nothing but a parish officer and a work house. Bring me another pot"; see Asa Briggs *The Age of Improvement* (1959) 58–9; cf *LS* (*CC*) 122 and n 1, 221–2, and *TT* 27 Apr 1823.

In close, though not perhaps obvious connection, with this, is the idea of moral freedom, as the ground of our proper responsibility. Speak to a young Liberal, fresh from Edinburgh or Hackney or the Hospitals, of Free-will, as implied in Free-agency, he will perhaps confess to you with a smile, that he is a Necessitarian,—[1] proceed[a] to assure you that the liberty of the will is an impossible conception, *a contradiction in terms*,* and finish by recommending you to read Jonathan Edwards,[3] or Dr. Crombie:[4] or as it may happen, he may declare the will itself a mere delusion, a non-entity, and ask you if you have read Mr. Lawrence's Lecture.[5] Converse on

* See AIDS TO REFLECTION, p. 226; where this is shewn to be one of the distinguishing characters of *ideas*, and marks at once the difference between an *idea* (a *truth-power* of the reason) and a conception of the understanding; viz. that the former, as expressed in words, is always, and necessarily, a *contradiction in terms*.[2]

[a] 1st ed: proceeds

[1] In the eighteenth century Edinburgh was one of the great centres of the Enlightenment, but C associates it particularly with the liberal Opposition: Lansdowne, Brougham, Horner, and Jeffrey were educated there. Hackney, long a centre of Dissent (Hazlitt had attended the now-defunct Academy), at this time boasted a Theological Seminary, a Protestant Dissenting Academy, and the Hackney... British School Association, which educated children of every denomination. See William Robinson *The History and Antiquities of the Parish of Hackney* (2 vols 1843) II 272–89, 290–302, 305–9. The London teaching hospitals, at one of which C's brother Luke studied, had a reputation for free-thought. Although C was himself a necessitarian in youth, influenced by David Hartley, author of *Observations on Man* (1749), and, briefly, by William Godwin, who developed Hartley's necessitarianism in *Political Justice* (1793), there was no place for a mechanistic view of choice in C's later thought.

[2] The passage in *AR* (1825) states that it "is the test and character of the truth" affirmed by the Reason "that in its own proper form it is *inconceivable*", and that a second test is "that it can come forth out of the moulds of the Understanding only in the disguise of two contradictory conceptions, each of which is partially true, and the conjunction of both conceptions becomes the representative or *expression* (the *exponent*) of a truth *beyond* conception and inexpressible. Examples: Before Abraham *was*, I *am*.—God is a Circle, the centre of which is everywhere, and the circumference nowhere. The soul is all in every part."

[3] Jonathan Edwards (1703–58), American Congregational divine, wrote an *Enquiry into...Freedom of Will* (1754); C's copy of the 5th ed (1790) is in VCL. In *AR* (1825) 153–4, C attacks his conception of the will as "absolutely passive, clay in the hands of the Potter", and in N 30 f 33v he says of Edwards that "his World is a Machine". The anonymous American author of *Coleridge and the Moral Tendency of His Writings* (NY 1844) 33 declares proudly that Edwards's treatise "will stand impregnable" when such philosophers as C are forgotten.

[4] Alexander Crombie (1762–1840), author of *A Defence of Philosophic Necessity* (1793), who ran a private school at Highgate.

[5] William Lawrence (1783–1867), surgeon, delivered lectures at the Royal College of Surgeons from 1815. He published the first series as *An Introduction to Comparative Anatomy and*

the same subject with a plain, single-minded, yet reflecting neighbour, and he may probably say (as St. Augustin had said long before him, in reply to the question, What is Time?) I know it well enough when you do not ask me.[1] But alike with both the supposed parties, the self-complacent student, just as certainly as with your less positive neighbour—attend to their actions, their feelings, and even to their words: and you will be in ill luck, if ten minutes pass without affording you full and satisfactory proof, that the *idea* of man's moral freedom possesses and modifies their whole practical being, in all they say, in all they feel, in all they do and are done to: even as the spirit of life, which is contained in no vessel, because it permeates all.

Just so is it with the *constitution. Ask any of our politicians what is meant by the constitution, and it is ten to one that he will give you a false explanation, *ex. gr.* that it is the body of our laws, or that it is the Bill of Rights; or perhaps, if he have read Tom Payne,[2] he may tell you, that we have not yet got one; and yet not an hour may have elapsed, since you heard the same individual denouncing, and possibly with good reason, this or that code of laws, the excise and revenue laws, or those for including pheasants,[3]

* I do not say, with the idea: for the constitution itself is an IDEA. This will sound like a paradox or a sneer to those with whom an Idea is but another word for *a fancy*, a something unreal; but not to those who in the ideas contemplate the most real of all realities, and of all operative powers the most *actual*.

Physiology (1816) and followed this with *On the Physiology, Zoology, and Natural History of Man* (1819), which was bitterly attacked for its supposed materialism and atheism. He argued that function was dependent on structure and attacked Hunterian vitalist theories. C supported the vitalist views of the distinguished surgeon John Abernethy (1764–1831) when they came under attack from Lawrence; cf *TL* (1848), *P Lects* Lect XII (1949) 353–5 and nn 35, 36 (p 457) and Introduction p 28, and *L&L* 16–23.

[1] "Quid est ergo tempus? si nemo ex me quaerat, scio; si quaerenti explicare velim, nescio." *Confessions* 11.14. "What is time then? If nobody asks me, I know: but if I were desirous to explain it to one that should ask me, plainly I know not." Tr W. Watts (LCL 1912) II 239.

[2] Thomas Paine *Rights of Man* (Everyman 1950) 48–9. In youth C recognised the strength of Paine's political writings, but despised his theological works; cf LRR III: *Lects 1795* (*CC*) 149 and n.

[3] An allusion to the Game Laws, which made it illegal for anyone to shoot or trap game or be in possession of guns or traps except those who were specially entitled: in the case of private land, this meant the landowner and those he licensed—for example, gamekeepers; in the case of crown land, this meant those licensed by the crown. After the Napoleonic wars, at a time of acute food shortage, Parliament passed an Act, in 1816, extending the scope of the Game Laws and making the penalties more severe. C's allusion was topical, as the laws had been even

or those for excluding Catholics, as altogether unconstitutional: and such and such acts of parliament as gross outrages on the constitution. Mr. Peel, who is rather remarkable for groundless and unlucky concessions, owned that the present Bill breaks in on the constitution of 1688:[1] [a]and, A.D. 1689, a[b] very imposing minority of the then House of Lords, with a decisive majority in the Lower House of Convocation, denounced the constitution of 1688, as breaking in on the English Constitution.

But a Constitution is an idea arising out of the idea of a state; and because our whole history from Alfred onward demonstrates the continued influence of such an idea, or ultimate aim, on the minds of our fore-fathers, in their characters and functions as public men; alike in what they resisted and in what they claimed; in the institutions and forms of polity which they established, and with regard to those, against which they more or less successfully contended; and because the result has been a progressive, though not always a direct, or equable advance in the gradual realization of the idea; and that it is actually, though even because it is an *idea* it cannot be *adequately*, represented in a correspondent scheme of means really existing;[c] we speak, and have a right to speak, of the idea itself, as actually existing, *i.e.*, as a *principle*, existing in the only way in which a principle can exist—in the minds and consciences of the persons, whose duties it prescribes, and whose rights it determines. In the same sense that the sciences of arithmetic and of geometry, that mind, that life itself, have reality; the constitution has real existence, and does not the less exist in reality, because it both *is*, and *exists as*, an IDEA.[d]

[a–b] 1st ed: and a [c] Copy W adds: —for all these reasons

[d] Copy W adds: The NATION, as distinguished from the aggregate of the people of a country at any moment in existence, is in like manner an IDEA, and as such a *real* Beings.

further extended in 1828. The Game Laws were used by a ruthless section of the propertied class to deter the destitute from stealing so that they might not starve; the laws were repealed in 1837.

[1] Sir Robert Peel, 2nd Bt (1788–1850), entered Parliament in the Tory interest in 1809 and held various offices under Lord Liverpool, including Chief Secretary for Ireland and Home Secretary. In 1828, as Home Secretary and Leader of the House of Commons under Wellington, he reversed his opposition to Catholic Emancipation and convinced Wellington of the necessity of introducing a simple straightforward measure for Catholic Relief. On 12 Feb 1829, Peel said that "it was with the utmost reluctance that he had at length consented to break in upon the constitutional settlement of 1688" by introducing a Bill for Catholic Relief. On 18 Mar he defended the phrase "breaking in upon the constitution", of which, he claimed, "such unfair and such unjust application had been made". *P Speeches* (1853) II 692 and 740. See Introduction, above, p li.

There is yet another ground for the affirmation of its reality; that, as the fundamental idea, it is at the same time, the final criterion by which all particular frames of government must be tried: for here only can we find the great constructive principles of our representative system (I use the term in its widest sense, in which the crown itself is included as representing the unity of the people, the true and primary sense of the word majesty);[1] those principles, I say, in the light of which it can alone be ascertained what are excrescences, symptoms of distemperature and marks of degeneration; and what are native growths, or changes naturally attendant on the progressive development of the original germ, symptoms of immaturity perhaps, but not of disease; or at worst, modifications of the growth by the defective or faulty, but remediless, or only gradually remediable, qualities of the soil and surrounding elements.

There are two other characters, distinguishing the class of substantive truths, or truth-powers here spoken of, that will, I trust, indemnify the reader for the delay of the two or three short sentences required for their explanation. The first is, that in distinction from the *conception* of a thing, which being abstracted or generalized from one or more particular states, or modes, is necessarily posterior in order of thought to the thing thus conceived,—an idea, on the contrary, is in order of thought always and of necessity contemplated as antecedent. In the idea or principle, Life, for instance—the vital *functions* are the result of the organization; but this organization supposes and pre-supposes the vital *principle*.[2] The bearings of the planets on the sun are determined by the ponderable matter of which they consist; but the *principle* of gravity, the *law* in the material creation, the *idea* of the Creator, is pre-supposed in order to the existence, yea, to the very conception of the existence, of matter itself.

[1] Cf *PD*, in which C interprets the word "majesty" as "the unity of the people", an interpretation repeated and justified on historical and etymological grounds in an essay in the *M Post* 28 Jan 1800. *Lects 1795* (*CC*) 295; *EOT* (*CC*) I 136. He is there pointing out (as he omits to do here) the etymological connexion between *majesty* (more probably from *magnus*, "great", meaning "greatness", "authority", etc) and *majority* (from *major*, "greater", as he supposes). From this it is a small step to argue that majesty meant the unity of the people. Cf also C's comment on Kant's reasons for the use of the royal "we": "Rather, from a relique of Democracy retained in the policy of Augustus, who merging in one of the most important magistracies would be addressed not as a person but as a Proxy of the Majority— = Majestas...". Annotation on Kant *Anthropologie* (1800) 9 (from *CM* ms). See below, p 30 and n.

[2] Cf *TL* (passim) and C's note on the vital principle in the "Essays on the Principles of Method" *Friend* (*CC*) I 493–4; cf also above, p 17 and n 4.

This is the first. The other distinctive mark may be most conveniently given in the form of a caution. We should be made aware, namely, that the particular form, construction, or model, that may be best fitted to render the idea intelligible, and most effectually serve the purpose of an instructive *diagram*, is not necessarily the mode or form in which it actually arrives at realization. In the works both of man and of nature—in the one by the imperfection of the means and materials, in the other by the multitude and complexity of simultaneous purposes—the fact is most often otherwise. A naturalist, (in the infancy of physiology, we will suppose, and before the first attempts at comparative anatomy) whose knowledge had been confined exclusively to the human frame, or that of animals similarly organized; [a]and who, by[b] this experience had been led inductively to the idea of respiration, as the copula and mediator of the vascular and the nervous systems,—might, very probably, have regarded the lungs, with their appurtenants, as the only form in which this idea, or ultimate aim, was realizable. Ignorant of the functions of the spiracula in the insects, and of the gills of the fish, he would, perhaps, with great confidence degrade both to the class of non-respirants. But alike in the works of nature and the institutions of man, there is no more effectual preservative against pedantry, and the positiveness of sciolism,[1] than to meditate on the law of compensation, and the principle of compromise; and to be fully impressed with the wide extent of the one, the necessity of the other, and the frequent occurrence of both.

Having (more than sufficiently, I fear), exercised your patience with these preparatory remarks, for which the anxiety to be fully understood by you is my best excuse, though in a moment of less excitement they might not have been without some claim to your attention for their own sake, I return to the idea, which forms the present subject—the English Constitution, which an old writer calls, "Lex Sacra, Mater Legum,[2] than which (says he), nothing can be

[a–b] 1st ed: and by

[1] Cf *P Lects* Lect VI (1949), in which C says that "feverish positiveness...so often deludes minds under the best impulses into the worst actions" and draws a distinction between positiveness and certainty, drawn also in *Friend* (*CC*) II 7 and n, and clarified in a late notebook: "O! if it were possible to impress on the young, and healthy, the utter difference between an *opinion*, a smatch of thoughts, and a truth grounded on a fact found by the Soul in itself!" N Q f 52v. For sciolism cf *SM* App D (*CC*) 94 and n 1, in which C says that it caused an "epidemic of a proud ignorance".

[2] "Sacred Law, Mother of Laws"; cf below, p 31 and n 1. Although the Latin phrase does not appear there, the main source for this passage

proposed more certain in its grounds, more pregnant in its consequences, or that hath more harmonical reason within itself: and which is so connatural and essential to the genius and innate disposition of this nation, it being formed (silk-worm like) as that no other law can possibly regulate it—a law not to be derived from Alured, or Alfred, or Canute, or other elder or later promulgators of particular laws, but which might say of itself—When reason and the laws of God first came, then came I with them."

[a]As, according to an old saying, "an ill foreknown is half disarmed," I will here notice an inconvenience in our language, which, without a greater inconvenience, I could not avoid, in the use of the term *State*, in a double sense, a larger, in which it is equivalent to Realm and includes the Church, and a narrower, in which it is distinguished *quasi per antithesin*[1] from the Church, as in the phrase, Church and State. But the context, I trust, will in every instance prevent ambiguity.[b]

[a–b] Added in 2nd ed

is probably the preface to Sir John Davies *Le Primer Report des Cases & Matters en Les Courts del Roy en Ireland* (Dublin 1615) *4: "Briefly, it is so framed and fitted to the nature & disposition of this people, as wee may properly say, it is *connatural* to the Nation....This lawe therefore doth demonstrate the strength of *witt and reason*...in the people of this land, which have made theire owne lawes out of their wisdome & experience (like a silke worme that formeth all her webb out of her selfe onely)....Lawe is nothing but a rule of reason...". But C has combined Davies with another seventeenth-century writer, William Hughes of Gray's Inn, who in his preface to his translation of Andrew Horn *The Mirrour of Justices* (1646) wrote (p vi): "That when the laws of God and Reason came first into *England*, then came I in." George Dyer *Four Letters on the English Constitution* (1812; C's copy inscribed by Dyer is in the BM) quoted the same passage (var) p 44 and may have led C to the work, for Alured, Alfred, etc are from Hughes's preface, in the previous paragraph. Cf also "The...common law is nothing else but pure and tried reason...containing the principles and maxims of law (consonant unto the laws of God)...". *Mirrour* vii–viii.

The attribution of sacred qualities to human institutions was a late mediaeval phenomenon. Ernst Kantorowicz *The King's Two Bodies* (Princeton 1957) traces the phrases *pater legis* and *mater juris* through the mediaeval glossators. Walter Ullmann *Law Quarterly Review* LVII (1942) 386ff cites the last of the great glossators, Baldus (1327–1406): "philosophia moralis est legum mater et janua"; and again "justitia...in abstracto, prout habet in se sua essentialia, circumscriptio omni legislatore...est mater et causa juris". An earlier gloss has: "Est jus a justitia sicut a matre sua". Although C refers to "an old writer", the notion of the constitution as a body of fundamental law that might be spoken of in the singular does not become differentiated until the end of the seventeenth century.

[1] "As if by antithesis".

[a]CHAPTER II

The idea of a State in the larger sense of the term, introductory to the constitution of the State in the narrower sense, as it exists in this Country[b]

A CONSTITUTION is the attribute of a state, *i.e.* of a body politic, having the principle of its unity within itself, whether by concentration of its forces, as a constitutional pure Monarchy, which, however, has hitherto continued to be *ens rationale*,[1] unknown in history (*B. Spinozae Tract. Pol. cap. VI. De Monarchiâ ex rationis praescripto*),[2]—or—with which we are alone concerned—by equipoise and interdependency: the *lex equilibrii*,[3] the principle prescribing the means and conditions by and under which this balance is to be established and preserved, being the constitution of the state. It is the chief of many blessings derived from the insular character and circumstances of our country, that our social institutions have formed themselves out of our proper needs and interests; that long and fierce as the birth-struggle and the growing pains have been, the antagonist powers have been of our own system, and have been allowed to work out their final balance with less disturbance from external forces, than was possible in the Continental states.

O ne'er enchain'd nor wholly vile,
O Albion! O my Mother Isle!
Thy valleys fair as Eden's bowers
Glitter green with sunny showers!
Thy[c] grassy uplands' gentle swells
Echo to the bleat of flocks;
Those grassy hills, those glittering dells,
Proudly ramparted with rocks:
And OCEAN 'mid his uproar wild
Speaks safety to his ISLAND-CHILD!
Hence thro' many a fearless Age
Has social Freedom lov'd the Land,

[a–b] 1st ed: CONCERNING THE RIGHT IDEA OF THE CONSTITUTION.
[c] 1st ed: The

[1] "Rational entity".

[2] *Tractatus politicus* 6.3, 5: *Opera* ed H. E. G. Paulus (2 vols Jena 1802–3) II 332–4. C suggested that this part of Spinoza should be read after Vico's *Scienza nuova*. *TT* 23 Apr 1832.

[3] "Law of balance".

Nor Alien Despot's jealous rage
Or warp'd thy growth or stamp'd the servile Brand.
ODE TO THE DEPARTING YEAR, *Dec.* 1796[1]

Now, in every country of civilized men, acknowledging the rights of property, and by means of determined boundaries and common laws united into one people or nation,[2] the two antagonist powers or opposite interests of the state, under which all other state interests are comprised, are those of PERMANENCE and of PROGRESSION.*

It will not be necessary to enumerate the several causes that combine to connect the permanence of a state with the land and the landed property.[6] To found a family, and to convert his wealth into

* Permit me to draw your attention to the essential difference between *opposite* and *contrary*.[3] Opposite powers are always of the same kind, and tend to union, either by equipoise or by a common product. Thus the + and − poles of the magnet, thus positive and negative electricity are opposites. Sweet and sour are opposites; sweet and bitter are contraries. The feminine character is *opposed* to the masculine; but the effeminate is its *contrary*. Even so in the present instance, the interest of permanence is opposed to that of progressiveness; but so far from being contrary interests, they, like the magnetic forces, suppose and require each other. Even the most mobile of creatures, the serpent, makes a *rest* of its own body, and drawing up its voluminous train from behind on this fulcrum, propels itself onward. On the other hand, it is a proverb in all languages, that (relatively to man at least) what would stand still must retrograde.[4] You, my dear Sir, who have long known my notions respecting the power and value of words, and the duty as well as advantage of using them appropriately, will forgive this.

Many years ago, in conversing with a friend, I expressed my belief, that in no instance had the false use of a word become current without some practical ill consequence, of far greater moment than would *primo aspectu*[5] have been thought possible. That friend, very lately referring to this remark, assured me, that not a month had passed since then, without some instance in proof of its truth having occurred in his own experience; and added, with a smile, that he had more than once amused himself with the thought of a verbarian Attorney-General, authorized to bring informations ex officio against the writer or editor of any work in extensive circulation, who, after due notice issued, should persevere in misusing a word.

[1] St 7 (var): *PW* (EHC) I 166–7, in which the last three lines are:

Has social Quiet lov'd thy shore;
Nor ever proud Invader's rage
Or sack'd thy towers, or stain'd thy fields with gore.

[2] Copy G contains a ms note by C at the foot of the page: "Mem. 'A Nation' is properly distinguished from 'a People'; it is the Unity of the successive Generations of a People. A *State*, again, is the conservative Form (therefore, at once the Form and the Power) of the unity of a People." For a description of Copy G, see App F, below.

[3] Cf *Friend* (*CC*) I 94 and n.

[4] Cf "...with states, as well as individuals, not to be progressive is to be retrograde". *Friend* (*CC*) I 253.

[5] "At first sight".

[6] For C's first recognition of the positive and beneficial function of property, see *M Post* 7 Dec 1799: *EOT* (*CC*) I 32, and for a later treatment see *Friend* (*CC*) I 199–202.

land, are twin thoughts, births of the same moment, in the mind of the opulent merchant, when he thinks of reposing from his labours. From the class of the Novi Homines[1] he redeems himself by[a] becoming the staple ring of the chain, by which the present will become connected with the past; and the test and evidence of permanency afforded. To the same principle appertain primogeniture and hereditary titles, and the influence which these exert in accumulating large masses of property, and in counteracting the antagonist and dispersive forces, which the follies, the vices, and misfortunes of individuals can scarcely fail to supply. To this, likewise, tends the proverbial obduracy of prejudices characteristic of the humbler tillers of the soil, and their aversion even to benefits that are offered in the form of innovations. But why need I attempt to explain a fact which no thinking man will deny, and where the admission of the fact is all that my argument requires?

On the other hand, with as little chance of contradiction, I may assert, that the progression of a state, in the arts and comforts of life, in the diffusion of the information and knowledge, useful or necessary for all; in short, all advances in civilization, and the rights and privileges of citizens, are especially connected with, and derived from the four classes of the mercantile, the manufacturing, the distributive, and the professional. To early Rome, war and conquest were the substitutes for trade and commerce. War was their trade.[2] As these wars became more frequent, on a larger scale, and with fewer interruptions, the liberties of the plebeians continued increasing: for even the sugar plantations of Jamaica would (in their present state, at least), present a softened picture of the hard and servile relation, in which the plebeian formerly stood to his patrician patron.

Italy is supposed at present to maintain a larger number of inhabitants than in the days of Trajan or in the best and most prosperous of the Roman empire.[3] With the single exception of the ecclesiastic state, the whole country is cultivated like a garden. You may find there

[a] Copy G: in

[1] "New men".

[2] Cf "War in republican Rome was the offspring of its intense aristocracy of spirit, and stood to the state in lieu of trade. As long as there was any thing *ab extra* to conquer, the state advanced: when nothing remained but what was Roman, then, as a matter of course, civil war began." *TT* 9 Jun 1832.

[3] Trajan (Marcus Ulpius Nerva Trajanus c 53–117), emperor from 98 until his death. According to one of C's reference books, Rees's *Cyclopaedia* (1819), under "Italy", in the time of Pliny (whether the elder, 23–79, or the younger, 61–c 112, is not stated) Italy "was said to contain 14,000,000", whereas the "present population" could not "be estimated at more than 13,000,000".

every gift of God—only not freedom. It is a country, rich in the proudest records of liberty, illustrious with the names of heroes, statesmen, legislators, philosophers. It hath a history all alive with the virtues and crimes of hostile parties, when the glories and the struggles of ancient Greece were acted over again in the proud republics of Venice, Genoa, and Florence. The life of every eminent citizen was in constant hazard from the furious factions of their[a] native city, and yet life had no charm out of its dear and honored walls. All the splendors of the hospitable palace, and the favor of princes, could not soothe the pining of Dante or Machiavel, exiles from their free, their beautiful Florence.[1] But[b] not a pulse of liberty survives. It was the profound policy of the Austrian and the Spanish courts, by every possible means to degrade the profession of trade; and even in Pisa and Florence themselves to introduce the feudal pride and prejudice of less happy, less enlightened countries. Agriculture, meanwhile, with its attendant population and plenty, was cultivated with increasing success; but from the Alps to the Straits of Messina, the Italians are slaves.[2]

We have thus divided the subjects of the state into two orders, the agricultural or possessors of land; and the merchant, manufacturer, the distributive, and the professional bodies, under the common name of citizens. And we have now to add that by the nature of things common to every civilized country, at all events by the course of events in this country, the first is subdivided into two classes, which, in imitation of our old law books, we may intitle the Major and Minor Barons; both these, either by their interests or by the very

[a] Copy G: his

[b] Copy G adds: Such Italy *was*. But *now*
Copy W adds: Such Italy *was*: and rich, fertile, populous, and beautiful Italy it remains. But

[1] Dante Alighieri (1265–1321) was exiled from his native Florence in 1302 for a variety of alleged crimes and moved from court to court and great city to great city; C probably has in mind a passage in the *Convivio* in which Dante speaks of Florence casting him "forth from her sweet bosom". Niccolò Machiavelli (1469–1527) was banished, imprisoned, and tortured when the Medici took possession of Florence in 1512, but was released when Leo x intervened and he then went into voluntary exile.

[2] When C was in Italy from the end of Sept 1805 until June 1806 on his way home from Malta, he observed the political and religious slavery of the people (*CN* II 2676–2868). After the settlement of 1814–15, Austria ruled or dominated much of Italy, and the popular uprisings in Naples and Piedmont in 1821 were easily quelled. The Italians were political slaves subject to foreign tyrants and moral slaves subject to the papacy. In this passage, C associates civil liberties closely with the commercial prosperity and independence of the great Italian cities. See C's footnote and Extract I on p 89, below.

effect of their situation, circumstances, and the nature of their employment, vitally connected with the permanency of the state, its institutions, rights, customs, manners, privileges—and as such, opposed to the inhabitants of ports, towns, and cities, who are in like manner and from like causes more especially connected with its progression. I scarcely need say, that in a very advanced stage of civilization, the two orders of society will more and more modify and leaven each other, yet never so completely but that the distinct character remains legible, and to use the words of the Roman Emperor, even in what is struck out the erasure is manifest.[1] At all times the lower of the two ranks, of which the first order consists, or[a] the Franklins, will, in their political sympathies, draw more nearly to the antagonist order than the first rank. On these facts, which must at all times have existed, though in very different degrees of prominence or maturity, the principle of our constitution was established. The total interests of the country, the interests of the STATE, were entrusted to a great council or parliament, composed of two Houses. The first consisting exclusively of the Major Barons, who at once stood as [b]the guardians and sentinels of their[c] several estates and privileges, and[d] the representatives of the common weal.[e] The Minor Barons, or Franklins, too numerous, and yet individually too weak, to sit and maintain their rights in person, were to choose among the worthiest of their own body representatives, and these in such number as to form an important though minor proportion of a second House—the majority of which was formed by the representatives chosen by the cities, ports, and boroughs; which representatives ought on principle to have been elected not only by, but from among, the members of the manufacturing, mercantile, distributive, and professional classes.[2]

These four classes, by an arbitrary but convenient use of the phrase,

[a] Copy W: viz.
[b–e] Copy G transposes to read: the representatives . . . weal and as the guardians . . . privileges.
[c] Copy G: their own [d] Copy G deletes

[1] The emperor was Claudius: Suetonius *Lives of the Caesars* 5.16.1–2. "When he had removed the mark of censure affixed to one man's name, yielding to the entreaties of the latter's friends, he said: 'But let the erasure be seen.'" Tr J. C. Rolfe (LCL 1914) II 33.

[2] C added in Copy G: "The two Interests, Permanence and Progression, represented, the first by the *Landed*, the second by the *Personal*; the term, personal, here expressing and comprizing, Manufacturers, Merchants, Shop-keepers, and Professional Men. —" This was written at the top of the page. It may have been intended to replace the last part of the paragraph, or as an addition, or as an explanatory note.

I will designate by the name of the Personal Interest, as the exponent of all moveable and personal possessions, including skill and acquired knowledge, the moral and intellectual stock in trade of the professional man and the artist, no less than the raw materials, and the means of elaborating, transporting, and distributing them.

Thus in the theory of the constitution it was provided, that even though both divisions of the Landed Interest should combine in any legislative attempt to encroach on the rights and privileges of the Personal Interest, yet the representatives of the latter forming the clear and effectual majority of the lower House, the attempt must be abortive: the majority of votes in both Houses being indispensable, in order to the presentation of a bill for the Completory Act,—that is, to make it a law of the land. By force of the same mechanism must every attack be baffled that should be made by the representatives of the minor landholders, in concert with the burgesses, on the existing rights and privileges of the peerage, and of the hereditary aristocracy, of which the peerage is the summit and the natural protector. Lastly, should the nobles join to invade the rights and franchises of the Franklins and the Yeomanry, the sympathy of interest, by which the inhabitants of cities, towns, and sea-ports, are linked to the great body of the agricultural fellow-commoners, who supply their markets and form their principal [a]customers, could not fail to secure a united and successful resistance.[1] Nor would this affinity of interest find a slight support in[b] the sympathy of feeling between the burgess senators and the county representatives, as members of the same House; [c]and in the consciousness, which the former have, of the dignity conferred on them by the latter. For[d] the notion of superior dignity will always be attached in the minds of men to that kind of property with which they have most associated the idea of permanence: and the land is the synonime of country.[e]

That the burgesses were not bound to elect representatives from among their own order, individuals bonâ fide belonging to one or other of the four divisions above enumerated; that the elective franchise of the towns, ports, &c., first invested with borough-rights,

[a–b] 1st ed: customers, and even

[c–d] 1st ed: and the consciousness of the dignity conferred by the latter on the former—for

[e] 1st ed: country—this affinity, I say, both of interest and fellow-feeling, could not fail to secure a united and successful resistance.

[1] For a similar account of the self-correcting balance of interests and power, see C's marginal notes on John Macdiarmid *Lives of British Statesmen* (1807): *NTP* 210–13.

was not made conditional,[1] and to a certain extent at least dependent on their retaining the same comparative wealth and independence, and rendered subject to a periodical revisal and re-adjustment; that in consequence of these and other causes, the very weights intended for the effectual counterpoise of the great land-holders, have, in the course of events, been shifted into the opposite scale; that they now constitute a large proportion of the political power and influence of the very class whose personal cupidity, and whose partial views of the landed interest at large they were meant to keep in check; these are no part of the constitution, no essential ingredients in the idea, but apparent defects and imperfections in its realization—which, however, we will neither regret nor set about amending, till we have seen whether an equivalent force had not arisen to supply the deficiency—a force great enough to have destroyed the equilibrium, had not such a transfer taken place previously to, or at the same time with, the operation of the new forces. Roads, canals, machinery, the press, the periodical and daily press, the might of public opinion, the consequent increasing desire of popularity among public men and functionaries of every description, and the increasing necessity of public character, as a means or condition of political influence—I need but mention these to stand acquitted of having started a vague and naked possibility in extenuation of an evident and palpable abuse.

But whether this[a] conjecture be well or ill grounded, the *principle* of the constitution remains the same. That harmonious balance of the two great correspondent, at once supporting and counterpoising, interests of the state, its permanence, and its progression: that balance of the landed and the personal interests was to be secured by a legislature of two Houses; the first consisting wholly of barons or landholders, permanent and hereditary senators; the second of the knights or minor barons, elected by, and as the representatives of, the remaining landed community, together with the burgesses, the representatives of the commercial, manufacturing, distributive, and professional classes,—the latter (the elected burgesses) constituting the major number. The king, meanwhile, in whom the executive power is vested, it will suffice at present to consider as the beam of

[a] 1st ed: my

[1] WW objected in Copy W: "they were so,—many instances occur ~~of~~ in our early history of the right to send Members to Parl. being withdrawn when a Borough fell into decay. W. W." For a description of Copy W, see App F, below.

the constitutional scales. A more comprehensive view of the kingly office must be deferred, till the remaining problem (the idea of a national church) has been solved.[1]

I must here intreat the reader to bear in mind what I have before endeavoured to impress on him, that I am not giving an historical account of the legislative body; nor[a] can I be supposed to assert that such was the earliest mode or form in which the national council was constructed. My assertion is simply this, that its formation has advanced in this direction. The line of evolution, however sinuous, has still tended to this point, sometimes with, sometimes without, not seldom, perhaps, against, the intention of the individual actors, but always as if a power, greater, and better, than the men themselves, had intended it for them. Nor let it be forgotten that every new growth, every power and privilege, bought or extorted, has uniformly been claimed by an antecedent right; not acknowledged as a boon conferred, but both demanded and received as what had always belonged to them, though withheld by violence and the injury of the times. This too,[b] in cases, where, if documents and historical records, or even consistent traditions, had been required in evidence, the monarch would have had the better of the argument. But, in truth, it was no more than a *practical* way of [c]saying: this or that[d] is contained in the *idea* of our government, and it is a

[a] 1st ed: or [b] Copy G adds: has been the language of our Parliaments even
[c–d] 1st ed: saying, it

[1] For his views here on the constitution C was indebted to Blackstone *Commentaries* Intro § II; cf *CN* III 3832. The discussion of the kingly office is deferred until ch 10, below. In ch 1 the function of the crown is related to the "primary sense of the word majesty" (p 20 and n); in N 3½ C refers to the king as the "natural Magnet" of society (ff 104^{v}–5) and in *CN* III 3843 he questions whether it is possible to place the safety of "the revenue of the Country, its Functionaries, Armies, Fleets & Colonies in any other Man or Men". The metaphor of the magnet is applied to the constitution at the end of the present chapter (p 31). In a marginal note on John Macdiarmid *Lives of British Statesmen* (1807), C declares that "the King is not an *Estate* of the Realm, but the Majesty of all three—that is, the Crown in its legislative character represents the Nation, its ancient Laws and Customs, ante-parliamentary as well as Parliamentary, and on his solemn oath alone (violent and extra-regular means not in question) does the Common-wealth depend for the continuance of its super-parliamentary Rights; while as the Executive Power, the Crown is the Agent and Trustee for all, chosen by the Nation, not elected by the Estates, or more truly appointed by Providence, as the Copula of all the complex Causes, the grounds and acts and results of which constitute the National History". C adds the comment: "Thus, my dear Gillman! without intending it I have left on record for you the sum of my political Religion, or the Constitutional Creed of S. T. Coleridge." *NTP* 213.

consequence of the "Lex, Mater Legum,"[1] which, in the very first law of [a]state ever[b] promulgated in the land, was pre-supposed as the ground of that first law.

Before I conclude this part of my subject, I must press on your attention, that the preceding is offered only as the constitutional idea of the *State*.[c][2] In order to correct views respecting the constitution, in the more enlarged sense of the term, viz. the constitution of the [d]*Nation*, we must, in addition to a grounded knowledge of the *State*,[e] have the right idea of the *National Church*. These[f] are two poles of the same magnet; the magnet itself, which is constituted by them, is the CONSTITUTION of the nation.[3]

[a–b] 1st ed: State that was [c] Copy G: *State*, in the narrower acceptation of the Word.
[d–e] 1st ed: *Nation* in addition to grounded knowledge of the *State*, we must
[f] Copy G: These, the National *State*, and the National *Church*,

1 Source untraced. "Law, Mother of Laws". See above, p 21.

2 On the front endleaf of a copy of *C&S* (2nd ed) presented to Jonathan Green, a medical writer, C stressed that his essay offered the idea, not the history, of the constitution: "this Essay—not on the history nor on the *actual form* of the British Legislature; but on the *Ultimate* Aims implied in the Constitution of the Same, by which ⟨alone⟩ as the regulative Idea, it can be rendered intelligible, and in reference to which as to its true Criterion, it must be judged. The convictions and conclusions of the Author may be thus briefly stated—:

"1. The British Legislature (= the King, the Lords, the Commons) *collectively* is an Organ for the Representation of the Interests of the Nation, not a Means for the transmission and collection of the Opinions or Wishes of the People.

"2. This holds equally of the House of Commons, as according to the practice of the Constitution the Common Arena of the three Powers.—

"3. All the Interests of the Nation are generalized in the two great Interests of *Permanence* and *Progression*: and to balance and reconcile these is the Ultimate Aim of the Constitution—". This inscribed copy is in the Berg Collection, NYPL; for details, see App F, below.

3 Cf above, p 30 n 1.

[a]CHAPTER III

On the Church; i.e. the National Church[b]

THE reading of *histories*, my dear Sir, may dispose a man to satire; but the science of [c]HISTORY,—History[d] studied in the light of philosophy, as the great drama of an ever unfolding Providence,—has a very different effect. It infuses hope and reverential thoughts of man and his destination.[1] To you, therefore, it will be no unwelcome result, though it should be made appear that something deeper and better than priestcraft and priest-ridden ignorance was at the bottom of the phrase, Church and State, and intitled it to be the form in which so many thousands of the men of England[e] clothed the wish for their country's weal.[f] But many things have conspired to draw off the attention from its true origin and import, and have led us to seek the reasons for thus connecting the two words, in facts and motives, that lie nearer the surface. I will mention one only, because, though less obvious than many other causes that have favoured the general misconception on this point, and though its action is indirect and negative, it is by no means the least operative. The immediate effect, indeed, may be confined to the men of education. But what influences these, will finally influence all. I am referring to the noticeable fact, arising out of the system of instruction pursued in all our classical schools and universities, that the annals of ancient Greece, and of republican and imperial Rome, though they are, in fact, but brilliant exceptions of history generally, do yet, partly from the depth and intensity of all early impressions, and in part, from the number and splendor of individual characters and particular events and exploits, so fill the imagination, as almost to be,—during the

[a–b] Added in 2nd ed [c–d] 1st ed: history, but history
[e] Copy G adds: during so many generations
[f] Copy G: weal, the ⟨solemn⟩ convivial *Toast* of loyal Englishmen!

[1] Cf *BL* ch 10 (1817) I 213–16; *SM* (*CC*) 11, in which C emphasises that history should be read for general principles and not simply for the facts, and *LS* (*CC*) 124n for history read as prophecy. See also above, p 10 n 7. C had little interest in "things contingent & transitory" (19 Apr 1804: *CN* II 2026), an attitude to history unlike Scott's, as C noted later (*TT* 4 Aug 1833).

period, when the groundwork of our minds is principally formed, and the direction given to our modes of thinking,—what we mean by HISTORY. Hence things, of which no instance or analogy is recollected in the customs, policy, and legisprudence[1] of Greece and Rome, lay little hold on our attention. Among these, I know not one more worthy of notice, than the principle of the division of property, which, if not, as I however think, universal in the earliest ages, was, at all events, common to the Scandinavian, Celtic, and Gothic tribes, with the Semitic, or the tribes descended from Shem.[2]

It is not the least among the obligations, which the antiquarian and the philosophic statist owe to a tribe of the last-mentioned race, the Hebrew I mean, that in the institutes of their great legislator,[a][3] who first formed them into a *state* or nation, they have preserved for us a practical illustration of this principle in question, which was by no means peculiar to the Hebrew people, though in their case it received a peculiar [b]sanction.

To[c] confound the inspiring spirit with the informing word, and both with the dictation of sentences and formal propositions; and to confine the office and purpose of inspiration to the miraculous immission, or infusion, of novelties, rebus nusquam prius visis, vel auditis,[4]—these, alas! are the current errors of Protestants without learning, and of bigots in spite of it;[5] but which I should have left

[a] 1st ed: legislators [b–c] 1st ed: sanction. But to

[1] A coinage, not recorded in *OED*. HNC's correction of "legisprudence" to the familiar "jurisprudence" in *C&S* (1839), which has no support in any of the surviving marked copies, is typical of his general process of smoothing out of C's original text; see Editorial Practice, above, p xiii.

[2] By "the principle of the division of property", C means the system of tithes, by which a tenth part of personal wealth is payable to the Church, and not any system of equal division of property, a point that becomes clearer in later paragraphs and in ch IV.

[3] Cf the extended discussion in LRR II on the legislation of Moses, in which C draws on Moses Lowman *A Dissertation on the Civil Government of the Hebrews* (1740), an interpretation of the texts in the Pentateuch that describe Moses' reception of "the two tables of stone, written with the finger of god" (Exod 31.18), and his implementation of Divine Law for the Jews, which was attractive to Dissenters and radicals because of its bearing on civil and religious liberty. *Lects 1795* (*CC*) 123–45. C ignores such radical interpretations in 1829.

[4] Source untraced. Tr: "Things nowhere previously seen or heard".

[5] Confounding two distinct conceptions, "the Revealing Word and the Inspiring Spirit" or "revelation by the Eternal Word and actuation of the Holy Spirit", led, C believed, to "indiscriminate Bibliolatry". See *CIS* passim, written as early as 1825 (see *AR*—1825—381 and Introduction, above, p liii), but not published until 1840. C rejected the view that the Bible was "throughout dictated, in word and thought, by an infallible Intelligence", likening such a "doctrine of infallible dictation" to the "Romish tenet of

unnoticed, but for the injurious influence which certain notions in close connexion with these errors have had on the present subject. The notion, I mean, that the Levitical institution[1] was not only enacted by an inspired Law-giver, not only a work of revealed *wisdom*, (which who denies?) but that it was a part of revealed *Religion*, having its *origin* in this particular [a]revelation, as a something[b] which could not have existed otherwise; yet, on the other hand, a part of the religion that had been *abolished* by Christianity. Had these reasoners contented themselves with asserting, that it did not *belong* to the Christian Religion, they would have said nothing more than the truth; and for this plain reason, that it forms no part of *religion* at all, in the Gospel sense of the word,—that is, *Religion* as contra-distinguished from *Law;* spiritual, as contra-distinguished from temporal or political.[2]

In answer to all these notions, it is enough to say, that not the principle itself, but the superior wisdom with which the principle was carried into effect, the greater perfection of the machinery, forms the true distinction, the *peculiar* worth, of the Hebrew constitution. [c]The principle itself[d] was common to Goth and Celt, or rather, I would say, to all the tribes that had not fallen off to either of the two *Aphelia*,[3] or extreme distances from the generic character of man, the wild or the barbarous state; but who remained either

[a–b] 1st ed: revelation, and [c–d] 1st ed: It

Infallibility"; "it is the spirit of the Bible, and not the detached words and sentences, that is infallible and absolute". *CIS* (1840) 32, 53, 73. The members of the interdenominational British and Foreign Bible Society, unlike C, believed that "the Bible was not to be regarded or reasoned about in the same way that other good books are or may be" and so issued their Bibles without "note or comment, catechism or liturgical preparation", leaving every reader free to pick and choose from Scripture and "find out for himself what he is bound to believe and practise". Ibid 56–7, 85. On the Bible Society cf *LS* (*CC*) 129n, 166n, 200–1, and nn; on the supposed "plainness and simplicity" of the Christian religion, ibid 176ff. Cf also C's poetic translation of a fragment from Heraclitus, of "the power of the informing Word" to sound "prophetic bodements": *PW* (EHC) II 1007, from an annotation on John Smith *Select Discourses* (1660). An adaptation of the original Heraclitus fragment is in *SM* (*CC*) 95; see ibid n 2.

[1] See p 37 and n 2, below.

[2] C is here arguing against all who place an excessive emphasis on a literal interpretation of the divine inspiration of everything in the OT. He also wishes to draw a firm distinction between the intrinsic value of the Mosaic Law and Constitution, and its status as divinely inspired. He may have had Dissenters and Unitarians chiefly in mind, but was probably thinking more widely.

[3] *OED* cites no earlier use of this word figuratively.

constituent[a] parts or appendages of the *stirps generosa seu historica*,[1] as a philosophic friend has named that portion of the Semitic and Japetic races,[2] that had not degenerated below the *conditions* of progressive civilization:—it was, I say, common to all the primitive races, that in taking possession of a new country, and in the division of the land into hereditable estates among the individual warriors or heads of families, a reserve should be made for the nation itself.

The sum total of these heritable portions, appropriated each to an individual Lineage, I beg leave to name the PROPRIETY; and to call the *reserve* above-mentioned the NATIONALTY; and likewise to employ the term wealth, in that primary and wide sense which it retains in the term, Commonwealth. In the establishment, then, of the landed *proprieties*, a *nationalty* was at the same time constituted: as a *wealth* not consisting of lands, but yet derivative from the land, and rightfully inseparable from the same. These, the *Propriety* and the *Nationalty*, were the two constituent factors, the opposite, but correspondent and reciprocally supporting, counter-weights, of the *commonwealth;* the existence of the one being the condition, and the perfecting, of the rightfulness of the other. Now as all polar forces, *i.e. opposite*, not *contrary*, powers, are necessarily *unius generis*,[3] homogeneous, so, in the present instance, each is that which it is called, relatively, by *predominance* of the one character or quality, not by the absolute exclusion of the other. The wealth appropriated was not so entirely a property as not to remain, to a certain extent, national; nor was the wealth reserved so exclusively national, as not to admit of individual tenure. It was only necessary that the mode and origin of the tenure should be different, and in *antithesis*, as it were. *Ex. gr.* If the one be hereditary, the

[a] Added in 2nd ed

[1] "Undegenerate or historic stock". The friend was probably Hyman Hurwitz (1770–1844), who conducted a Hebrew academy for boys at Highgate and became Professor of Hebrew at University College, London, in 1829; see also below, pp 122–3n. C consulted him frequently as an authority: *CL* IV 871.

[2] Gen 10. C alludes to the traditional division of the races of the world into three derived from Noah's sons: Shem (Semitic), Ham (Negro), and Japheth (Indo-European); cf *CN* III 4384, a draft of the literary lectures of 1818, which contains material on this subject.

[3] "Of one kind"; C has already used the poles of the magnet as an example of opposing as distinct from contrary forces (see his footnote above, p 24). The idea of polarity came to assume central importance in the philosophy of C and his German contemporaries, in which the dynamic unity of nature, of life, and of thought was conceived as arising from a synthesis of opposing forces.

other must be elective; if the one be lineal, the other must be circulative.[1]

[1] In a marginal note in *Reliquiae Baxterianae* (1696), C asserted that the "Decline or Progress of this Country" depended on "the restoration of a National and Circulating Property in counterpoise of individual Possession, disposable & heritable". *C 17th C* 355, dated 12 Jul 1827. This long note contains a detailed exposition of the "two Senses in which the words, Church of England, may be used", together with an account of a "permanent learned Class". The phrasing anticipates C's account of the clerisy in *C & S*; cf below, pp 46, 53, and nn.

[a]CHAPTER IV

Illustration of the preceding Chapter from History, and principally that of the Hebrew Commonwealth[b]

IN the unfolding and exposition of any idea, we naturally seek assistance and the means of illustration from the historical instance, in which it has been most nearly realized, or of which we possess the most exact and satisfactory records. Both of these recommendations are found in the formation of the Hebrew Commonwealth. But, in availing ourselves of examples from history, there is always danger, lest that, which was to assist us in attaining a clear insight into truth, should be the means of disturbing or falsifying it, so that we attribute to the object what was but the effect of flaws, or other accidents in the glass, through which we looked at it.[1] To secure ourselves from this danger, we must constantly bear in mind, that in the actual realization of every great idea or principle, there will always exist disturbing forces, modifying the product, either from the imperfection of their agents, or from especial circumstances overruling them: or from the defect of the materials; or lastly, and which most particularly applies to the instances we have here in view, from the co-existence of some yet greater idea, some yet more important purpose, with which the former must be combined, but likewise subordinated. Nevertheless, these are no essentials of the idea, no exemplary parts in the particular construction adduced for its illustration. On the contrary, they are deviations from the idea, from which we must abstract, which we must put aside, before we can make a safe and fearless use of the example.

Such, for instance, was the settlement of the NATIONALTY in one tribe,[2] which, to the exclusion of the eleven other divisions of

[a–b] Added in 2nd ed

[1] In the MS "Observations of Egypt" (BM MS Egerton 2800 ff 118–26) drawn up in Malta, C declared that a "blind faith in false analogies of the Past" was a characteristic fault of the unthinking. But in his *M Post* essays he recognised the value of historical analogy; see esp "Letters to Fox" II (9 Nov 1802); *EOT* (*CC*) I 392. Cf *BL* ch 10 (1907) I 146–8.

[2] The Levites; cf Num 3.5ff and Num 18; for reversion of "sanctified" property to the priesthood, see Lev 27.14ff. Cf *Lects 1795* (*CC*) 137 and n.

the Hebrew confederacy, was to be invested with its[1] rights, and to be capable of discharging its duties.[2] This was, indeed, in some measure, corrected by the institution of the *Nabim*, or Prophets, who might be of any tribe, and who formed a numerous body, uniting the functions and three-fold character of the Roman Censors, the Tribunes of the people, and the sacred college of Augurs; protectors of the Nation and privileged state-moralists, whom, you will recollect, our Milton has already compared* to the orators of the Greek Democracies. Still the most satisfactory justification of this exclusive policy, is to be found, I think, in the fact, that the Jewish Theocracy itself was but a means to a further and greater end; and that the effects of the policy were subordinated to an interest, far more momentous than that of any single kingdom or commonwealth could be. The unfitness and insufficiency of the Jewish character for the reception and execution of the great legislator's scheme were not less important parts of the sublime purpose of Providence in the separation of the chosen people, than their characteristic virtues. Their frequent relapses, and the never-failing return of a certain number to the national faith and customs, were alike subservient to the ultimate object, the final cause, of the Mosaic dispensation.[4]

* The lines which our sage and learned poet puts in the Saviour's mouth, both from their truth and from their appositeness to the present subject, well deserve to be quoted:—

> Their orators thou then extoll'st, as those
> The top of eloquence:—Statists indeed
> And lovers of their country as may seem;
> But herein to our prophets far beneath,
> As men divinely taught and better teaching
> The solid rules of civil government,
> In their majestic, unaffected style,
> Than all the oratory of Greece and Rome.
> In them is plainest taught and easiest learnt
> What makes a nation happy, and keeps it so.
>
> Par. Reg. B. iv[3]

[1] In answer to a pencil query "whose" in Copy G, C remarked: "evidently, those of the Nationalty: i.e. the sacred portion of the common Wealth reserved for purposes common to all in every class—viz, those of civilization."

[2] From 1795, when C advocated that the true friend of freedom "should be *personally* among the Poor, and teach them their *Duties* in order that he may render them susceptible of their *Rights*" (*Lects 1795—CC*—43), he habitually coupled rights and duties; cf *Friend* (*CC*) I 166.

[3] *Paradise Regained* IV 353–62. Quoted also in *SM* (*CC*) 8.

[4] In other words, "to preserve one nation free from Idolatry in order that it might be a safe receptacle for the precursive Evidences of Christianity"; cf C's remarks on the Levites, LRR II: *Lects 1795* (*CC*) 137.

Without pain or reluctance, therefore, I should state this provision, by which a particular lineage was made a necessary qualification for the trustees and functionaries of the reserved NATIONALTY, as the main cause of the comparatively little effect, which the Levitical establishment produced on the moral and intellectual character of the Jewish people, during the whole period of their existence as an independent state.

With this exception, however, the scheme of the Hebrew polity may be profitably made use of, as the diagram or illustrative model[1] of a principle which actuated the primitive races generally under similar circumstances. With this and one other exception, likewise arising out of the peculiar purpose of Providence, as before stated, namely, the discouragement of trade and commerce in the Hebrew policy,[2] a principle so inwoven in the whole fabric, that the revolution in this respect effected by Solomon had no small share in the quickly succeeding dissolution of the confederacy,[3] it may be profitably considered even under existing circumstances.

And first, let me observe, with the Celtic, Gothic, and Scandinavian, equally as with the Hebrew tribes, Property by absolute right existed only in a tolerated alien; and there was everywhere a prejudice against the occupation expressly directed to its acquirement, viz. the trafficking with the current representatives of wealth.[4] Even in that species of possession, in which the right of the individual was the prominent relative character, the institution of the Jubilee[5] provided against its degeneracy into the merely *personal;* reclaimed it for the state,—that is, for the *line*, the *heritage*, as one of the permanent units, or integral parts, the aggregate of which constitutes the STATE, in that narrower and especial sense, in which it has been

[1] Cf above, pp 8 and 21, in which C reminds his readers "that the scheme or diagram...may be very different from the form in which it is or may be most adequately *realized*".

[2] On the anti-commercial laws of the Hebrews cf *LS* (*CC*) 223 and n 3.

[3] Cf *SM* (*CC*) 33. By the revolution effected by Solomon, C means the introduction of large-scale commercialism, bringing the antagonist powers into play and leading to the dissolution of the state.

[4] Cf C's account, in *LS* (1817), of the historic growth of the idea of "*individual* or private property" associated mainly with "moveable things", in which he suggests that "the minds of men were most familiar with the idea in the case of Jews and Aliens" in Europe. *LS* (*CC*) 215n.

[5] The jubilee provided that every fiftieth year all land was restored to those owners who had sold it during that period; all who through poverty had to hire themselves were released from bondage, except aliens; and all debts were remitted. Lev 25. C makes his own very personal application of the Jewish text to English history; cf his earlier treatment of the jubilee in LRR II: *Lects 1795* (*CC*) 125–7.

distinguished from the *nation*. And to these permanent units the calculating and governing *mind* of the state directs its attention, even as it is the depths, breadths, bays, and windings or reaches of a river, that are the subject of the hydrographer, not the water-drops, that at any one moment constitute the stream. And on this point the greatest stress should be laid; this should be deeply impressed, carefully borne in mind, that the abiding interests, the *estates*, and ostensible tangible properties, not the *persons* as *persons*,[1] are the proper subjects of the *state* in this sense, or of the power of the parliament or supreme council, as the representatives and plenipotentiaries of the state, *i.e.* of the PROPRIETY, and in distinction from the commonwealth, in which I comprise both the Propriety and the Nationalty.

And here permit me, for the last time, I trust, to encroach on your patience, by remarking, that the records of the Hebrew policy are rendered far less instructive as lessons of political wisdom, by the disposition to regard the Jehovah in that universal and spiritual acceptation, in which we use the word as Christians. But relatively to the Jewish polity, the Jehovah was their covenanted king: and if we draw any inference from the former, the Christian sense of the term, it should be this—that God is the unity of every nation; that the convictions and the will, which are one, the same, and simultaneously acting in a multitude of individual agents, are not the birth of any individual; "that when the people speak loudly and unanimously, it is from their being strongly impressed by the godhead or the demon. Only exclude the [a](by no means extravagant)[b] supposition of a demoniac possession, and *then* Vox Populi Vox Dei."[2]

[a–b] Added in 2nd ed

[1] A frequently reiterated principle; cf "Jack, Tom, and Harry have no existence in the eye of Law, except as included in some form or other of the *permanent Property* of the Realm. . . . Law knows nothing of Persons other than as Proprietors, Officiaries, Subjects. The preambles of our old Statutes concerning aliens (as foreign Merchants) and Jews, are all so many illustrations of my principle". Letter to Stuart 29 Oct 1814: *CL* III 537.

[2] In *PD* C had committed himself to the idea that the voice of the people is the voice of God. *Lects 1795* (*CC*) 312–13. Here he re-echoes WW: "For, when the people speak loudly, it is from being strongly possessed by the Godhead or the Demon . . .". *Convention of Cintra: Prose Works* ed A. B. Grosart I 113. C quoted this in *Friend* (*CC*) I 182 (II 108). Cf WW's earlier passage on "Philosophers" asserting "that the voice of the people is the voice of God". *Prose Works* I 64. C later denied that he had ever "said that the *vox populi* was of course the *vox Dei*. It may be; but it may be, and with equal probability, *a priori*, *vox Diaboli*. That the voice of ten millions of men calling for the same thing, is a spirit, I believe; but whether that be a spirit

So thought Sir Philip Sydney, who in the great revolution of the Netherlands considered the universal and simultaneous adoption of the same principles, as a proof of the divine presence; and on that belief, and on that alone, grounded his assurance of its successful result.[1] And that I may apply this to the present subject, it was in the character of the king, as the majesty, or symbolic unity of the whole nation, both of the state and of the persons;[2] it was in the name of the KING, in whom both the propriety and the nationalty ideally centered, and from whom, as from a fountain, they are ideally supposed to [a]flow—it was in the name of the KING, that[b] the proclamation throughout the land, by sound of trumpet, was made to all possessors: "The land is not your's, saith the Lord, the land is mine. To you I lent it."[3] The voice of the trumpets is not, indeed, heard in this country. But [c]no less[d] intelligibly is it declared by the spirit and history of our laws, that the possession of a property, not connected with especial duties, a property not fiduciary or official, but arbitrary and unconditional, was in the light of our forefathers the brand of a Jew and an alien; not the distinction, not the right, or honour, of an English baron or gentleman.[4]

a–b 1st ed: flow, that *c–d* 1st ed: as

of Heaven or Hell, I can only know by trying the thing called for by the prescript of reason and God's will." *TT* 29 Apr 1832.

[1] Cf "When Sir Philip Sidney saw the enthusiasm which agitated every man, woman, and child in the Netherlands against Philip and D'Alva, he told Queen Elizabeth that it was the Spirit of God, and that it was invincible." *TT* 17 May 1833. The source is a life of Sidney: "In one of his letters there is so strong a proof that he considered the cause of the persecuted inhabitants of the Netherlands as the cause of God, that it would be improper to deny the Protestant reader the pleasure of perusing it. 'If her Majesty...wear the fountain, I wold fear, considering what I daily find, that we shold wax dry. But she is but a means whom God useth. And I know not whether I am deceaved; but I am faithfully persuaded, that, if she shold withdraw herself, other springes wold rise up to help this action. For, methinkes, I see the great work indeed in hand against the abusers of the world, wherein it is no greater fault to have confidence in man's power, than it is too hastily to despair of God's work.'" Thomas Zouch *Memoirs of the Life and Writings of Sir Philip Sidney* (York 1808) 238–9, citing a ms life. C quoted part of the letter in *Friend* No 7; WW, all of it in *Cintra*: see *Friend* (*CC*) II 108 (I 182) and WW *Prose Works* I 170.

[2] Cf above, p 16 and n.

[3] Cf Lev 25.23; also LRR II: *Lects 1795* (*CC*) 127.

[4] Cf the letter to Stuart quoted above, p 40 n 1, and C's note, "A landed estate is a Trust for determinate use—and one of the uses is the existence of *enduring* Families, and of *estates* in a graduated ascent, of magnitude and number in inverse ratio", on Henry Brougham *A Speech on the Present State of the Law of the Country; Delivered in the House of Commons, on Thursday, February 7, 1828* (1828) 43–4. Cf *TT* 31 Mar 1833.

[a]CHAPTER V

Of the Church of England, or National Clergy, according to the Constitution: its characteristic ends, purposes and functions: and of the persons comprehended under the Clergy, or the Functionaries of the National Church[b]

AFTER these introductory preparations, I can have no difficulty in setting forth the right idea of a national church as in the language of Elizabeth the *third* great venerable estate of the realm.[1] The first being the estate of the land-owners or possessors of fixed property, consisting of the two classes of the Barons and the Franklins; the second comprising the merchants, the manufacturers, free artizans, and the distributive class. To comprehend, therefore, this third estate, in whom the reserved nationalty was vested, we must first ascertain the end, or national purpose, for which it was reserved.

Now, as in the former state, the permanency of the nation was provided for; and in the second estate its progressiveness, and personal freedom; while in the king the cohesion by interdependence, and the unity of the country, were established; there remains for the third estate only that interest, which is the ground, the necessary antecedent condition, of both the former. Now[c] these depend on a continuing and progressive [d]civilization. But[e] civilization is itself but a mixed good, if not far more a corrupting influence, the hectic of disease, not the bloom of health, and a nation so distinguished more fitly to be called a varnished than a polished people; where this civilization is not grounded in *cultivation*,[2] in the harmonious develope-

[a–b] Added in 2nd ed   [c] 1st ed: All   [d–e] 1st ed: civilization, but

[1] The term estates of the realm applies to the classes of men invested with political rights in the state. Originally the three estates were the clergy, barons, and commons, but today as the result of the growth of parliamentary power and the elimination of the clergy as a separate body, the estates consist of Lords Spiritual (bishops), Lords Temporal (peers entitled to vote in the House of Lords), and the Commons (representing the whole electorate). The sovereign and these three estates form the body politic. According to Stubbs *Constitutional History* ch 15, § 184, the first estate was always the Church, but C is recalling that the Church was occasionally called the third estate by some Elizabethan writers.

[2] In England the verbal distinction between civilisation and cultivation

ment of those qualities and faculties that characterise our *humanity*.[1] We[a] must be men in order to be citizens.[2]

The Nationalty, therefore, was reserved for the support and maintenance of a permanent class or order, with the following duties. A certain smaller number were to remain at the fountain heads of the humanities, in cultivating and enlarging the knowledge already possessed, and in watching over the interests of physical and moral science; being, likewise, the instructors of such as constituted, or were to constitute, the remaining more numerous classes of the order. This latter and far more numerous body were to be distributed throughout the country, so as not to leave even the smallest integral part or division without a resident guide, guardian, and instructor; the objects[b] and final intention of the whole order being [c]these—to[d] preserve the stores, to guard the treasures, of past civilization, and thus to bind the present with the past; to perfect and add to the

[a] 1st ed: In short, we [b] 1st ed: object [c–d] 1st ed: thus to

has not achieved wide currency, but the idea of a distinction between material prosperity and cultural health (for the individual and the whole society) that it expresses certainly has. For its influence on nineteenth-century thought, see Raymond Williams *Culture and Society, 1780–1950* (Penguin 1961) 75–7, and for more recent influence, see T. S. Eliot *Notes Towards a Definition of Culture* (1949) 23. C used the distinction as early as 1818 in the "Essays on the Principles of Method" IX: *Friend* (*CC*) I 494. In the next essay he expanded it by speaking of "young men the most anxiously and expensively be-school-mastered, be-tutored, be-lectured, any thing but *educated;* who have received arms and ammunition, instead of skill, strength, and courage; varnished rather than polished; perilously over-civilized, and most pitiably uncultivated!" *Friend* (*CC*) I 500. Cf *P Lects* (1949) 110, in which C describes the state of India and Egypt as having been "a state of high civilization and of all that can arise out of civilization, but without any cultivation"; cf also *AR* (1825) xviii.

[1] The idea of harmonious development influenced many nineteenth-century writers, including Thomas Arnold in his *Fragment on the Church* (1844) and Matthew Arnold in *Culture and Anarchy*: "One may say that to be reared a member of a national Church is in itself a lesson of religious moderation, and a help towards culture and harmonious perfection." *Culture and Anarchy* ed J. D. Wilson (1960) 15. For a general discussion see Introduction, above, p lxii, and Williams *Culture and Society* 248.

[2] Copy G adds: "With equal truth ~~it may be affirmed~~ two apparently contradictory Positions may be affirmed.—1. We must be citizens in order to be men: and 2. We must be men in order to be citizens. The contradiction disappears by the insertion of an explanatory adjective in each instance. We must be *potential* men in order to be made Citizens, but likewise we must be citizens in order to [be]come actual Men. The shew of *contradiction* is removed; but still the *Cycle* remains, a fact." The note is written above the chapter head but clearly refers to the last sentence of this paragraph.

same, and thus to connect the present with the future; but especially to diffuse through the whole community, and to every native entitled to its laws and rights, that quantity and quality of knowledge which was indispensable both for the understanding of those rights, and for the performance of the duties correspondent. Finally, to secure for the nation, if not a superiority over the neighbouring states, yet an equality at least, in that character of general civilization, which equally with, or rather more than, fleets, armies, and revenue, forms the ground of its defensive and offensive power. The object of the two former estates of the realm, which conjointly form the STATE, was to reconcile the interests of permanence with that of progression —law with liberty. The object of the National Church, the third remaining estate of the realm, was to secure and improve that civilization, without which the nation could be neither permanent nor progressive.[1]

That in all ages, individuals who have directed their meditations and their studies to the nobler characters of our nature, to the cultivation of those powers and instincts which constitute the man, at least separate him from the animal, and distinguish the nobler from the animal part of his own being, will be led by the *supernatural* in themselves[2] to the contemplation of a power which is likewise super-*human;* that science, and especially moral science, will lead to religion, and remain blended with it—this, I say, will, in all ages, be the course of things. That in the earlier ages, and in the dawn of civility, there will be a twilight in which science and religion give

[1] In *The Friend* C defined instruction as one of the ends of government. *Friend* (*CC*) I 253. In a letter to C. A. Tulk [12 Feb 1821] he refers to the importance of a permanent learned order and uses the word "clerisy": *CL* v 138; cf also the passage in N 28, quoted below, p 46 n 1, and *C 17th C* 137–8 and *SM* passim. The idea of the continuity of civilisation owes much to Burke; see Alfred Cobban *Edmund Burke and the Revolt Against the Eighteenth Century* (1929, 2nd ed 1960) 177–86. The idea of the correlative nature of rights and duties (often repeated) stresses the social rôle of education. Charles James Blomfield, bp of London, one of the Grasmere–Keswick circle, introduced administrative reforms in the 1830's to make the Church more effective in educating the nation. For C's marginal comments on Blomfield's *Charge* (1830) see Introduction, above, p lxv and n 7.

[2] There is a close connexion between C's poetic exploration of the supernatural and his psychological and religious speculations, a connexion that might have been further explored had he ever written his projected essay on the supernatural (*BL* ch 13—1907—I 202; see I 272; and *CL* IV 561). In *Blackwoods* XI (Jan 1822) 6, C remarked that "the age is so fully attached to the unnatural in taste, the praeternatural in life, and the contranatural in philosophy as to have left little room for the super-natural . . .". Cf "...My great aim and object is to assert the *Superhuman* in order to diffuse more & more widely the faith in the *Supernatural.*" N Q f 64.

light, but a light refracted through the dense and the dark, a superstition—this is what we learn from history, and what philosophy would have taught us to expect. But we affirm, that in the spiritual purpose of the word, and as understood in reference to a future state, and to the abiding essential interest of the individual as a person, and not as the citizen, neighbour, or subject, religion may be an indispensable ally, but is not the essential constitutive end of that national institute, which is unfortunately, at least improperly, styled a church—a name which, in its best sense is exclusively appropriate to the church of Christ. If this latter be ecclesia, the communion of such as are called out of the world, *i.e.* in reference to the especial ends and purposes of that communion; this other might more expressively have been entitled *enclesia*, or an order of men, chosen in and of the realm, and constituting an estate of that realm.[1] And in fact, such was the original and proper sense of the more appropriately named CLERGY. It comprehended the learned of all names, and the CLERK was the synonyme of the man of learning.[2] Nor can any fact more strikingly illustrate the conviction entertained by our ancestors, respecting the intimate connexion of this clergy with the peace and weal of the nation, than the privilege formerly recognized by our laws, in the well-known phrase, "benefit of clergy."[3]

[1] *Ecclesia* (derived from ἐκ, out, καλέω, call) was the normal Greek word for an assembly of citizens; in the Septuagint it is used for the assembly of the Jewish nation and was adopted (rather than *synagogue*, which had become the more common word) by the Christians for their assemblies. Jeremy Taylor e.g. noted: "Now by *Translation* this word is used among Christians to signifie *all them who out of the whole mass of mankind are called and come and are gathered together by the voice and call of God*...". *A Dissuasive from Popery* pt 2 sec 1: Σύμβολον Θεολογικόν, *or a Collection of Polemicall Discourses* (1674) 382. *Enclesia* is C's own coinage. It was the problem of "Christian Discipline in a Church established by Law" that first led C, he claimed, to the distinction between *ecclesia* and *enclesia*; see his annotation on Philip Skelton *Complete Works* (6 vols 1824) III 394–9: *LR* IV 277–9. He did not deny that a man could belong to both societies and believed that Archbishop Grindal (1519–83) "saw the *whole* truth; and saw, that the functions of the *En*clesiastic and those of the *Ec*clesiastic were not the less distinct, because both were capable of being exercised by the same Person; & vice-versâ, not the less compatible in the same subject because distinct in themselves. The Lord Chief Justice of the King's Bench is a Fellow of the Royal Society." Marginal comment on Hooker *Works* (1682) 56: *C 17th C* 145. Cf *AR* (1825) 166, *C 17th C* 217–18, and below, p 46.

[2] Cf C's definition of the intended audience for *SM* in 1816: "exclusively *ad clerum*; i.e. (in the old and wise sense of the word) to men of *clerkly* acquirements, of whatever profession". *SM* (*CC*) 36.

[3] Originally, the privilege of exemption from arrest and criminal trial enjoyed by the clergy (those claiming benefit of clergy had to be able to read), it was later extended to laymen and

[a]Deeply do I feel, for clearly do I see, the importance of my Theme. And had I equal confidence in my ability to awaken the same interest in the minds of others, I should dismiss as affronting to my readers all apprehension of being charged with prolixity, while I am labouring to compress in two or three brief Chapters, the principal sides and aspects of a subject so large and multilateral as to require a volume for its full exposition. With what success will be seen in what follows, commencing with the Churchmen, or (a far apter and less objectionable designation,) the National CLERISY.[b][1]

THE CLERISY of the [c]nation, or[d] national church, in its primary acceptation and original intention comprehended the learned of all denominations;—the sages and professors of the[e] law and jurisprudence; of medicine and physiology; of music; of military and civil architecture; of the physical sciences; with the mathematical as the common *organ* of the preceding; in short, all the so called liberal arts and sciences, the possession and application of which constitute the civilization of a country, as well as the Theological. The last was, indeed, placed at the head of all; and of good right did it claim the precedence. But why? Because under the name of Theology, or

[a–b] 1st ed: From the narrow limits prescribed by my object in *compressing* the substance of my letters to you, I am driven to apologise for prolixity, even while I am pondering on the means of presenting, in three or four numbered paragraphs, the principal sides and aspects of a subject so large and multilateral as to require a volume for their full exposition. Regard the following, then, as the text. The commentary may be given hereafter:—PARAGRAPH THE FIRST.

[c–d] 1st ed: nation (a far apter exponent of the thing meant, than the term which the usus norma loquendi forces on me), the clerisy, I say, or

[e] Added in 2nd ed

women. So numerous did the exemptions from punishment for crime grow that Parliament made certain offences "felony, without benefit of clergy". The Criminal Law Act of 1827 finally abolished benefit of clergy, "a benefit the very name of which, always keeping alive the remembrance of its rude origin, excites our wonder that it should still have survived, even in the forms of law, in the nineteenth century". *A Reg* (1827) 185.

[1] C coined the word, meaning learned men as a body, scholars, on the German *Clerisei*, late Latin *clericia*. It has survived, but usually in passages relating to or alluding to C. Expounding the idea that all harmony is founded on a relation to rest, C referred to "the clerisy of a nation, that is, its learned men, whether poets, or philosophers, or scholars" as "these points of relative rest. There could be no order, no harmony of the whole, without them." *TT* 10 Apr 1832. Cf "Clearer than the inference of Heat and Light from the relative position of the Earth to the Sun, is this to me. A nation that substitutes Locke for Logic, and Paley for Morality, and both this and that for Polity, Philosophy and Theology cannot but be slaves. But if this be the case with the Gentry, Clerisy, & the learned in all liberal professions, it is so with the Nation—or a Revolution is at hand." N 28 f 59[v]. Cf also *Lects 1795* (*CC*) 218 and n, letter to C. A. Tulk [12 Feb 1821]: *CL* v 138, *AR* (1825) 290, and above, pp 43, and below, pp 52–3 and nn.

Divinity, were contained the interpretation of languages; the conservation and tradition of past events; the momentous epochs, and revolutions of the race and nation; the continuation of the records; logic, ethics, and the determination of ethical science, in application to the rights and duties of men in all their various relations, social and civil; and lastly, the ground-knowledge, the prima scientia[1] as it was named,—PHILOSOPHY, or the doctrine and discipline* of *ideas*.

Theology formed only a part of the objects, the Theologians formed only a portion of the clerks or clergy of the national church. The theological order had precedency indeed, and deservedly; but not because its members were priests, whose office was to conciliate the invisible powers, and to superintend the interests that survive the grave; not as being exclusively, or even principally, sacerdotal or templar, which, when it did occur, is to be considered as an accident of the age, a mis-growth of ignorance and oppression, a falsification of the constitutive principle, not a constituent part of the same. No! The Theologians took the lead, because the SCIENCE of Theology was the root and the trunk of the knowledges that civilized man, because it gave unity and the circulating sap of life to all other sciences, by virtue of which alone they could be contemplated as forming, collectively, the living tree of knowledge.[7] It had the

* That is, of knowledges immediate, yet real, and herein distinguished *in kind* from logical and mathematical truths, which express not realities, but only the necessary *forms* of conceiving and perceiving, and are therefore named the *formal* or *abstract* sciences. Ideas, on the other hand, or the truths of philosophy, properly so called, correspond to substantial beings, to objects whose actual subsistence is *implied* in their idea, though only *by* the idea revealable.[2] To adopt the language of the great philosophic apostle,[3] they are "*spiritual realities that can only spiritually be discerned*,"[4] and the inherent aptitude and moral *preconfiguration* to which constitutes what we mean by ideas, and by the presence of *ideal* truth, and of *ideal* power, in the human being. They, in fact, constitute his *humanity*.[5] For try to conceive a *man* without the ideas of God, eternity, freedom, will, absolute truth, of the good, the true, the beautiful, the infinite. An *animal* endowed with a memory of appearances and of facts might remain. But the *man* will have vanished, and you have instead a creature, "more subtile than any beast of the field, but likewise cursed above every beast of the field; upon the belly must it go and dust must it eat all the days of its life."[6] But I recal myself from a train of thoughts, little likely to find favour in this age of sense and selfishness.

1 "First knowledge". C had argued earlier (*LS* 1817 passim) that neglect of theology had led to the overbalance of the commercial spirit in the country.

2 Cf above, pp 12–13, and *Friend* (*CC*) I 520–4.

3 St Paul.

4 Cf 1 Cor 2.14.

5 Cf above, p 43.

6 Gen 3.1, 14 (var).

7 Gen 2.9. C adds the organic metaphor.

precedency, because, under the name theology, were comprised all the main aids, instruments, and materials of NATIONAL EDUCATION, the *nisus formativus*[1] of the body politic, the shaping and informing spirit, which *educing*,[2] *i.e.* eliciting, the latent *man* in all the natives of the soil,[3] *trains them up* to citizens of the country, free subjects of the realm. And lastly, because to divinity belong those fundamental truths, which are the common ground-work of our civil and our religious duties, not less indispensable to a right view of our temporal concerns, than to a rational faith respecting our immortal well-being. (Not without celestial observations, can even terrestrial charts be accurately constructed.) And of especial importance is it to the objects here contemplated, that only by the vital warmth diffused by these truths throughout the MANY, and by the guiding light from the philosophy, which is the basis of *divinity*, possessed by the FEW,[4] can either the community or its rulers fully comprehend, or rightly

[1] Writers in many fields seized on this phrase, which means "formative urge, impulse, or force", with its German equivalent, *Bildungstrieb*. It was used by J. F. Blumenbach (whose lectures C had attended in 1798–9) in his defence of epigenesis (on which Darwinian evolution depended) against preformation (which was preferred by the literal interpreters of Genesis). C used it figuratively, as here, in *The Friend* (1818), having already forgotten its origin or dismissed its special significance: *Friend* (*CC*) I 493 and n, in which he says that medical writers translate Blumenbach's *Bildungstrieb* as *nisus formativus*. Apparently C forgot that Blumenbach himself used the Latin phrase. See also *CN* III 3744 and n, 3840n.

[2] In *SM* (1816) C defined the function of education as "*educing* the faculties, and forming the habits", and in a footnote in *The Friend* as consisting in "*educing*, or to adopt Dr. Bell's own expression, *eliciting* the faculties of the human mind, and at the same time subordinating them to the reason and conscience; varying the means of this common end according to the sphere and particular mode, in which the individual is likely to act and become useful". *SM* (*CC*) 40; *Friend* (*CC*) I 540n. C's distinction between education and instruction has become a commonplace in educational theory; it was not so then. T. S. Eliot acknowledges the Coleridgian origin in *The Idea of a Christian Society* (1939) 41.

[3] C's idea of developing the latent man extends to the native populations in Africa, Malta, and India. His letters, notebooks, and scattered comments reveal a sympathetic interest in their ways of life, development, and right to independent existence. In his notes (BM MS Egerton 2800 ff 118–21) on Brougham's *Inquiry into the Colonial Policy of the European Powers* (2 vols Edinburgh 1802), C wrote: "I am deeply convinced, that as soon as a colony can maintain itself, the Mother Country ought to make it an equal, true, integral part of herself—& give to it all the privileges, it could enjoy as an independent State." He was bitterly critical of British colonial policy, and criticised politicians and public servants for their imaginative failure to understand the peoples they governed.

[4] Cf "...The most important changes in the commercial relations of the world had their origin in the closets or lonely walks of uninterested theorists". *SM* (*CC*) 14. Cf also *Friend* (*CC*) I 62.

appreciate, the permanent *distinction*, and the occasional *contrast*, between cultivation and civilization; or be made to understand this most valuable of the lessons taught by history, and exemplified alike in her oldest and her most recent records—that a nation can never be a too cultivated, but may easily become an over-civilized race.[1]

[1] See above, p 42 n 2, especially the passage from *Friend* (*CC*) I 500.

[a]CHAPTER VI

Secessions or offsets from the National Clerisy. Usurpations and abuses previous to the Reformation. Henry VIII. What he might and should have done. The main End and Final Cause of the Nationalty: and the duties, which the State may demand of the National Clerisy. A question, and the answer to it[b]

As a natural consequence of the full developement and expansion of the mercantile and commercial order, which in the earlier epochs of the constitution, only existed, as it were, potentially and in the bud; the students and possessors of those sciences, and those sorts of learning, the use and necessity of which were indeed constant and perpetual to the *nation*, but only accidental and occasional to *individuals*, gradually detached themselves from the nationalty and the national clergy, and passed to the order, with the growth and thriving condition of which their emoluments were found to increase in equal proportion. Rather, perhaps, it should be said, that under the common name of professional, the learned in the departments of law, medicine, &c., formed an intermediate link between the established clergy and the burgesses.

This circumstance, however, can in no way affect the principle, nor alter the tenure, nor annul the rights of those who remained, and who, as members of the permanent learned class, were planted throughout the realm, each in his appointed place, as the immediate agents and instruments in the great and indispensable work of perpetuating, promoting, and increasing the civilization of the nation, and who thus fulfilling the purposes for which the determinate portion of the total wealth from the land had been reserved, are entitled to remain its trustees, and usufructuary proprietors. But, remember, I do not assert that the proceeds from the nationalty cannot be rightfully vested, except in what we now mean by clergymen, and the established clergy.[1] I have every where implied the

[a–b] 1st ed: PARAGRAPH THE SECOND.

[1] Cf C's views on private ownership as a "trust" (at the end of ch 4, above, p 41). John Stuart Mill, in "Corporation and Church Property", praised C's idea of a "permanent learned class", but suggested that the state

contrary. But I do assert, that the nationalty cannot rightfully, and that without foul wrong to the nation it never has been, alienated from its original purposes. I assert that those who, being duly elected and appointed thereto, exercise the functions, and perform the duties, attached to the nationalty—that these collectively possess an unalienable, indefeasible title to the same—and this by a *Jure Divino*,[1] to which the thunders from Mount Sinai[2] might give additional authority, but not additional evidence.

COROLLARY.[a]—During the dark times, when the incubus of superstition lay heavy across the breast of the living and the dying; and when all the familiar "tricksy spirits"[3] in the service of an alien, self-expatriated and anti-national priesthood were at work in all forms, and in all directions, to aggrandize and enrich a "kingdom of this world;"[4] large masses were alienated from the heritable proprieties of the realm, and confounded with the Nationalty under the common name of church property. Had every rood, every pepper-corn, every stone, brick, and beam, been re-transferred, and made heritable, at the Reformation, no right would have been invaded, no principle of justice violated. What the state, by law—that is, by the collective will of its functionaries at any one time assembled—can do or suffer to be done; that the state, by law, can undo or inhibit. And in *principle*, such bequests and donations were vitious *ab initio*, implying in the donor an absolute property in land, unknown to the constitution of the realm, and in defeasance of that immutable reason, which in the name of the nation and the national majesty proclaims:—"The land is not yours; it was vested in your *lineage* in trust for the nation."[5] And though, in change of times and circumstances, the interest of progression, with the means and motives for the same—Hope, Industry, Enterprise—may render it the wisdom of the state to facilitate the transfer from line to line, still it must be

[a] 1st ed: COROLLARY to Paragraph II.

was at liberty to withdraw the endowment from its original possessors, the National Church, if it failed to fulfil duties as trustee, and hand it over to any body that was better able to accomplish the ends for which the endowment had been made. Thus, unwittingly C provided Mill with a powerful argument for a rational, utilitarian redistribution of national wealth for secular ends. Mill *Collected Works* IV 220–2; see also Introduction, above, p lxiii, and *C&S* (Ev ed) xxvi–xxviii.

[1] "Divine Law", or "Divine Right". Cf *SM* (*CC*) 33.

[2] Exod 19.16.

[3] Shakespeare *The Tempest* v i 226.

[4] Cf John 18.36 and Rev 11.15; cf below, pp 55 and 103, 114.

[5] Cf Lev 25.23.

within the same scale, and with preservation of the balance.[1] The *most* honest of our English historians, and with no *superior* in industry and research, Mr. Sharon Turner,[2] has labored successfully in detaching from the portrait of our first Protestant king the layers of soot and blood, with which pseudo-Catholic hate and pseudo-Protestant candour had coated it. But the name of Henry VIII. would outshine that of Alfred, and with a splendor, which not even the ominous shadow of his declining life would have eclipsed—had he retained the will and possessed the power of effecting, what in part, he promised and proposed to do—if he had availed himself of the wealth, and landed masses that had been unconstitutionally alienated from the state, *i.e.* transferred from the scale of heritable lands and revenues, to purchase and win back whatever had been alienated from the opposite scale of the nationalty. *Wrongfully* alienated: for it was a possession, in which every free subject in the nation has a living interest, a permanent, and likewise a possible personal and reversionary interest! *Sacrilegiously* alienated: for it had been consecrated τῷ Θεῷ οἰκείῳ,[3] to the potential divinity in every man, which is the ground and condition of his *civil* existence, that without which a man can be neither free nor obliged, and by which alone, therefore, he is capable of being a free subject—a citizen.[4]

If, having thus righted the balance on both sides, HENRY had then directed the nationalty to its true national purposes, (in order to which, however, a different division and sub-division of the kingdom must have superseded the present barbarism, which forms an obstacle to the improvement of the country, of much greater magnitude than men are generally aware of)—if the Nationalty had been distributed in proportionate channels, to the maintenance,—1, Of universities, and the great schools of liberal learning: 2, Of a

[1] C recognises the need for circulation of property, but neither here nor elsewhere suggests how the state is to achieve this desirable end.

[2] Sharon Turner (1768–1847) published a *History of the Reign of Henry VIII* in 1826 and a *History of the Reigns of Edward the Sixth, Mary, and Elizabeth* in 1829, the two together forming his *Modern History of England*. Turner claims that Henry VIII has been unfairly maligned by previous historians and twice compares him to Alfred.

[3] "To the indwelling God"; C translates more expansively "to the potential divinity in every man". Cf an annotation on W. G. Tennemann *Geschichte der Philosophie* in which he tr the phrase "domestic God, or Divine Familiar". *P Lects* (1949) 408 (n 31). Cf also *CN* III 3911 and n and *Friend* (*CC*) I 150.

[4] In the political essays in *The Friend* Sec I, C argues that the potential divinity in every man makes him fit for both freedom and civil obedience through the possession of reason and conscience. *Friend* (*CC*) I 191.

pastor, presbyter, or *parson** in every parish: 3, Of a school-master in every parish, who in due time, and under condition of a faithful performance of his arduous duties, should succeed to the pastorate; so that both should be labourers in different compartments of the same field, workmen engaged in different stages of the same process, with such difference of rank, as might be suggested in the names pastor and sub-pastor, or as now exists between curate and rector, deacon and elder. Both alike, I say, members and ministers of the national clerisy or church, working to the same end, and determined in the choice of their means and the direction of their labours, by one and the same object—namely, in producing and re-producing,[3] in preserving, continuing and perfecting, the necessary sources and conditions of national civilization; this being itself an indispensable condition of national safety, power and welfare, the strongest security and the surest provision, both for the permanence and the progressive advance of whatever (laws, institutions, tenures, rights, privileges, freedoms, obligations, &c. &c.) constitute the public weal: these parochial clerks being the great majority of the national clergy, and

* *i.e.* Persona κατ' ἐξοχήν; persona *exemplaris*;[1] the representative and exemplar of the *personal* character of the community or parish; of their duties and rights, of their hopes, privileges and requisite qualifications, as moral *persons*, and not merely living things. But this the pastoral clergy cannot be other than imperfectly—they cannot be that which it is the paramount end and object of their establishment and distribution throughout the country, that they should be—each in his sphere the germ and nucleus of the progressive civilization[2]—unless they are *in the rule* married men and heads of families. This, however, is adduced only as an accessary to the great principle stated in a following page, as an instance of its beneficial consequences, not as the grounds of its validity.

[1] "A person in the highest sense; a *model* person". C is noting that "parson" is the same word as the Latin *persona*; cf *OED* under "parson" (end-note).

[2] Cf "...and last not least, by the example and influence of a Pastor and a School Master placed, as a germ of civilization and cultivation, in every Parish throughout the Realm": a note (c Jun 1820) on the end-pages of Baxter *Reliquiae*, in which C defines the "two Senses of the words, Church of England" and outlines the "*Idea* of the Church as an Estate", in language similar to that used in *C&S*: *C 17th C* 354–5. In the notes of 1820 and here, C's insistence that the clergy should be married men and heads of families sharply distinguishes them from the members of the Roman Catholic orders. For remarks on the enforced celibacy of the latter see below, p 113. In some notes he prepared (probably for Green or one of his pupils, as EHC notes on the ms), C listed no less than seven functions of a priesthood. The ms "On the origin of the Priesthood or priestly caste" (now in PML: M.A. 2033G) is reproduced in App D 2, below, pp 229–30.

[3] C's ms draft of the latter part of this ch 6 (with chs 7 and 8), in the BM, begins here: Add Ms 34225 f 115. For the text see App C, below, pp 213–21.

the comparatively small remainder, being principally* *in* ordine *ad hos*, Cleri doctores ut Clerus Populi.[3]

I may be allowed, therefore, to express the final cause of the whole by the office and purpose of the greater part—and this is, to form and train up the people of the country to obedient, free, useful, organizable subjects, citizens, and patriots, living to the benefit of the state, and prepared to die for its defence.[4] The proper *object* and end of the National Church is civilization with freedom; and the duty of its ministers, could they be contemplated merely and exclusively as officiaries of the *National* Church, would be fulfilled in the communication of that degree and kind of knowledge to all, the possession of which is necessary for all in order to their CIVILITY. By civility I mean all the qualities essential to a citizen, and devoid of which no people or class of the people can be calculated on by the rulers and leaders of the state for the conservation or promotion of its essential interests.

It follows therefore, that in regard of the grounds and principles of action and conduct, the State has a right to demand of the National Church, that its instructions should be fitted to diffuse throughout the people [a]*legality*, that is, the[b] obligations of a well-calculated self-interest, [c]under the conditions of a common interest determined by common laws.[d] At least, whatever of higher origin and nobler and wider aim the ministers of the National Church, in some other capacity, and in the performance of other duties, might labour to implant and cultivate in the minds and hearts of their congregations

* Considered, I mean, in their national relations, and in that which forms their *ordinary*, their most *conspicuous* purpose and utility; for Heaven forbid, I should deny or forget, that the sciences, and not only the sciences both abstract and experimental, but the Literae Humaniores,[1] the products of genial power, of whatever name, have an immediate and positive value, even in their bearings on the national interests.[2]

[a–b] 1st ed: *Legality*, the

[c–d] 1st ed: enlivened by the affections and the warrantable prejudices of nationality.

[1] Humane Letters, or branches of study that tend to humanise or refine, such as the ancient classics.

[2] Behind the phrase "products of genial power" lies C's belief that it is the creative imagination that leads to growth in all areas of human activity. The imagination is as necessary to the scientist as to the poet.

[3] "*In* order *to these*, teachers of the Clergy, as the Clergy are [teachers] of the People". In the ms (see App C, below, p 213) C first wrote "in reference".

[4] On the willingness to die for the state, see the passage describing the "warm-hearted Tenantry...ready to march off at the first call of their country with a SON OF THE HOUSE at their head": *LS* (*CC*) 218. R. J. White illustrated the development of C's views on the relationship of the individual and the state: *The Political Thought of Samuel Taylor Coleridge* (1938) 139–42.

and seminaries, should include the practical consequences of the *legality* above mentioned. The State requires that the basin should be kept full, and that the stream which supplies the hamlet and turns the mill, and waters the meadow-fields, should be fed and kept flowing. If this be done, the State is content, indifferent for the rest, whether the basin be filled by the spring in its first ascent, and rising but a hand's-breadth above the bed; or whether drawn from a more elevated source, shooting aloft in a stately column, that reflects the light of heaven from its shaft, and bears the "Iris, Coeli decus, promissumque Iovis lucidum,"[1] on its spray, it fills the basin in its descent.

In what relation then do you place Christianity to the National Church? Though unwilling to anticipate what belongs to a part of my subject yet to come,[2] namely, the idea of the Catholic or Christian church, yet I am still more averse to leave this question, even for a moment, unanswered. And this is my answer.

In relation to the National Church, Christianity, or the Church of Christ, is a blessed* accident,[3] a providential boon, a grace of God, a mightly and faithful friend, the envoy indeed and liege subject of another state, but which can neither administer the laws nor promote the ends of [b]this other State,[c] which is *not* of the world,[4] without advantage, direct and indirect, to the true interests of the States, the aggregate of which is what we† mean by the WORLD[d]—*i.e.*

* Let not the religious reader be offended with this phrase. The writer means only that Christianity is an aid and instrument, which no State or Realm could have produced out of its own elements—which no State had a right to expect. It was, most awfully, a GOD-SEND![a]

† What we ought to mean, at least: for I blush to think, current as the term is among the religious public in consequence of its frequent occurrence in the New Testament, how many discourses I have heard, in which the preacher has made it only too evident that he understood by the term the earth which turns round with us, the planet TELLUS of the astronomers![5]

[a] Footnote added in 2nd ed   [b–c] 1st ed: this State,   [d] 1st ed: world

[1] C's Latin; cf the ms (App C, below, p 214) for his first version, which included a phrase from Virgil. Tr: "Rainbow, glory of heaven, and Jove's bright promise". An allusion to Gen 9.8–17. Cf "Diana, lucidum caeli decus..." (Horace *Carmen saeculare* 1–2) and "Iri, decus caeli" (Virgil *Aeneid* 9.18).

[2] In the section "Idea of a Christian Church"; see below, pp 111–28.

[3] Gladstone referred with approval to "what Mr. Coleridge had felicitously termed the...'happy accident' of the Christian Church". *The State in Its Relations with the Church* ch 1 (1838) 22.

[4] John 18.36 (var) and Rev 11.15 (var); cf similar allusions by C at pp 51 and 103, 114.

[5] In the ms and *C&S* (1st ed) the explanatory sentence: "What we ought...the planet Tellus of the astronomers!" appeared in the text here and not as a footnote.

the civilized world. As the olive tree is said in its growth to fertilize the surrounding [a]soil; to[b] invigorate the roots of the vines in its immediate neighbourhood, and [c]to improve[d] the strength and flavour of the wines—such is the relation of the Christian and the National Church. But as the olive is not the same plant with the vine, or with the elm or poplar (*i.e.* the State) with which the vine is wedded; and as the vine with its prop may exist, though in less perfection, without the olive, or prior to its implantation—even so is Christianity,[1] and à fortiori any particular scheme of Theology derived and supposed (by its partizans) to be *deduced* from Christianity, no essential part of the *Being* of the *National* Church, however conducive or even indispensable it may be to its *well* being. And even so a National Church might exist, and has existed, without, because before the institution of the *Christian* Church—as the Levitical Church in the Hebrew Constitution, the Druidical in the Celtic, would suffice to prove.

But here I earnestly intreat, that two things may be remembered—first, that it is my object to present the *Idea* of a National Church, as the only safe criterion, by which the judgment can decide on the existing state of things; for when we are in full and clear possession of the ultimate aim of an Institution, it is comparatively easy to ascertain, in what respects this aim has been attained in other ways, arising out of the growth of the Nation, and the gradual and successive expansion of its germs; in what respects the aim has been frustrated by errors and diseases in the body politic; and in what respects the existing institution still answers the original purpose, and continues to be a mean to necessary or most important ends, for

[a–b] 1st ed: soil, and to [c–d] 1st ed: improve

[1] Cf "An Olive-tree (said *Luther*) will stand, endure, and bear fruit the space of two hundred years, and it is a fair similitude of the Church; for *oil* signifieth the Amitie and Love of the Gospel; but *wine* signifieth the Doctrine of the Law. There is such a natural unitie and affinitie between the Vine and the Olive-tree, that when the Vine branch is grafted and set upon an Olive-tree, then it beareth both Grapes and Olives. In like manner when the Church (which is God's word) is planted in people's hearts, then it ringeth, soundeth out, and teacheth both the Law and the Gospel, it useth both Doctrines, and from both bringeth fruit." *Colloquia Mensalia: or, Dr Martin Luther's Divine Discourses at His Table* ch 20 (1652) 271—a work C heavily annotated. In 1826 he wrote to the Rev Edward Coleridge that Luther's *Table Talk* was "next to the Scriptures" his "main book of meditation, deep, seminative, pauline" and that "beyond all other works... *potenziates* both my Thoughts and my Will". *CL* VI 461. If C took the imagery from Luther, he attempted to correct Luther's mistaken notions of viticulture. See also below, p 103 and n 1, p 112 and n 1, and p 177.

which no adequate substitute can be found.[1] First, I say, let it be borne in mind, that my object has been to present the *idea* of a National Church, not the history of *the* Church established in this nation.[2] Secondly, that two distinct functions do not necessarily imply or require two different functionaries.[3] Nay, the perfection of each may require the union of both in the same person. And in the instance now in question, great and grievous errors have arisen from confounding the functions; and fearfully great and grievous will be the evils from the success of an attempt to separate them—an attempt long and passionately pursued, in many forms, and through many various channels, by a numerous party, who[a] has already the ascendancy in the *State;* and which, unless far other minds and far other principles than the opponents of this party have hitherto allied with their cause, are called into action, *will* obtain the ascendancy in the *Nation*.[4]

[a] Copy G: which

[1] C stated the general principle in 1817: "The corruptions of a system can be duly appreciated by those only who have contemplated the system in that ideal state of perfection exhibited by the reason: the nearest possible approximation to which under existing circumstances it is the business of the prudential understanding to realize. Those, on the other hand, who commence the examination of a system by identifying it with its abuses or imperfections, degrade their understanding into the pander of their passions, and are sure to prescribe remedies more dangerous than the disease." *LS* (*CC*) 156.

[2] In fact, C moves uneasily between "idea" and "history". Both Thomas Arnold (1795–1842) and the great German historian Bartold Georg Niebuhr (1776–1831) thought that *C&S* was historically faulty, although Arnold was pained to hear that Niebuhr had spoken "with strong disrespect of Coleridge's Church and State" and on 16 Jan 1840 asked J. C. Hare, one of Niebuhr's translators, for further details of his objection. A. P. Stanley *Life*...*Thomas Arnold* (2 vols 2nd ed 1880) II 165. A letter of 16 Jun 1825 (*CL* v 470), which refers to a review (by Arnold) of Niebuhr's *Römische Geschichte*, seems to imply that C had read the original work in German (first published 1811–12), but in May 1828, after reading 125 pages of the English translation, *History of Rome* (Cambridge and London 1828–42), he commented that if anyone could tell him what he had been reading, he would appoint him his "Archimage, by the name of Daniel Redivivus". N 37 f 75.

[3] Cf "O that our clergy did but know & see that their Tythes &c belong to them, as Officers & Functionaries of the Nationalty, as *Clerks*, & not exclusively as Theologians, ⟨and not at all, as Ministers of the Gospel;⟩ but they *are* likewise Ministers of the Church of *Christ*, and that their claims & the powers of that Church, are no more alienated or affected by their being at the same time, the established Clergy, than they are by the casual co-incidence of being Justices of the Peace, or heirs to an Estate or Fund-owners.—The Romish Divines placed the Church *above* the Scriptures, our present Divines give it no place at all." Note on Donne *LXXX Sermons* (1640) 71: *C 17th C* 181.

[4] Not only the Whig party, but the combined forces of nonconformity and philosophical radicalism, C thought, were trying to reduce the National Church to the status of a sect.

I have already said, that the subjects, which lie right and left of my road, or even jut into it, are so many and so important, that I offer [a]these Chapters[b] but as a catalogue *raisonné* of texts and theses, that will have answered their purpose if they excite a certain class of readers to desire or to supply the commentary.[1] But [c]there will not be wanting among my readers men who are no strangers to the ways, in which my thoughts travel: and the jointless sentences that make up the following Chapter or Inventory of regrets and apprehensions, will suffice to possess them of the chief points that press on my mind.[2]

The commanding knowledge, the *power* of truth, given or obtained by contemplating the subject in the fontal mirror of the Idea, is in Scripture ordinarily expressed by Vision: and no dissimilar gift, if not rather in its essential characters the same, does a great living Poet speak of, as

The VISION and the Faculty divine.[3]

And of the many political *ground-truths* contained in the Old Testament, I cannot recall one more worthy to be selected as the *Moral* and L'ENVOY of a Universal History, than the text in Proverbs, WHERE NO VISION IS, THE PEOPLE PERISHETH.[4]

It is now thirty years since the diversity of REASON and the UNDERSTANDING, of an Idea and a Conception, and the practical importance of distinguishing the one from the other, were first made evident to me.[5] And scarcely a month has passed during this long interval in which either books, or conversation, or the experience of life, have not supplied or suggested some fresh proof and instance of the mischiefs and mistakes, derived from that ignorance of this

[a–b] 1st ed: this epistolary pamphlet

[c–a] (p 60) 1st ed: you, Sir, are no stranger to the ways in which my thoughts travel; and a few jointless sentences will possess you of the chief points that press on my mind—to show

[1] In Copy G the last few words are underlined in pencil and Gillman has written below: "I desire but cannot supply it."

[2] C added the following five new paragraphs in the 2nd ed. He returns to the text of the 1st ed at the beginning of the quotation from Isaiah; see textual n above, also the ms draft of this passage, App C, below, p 215.

[3] WW *The Excursion* bk I line 79.

[4] Prov 29.18 (var); cf "But truly there is no vision in the land, and the people accordingly perisheth." *TT* 5 Feb 1833.

[5] A strict interpretation would attribute the first recognition of these principles to C's residence in Germany 1798–9. They were not worked out until later. For detailed discussions, see *SM* App C (*CC*) 59–93 and *Friend* (*CC*) I 153–61, and the letter in which he explained that "in the last Essay of the first 'Landing-Place'" of the revised *Friend* of 1818, "you will find the *pre-desiderata* to the Appendix of my first Lay-sermon". *CL* IV 851.

Truth, which I have elsewhere called the Queen-bee in the Hive of Error.[1]

Well and truly has the understanding been defined; *Facultas mediata et Mediorum:*—the Faculty of means to medial Ends,[2] that is to *Purposes*, or such ends as are themselves but means to some ulterior end.

My eye at this moment rests on a volume newly read by me, containing a well-written history of the Inventions, Discoveries, Public Improvements, Docks, Rail-ways, Canals, &c. for about the same period, in England and Scotland.[3] I closed it under the strongest impressions of awe, and admiration akin to wonder. We live, I exclaimed, under the dynasty of the understanding: and this is its golden age.

It is the faculty of means to medial ends. With these [a]the age,[b] this favoured land, teems: they spring up, the armed host, ("seges clypeata") from the serpent's teeth sown by Cadmus: "mortalia semina, dentes."[4] In every direction they advance, conquering and to conquer. Sea, and Land, Rock, Mountain, Lake and Moor, yea Nature and all her Elements, sink before them, or yield themselves captive! But the *ultimate* ends? Where shall I seek for information concerning these? By what name shall I seek for the historiographer of REASON? Where shall I find the annals of *her* recent campaigns? the records of her conquests? In the facts disclosed by the Mendicant Society?[5] In the reports on the increase of crimes, commitments?

[a–b] Copy G: this age, with these

[1] The Queen Bee figure was a favourite one, used of "the aversion to all intellectual effort" of most people, in *Friend* (*CC*) I 22 (II 152), of "the Popish Error...concerning Faith and Works" in *CN* II 2434, and of irrational faith—"This is, me saltem judice, the Queen Bee in the Hive of Romish—would that I dare say only of Romish Error" in a marginal note on *Faith, Hope and Charity: the Substance of a Sermon Preached...July 27 1825* (1827) by Peter Augustine Baines. Cf below, p 171.

[2] Source untraced; cf C's definition of the understanding in *AR* (1825) 250n and in annotations on *SM*: *SM* (*CC*) 19n, 61n.

[3] *A History of Inventions and Discoveries* by Francis Sellon White (1827), in which the inventions are arranged alphabetically and cover the entire period of history down to modern times.

[4] Ovid *Metamorphoses* 3.110, 105. Tr: "the shield-bearing crop", "the man-producing seed, the teeth". Cf *Friend* (*CC*) I 46.

[5] The Society for the Suppression of Mendicity, called briefly the London Mendicity Society, was founded on 25 Mar 1818; it issued tokens to its subscribers to give beggars, who could then call on the Society for help, when their position was carefully investigated; it also published annual reports of the beggars who had been helped and the undeserving beggars who had subsequently been prosecuted.

In the proceedings of the Police? Or in the accumulating volumes on the horrors and perils of population?[1]

O voice, once heard
Delightfully, *Increase and multiply!*
Now death to hear! For what can we increase
Or multiply, *but penury, woe and crime?*
PAR. LOST[2]

Alas! for a certain class, the following Chapter will, I fear, but too vividly shew[a] "the burden of the valley of vision, even the burden upon the crowned isle, whose merchants are princes, whose traffickers the honourable of the earth; who stretcheth out her hand over the sea, and she is the mart of nations!" (Isaiah, xxiii.)[3]

[c] (p 58)–[a] See p 58, above

[1] C did not share the strong Malthusian fear of rising population common to the age, but was concerned at the increase of "penury, woe and crime", as his emendation to the lines from *Paradise Lost*, above, indicates; cf marginalia on Malthus *An Essay on the Principles of Population* (2nd ed 1803), published by G. R. Potter *PMLA* LI (1936) 1061–8.

[2] Adapted from *Paradise Lost* X 729–32. C substitutes "but penury, woe and crime" for "but curses on my head".

[3] Isa 22.1; 23.8 (var), 11 (var), 3 (var).

[a]# CHAPTER VII

Regrets and Apprehensions[b]

THE National Church was deemed in the *dark age* of Queen Elizabeth, in the unenlightened times of Burleigh, Hooker, Spenser, Shakspeare, and Lord Bacon, A GREAT VENERABLE ESTATE OF THE REALM;[1] but now by "*all* the intellect of the kingdom," it has been determined to be one of the many theological sects, churches or communities, established in the realm; but distinguished from the rest by having its priesthood *endowed*, durante bene placito,[2] by favour of the legislature—that is, of the majority, for the time being, of the two Houses of Parliament. The Church being thus reduced to *a* religion, Religion *in genere*[3] is consequently separated from the church, and made a subject of parliamentary determination, independent of this church. The poor withdrawn from the discipline of the church.[4] The education of the people detached from the ministry of the church.[5] Religion, a *noun of multitude*, or nomen collectivum, expressing the aggregate of all the different groups of notions and ceremonies connected with the invisible and supernatural. On the plausible (and in *this* sense of the word, unanswerable) pretext of the multitude and variety of *Religions*,[6] and for the suppression of bigotry and negative persecution,

[a–b] Added in 2nd ed

[1] Cf n above, p 42.

[2] A legal phrase. "During the good pleasure [of the granter of an office]".

[3] "In general".

[4] Cf "The injury to Religion, to the Church, to the State, to general morality & industry, & in all these & in many other respects, to the Poor themselves, that arises from the disjunction of the Poor Laws from the Church—which yet in name they belong to?—Surely, this has been strangely overlooked by the Reformers on this important Subject! *Reform?* then look back at the original form—& see how far it is applicable to the present Times." N 24 f 31^v. For C on the rôle of the Church as a mediator between rich and poor, see *TT* 8 Sept 1830.

[5] C's marginal comments on Blomfield's *Charge* to the London clergy of 1830 stress that a clergyman's attention to parochial schools was the "most helpful part of his administrative duties". See also Introduction, above, p lxv, and p 44, above.

[6] In 1814, the British and Foreign Schools Society was set up to secure general and non-denominational religious instruction in the schools. It drew its membership mainly but not exclusively from Dissenters. The main

National Education to be finally sundered from all religion, but speedily and decisively emancipated from the superintendence of the National Clergy.[1] Education reformed. Defined as synonimous with Instruction.[2] *Axiom of Education so defined.* Knowledge being power,[3] those attainments, which give a man the power of doing what he [a]wishes in order[b] to obtain what he desires, are alone to be considered as knowledge, or to be admitted into the scheme of National Education. Subjects to be taught in the National Schools. Reading, writing, arithmetic, the mechanic arts, elements and results of physical science, but to be taught, as much as possible, empirically.[4] For all knowledge being derived from the Senses, the closer men are kept to the fountain head, the *knowinger* they must become. —POPULAR ETHICS, *i.e.* a Digest of the Criminal Laws, and the evidence requisite for conviction under the same: Lectures on Diet, on Digestion, on Infection, and the nature and effects of a specific virus incidental to and communicable by living bodies in the intercourse of society. N.B. In order to balance the Interests of Individuals and the Interests of the State, the Dietetic and Peptic Text Books, to be under the censorship of the Board of Excise.[5]

[a–b] 1st ed: wishes

issue, which C does not face here or elsewhere in *C&S*, was not between religious and secular education, but the voluntary principle; cf below, p 69 and n 1.

[1] See the continuation of this passage in the ms draft, below, App C, p 216.

[2] Cf above, p 48 and n 2.

[3] Cf *SM* (*CC*) 24 and n 2, which cites Bacon's *Novum Organum*, and cf *The Watchman* (*CC*) 4 and n 2. The speech made by George Birkbeck (1776–1841) at the laying of the foundation-stone of the London Mechanics' Institution in 1824 illustrates the kind of utilitarian interpretation of Bacon's phrase that C is attacking: "Whilst I remind you that the illustrious Bacon, long ago, maintained that 'Knowledge is power,' I may apprize you that it has, since his time, been established that knowledge is wealth—is comfort—is security—is enjoyment—is happiness." Hone's *Every-day Book* I 1550. Birkbeck, a doctor, was first active in bringing education to working-men in Glasgow, where he was Professor of Natural Philosophy, and then continued these activities when he moved to London and helped to form the Mechanics' Institution, of which he became the first president.

[4] Cf the ms draft of this passage, below, App C, p 216.

[5] C was opposed not simply to the secular organisation but to the increasingly utilitarian conception of the aims and content of national education. The Mechanics' Institution was founded in 1824 (see above, n 3). Brougham's *Practical Observations upon the Education of the People* (1825), dedicated to George Birkbeck, helped to popularise "the gospel of the alphabet", while the Society for the Diffusion of Useful Knowledge, established in 1825 as the result of Brougham's observations, carried out his plan for the publication of cheap and useful works.

Shall I proceed with my chapter of hints? Game Laws,[1] Corn Laws,[2] Cotton Factories,[3] Spitalfields,[4] the tillers of the land paid by poor-rates,[5] and the remainder of the population mechanized into engines for the manufactory of new rich men[6]—yea, the machinery of the wealth of the nation made up of the wretchedness, disease and depravity of those who should constitute the strength of the nation! Disease, I say, and vice, while the wheels are in full motion; but at the first stop the magic wealth-machine is converted into an intolerable weight of pauperism![7] But this partakes of History. The head and neck of the huge Serpent are out of the den: the voluminous train is to come. What next? May I not whisper as a fear, what Senators have promised to demand as a right? Yes! the next in my filial bodings is Spoliation.[8]—Spoliation of the NATIONALTY,

[1] For Game Laws, see above, p 18 n 3.

[2] The price of bread fell sharply in England in 1814, but instead of the poor benefiting from lower prices, the notorious Corn Law prohibiting the import of corn unless the price of wheat was eighty shillings a quarter was passed in 1815. This law, like the Game Laws, protected the interests of the landlords at the expense of the hungry poor. Mounted "on the Butcher's Table" in the Calne market-place, C had made a "butcherly sort of Speech of an hour long" against it. *CL* IV 549. See also below, p 90 and n 2.

[3] C supported the elder Peel's Bill to reduce the hours of juvenile labour in the cotton factories, writing several pamphlets: *Remarks on the Objections Which Have Been Urged Against the Principles of Sir Robert Peel's Bill* (18 Apr 1818) and *The Grounds of Sir Robert Peel's Bill Vindicated* (24 Apr 1818). A transcript of part of a third pamphlet, dated 15 May 1818 and apparently published, is in VCL.

[4] An allusion to the repeal of the Spitalfields Acts in 1824. These Acts, passed first in 1773, confirmed in 1782 and 1801, empowered justices to fix wages for the silk workers. The silk trade at Spitalfields had been the most protected of any industry (and the repeal in 1824 was part of Huskisson's free-trade policy). Silk soon fell in price and became a commodity available to the middle as well as the upper classes.

[5] See above, p 16 and n 4.

[6] Possibly an allusion to the shipping of children to the North to labour in the manufactories.

[7] Cf the moving passage in which C speaks in 1817 of the long-term effects on the health of the workers of the thousand wheels of some vast manufactory remaining "silent as a frozen water-fall". *LS* (*CC*) 206–7.

[8] HNC in the Preface to *TT* (1835) I xxviii explained that, though no party man, C threw his weight in the Tory scale "because the National Church was to him the ark of the covenant of his beloved country, and he saw the Whigs about to coalesce with those whose avowed principles lead them to lay the hand of Spoliation upon it". He went on to quote C as saying "once invade that truly national and essentially popular institution, the Church, and divert its funds to the relief or aid of individual charity or public taxation—how specious soever that pretext may be—and you will never thereafter recover the lost means of perpetual cultivation." HNC reported that on this subject his uncle spoke with an emotion which he "never saw him betray upon any topic of common politics, however decided his opinion might be". Ibid I xxix–xxx. See also below, p 161.

half thereof to be distributed among the land-owners, and the other half among the stock-brokers, and stock-owners, who are to receive it in lieu of the interest formerly due to them.

But enough! I will ask only one question. Has the national welfare, have the *weal*[a] and happiness of the people, advanced with the increase of the circumstantial prosperity?[1] Is the increasing number of wealthy individuals that which ought to be understood by the wealth of the nation? In answer to this, permit me to annex the following chapter of contents of the moral history of the last 130 years.[2]

A. Declarative act, respecting certain parts of the constitution, with provisions against further violation of the same, erroneously entitled, "THE REVOLUTION of 1688."

B. The Mechanico-corpuscular Theory raised to the Title of the Mechanic Philosophy, and espoused as a revolution in philosophy, by the actors and partizans of the (so called) Revolution in the state.[3]

C.[4] Result illustrated, in the remarkable contrast between the acceptation of the word, Idea, *before* the Restoration, and the *present* use of the same word. *Before* 1660, the magnificent SON OF COSMO[5] was wont to discourse with FICINO,[6] POLITIAN[7] and the princely MIRANDULA[8] on the IDEAS of Will, God, Free-

[a] 1st ed: wealth

[1] Once again, as in the earlier distinction between civilisation and cultivation (above, pp 42–3), C makes a sharp distinction between the wealth and the welfare of the nation. Cf *LS* (*CC*) 157 and n 3, 205 n 1.

[2] In the ms draft this was a "brief history...by a lover of Old England". A footnote to the word "history" in Copy G runs: "With the exception of the last sentence, which is extracted from my '*Aids to Reflection*', p 293, this 'brief history' was written about the year 1808, and republished in the *Friend*, vol. III, p. 130." This footnote also appears in the ms draft; see below, App C, p 217. Cf *Friend* (*CC*) I 446–7.

[3] Repeated (var) from *Friend* (*CC*) I 446–7. C is here attacking Locke and his modern followers; cf *SM* App E (*CC*) 108–10.

[4] Except for the first sentence, the whole of § C is taken from the beginning of *SM* App E (*CC*) 101–2.

[5] Lorenzo the Magnificent (1449–92), Duke of Florence, was the grandson, not the son, of Cosimo de' Medici (1389–1464); he founded his famous academy for the study of the antique and completed the great Laurentian library.

[6] Marsilio Ficino (1433–99), Italian philosopher, who enjoyed the patronage of Cosimo and who awakened interest in Greek philosophy by his translation of Plato. C's copy of Ficino's *Platonica theologia* (Venice 1525), bought at Messina on 9 Oct 1805, contains a comment on the contempt for Platonism that had developed from the time of Bacon to Condillac. *IS* 127–8.

[7] Angelo Politian or Poliziano (1454–94), Italian humanist, enjoyed Lorenzo's patronage.

[8] Giovanni Pico della Mirandola, Conte della Concordia (1463–94), Italian philosopher, friend of Politian, Ficino, and Lorenzo. Cf *P Lects* Lect X (1949) 294–5, on the revival of Platonism.

dom. SIR PHILIP SIDNEY, the star of serenest brilliance in the glorious constellation of Elizabeth's court, communed with SPENSER, on the IDEA of the beautiful:[1] and the younger ALGERNON[2]—Soldier, Patriot, and Statesman—with HARRINGTON,[3] MILTON, and NEVIL[4] on the IDEA of the STATE: and in what sense it may be more truly affirmed, that the people (*i.e.* the component particles of the body politic, at any moment existing as such) are in order to the state, than that the state exists for the sake of the people.[5]

1 C's precise source is unknown, but it was common knowledge that Sir Philip Sidney (1554–86) and Edmund Spenser (c 1552–99) both believed in a Platonic idea of the beautiful. They saw much of each other after Spenser obtained a post in Leicester's household in 1578; from 1579 they were fellow-members of the Areopagus club, which aimed to naturalise classical metres in English poetry.

2 Algernon Sidney (1622–83), son of Robert Sidney, 2nd Earl of Leicester, was sentenced to death by Jeffreys in Nov 1683 for his part in the Rye House Plot and was executed 7 Dec. His *Discourses Concerning Government* was published in 1698; for C's marginal comments on the *Discourses* see *NTP* 189–93 and *CN* II 3117, 3118 and n. As the editor of *The Watchman* (*CC*) 176 notes, Sidney was one of C's lifelong heroes.

3 James Harrington or Harington (1611–77) served Charles I during his imprisonment and on the King's death wrote *Oceana*, a work that outlines a scheme for an oligarchical republic. On 21 Jan 1800 Poole advised C to read this "neglected book" (*Poole* II 4), which he did (*CN* I 639–43), and nine years later in preparing the political section of *The Friend* C studied it with care and quoted from it with qualified approval: *Friend* (*CC*) I 274.

4 Henry Neville (1620–94), a writer who took an active interest in politics, was banished from London by Cromwell in 1654, and in 1663 was arrested and acquitted on a charge of complicity in the Yorkshire rising. He translated Machiavelli's works (1675). His *Plato Redivivus* (1681) reflected Harrington's ideas so closely that it was included in the Dublin edition of Harrington's works.

5 All these great political writers of the seventeenth century were deeply imbued with Platonic ideas. They were also concerned with planning an ideal republican government and with emphasising the importance of institutions. Whether they discussed the question C poses is problematic, but Lessing's Ernst and Falk, in the second dialogue of the work of that name, did: "FALK. Do you believe that the people are created for the states. Or that the states are for the people? ERNST. Some seem to assert the former. But the latter is probably the more accurate." C's annotation on this passage, in his edition of Lessing now in the BM, reads: "...I hold, that the former Position (to wit, that ⟨*the*⟩ Men were made for, i.e. have their final cause in, the State, *rather* than the State for *the* Men) is capable of being maintained in a weighty and even sublime sense. I say *rather*, because both may be true. Not only is the Whole greater than a Part; but where it is a Whole, and not a mere All or Aggregate, it makes each part that which it is." *Sämmtliche Schriften* (30 pts in 15 vols Berlin 1784–98) IV pt VII 245–6. For C's recommendation of *Ernst und Falk* see below, p 114n.

PRESENT USE OF THE WORD

Dr. HOLOFERNES, in a lecture on metaphysics, delivered at one of the Mechanics' Institutions, explodes all *ideas* but those of sensation; and his friend, DEPUTY COSTARD, has no *idea* of a better flavored haunch of venison, than he dined off at the London Tavern last week.[1] He admits, (for the deputy has travelled) that the French have an excellent *idea* of cooking in general; but holds that their most accomplished *Maitres du Cuisine* have no more *idea* of dressing a turtle, than the Parisian Gourmands themselves have any *real* idea of the true *taste* and *colour* of the fat.

D. Consequences exemplified. State of nature, or the Ouran Outang theology[a] of the origin of the human race, substituted for the Book of Genesis, ch. I.–X.[2] Rights of nature for the duties and privileges of citizens.[3] Idealess facts, misnamed proofs from history, grounds of experience, &c., substituted for principles and the insight derived from them. State-policy, a Cyclops with one eye, and that in the back of the head![4] Our measures of policy, either a

[a] 1st ed: theory

1 Schoolmaster and clown in Shakespeare's *Love's Labour's Lost*. In *SM* App E the passage reads: "But these lights shine no longer, or for a few. Exeunt: and enter in their stead Holofernes and Costard! masked as Metaphysics and Commonsense." *SM* (*CC*) 102. (The remainder of the paragraph is also taken from *SM*; see ibid 102–3.) The reference to "Mechanics' Institutions" indicates that C thought this form of popular education, supported by the utilitarians and philosophical radicals, helped to perpetuate Locke's sensational mechanistic philosophy. Cf "What are all these Mechanics' Institutions, Societies for spreading Knowlege, &c but so many confessions of the necessity & of the absence of a *National Church*?" BM MS Egerton 2801 f 210. Cf above, p 62 nn 3, 5.

2 Theories of evolution were aired long before Darwin's *The Origin of Species* (1859) founded upon the work of such men as Edward Tyson, who in his *Orang-Outang, Sive Homo Sylvestris: or, The Anatomy of a Pygmie* (1699), illustrated the anatomical similarity "between the lowest rank of men, and the highest of animals". In 1815 C wrote to WW that he expected him in *The Excursion* to explode "the absurd notion of Pope's Essay on Man, Darwin, and all the countless Believers —even (strange to say) among Xtians of Man's having progressed from an Ouran Outang state". *CL* IV 574; cf VI 723 and *P Lects* Lect VII (1949) 239. In 1826 C outlined a scheme expressing the degeneracy of man rather than his "progressive Developement (as Dr Prichard from the Negro, or Oken from the Orang Outang)". N 26 ff 99–100.

3 The correlative nature of rights and duties is first stated in 1795 in the Bristol political lectures (*Lects 1795—CC*—43) and often repeated in later works. In C's eyes the cardinal error of contemporary revolutionary and radical thought was the substitution of abstract political rights for social duties.

4 A favourite figure adapted according to context to characterise the triumph of expedience in various human affairs. A ms note in a copy of

series of anachronisms, or a truckling to events substituted for the science, that should command them; for all true insight is foresight.[1] (Documents. The measures of the British Cabinet from the Boston Port-Bill, March, 1774; but particularly from 1789, to the Union of Ireland, and the Peace of Amiens.)[2] Mean time, the true historical feeling, the immortal life of an historical Nation, generation linked to generation by faith, freedom, heraldry, and ancestral fame, languishing, and giving place to the superstitions of wealth, and newspaper reputation.[3]

E. Talents without genius:[4] a swarm of clever, well-informed men: an anarchy of minds, a despotism of maxims.[5] Despotism of finance in government and legislation—of vanity and sciolism in the inter-

---

SM is typical: "Mere Experience 〈I mean a Statesman so endowed)〉 unenlightened by Philosophy a Cyclops with one eye, and that in the back of his head. Such a statesman was Mr Pitt". *SM* (*CC*) 43 n 1. In *TT* 24 Jun 1827 a man of maxims as opposed to a man of ideas "is like a Cyclops with one eye, and that eye placed in the back of his head".

1 In *BL* ch 10 a discussion of Burke as a "*scientific* statesman" develops the theme that foresight is the natural result of habitually referring political affairs to principles. *BL* (1907) I 124–5. Copy G contains a pencil note that the "same complaints were made by 〈Bacon〉 Harrington & Milton in their day" and supplies brief quotations from Harrington's *Oceana* and Milton's *On Reformation in England.* Though not in C's hand, it may be based on information supplied by C.

2 The Boston Port Bill, which removed the customhouse and closed the port after the destruction of British-taxed tea, precipitated the American War; 1789 marked the beginning of the French Revolution; the Union of Ireland took place in 1800; and the Peace of Amiens between England and France lasted from 1802 to 1803. Some of the measures of the British Cabinet between 1789 and 1803 that C had in mind were those that he had attacked earlier in *The Watchman* and *M Post* essays; for example, the British Cabinet's support of the European despots against France, its condoning of the slave-trade, its refusal to negotiate with France in 1799, its Irish policy. C was critical of the Union with Ireland and the Peace of Amiens on the grounds that both were prompted by expedience and not by principle.

3 For this "true historical feeling" of the nation, C was deeply indebted to Burke. Cf *LS* (*CC*) 170, which also has the phrase "grosser superstition for wealth", to which annotated copies add "reverence for *ancientry*" (ibid 170 textual note *a*).

4 A favourite distinction used by C (see also below p 87 and n 3), genius being the product of reason and talents of understanding: "In short, I define Genius, as originality in intellectual construction: the moral accompaniment, and actuating principle of which consists, perhaps, in the carrying on of the freshness and feelings of childhood into the powers of manhood. By Talent, on the other hand, I mean the comparative facility of acquiring, arranging, and applying the stock furnished by others and already existing in books and other conservatories of intellect." *Friend* (*CC*) I 419. The distinction occurs strikingly in the *M Post* essay on Pitt: *EOT* (*CC*) I 220.

5 C habitually distinguished between maxims and principles, e.g. *Friend* (*CC*) I 180. See also below, p 84 and n 2.

course of life—of presumption, temerity, and hardness of heart, in political economy.[1]

F. The Guess-work of general consequences substituted for moral and political philosophy, adopted as a text book in one of the Universities, and cited, as authority, in the legislature:[2] Plebs pro Senatu Populoque;[3] the wealth of the nation (*i.e.* of the wealthy individuals thereof, and the magnitude of the Revenue) for the well-being of the people.

G. Gin consumed by paupers to the value of about eighteen millions yearly. Government by journeymen clubs; by saint and sinner societies,[4] committees, institutions; by reviews, magazines, and above all by newspapers.[5] Lastly, crimes quadrupled for the whole country, and in some counties decupled.[6]

Concluding address to the parliamentary leaders of the Liberalists and Utilitarians. I respect the talents of many, and the motives and character of some among you too sincerely to court the scorn, which

[1] A further allusion to Malthus and current utilitarian political thought.

[2] William Paley's *The Principles of Moral and Political Philosophy* (1785), which was prescribed reading at Cambridge. C came to hate its utilitarian scheme of ethics. Cf *LS* (*CC*) 186n–7. Ben Ross Schneider, Jr *Wordsworth's Cambridge Education* (1957) points out that although Paley gave his principles a conservative application, they "could serve as a radical text almost as well as they could serve a Tory one. This was how it was read by the young Cambridge radicals."

[3] "The lower classes for the Senate and People" (S and P was the normal way of referring to the whole body of Roman citizens); cf *CL* III 189.

[4] C refers to the various societies created by the Evangelicals, or "Saints", who were often more concerned with making the poor moral than with relieving their distresses and who made adherence to strict Christian morality a condition of help. Their chief spokesman, William Wilberforce (1759–1833), a reformed sinner himself, helped to found or took an active interest in many of these societies, including the Proclamation Society (1787) originating in George III's Royal Proclamation against Vice and Immorality, which was later replaced by the more active and zealous Society for the Suppression of Vice, described by Sydney Smith as a corporation of informers supported by large contributions and bent on suppressing not the vices of the rich but the pleasures of the poor. C's feelings about Wilberforce were mixed: he valued his anti-slavery activities but thought they were "over rated" (*CL* III 148) and more concerned with saving his own soul than the lives of the slaves; he admired his concern with social evil, but distrusted his hell-fire theology (*IS* 115) and narrow sabbatarianism; and, to add further complication, Wilberforce took drugs, like C (*CL* IV 674–5).

[5] Suspicion of the inherent danger of any *imperium in imperio* led C to attack all clubs and societies; cf "Letters to Mr Justice Fletcher" (1814): *EOT* (*CC*) II 381. For C's attacks on newspapers see *Lects 1795* (*CC*) 265–6, *Watchman* (*CC*) 4; cf *CN* III 3454n.

[6] This re-echoes the note (added to *SM* 1839 and dated 28 Sept 1828) on the increase of crime, based on the Report of the House of Commons Committee. *SM* (*CC*) 42 n 1.

I anticipate. But neither shall the fear of it prevent me from declaring aloud, and as a truth which I hold it the disgrace and calamity of a professed statesman not to know and acknowledge, that a permanent, nationalized, learned order, a national clerisy or church, is an essential element of a rightly constituted nation, without which it wants the best security alike for its permanence and its progression; and for which neither tract societies nor conventicles, nor Lancasterian schools,[1] nor mechanics' institutions, nor lecture-bazaars under the absurd name of universities,[2] nor all these collectively, can be a substitute. For they are all marked with the same asterisk of spuriousness,[3] shew the same distemper-spot on the front, that they are empirical specifics for morbid *symptoms* that help to feed and continue the disease.

But you wish for *general* illumination:[4] you would spur-arm the toes of society: you would enlighten the higher ranks per ascensum ab imis.[5] You begin, therefore, with the attempt to *popularize* science: but you will only effect its *plebification*.[6] It is folly to think of making all, or the many, philosophers, or even men of science and systematic knowledge. But it is duty and wisdom to aim at making as many as possible soberly and steadily religious;—inasmuch as the morality which the state requires in its citizens for its own well-being and ideal immortality, and without reference to their spiritual interest as individuals, can only exist for the people in the form of religion.[7] But the existence of a true philosophy, or the

[1] C was opposed to the schools organised on the model supplied by Joseph Lancaster (1778–1838) in *Improvements in Education* (1803). He supported the Bell monitorial system used in the Church of England schools. Cf *SM* (*CC*) 40–1, and above, p 61 n 6.

[2] Probably a reference to University College, London (founded 1826 and opened Oct 1828), an object of distrust and suspicion owing to its connexion with Bentham and other philosophical radicals, and its purely secular character. In a letter to Allsop 10 May 1825, C speaks of a plan to give a series of three lectures on "the subject of a Metropolitan University" (*CL* v 445); they were never given, but the plan indicates an active interest in the special problems connected with founding such a university. Cf *L&L* 41–4 and see Introduction, above, p lxi, for C's influence at King's College, London.

[3] Classical scholars often used an asterisk to indicate a corruption in the text or the conjectural nature of an attribution. St Jerome, in his translation of the Bible, indicated by asterisks those passages of the Hebrew text not in the Septuagint.

[4] By contrast C had argued in 1795: "That general Illumination should precede Revolution, is a truth as obvious, as that the Vessel should be cleansed before we fill it with a pure Liquor." *Lects 1795* (*CC*) 43.

[5] Tr: "by ascent from the lowest levels".

[6] Cf *Friend* (*CC*) I 447, of which this passage is an expansion; *OED* credits C with earliest use of "plebification".

[7] Cf the ms draft of this passage, below, App C, p 219.

power and habit of contemplating particulars in the unity and fontal mirror of the idea—this in the rulers and teachers of a nation is indispensable to a sound state of religion in all classes.[1] In fine, Religion, true or false, is and ever has been the centre of gravity in a realm, to which all other things must and will accommodate themselves.[2]

[1] Cf the more extensive treatment added to *SM* and dated 28 Sept 1828—*SM* (*CC*) 42 and n 1—and C's belief that "an excess in our attachment to temporal and personal objects can be counteracted only by a pre-occupation of the intellect and the affections with permanent, universal, and eternal truths", an application of the Platonic concept of the particular in the universal: *LS* (*CC*) 173; cf *SM* (*CC*) 62, 64. Cf also C's letter to Lord Liverpool 28 Jul 1817: *CL* IV 757–64.

[2] Cf *Friend* (*CC*) I 447 and *P Lects* Lect IX (1949) 265–8.

[a]CHAPTER VIII

The subject resumed—viz. the proper aims and characteristic directions and channels of the Nationalty. The Benefits of the National Church in time past. The present beneficial influences and workings of the same.[b]

THE[1] deep interest which, during the far larger portion of my life since early manhood,[2] I have attached to these convictions, has, I perceive, hurried me onwards as by the rush from the letting forth of accumulated waters by the sudden opening of the sluice gates. It is high time that I should return to my subject. And I have no better way of taking up the thread of my argument, than by re-stating my opinion,[3] that our Eighth Henry would have acted in correspondence to the great principles of our constitution, if having restored the original balance on both sides, he had determined the nationalty to the following objects: 1st. To the maintenance of the Universities and the great liberal schools. 2ndly. To the maintenance of a pastor and schoolmaster in every parish. 3rdly. To the raising and keeping in repair of the churches, schools, &c., and, Lastly: To the maintenance of the proper, that is, the infirm, poor whether from age or sickness: one of the original purposes of the national Reserve being the alleviation of those evils, which in the best forms of worldly states must arise and must have been foreseen as arising from the institution of individual properties and primogeniture. If these duties were efficiently performed, and these purposes adequately fulfilled, the very increase of the population, (which would, however, by these very means have been prevented from becoming a vicious population,) would have more than counterbalanced those savings in the expenditure of the nationalty occasioned by the detachment of the practitioners of law, medicine, &c., from the national clergy. That this transfer of the national reserve from what had become national evils to its original and inherent purpose of national

[a–b] Added in 2nd ed

[1] In the ms draft (see App C, below, p 219) from here until the end, the hand is J. H. Green's, the punctuation is light and inaccurate, and obvious words are omitted.

[2] For C's early interest in Church and State and the development of his thought, see Introduction, above, pp li–lvii.

[3] See above, p 52.

benefits, instead of the sacrilegious alienation which actually took place—that this was impracticable, is historically true: but no less true is it philosophically that this impracticability, arising wholly from moral causes—that is, from loose manners and corrupt principles—does not rescue this wholesale sacrilege from deserving the character of the first and deadliest wound inflicted on the constitution of the kingdom: which term constitution in the body politic, as in bodies natural, expresses not only what has been actually evolved, but likewise whatever is potentially contained in the seminal principle of the particular body, and would in its due time have appeared but for emasculation or disease. Other wounds, by which indeed the constitution of the nation has suffered, but which much more immediately concern the constitution of the church, we shall perhaps find another place to mention.[a]

The mercantile and commercial class, in which I here comprise all the four classes that I have put in antithesis to the Landed Order, the guardian, and depository of the *Permanence* of the Realm, as more characteristically conspiring to the interests of its progression, the improvement and general freedom of the country—this class did as I have already remarked, in the earlier states of the constitution, exist but as in the bud. But during all this period of potential existence, or what we may call the minority of the burgess order, the National Church was the substitute for the most important national benefits resulting from the same. The National Church presented the only breathing hole of hope. The church alone relaxed the iron fate by which feudal dependency, primogeniture, and entail would otherwise have predestined every native of the realm to be lord or vassal. To the Church alone could the nation look for the benefits of existing knowledge, and for the means of future civilization. Lastly, let it never be forgotten, that under the fostering wing[b] of the church, the class of free citizens and burgers were reared. To the feudal system we owe the *forms*, to the church the *substance*, of our liberty.[1] We mention only two of many facts that would form the proof and comment of the above; first, the origin of towns and cities,[2] in the privileges attached to the vicinity of churches and monasteries, and which preparing an asylum for the fugitive Vassal and oppressed Franklin, thus laid the first foundation of a class of freemen detached from the land. Secondly, the holy war, which the

[a] 1st ed: mention. PARAGRAPH THE THIRD.

[b] 1st ed: wings

[1] Cf *LS* (*CC*) 215n.

[2] This and the following sentence are a revision of the footnote in *LS*.

national clergy, in this instance faithful to their national duties, waged against slavery and villenage, and with such success, that in the reign of Charles II., the law which declared every native of the realm free by birth,[1] had merely to sanction an opus jam consummatum.[2] Our Maker has distinguished man from the brute that perishes, by making hope first an instinct of his nature;[3] and secondly, an indispensable condition of his [a]moral and intellectual[b] progression:[4]

> For every gift of noble origin
> Is breathed upon by Hope's perpetual breath.
>
> WORDSWORTH[5]

But a natural instinct constitutes a right, as far as its gratification is compatible with the equal rights of [c]others. And this principle we may expand, and apply to[d] the idea of the National Church.

Among the primary ends of a STATE, (in that highest sense of the word, in which it is equivalent to the nation, considered as one body politic, and therefore includes the National Church), there are two, of which the National Church (according to its idea), is the especial and constitutional organ and means. The one is, to secure to the subjects of the realm generally, the hope, the chance, of bettering their own or their children's condition.[6] And though during

a–b 1st ed: moral intellectual

c–d 1st ed: others. PARAGRAPH THE FOURTH. RECAPITULATION of the preceding, in respect of

1 HNC in *C&S* (1839) 75n refers to the Act passed at the Restoration, 12 C. II c 24, and quotes Blackstone II c 6. 96: "And these encroachments grew to be so universal, that when tenure in villenage was virtually abolished (though copyholds were preserved) by the statute of Charles II, there was hardly a pure villein left in the nation."

2 "Work already completed".

3 Hope is one of the most important single themes in C's works. The very fact that it proved so elusive in his own life (e.g. *Dejection* and *Work Without Hope*) deepened his psychological understanding of its importance for others, especially children, "the Hope of the race". He constantly emphasises the rôle of hope in the moral and spiritual development of the individual. In saying that what makes a slave a slave "is the being in a state out of which he cannot hope to rise" and in defining the "Ideal of a Government" as "that which...most effectually affords Security to the Possessors, Facility to the Acquirers, and *Hope* to all" (*IS* 35, 366), C reveals the central place that hope occupies in his political thought; see John Colmer "Coleridge and the Life of Hope" *Studies in Romanticism* II (1972) 332–41.

4 Cf *Friend* (*CC*) II 201 (I 252–3) and *LS* (*CC*) 216n.

5 "These times strike monied worldlings with dismay" lines 10–11 (var): *WPW* III 119.

6 Cf a marginal comment on Heinrich Steffens *Caricaturen des Heiligsten* (2 vols Leipzig I 1819) 219: "A Peasant does not wish to be a Lord—no, nor perhaps does he wish to be a Parson,

the last three or four centuries, the National church has found a most powerful surrogate and ally for the effectuation of this great purpose in her former wards and foster-children, *i.e.* in trade, commerce, free industry, and the arts—yet still the nationalty, under all defalcations, continues to feed the higher ranks by drawing up whatever is worthiest from below, and thus maintains the principle of Hope in the humblest families, while it secures the possessions of the rich and noble. This is one of the two ends.[1]

The other is, to develope, in every native of the country, those faculties, and to provide for every native that knowledge and those attainments, which are necessary to qualify him for a member of the state, the free subject of a civilized realm. We do not mean those degrees of moral and intellectual cultivation which distinguish man from man in the same civilized society, much less those that separate the Christian from the this-worldian;[2] but those only that constitute the civilized man in contra-distinction from the barbarian, the savage, and the animal.

I have now brought together all that seemed requisite to put the intelligent reader in full possession of (what I believe to be) the right Idea of the National Clergy, as an estate of the realm. But I cannot think my task finished without an attempt to rectify the too frequent false feeling on this subject, and to remove certain vulgar errors, errors, alas! not confined to those whom the world call the vulgar. Ma nel mondo non è se non volgo, says Machiavel.[3] I shall make no apology therefore, for interposing between the preceding statements, and the practical conclusion from them, the following paragraph, extracted from a work long out of print, and of such

---

or a Doctor, but he would have the Soul of a Slave if he did not desire that there should be a *possibility* of his Children or Grand-children becoming such." C's copy is in BM; see *IS* 318.

[1] This whole paragraph is a revision of *Friend* (*CC*) II 202 (I 253) as revised for *LS* (*CC*) 216–17; the passage is closer to *LS*, though again revised. Cf also the ms draft, below, App C, p 221.

[2] *OED* cites as earliest use.

[3] *Il Principe* ch 18 (var). Tr: "But in the world there are only the vulgar". C entered the Machiavelli passage in a notebook in May 1807: *CN* II 3015. Cf C's note in N Q dated 9 Dec 1833: "O what a work could I write upon Vulgar Errors, with Machiavel's sentence for the Motto—Tutto il Mundo è il Vulgo. Politicians, Corn Laws—in short, all the favorite Degenerates of the Times. M. Chronicle, Eding. Review—of Lord Brougham, & Althorp—of Sects, Saints, and Radicals! But inopem me Copia fecit. I could supply Subjects and Thoughts, Title pages & Chapters of Contents, for half a dozen Authors. ⟨(I had almost said Southeys.)⟩—I say this not in pride but in grief, hopelessness and self-reproach, the Ghosts of all my many idle hours haunting and accusing me.—" N Q ff 59^{v}–60.

very limited circulation that I might have stolen from myself with little risk of detection, had it not been my wish to shew that the convictions expressed in the preceding pages, are not the offspring of the moment, brought forth for the present occasion; but an expansion of sentiments and principles publicly avowed in the year 1817.[1]

Among the numerous blessings of the English Constitution,[2] the introduction of an established Church makes an especial claim on the gratitude of scholars and philosophers; in England, at least, where the principles of Protestantism have conspired with the freedom of the government to double all its salutary powers by the removal of its abuses.

That the maxims of a pure morality,[3] and those sublime truths of the divine unity and attributes, which a Plato found hard to learn, and more difficult to reveal; that these should have become the almost hereditary property of childhood and poverty, of the hovel and the workshop; that even to the unlettered they sound as *common place;* this is a phenomenon which must withhold all but minds of the most vulgar cast from undervaluing the services even of the pulpit and the reading desk. Yet he who should *confine* the efficiency of an Established Church to these, can hardly be placed in a much higher rank of intellect. That to every parish throughout the kingdom there is transplanted a germ of civilization; that in the remotest villages there is a nucleus, round which the capabilities of the place may crystallise and brighten; a model sufficiently superior to excite, yet sufficiently near to encourage and facilitate, imitation; *this* unobtrusive, continuous agency of a Protestant Church Establishment, *this* it is, which the patriot, and the philanthropist, who would fain unite the love of peace with the faith in the progressive amelioration of mankind, cannot estimate at too high a price—"It cannot be valued with the gold of Ophir, with the precious onyx, or the sapphire. No mention shall be made of coral or of pearls: for the price of wisdom is above rubies."[4]—The clergyman is with his parishioners and among them; he is neither in the cloistered cell, nor in the wilderness, but a neighbour and family-man, whose education and rank admit him to the mansion of the rich landholder, while his duties make him

[1] The paragraphs that follow until the end of the chapter were taken (var) from *BL* ch 11 (1817) I 226–8. From the ms draft it is clear that they were intended to be printed as PARAGRAPH THE FIFTH in the 1st ed, but no new heading was supplied; see below, App C, p 222.

[2] "Among the numerous blessings of Christianity" in *BL* (1817) I 226.

[3] In *BL* (1817) C interposed lines 261–4 from *Paradise Regained* IV.

[4] Job 28.16, 18.

the frequent visitor of the farmhouse and the cottage. He is, or he may become, connected with the families of his parish or its vicinity by marriage. And among the instances of the blindness or at best of the short-sightedness, which it is the nature of cupidity to inflict, I know few more striking, than the clamours of the farmers against church property. Whatever was not paid to the clergymen would inevitably at the next lease be paid to the landholder, while, as the case at present stands, the revenues of the church are in some sort the reversionary property of every family that may have a member educated for the church, or a daughter that may marry a clergyman. Instead of being *fore closed* and immoveable, it is, in fact, the only species of landed property that is essentially moving and circulative. That there exist[a] no inconveniencies, who will pretend to assert? But I have yet to expect the proof, that the inconveniences are greater in this than in any other species; or that either the farmers or the clergy would be benefited by forcing the latter to become either *trullibers*[1] or salaried *placemen*. Nay, I do not hesitate to declare my firm persuasion that whatever *reason* of discontent the farmers may assign, the true *cause* is that they may cheat the *Parson* but cannot cheat the steward; and they are disappointed if they should have been able to withhold only two pounds less than the legal claim, having expected to withhold five.

[a] 1st ed: exists

1 Parson Trulliber, the boorish parson-farmer in Fielding's *Joseph Andrews*.

[a]CHAPTER IX

Practical Conclusion: What unfits; and what excludes from the National Church[b]

THE clerisy, or National Church, being an estate of the realm, the Church and State with the king as the sovereign head of both constituting the Body Politic, the State in the large sense of the word, or the NATION dynamically considered (ἐν δυνάμει κατὰ πνεῦμα,[1] *i.e.* as an *ideal*, but not the less *actual* and abiding, unity); and in like manner, the Nationalty being one of the two constitutional modes or species, of which the common wealth of the nation consists; it follows by the immediate consequence, that of the qualifications for the trusteeship, absolutely to be required of the order collectively, and of every individual person as the conditions of his admission into this order, and of his liability[c] to the usufruct or life-interest of any part or parcel of the Nationalty, the first and most indispensable qualification and pre-condition, that without which all others are null and void,—is that the National Clergy, and every member of the same from the highest to the lowest, shall be fully and exclusively citizens of the State, neither acknowledging the authority, nor within the influence of any other State in the world—full and undistracted subjects of this kingdom, and in no capacity, and under no pretences, owning any other earthly sovereign or visible head but the king, in whom alone the majesty of the nation is *apparent*, and by whom alone the unity of the nation in will and in deed is symbolically expressed and impersonated.

The full extent of this first and absolutely necessary qualification will be best seen in stating the contrary, that is, the absolute disqualifications, the existence of which in any individual, and in any class or order of men, constitutionally incapacitates such individual and class or order from being inducted into the National Trust: and this on a principle so vitally concerning the health and integrity of the body politic, as to render the voluntary transfer of the

[a–b] 1st ed: PRACTICAL CONCLUSION. [c] 1st ed: eligibility

[1] Rom 1.4: "with power, according to the spirit".

nationalty, whole or part, direct or indirect, to an order notoriously thus disqualified, a foul treason against the most fundamental rights and interests of the realm, and of all classes of its citizens and free subjects, the individuals of the very order itself, *as* citizens and subjects, not excepted. Now there are two things, and but two, which evidently and predeterminably disqualify for this great trust: the first absolutely, and the second, which in its collective operation, and as an attribute of the whole class, would, of itself, constitute the greatest possible unfitness for the proper ends and purposes of the National Church, as explained and specified in the preceding paragraphs, and the heaviest drawback from the civilizing influence of the National Clergy in their pastoral and parochial character—the second, I say, by implying the former, becomes likewise an *absolute* ground of disqualification. It is scarcely necessary to add, what the reader will have anticipated, that the first absolute disqualification is allegiance to a foreign power: the second, the abjuration—under the command and authority of this power, and as by the rule of their order its professed Lieges (Alligati)[1]—of that bond, which more than all other ties connects the citizen with his country; which beyond all other securities affords the surest pledge to the state for the fealty of its citizens, and that which (when the rule is applied to any body or class of men, under whatever name united, where the number is sufficiently great to neutralize the accidents of individual temperament and circumstances) enables the State to calculate on their constant adhesion to its interests, and to rely on their faith and singleness of heart in the due execution of whatever public or national trust might be assigned to them.

But we shall, perhaps, express the nature of this security more adequately by the negative. The Marriage Tie is a Bond, the preclusion of which by an antecedent obligation, that overrules the accidents of individual character and is common to the whole order, deprives the State of a security with which it cannot dispense. I will not [a]say, that it is a security which the State may rightfully demand of all its adult citizens, competently circumstanced, by positive enactment: though[b] I might shelter the position under the authority of the great Publicists and State-Lawyers of the Augustan Age, who, in the Lex Julia Papia, enforced anew a principle common to the old

[a–b] 1st ed: say, though

[1] "Bondsmen"; actually "liege" comes from an OHG word meaning free, unfettered, not from the Latin *ligatus*, "bound"; but the meaning of the word "allegiance" was affected by the false derivation.

Roman Constitution with that of Sparta.[a] [1] But without the least fear of confutation, though in the full foresight of vehement contradiction, I do assert, that the State may rightfully demand of any number of its subjects united in one body or order the *absence* of all customs, initiative vows, covenants and by-laws in that order, precluding the members of the said body collectively and individually from affording this security. In strictness of principle, I might here conclude the sentence—though as it now stands it would involve the assertion of a right in the state to suppress any order confederated under laws so anti-civic. But I am no friend to any rights that can be disjoined from the *duty* of enforcing them. I therefore at once confine and complete the sentence thus:—The State not only possesses the [b]right of demanding, but[c] is in duty bound to demand, the above as a *necessary condition* of its entrusting to any order of men, and to any individual as a member of a known order, the titles, functions, and investments of the *National* Church.

But if any doubt could attach to the proposition, whether thus stated or in the perfectly equivalent *Converse*, *i.e.* that the existence and known enforcement of the injunction or prohibitory by-law, before described, in any Order or Incorporation constitutes an *a priori* disqualification for the Trusteeship of the Nationalty, and an insuperable obstacle to the establishment of such an order, or of any members of the same as a National Clergy—such doubt would be removed, as soon as the fact of this injunction, or vow exacted and given, or whatever else it may be, by which the members of the Order, collectively and as such, incapacitate themselves from affording this security for their full, faithful, and unbiassed application of a *National* Trust to its proper and national purposes, is found[d] in conjunction with, and aggravated by, the three following circumstances. First, that this incapacitation originates in, and forms part of, the allegiance of the order to a foreign Sovereignty: Secondly, that it is notorious, that the Canon or Prescript, on which it is grounded, was first enforced on the secular clergy universally, after

[a] 1st ed: Sparta, that it is a security which the State may rightfully demand of all its adult citizens, competently circumstanced, by positive enactment.

[b–c] 1st ed: right, but [d] 1st ed: formed

[1] The *Lex Julia de maritandis ordinibus* of 18 B.C. and the *Lex Papia Poppaea* of A.D. 9 discouraged celibacy and childlessness, forbade misalliances, and regulated divorce. In early Rome marriage was a matter of fact and custom rather than a form amenable to legislation. In Sparta there were severe penalties for celibacy, as is pointed out by John Potter *Archaeologia Graeca* bk 4 ch 11 (2 vols 1697–9, frequently reprinted), which C claimed to have had at his fingers' ends at school (*CL* VI 843).

long and obstinate reluctation on their side, and on that of their natural sovereigns in[a] the several realms, to which as subjects they belonged; and that it is still retained in force, and its revocation inflexibly refused, as the direct and only adequate means of *supporting* that usurped and foreign Sovereignty, and of securing by virtue of the expatriating and insulating effect of its operation, the devotion, and allegiance of the order* to their visible Head, and Sovereign. And thirdly, that the operation of the interdict precludes one of the most constant and influencive ways and means of promoting

* For the fullest and ablest exposition of this point, I refer to the Reverend Blanco White's "Practical and Internal Evidence,"[1] and to that admirable work, "Reforma d'Italia,"written"[2] by a professed and apparently sincere

[a] 1st ed: on

[1] In acknowledging receipt of Joseph Blanco White's *Practical and Internal Evidence Against Catholicism, with Occasional Strictures on Mr. Butler's Book of the Roman Catholic Church* (1825) in July 1825, C noted a similarity between it and the latter part of a small work he was on the point of putting to the press. He wrote: "tho' I cannot ascribe to the perusal of your work what had been written before it's publication, I shall feel myself induced by prudence as well as constrained by Justice, to express my sense of it's worth & value, and the delight, I have received from the unexpected confirmation of my own Convictions, in fuller terms than I may address to yourself". *CL* v 485. The promise was fulfilled in 1830 in *C&S*. In Letter v White gives a graphic account of the evil effects of compulsory celibacy and describes the death of his sister in one of the gloomiest nunneries in Seville ("Bastilles of Superstition"): *Practical and Internal Evidence* pp 123–43. José María Blanco y Crespo, later known as Blanco White (1775–1841), of mixed Irish–Spanish parentage, lived his early life in Spain, was a Catholic priest, came to England in 1810 and joined the Anglican Church in 1814, contributed to the debate between RS and Charles Butler on the rival merits of the Anglican and Catholic Churches, and ended his life a Unitarian. C read his other works with interest and his own copies of *Practical and Internal Evidence*, *The Poor Man's Preservative Against Popery* (1825), *Letters from Spain* (2nd ed 1825) published under the pseudonym Don Leucadio Doblado, and *A Letter to Charles Butler, Esq.* (1826), now in the BM, contain marginal comments; those on *Letters* were printed in *NTP* 131–5. In N 41 ff 57–8ᵛ, C speaks of having seen White only twice, praises his *Poor Man's Preservative*, and regrets that he has not been suitably rewarded for his "service to Protestantism".

[2] The work referred to, *Di una Riforma d'Italia ossia Dei mezzi di riformare i più cattivi costumi e le più perniciose leggi d'Italia* (Venice 1767), was published anonymously; an expanded 3rd ed (3 vols) was published in London 1786. Its author was Carlo Antonio di Pilati di Tassulo (1733–1802), an Italian political and historical writer, a keen student of the works of Machiavelli and Sarpi. His works were imbued with the idea of spiritual freedom and the desire to subordinate the Church to the State, suppress the religious orders and their privileges, and educate the laity. See also below, p 122 and n 2.

the great paramount end of a National Church, the progressive civilization of the community. Emollit mores nec sinit esse feros.[1]

And now let me conclude these preparatory Notices by compressing the sum and substance of my argument into this one sentence. Though many things may detract from the comparative fitness of individuals, or of particular classes, for the Trust and Functions of the NATIONALTY, there are only two *absolute* Disqualifications: and these are, Allegiance to a Foreign Power, or the Acknowledgement of any other visible HEAD OF THE CHURCH, but our Sovereign Lord the King: and compulsory celibacy in connection with, and in dependence on, a foreign and extra-national head.[2]

Catholic, a work which well merits translation. I know no work so well fitted to soften the prejudices against the theoretical doctrines of the Latin Church, and to deepen our reprobation of what it actually and practically *is*, in all countries where the expediency of keeping up appearances, as in Protestant neighbourhoods, does not operate.

1 Ovid *Epistulae ex Ponto* 2.9.48. "[A faithful study of the liberal arts] humanizes character and permits it not to be cruel." Tr A. L. Wheeler (LCL 1924) 363. C quotes it again below, p 113.

2 On the celibacy of the clergy see also *TT* 18 Apr 1833.

CHAPTER X[a]

On the King and the Nation

A TREATISE? why, the subjects might, I own, excite some apprehension of the sort. But it will be found like sundry Greek Treatises among the tinder-rolls of Herculaneum,[1] with titles of as large promise, somewhat largely and irregularly abbreviated in the process of unrolling. In fact, neither my purpose nor my limits permit more than a few hints, that may prepare the reader for some of the positions assumed in the second part of this volume.

Of the King with the two Houses of Parliament, as constituting the STATE (in the special and antithetic sense of the word) we have already spoken: and it remains only to determine the proper and legitimate objects of its superintendence and control. On what is the power of the State rightfully exercised? Now, I am not arguing in a court of law; and my purpose would be grievously misunderstood if what I say should be taken as intended for an assertion of the *fact*. Neither of facts, nor of statutory and demandable rights do I speak; but exclusively of the STATE according to the *idea*. And, in accordance with the *idea* of the State, I do not hesitate to answer, that the legitimate objects of its power comprise all the interests and concerns of the PROPRIETAGE,[2] both landed and personal, and whether inheritably vested in the lineage or in the individual citizen; and these alone. Even in the lives and limbs of the lieges, the King, as the head and arm of the State, has an interest of property: and in any trespass against them the King appears as plaintiff.

The chief object, for which men who from the beginning existed as[b] a social bond, first formed themselves into a *State*, and on the social super-induced the political relation, was not the protection of their lives but of their property. The natural man is too proud

[a] Added in 2nd ed [b] 1st ed: under

[1] Excavations at Herculaneum, destroyed by an eruption of Mt Vesuvius in A.D. 79, revealed a library of valuable Greek papyri including works by Epicurus, Philodemus, and others. The main excavations continued from 1738 to 1780 and were briefly resumed in 1827. In Italy or Sicily C acquired a list of papyri found in Herculaneum: *CN* II App B p 410. See also *CN* III 4157 and n.

[2] See p 108 and n 2, below.

an animal to admit that he needs any other protection for his life than his own courage and that of his clan can bestow. Where the nature of the soil and climate has precluded all property but personal, and admitted that only in its simplest forms, as in Greenland for instance—there men remain in the domestic state and form neighbourhoods, not governments. And in North America, the chiefs appear to exercise government in those tribes only which possess individual landed property. Among the rest the chief is the general, a leader in war; not a magistrate. To property and to its necessary inequalities must be referred all human laws, that would not be laws without and independent of any conventional enactment: *i.e.* all State-legislation.—FRIEND, vol i. 351.[1]

Next comes the King, as the Head of the National Church, or Clerisy, and the Protector and Supreme Trustee of the NATIONALTY: the power of the same in relation to its proper objects being exercised by the King and the Houses of Convocation, of which, as before of the State, the King is the head and arm. And here if it had been my purpose to enter at once on the development of this position, together with the conclusions to be drawn from it, I should need with increased earnestness remind the reader, that I am neither describing what the National Church now is, nor determining what it ought to be. My statements respect the idea alone, as deduced from its original purpose and ultimate aim: and of the *idea* only must my assertions be understood. But the full exposition of this point is not necessary for the appreciation of the late Bill which is the subject of the following part of the volume. It belongs indeed to the chapter with which I had [a]intended to conclude this volume, and which, should my health permit, and the circumstances warrant it, it is still my intention to let follow the present work[b]—namely, my humble contribution towards an answer to the question, What is to be done now?[2] For the present, therefore, it will be sufficient, if I recal to the

[a–b] 1st ed: intended, and should my health permit it, still intend to conclude this volume

[1] Quoted (var and with an omission) from *Friend* (*CC*) I 199–200. C expanded the first sentence in *C&S* to make it clear that the social bond had existed from the beginning. In *The Friend* it ran: "The chief object for which men first formed themselves into a State was not the protection of their lives but of their property." He also added a new second sentence. See also C's footnote and Extract II on p 89, below.

[2] See C's letter of Sept 1829 to Thomas Hurst, the publisher of *C&S*: "I have before me & needing little more than transcription, a Chapter that would amount to half a sheet, or more—with the title—What is to be done now?—addressed principally to the Clergy of the Establishment—and which would prove an interesting addition to the Volume and give an air of completeness to it." *CL* VI 819. See also a letter to HNC 6 Jan 1830: *CL*

reader's recollection, that formerly the National Clerisy, in the two Houses of Convocation duly assembled and represented, taxed themselves.[1] But as to the proper objects, on which the authority of the convocation with the King as its head was to be exercised—these the reader will himself without difficulty decypher by referring to what has been already said respecting the proper and distinguishing ends and purposes of a National Church.

I pass, therefore, at once to the relations of the Nation, or the State in the larger sense of the word, to the State especially[a] so named, and to the Crown. And on this subject again I shall confine myself to a few important, yet, I trust, not common nor obvious, remarks respecting the conditions requisite or especially favorable to the health and vigor of the[b] realm. From these again I separate those, the nature and importance of which cannot be adequately exhibited but by adverting to the consequences which have followed their neglect or inobservance, reserving them for another place: while for the present occasion I select two only; but these, I dare believe, not unworthy the name of Political Principles, or *Maxims*, *i.e.* regulae quae inter *maximas* numerari merentur.[2] And both of them forcibly confirm and exemplify a remark, often and in various ways suggested to my mind, that with, perhaps, one* exception, it

* That namely of the WORD (*Gosp. of John*, I. 1.) for the Divine Alterity, the Deus Alter et idem of Philo; *Deitas Objectiva*.[3]

[a] 1st ed: specially [b] 1st ed: a

VI 826 and the Advertisement to *C&S* above, p 7; also Introduction, above, p lvii.

[1] C alludes to the situation that existed before 1664, when the clergy ceased to tax themselves. Convocations were called together by the Archbishops of Canterbury and York from the eighth century onwards and became fully established by the reign of Edward I. From early on they enjoyed the right to tax themselves. At first the bishops and lower clergy sat together, but from the fifteenth century they sat as two Houses, the "Upper" and the "Lower". In 1664 they surrendered the right to tax themselves; in 1717 Convocation was prorogued because of a lack of submission by the Lower House (see below, p 99 and n 3) and its powers remained in abeyance until 1852.

[2] "Rules that deserve to be numbered among the *most important*". In a ms he defined "maxim" as "Regula *Maxima* or Supreme Rule". BM MS Egerton 2801 f 217. Elsewhere, e.g. *Friend* (*CC*) I 122–4, C drew a sharp distinction between maxims and principles, maxims being products of the prudential understanding, principles of the higher power, the reason.

[3] "The God Other and the same... *Objective Deity*". Philo Judaeus (c 25 B.C.–c A.D. 50) interpreted the Old Testament along neoplatonic lines and had much influence on Christian theology. He described the Logos as "second God", frequently as "son of God" and "God's image", but never as "the same", as is implied in John

would be difficult in the whole compass of language, to find a metaphor so commensurate, so pregnant, or suggesting so many points of elucidation, as that of *Body Politic*, as the exponent of a State or Realm. I admire, as little as you do, the many-jointed similitudes of Flavel,[a][1] and other finders of moral and spiritual meanings in the works of Art and Nature, where the proportion of the likeness to the difference not seldom reminds us of the celebrated comparison of the Morning Twilight to a Boiled Lobster.[2] But the correspondence between the Body Politic to the Body Natural holds even in the detail of application. Let it not however be supposed, that I expect to derive any proof of my positions from this analogy. My object in thus prefacing them is answered, if I have shown cause for the use of the physiological terms by which I have sought to render my meaning intelligible.[3]

The first condition then required, in order to a sound constitution of the Body Politic, is a due proportion of the free and permeative life and energy of the Nation to the organized powers brought within containing channels.[4] What those vital forces that seem to bear an

[a] 1st ed: Fleming

1.1: "In the beginning was the Word, and the Word was with God, and the Word was God". Cf J. Robert Barth *Coleridge and Christian Doctrine* (Cambridge, Mass. 1969) 89–90, 93–4, esp the passage quoted from the *Opus Maximum*; cf also *SM* App D (*CC*) 95 and *TT* 6 Jan 1823. On *Deitas objectiva* cf C's "Formula Fidei: the Alterity" *LR* III 2.

[1] John Flavel (c 1630–91), a Presbyterian divine, wrote *England's Duty under the Present Gospel Liberty* (1689), which consists of discourses on the text "I stand at the door, and knock" (Rev 3.20). A characteristic feature is the expansion of the text by ill-assorted similes such as "the Iron Bar of Law, that thundering terrible Law, cannot force open the Heart of an Unbeliever; all the dreadful curses flying out of its fiery mouth, make no more impression than a tennis-ball against a wall of Marble". *England's Duty* (2nd ed 1701) 68. In 1824 C knew nothing of Flavel; see *CL* v 326. In *C&S* (1st ed) the name appeared as Fleming, presumably Robert Fleming the Younger (1660–1716), whose *Apocalyptical Key* (1701) was re-issued in 1793 with a brief postcript by the editor and an explanation on the title-page of the relevance to the French Revolution, and in 1809 with an Appendix introducing similitudes relating to the French Revolution.

[2] The Sun had long since, in the lap
Of Thetis, taken out his nap,
And like a lobster boiled, the morn,
From black to red began to turn...

Samuel Butler *Hudibras* pt 2 canto 2 lines 29–32. C quoted the lines as an example of the "excellence of men of discontinuous minds" in *CN* II 2112, and in *TT* 23 Jun 1834 as an example of fancy as distinct from imagination.

[3] A further indication of C's taste for organic and physiological or biological metaphors for social institutions.

[4] The implied distinction between free energy and organised powers is the second main element in C's view of the dynamic nature of the state. The first is his distinction between the forces of permanence and progression, for which see above, p 24.

analogy to the imponderable agents, magnetic, or galvanic, in bodies inorganic,[1] if indeed, they are not the same in a higher energy and under a different law of action—what these, I say, are in the living body in distinction from the fluids in the glands and vessels—the same, or at least a like relation, do the indeterminable, but yet actual influences of intellect, information, prevailing principles and tendencies, [a](to which we must add[b] the influence of property, or income, where it exists without right of suffrage attached thereto), hold to the regular, definite, and legally recognised Powers, in the Body Politic.[2] But as no simile runs on all four legs (*nihil simile est idem*),[3] so here the difference in respect of the Body Politic is, that in sundry instances the [c]former, *i.e.* the permeative, species[d] of force is capable of being converted into the latter, of being as it were organized and rendered a part of the vascular system, by attaching a measured and determinate political right, or privilege thereto.

What the exact proportion, however, of the two kinds of force should be, it is impossible to pre-determine. But the existence of a disproportion is sure to be detected, sooner or later, by the effects. Thus: the ancient Greek democracies, the *hot-beds* of Art, Science, Genius, and Civilization, fell into dissolution from the excess of the former, the permeative power deranging the functions, and by explosions shattering the organic structures, they should have enlivened. On the contrary, the Republic of Venice fell by the contrary extremes.[4] All political power was confined to the determinate vessels, and these becoming more and more rigid, even to an ossification of the arteries, the State, in which the people were nothing, lost all power of resistance ad extra.[5]

a–b 1st ed: with *c–d* 1st ed: former species

[1] For a suitable analogy C turns to the rapidly developing sciences of electricity and magnetism. The discovery of electrical energy—i.e. vital forces in inorganic matter—offered a new source of inspiration and speculation for philosophers like C, who interpreted nature along dynamic, vitalist lines. For some informal speculations on magnetic, galvanic, electrical forces, see *TT* 15 Jun 1827 and 8 Aug 1831.

[2] Cf other attempts to discover analogous laws in different orders of being: e.g. in the "Essays on Method", originally written for the *Encyclopaedia Metropolitana* but later expanded and incorporated in *Friend* (*CC*) I 448–524.

[3] "Nothing similar is the same". Proverbial since scholastic times. C used the expression in N Q in comparing Church doctrines to the Scriptures as banknotes to bullion, adding: "No simile goes on all *fours*. Every simile necessarily *limps* with this understanding. . .". N Q f 7ᵛ.

[4] In 1797, to Napoleon; cf Vittorio Barzoni *Rivoluzioni della repubblica Veneta* (Valletta 1804) ch 11. On Barzoni and C see *CN* II App D pp 416–17.

[5] "Externally".

Under this head, in short, there are three possible sorts of malformation to be noticed, namely,—The adjunction or concession of direct political power to *personal* force and influence, whether physical or intellectual, existing in classes or aggregates of individuals, without those fixed or tangible possessions, freehold, copyhold, or leasehold, in land, house, or stock.[1] The power resulting from the acquisition of knowledge or skill, and from the superior developement of the understanding is, doubtless, of a far nobler kind than mere physical strength and fierceness, the one being *peculiar* to the animal *Man*, the other common to him with the Bear, the Buffalo, and the Mastiff. And if superior Talents, and the mere possession of knowledges, such as can be learnt at Mechanics' Institutions,[2] were regularly accompanied with a Will in harmony with the Reason, and a consequent subordination of the appetites and passions to the ultimate ends of our Being: if intellectual gifts and attainments were infallible signs of wisdom and goodness in the same proportion, and the knowing, clever, and *talented* (a vile word!)[3] were always *rational;* if the mere facts of science conferred or superseded the soft'ning humanizing influences of the moral world, that habitual presence of the beautiful or the seemly, and that exemption from all familiarity with the gross, the mean, and the disorderly, whether in look or language, or in the surrounding objects, in which the main efficacy of a liberal education consists; and if, lastly, these acquirements and powers of the understanding could be shared equally by the whole class, and did not, as by a necessity of nature they ever must do, fall to the lot of two or three in each several group, club, or neighbourhood;—then, indeed, by an enlargement of the Chinese system, political power might not unwisely be conferred as the honorarium or privilege on having passed through all the forms in the National Schools, without the security of political ties, without those fastenings and radical fibres of a collective and registrable property, by which the Citizen inheres in and belongs to the Commonwealth, as a constituent part either of the Proprietage, or of the Nationalty; either of the State, or of the National Church.[4] But as the contrary of all these suppositions may be more safely assumed, the practical

1 Cf *TT* 20 Nov 1831.

2 Cf above, p 62 and nn 3, 5.

3 Cf the distinction between genius and talent in *BL* ch 11 (1907) I 153; see also above, p 67 and n 4. In *TT* 8 Jul 1832 C says that such "vile and barbarous" slang words as "talented" came from America.

4 Cf *M Post* 7 Dec 1799: *EOT* (*CC*) I 32; for a discussion of C's ideas on property see Colmer *Coleridge: Critic of Society* (Oxford 1959) 55–7, 103–5, and passim.

conclusion will be—not that the requisite means of intellectual developement and growth should be withheld from any native of the soil, which it was at all times wicked to wish, and which it would be now silly to attempt; but—that the gifts of the understanding, whether the boon of a genial nature, or the reward of more persistent application, should be allowed fair play in the acquiring of that proprietorship, to which a certain portion of political power belongs, as its proper function. For in this way there is at least a strong probability, that intellectual power will be armed with political power, only where it has previously been combined with and guarded by the moral qualities of prudence, industry, and self-control. And this is the first of the three kinds of mal-organization in a [a]state: viz. direct political power without cognizable possession.[b]

The second is: the exclusion of any class or numerous body of individuals, who have notoriously risen into possession, and the influence inevitably connected with known possession, under pretence of impediments that do not directly or essentially affect the character of the individuals as citizens, or absolutely disqualify them for the performance of civic duties. Imperfect, yet oppressive, and irritating ligatures that peril the trunk, whose circulating current they would withhold, even more than the limb which they would fain excommunicate![1]

The third and last is: a gross incorrespondency of the proportion of the antagonist interests of the Body Politic in the representative body—*i.e.* (in relation to our own country,) in the two Houses of Parliament—to the actual proportion of the same interests, and of the public influence exerted by the same in the Nation at large. Whether in consequence of the gradual revolution which has transferred to the Magnates of the Landed Interest so large a portion of that Borough Representation which was to have been its counterbalance; whether the same causes which have deranged the equilibrium of the Landed and the *Monied Interests in the Legislation, have not

* *Monied*, used arbitrarily, as in preceding pages the words, *Personal* and *Independent*, from my inability to find any one self-interpreting word, that would serve for the generic name of the four classes, on which I have stated the Interest of *Progression* more especially to depend, and with it the Freedom which is the indispensable *condition* and propelling force of all national progress: even as the Counter-pole, the other great Interest of the Body Politic, its *Permanency*, is more especially committed to the Landed Order, as its natural Guardian and

[a–b] 1st ed: State.

[1] The Test and Corporation Acts, which prevented Dissenters and Roman Catholics from taking an active part in national and municipal life, were repealed in Apr 1828. The above paragraph may have been drafted before the repeal.

likewise deranged the balance between the two unequal divisions of the Landed Interest itself, viz., the Major Barons, or great Land-

Depository. I have therefore had recourse to the convenient figure of speech, by which a conspicuous part or feature of a subject is used to express the whole; and the reader will be so good as to understand, that the Monied Order in this place comprehends and stands for, the Commercial, Manufacturing, Distributive, and Professional classes of the Community.

Only a few days ago, an accident placed in my hand a work of which, from my very limited opportunities of seeing new publications, I had never before heard. Mr. CRAWFURD's History of the Indian Archipelago—the work of a wise as well as of an able and well-informed man![1] Need I add, that it was no ordinary gratification to find, that in respect of certain prominent positions, maintained in this volume, I had unconsciously been fighting behind the shield of one whom I deem it an honour to follow. But the sheets containing the passages, having been printed off,[2] I avail myself of this note, to insert the sentences from Mr. Crawfurd's History, rather than lose the confirmation which a coincidence with so high an authority has produced on my own mind, and the additional weight which my sentiments, will receive in the judgment of others. The first of the two Extracts the reader will consider as annexed to pp. 25–26 of this volume; the second to the paragraph on the protection of property, as the end chiefly proposed in the formation of a fixed government, quoted from a work of my own, (viz. *The Friend*),[3] published ten or eleven years before the appearance of Mr. Crawfurd's History, which I notice in the work to give the principle in question that probability of its being grounded in fact, which is derived from the agreement of two independent minds. The first extract, Mr. Crawfurd introduces by the remark, that the possession of wealth, derived from a fertile soil, encouraged the progress of absolute power in Java. He then proceeds—

EXTRACT I

The devotion of a people to agricultural industry, by rendering themselves more tame, and their property more tangible, went still farther towards it: *for wherever Agriculture is the principal pursuit, there it may certainly be reckoned, that the People will be found living under an absolute government.*

HISTORY OF THE INDIAN ARCHIPELAGO: vol. iii. p. 24[4]

EXTRACT II

In cases of murder, no distinction is made (*i.e. in the Ancient Laws of the Indian Islanders*), between wilful murder and chance medley. *It is the Loss, which the family or tribe sustains, that is considered, and the pecuniary compensation was calculated to make up that loss.*

DITTO, DITTO, p. 123[5]

[1] John Crawfurd (1783–1868) obtained his information from first-hand experience and observation. After training as a doctor at Edinburgh, he first served in the North-West Province in India, then obtained extensive knowledge of the language and people in Penang and later Java, where he held most of the main civil and political posts. On his return to England in 1817 he wrote his *History of the Indian Archipelago* (3 vols Edinburgh 1820). As an advanced radical he unsuccessfully contested Glasgow, Paisley, Stirling, and Preston (1832–7).

[2] This long note was probably added at proof stage, one of the many indications that composition and printing proceeded erratically. Cf the long note on Edward Irving, below, pp 139–44.

[3] See above, p 83, in which C quotes from *Friend* (*CC*) I 199–200.

[4] Var, with omissions: C's italics.

[5] C's parenthesis and italics.

owners, with or without title, and the great body of the Agricultural Community, and thus giving to the real or imagined interests of the comparatively few, the imposing name of the Interest of the whole—the landed Interest!—these are questions, to which the obdurate adherence to the jail-crowding Game Laws, (which during the reading of our Church Litany, I have sometimes been tempted to include, by a sort of *subintellige*,[1] in the petitions—"from envy, hatred, and malice, and all uncharitableness; from battle, murder, and sudden death, Good Lord, deliver us!") to which the Corn Laws,[2] the exclusion of the produce of our own colonies from our distilleries, &c., during the war, against the earnest recommendation of the government,[3] the retention of the Statutes against Usury,[4] and

[1] "Understand" or "supply in thought"; cf *subintelligitur* in *OED*. For earlier reference to Game Laws, see above, p 18 and n 3.

[2] Cf *TT* 3 May and 20 Jun 1834, in which C supports retention of the Corn Laws on the grounds that agriculture is a positive good in the state and must therefore be protected. In 1828–9, he recognised that the laws that prohibited import of foreign corn until the home price reached a specific figure caused wide distress and favoured the "great Land-owners", but he nevertheless saw the need for some form of Corn Law. In a passage prophesying "the utter oblivion of the *State*", C wrote: "No Corn Laws—why should we maintain a set of Aristocrats?—instead of, what will the Nation become without an Aristocracy?—No tythes!—why should we maintain a set of lazy Parsons?—Instead of—Can a Nation subsist in health and dignity without a CHURCH, the representative of its *Personality*, as the State is the representative of its *Reality*—i.e. its *Things*? Remove the Corn-laws—& ⟨one of⟩ two things must follow. Either it will have no sensible effect on the price of provisions (nominally, I mean, for virtually, none *can* be produced, as wages will ever follow the price of subsistence) or G. Britain will be a lax confederacy of Tyres, and Sidons—Liverpool will become a Republic for itself, as much as Carthage." Written on p iv of a notebook used for copying out the *Courier* Judge Fletcher articles and now in the Berg Collection (NYPL). It is a comment on *Times* correspondent Joseph Durham on the Corn Laws 1832. See above, p 63 and n 2.

[3] An Act was passed 2 Jul 1808 to prohibit the distillation of spirits from corn and grain for a limited time. A committee had been appointed to examine the advantages of using sugar and molasses in addition to grain, and its chairman, Lord Binning, showed that in the light of Britain's dependence for a sufficient supply of corn on imports now cut off by war, and the reduction of the home supply of bad crops, it would be a sensible precautionary measure against famine to stop the distillation of corn. After a great struggle the Act was passed, the chief opposition coming from the landed interest.

[4] The laws against usury, which regulated conditions and maximum rates of interest for lending money, came under strenuous attack from the utilitarians, especially Bentham, who wrote: "...that no man of ripe years and of sound mind, acting freely and with eyes open, ought to be hindered with a view to his advantage, from making such a bargain, in the way of obtaining money, as he thinks fit: nor, (what is a necessary consequence) anybody hindered from supplying him

other points, of minor importance or of less safe handling, may seem at a first view to suggest an answer in the affirmative; but which, for reasons before assigned, I shall leave unresolved, content if only I have made the Principle itself intelligible.

The following anecdote, for I have no means of ascertaining its truth, and no warrant to offer for its accuracy, I give not as a fact in proof of an overbalance of the Landed Interest, but as an indistinctly remembered hearsay, in elucidation of what is meant by the words. Some eighteen or twenty years ago—for so long I think it must have been, since the circumstance was first related to me—my illustrious (alas! I must add, I fear, my *late*) friend, Sir Humphrey Davy,[1] at Sir Joseph Banks's request,[2] analysed a portion of an East Indian import, known by the names of cutch, and Terra Japonica;[3] but which he ascertained to be a vegetable extract, consisting almost wholly of pure *tannin:* and further trials, with less pure specimens, still led to the conclusion, that the average product would be seven parts in ten of the tanning principle. This discovery

---

upon any terms he thinks proper to accede to". Jeremy Bentham *Defence of Usury* Letter I: *Works* ed John Bowring (11 vols 1838–43) III 3. C would have had little sympathy with Bentham's grounding his case for repeal on the "infallible" principle of utility, but he seems to agree with Bentham that the laws against usury had become only a legal fiction and were being continuously circumvented. They were not finally repealed until 1854.

[1] Sir Humphry Davy (1778–1829) first met C at Dr Beddoes's Pneumatic Institute in Bristol and did much to stimulate the poet's interest in science. Soon after his arrival as chemist at the Royal Institution, he was requested to give his attention to tanning. The results of his researches were communicated to the Royal Society in 1803 and published in *Philosophical Transactions* with the title "An Account of Some Experiments and Observations on the Constituent Parts of Certain Astringent Vegetables". As Davy died on 29 May 1829, this part of the work must have been written after that date.

[2] Sir Joseph Banks (1743–1820), naturalist and explorer, President of the Royal Society. C thought highly of his library (now in the BM), and a note (in *Poole* I 95n) records that Purkis's article on the art of tanning in the *Encyclopaedia Britannica* was written after obtaining somewhat reluctant permission to use Banks's books. Purkis acted as an intermediary between C and Banks to obtain a small quantity of bhang; Banks had supplies, and Tom Wedgwood and C both experimented with this narcotic drug. *CL* II 919, 933.

[3] Catechu or Terra Japonica, astringent substances, containing 40 to 55 per cent of tannin, which are obtained from *Acacia Catechu* and other Eastern trees and shrubs. According to Davy's paper read to the Royal Society, "about half a pound of catechu would answer the same purpose" in the tanning process as four to five pounds of common oak bark, and a footnote in the *Transactions* (1803) 273 states that this estimate agrees well with that made by Purkis, that "one pound of catechu was equivalent to seven or eight of oak bark".

was *communicated to the trade; and on inquiry made at the India House it was found that this cutch could be prepared in large

* And, (if I recollect right, though it was not from him, that I received the anecdote) by a friend of Sir Humphrey's,[1] whom I am proud to think *my* friend likewise, and by an elder claim.—A man whom I have seen now in his harvest field, or the market, now in a committee-room, with the Rickmans[2] and Ricardos[3] of the age; at another time with Davy, Woolaston,[4] and the Wedgewoods;[5] now with Wordsworth, Southey, and other friends not unheard of in the republic of letters; now in the drawing-rooms of the rich and the noble, and now presiding at the annual dinner of a Village Benefit Society; and in each seeming to be in the very place he was intended for, and taking the part to which his tastes, talents, and attainments, gave him an admitted right. And yet this is not the most remarkable, not the individualising trait of our friend's character. It is almost overlooked in the originality and raciness of his intellect; in the life, freshness and practical value of his remarks and notices, truths plucked as they are growing, and delivered to you with the dew on them, the fair earnings of an observing eye, armed[6] and kept on the watch by thought and meditation; and above all, in the integrity, *i.e. entireness* of his being, (*integrum et sine cerâ vas*),[7] the steadiness

[1] Thomas Poole (1765–1837), a lifelong friend of C, was a tanner and therefore directly interested. In July 1830 the author sent Poole a copy of the 2nd ed of *C&S*, directed his attention to later pages, but made no specific reference to this passage. *CL* VI 842, *Poole* II 320–1. Davy dedicated his *Consolations in Travel* to Poole "in remembrance of thirty years of continual and faithful friendship".

[2] In 1803 John Rickman (1771–1840), who conducted the first census in Great Britain, invited Poole to supervise the analysis of the Poor Law returns and thus initiated him into the world of public administration.

[3] David Ricardo (1772–1823), economist. He is mentioned to complete the alliterative phrase; there is no evidence to suggest that Poole met Ricardo, though he may have done so on Poor Law and currency committees. For a detailed comparison of C's economic thought with that of Malthus and Ricardo, see W. F. Kennedy *Humanist Versus Economist* (1958) 22–9.

[4] William Hyde Wollaston (1766–1828), natural philosopher and chemist. Again choice of name was probably determined by alliteration, and by association (with Davy, also a chemist). The text reproduces C's spelling Woolaston; in a note on the flysheet of Eichhorn *Commentarius in Apocalypsin Joannis* (1791) I, the name is similarly spelt and listed with that of Davy as the "Chemical Magnates of this All-chemical Generation"; cf also the reference to "Woolaston" in a letter to Allsop [early Feb 1825]: *CL* V 410. C links Davy and Wollaston also in *Friend* (*CC*) I 471.

[5] Poole probably first met the Wedgwoods, Thomas (1771–1805) and Josiah (1769–1843), through Dr Beddoes. He introduced C to them in 1797; their annuity of £150 was offered to C before the year was out. In offering the annuity Tom Wedwood wrote: "...we have been accustomed, for some time, to regard ourselves rather as Trustees than Proprietors" of our wealth (*CL* I 373n), an interesting parallel with C's ideas on wealth as a trust.

[6] Cf *SM* (*CC*) 24 and n 3 and *LS* (*CC*) 136.

[7] Untraced. Tr: "a flawless vessel without wax". An allusion to the old (and unsound) etymology of *sincerus*, "clean", "pure", "whole", "genuine", etc and to the frequent symbolical use of "vessel" in the Bible and elsewhere. The implication is probably that the vessel in this case needs no lining or repairing of cracks with wax to make it usable or that being free from wax it will not spoil the taste of its contents.

quantities, and imported at a price which, after an ample profit to the importers, it would very well answer the purposes of the tanners to give. The trade itself, too, was likely to be greatly benefitted and enlarged by being rendered less dependent on [a]particular situations; while[b] the reduction of the price at which it could be offered to the foreign consumer, acting[c] in conjunction with the universally admitted superiority of the English leather, might be reasonably calculated on as enabling us to undersell our foreign rivals in their own markets. Accordingly, an offer was made, on the part of the principal persons interested in the leather trade, to purchase, at any price below the sum that had been stated to them as the highest, or extreme price, as large a quantity as it was probable that the Company would find it feasible or convenient to import in the first instance. Well! the ships went out, and the ships returned, again and again: and no increase in the amount of the said desideratum appearing among the imports, enough only being imported to meet the former demand of the druggists, and (it is whispered) of certain transmuters of Bohea into Hyson[1]—my memory does not enable me to determine whether the inquiry into the occasion of this disappointment was *made*, or whether it was anticipated, by a discovery that it would be useless. But it *was generally understood*, that the Tanners had not been the only persons, whose attention had been drawn to the qualities of the article, and the consequences of its importation; and that a very intelligible hint had been given to persons of known influence in Leadenhall-street, that in case of any such importation being allowed, the East-India Company must not expect any support from the *Landed Interest* in parliament, at the next renewal, or motion for the renewal of their Charter. The East

---

of his attachments, and the activity and persistency of a benevolence, which so graciously presses a warm temper into the service of a yet warmer heart, and so lights up the little flaws and imperfections, incident to humanity in its choicest specimens, that were their removal at the option of his friends, (and few have, or deserve to have so many!) not a man among them but would vote for leaving him as he is.

This is a note *digressive;* but, as the height of the offence is, that the Garnish is too good for the Dish, I shall confine my apology to a confession of the fault.

S. T. C.

[a–b] 1st ed: a particular situation, and by [c] 1st ed: which,

[1] C suggests that cutch was used to transform black tea into more expensive green tea.

India Company might reduce the price of Bark, one half, or more: and the British Navy, and the grandsons of our present Senators, might thank them for thousands and myriads of noble oaks, left unstript in consequence—this may be true; but no less true is it, that the Free Merchants would soon reduce the price of good Tea, in the same proportion, and monopolists ought to have a feeling for each other.

[a]CHAPTER XI

The relations of the potential to the actual. The omnipotence of Parliament: of what kind[b]

So much, in explanation of the first of the two *Conditions* of the health and vigour of a Body Politic: and far more, I must confess, than I had myself reckoned on. I will endeavour to indemnify the reader, by despatching the second in a few sentences, which could not so easily have been accomplished, but for the explanations given in the preceding paragraphs. For as we have found the first condition in[c] the due proportion of the free and permeative Life of the State to the Powers organized, and severally determined by their appropriate and containing, or conducting nerves, or vessels; the Second Condition is—

A due proportion of the *potential* (latent, dormant) to the *actual* Power.[1] In the [d]first Condition,[e] both Powers alike are awake and in act. The Balance is produced by the *polarization*[2] of the Actual Power, *i.e.* the opposition of the Actual Power organized, to the Actual Power free and permeating the organs. In the Second, the Actual Power, *in toto*, is opposed to the Potential. It has been frequently and truly observed, that in England, where the ground plan, the skeleton, as it were, of the government is a monarchy, at once buttressed and limited by the Aristocracy, (the assertions of its popular character finding a better support in the harangues and theories of popular men, than in state-documents and the records of clear History), a far greater degree of liberty is, and long has been enjoyed, than ever existed in the ostensibly freest, that is, most

[a–b] Added in 2nd ed   [c] 1st ed: on   [d–e] 1st ed: former

[1] This distinction was influential and formed an important contribution to nineteenth-century political thought.

[2] The principle of polarity became C's key to explain the operation of different forces. He found the idea in Greek thought (Heraclitus), in Giordano Bruno (1548–1600), and in contemporary German philosophy. His clearest definition of the principle is: "EVERY POWER IN NATURE AND IN SPIRIT *must evolve an opposite, as the sole means and condition of its manifestation:* AND ALL OPPOSITION IS A TENDENCY TO RE-UNION." *Friend* (*CC*) I 94 and n. Cf *TL* (1848) 50–9. See above, pp 24, 35.

democratic, Commonwealths of ancient or of modern times—greater, indeed, and with a more decisive predominance of the Spirit of Freedom, than the wisest and most philanthropic statesmen of antiquity, or than the great Commonwealth's-men (the stars of that narrow interspace of blue sky between the black clouds of the first and second Charles's reigns) believed compatible, the one with the safety of the State, the other with the interests of Morality.

Yes! for little less than a century and a half Englishmen have collectively, and individually, lived and acted with fewer restraints on their free-agency, than the citizens of any known *Republic, past or present. The fact is certain. It has been often boasted of, but never, I think, clearly explained. The solution of the phenomenon must, it is obvious, be sought for in the combination of circumstances, to which we owe the insular privilege of a self-evolving Constitution: and the following will, I think, be found the main cause of the fact in question. Extremes meet—an adage of inexhaustible exemplification.[1] A democratic Republic and an Absolute Monarchy agree in this; that in both alike, the Nation, or People, delegates its whole power. Nothing is left obscure,[2] nothing suffered to remain in the Idea, unevolved and only acknowledged as an existing, yet indeterminable[c] Right. A Constitution such states can scarcely be said to possess. The whole Will of the Body Politic is in act at every moment. But in the Constitution of England according to the Idea, (which in this instance has demonstrated its actuality by its practical influence, and this too though counter-worked by fashionable errors and maxims, that left their validity behind in the Law-Courts, from which they were borrowed)

* It will be thought, perhaps, that the United States of North America should have been excepted. But the identity of Stock, Language, Customs, Manners and Laws scarcely allows us to consider this an exception: even tho' it were quite certain both that it is and that it will continue such. It was, at all events, a remark worth remembering, which I once heard from a Traveller (a prejudiced one I must admit) that where every man may take liberties, there is little Liberty for any [a]man—or, that where every man takes liberties, no man can enjoy any.[b]

a–b 1st ed: man.
c 1st ed: indeterminable
2nd ed: interminable

1 Cf *Friend* (*CC*) I 110, *CN* I 1725 and II 2066; one of C's favourite adages.

2 In his attitude to language, in his literary criticism, and in his observations on nature and psychological phenomena, as well as in his thoughts on the constitution, C recognises that there are shadowy areas that defy exact analysis. In such cases to offer exact analysis is to falsify experience. Unfortunately, C's critics have sometimes mistaken respect for obscurity for love of obscurity.

the Nation has delegated its power, not without measure and circumscription, whether in respect of the duration of the Trust, or of the particular interests entrusted.

The Omnipotence of Parliament, in the mouth of a lawyer, and understood exclusively of the restraints and remedies within the competence of our Law-courts, is objectionable only as bombast. It is but a puffing pompous way of stating a plain matter of fact. Yet in the times preceding the Restoration, even this was not universally admitted. And it is not without a fair show of reason, that the shrewd and learned author of "THE ROYALIST'S DEFENCE;" printed in the year 1648, (a tract of 172 pages, small quarto, from which I now transcribe) thus sums up his argument and evidences:[1]

"Upon the whole matter clear it is, the Parliament itself (that is, the King, the Lords, and Commons) although unanimously consenting, are *not boundless:* the Judges of the Realm by the *fundamental* Law of *England* have power to determine which Acts of Parliament are binding and which void." p. 48.—That a unanimous declaration of the Judges of the realm, that any given Act of Parliament was against right reason and the fundamental law of the land (*i.e.* the Constitution of the realm), render such Act null and void, was a principle that did not want defenders among the lawyers of elder times. And in a state of society in which the competently informed and influencive members of the community, (the National Clerisy not included), scarcely perhaps trebled the number of the members of the two Houses, and Parliaments were so often tumultuary congresses of a victorious party rather than representatives of the State, the right and Power here asserted might have been wisely vested in the Judges of the realm: and with at least equal wisdom, under change of circumstances, has the right been suffered to fall into abeyance. Therefore let the potency of Parliament be that highest and uttermost, beyond which a court of Law looketh not: and within the sphere of the Courts quicquid Rex cum Parliamento voluit, *Fatum* sit![2]

[1] The author was Charles Dallison, Recorder of Lincoln; the tract has 142, not 172 pages. In *Friend* (*CC*) I 410, C regretted that greater use had not been made of "books, pamphlets, and flying sheets of that momentous period, during which all the possible forms of truth and error... bubbled up on the surface of the public mind, as in a ferment of a chaos". For marginalia in this and other political tracts, see *NTP* 169–223, esp 205, 206.

[2] Source untraced. A deliberate alteration of *factum sit*, "let it be done"? In N F° f 41ᵛ C writes: "...the Decree hath been pronounced —FATUM *est*—it is *Fate*...". Tr: "Whatever the King with Parliament has decided, let it be *pronounced* [or let it be *Fate*]!"

But if the strutting phrase be taken, as from sundry recent speeches respecting the fundamental institutions of the realm it may be reasonably inferred, that it has been taken, *i.e.* absolutely, and in [a]reference, not to our Courts of Law exclusively, but to[b] the Nation, to England with all her venerable heir-looms, and with all her germs of reversionary wealth—thus used and understood, the Omnipotence of Parliament is an hyperbole, that would contain mischief in it, were it only that it tends to provoke a detailed analysis of the materials of the joint-stock company,[1] to which so terrific an attribute belongs, and the competence of the shareholders in this earthly omnipotence to exercise the same. And on this head the observations and descriptive statements given in Chap. v. of the old tract, just cited, retain all their force;[2] or if any have fallen off, their place has been abundantly filled up by new growths. The degree and sort of knowledge, talent, probity, and prescience, which[c] it would be only too easy, were it not too invidious, to prove from acts and measures presented by the history of the last half century, are but *scant* [d]*measure* even when exerted within the sphere and circumscription of the constitution, and on the matters properly and peculiarly appertaining to the State according to the idea—this portion of moral and mental endowment placed[e] by the side of the plusquam-gigantic height and amplitude of power, implied in the unqualified use of the phrase, Omnipotence of Parliament, and with its dwarfdom exaggerated by the contrast, would threaten to distort the countenance of truth itself with the sardonic laugh of irony.*

* I have not in my possession the morning paper in which I read it, or I should with great pleasure transcribe an admirable passage from the present King of Sweden's Address to the STORTHING, *i.e.* Parliament of Norway, on the necessary

[a–b] 1st ed: reference to

[c] 1st ed: which even when exerted within the sphere and circumscription of the constitution, and on the matters properly and peculiarly appertaining to the State according to the idea (*i.e.*, the interests of the proprietage of the realm, and (though not directly or formally, yet actually), the interests of the realm in its foreign relations, as affecting the weal, and requiring the aid of the proprietors),

[d–e] 1st ed: *measure*—placed

[1] C here uses Burke's metaphor in *Reflections* (Everyman 1950) 84 and 93, but the phrase became very much his own; cf "a joint-stock Company Pope", an annotation on the Rev Samuel Johnson *Works* (1710) 155 (C's copy in the BM).

[2] The heading of ch 5 states the argument that C is here endorsing: "That the Judges of the Kings Bench, of the Common Pleas, and the Barons of the Exchequer, are the Judges of the Realme, unto whom the people are bound lastly and finally". *The Royalist's Defence* p 49. Dallison argues that since few members of either House possess legal knowledge it is presumptuous for Parliament to claim to be omnipotent judge of the legality of its laws. But C's reference to "Chap. v" may be an error for "iv", which he has just cited.

The non-resistance of successive generations has ever been, and with evident reason, deemed equivalent to a tacit consent, on the part of the[a] nation, and as finally legitimating the act thus acquiesced in, however great the dereliction of principle, and breach of trust, the original enactment may have been. I hope, therefore, that without offence I may venture to designate the Septennial Act, as an act of usurpation, tenfold more dangerous to the true Liberty of the Nation, than the pretext for the measure, viz. the apprehended Jacobite[b] leaven from a new election, was at all likely to have proved:[2] and I repeat the conviction, I have expressed in reference to the practical suppression of the CONVOCATION,[2] that no great prin-

limits of Parliamentary Power, consistently with the existence of a CONSTITUTION.[1] But I can with confidence refer the reader to the speech, as worthy of an Alfred. Every thing indeed, that I have heard or read of this sovereign, has contributed to the impression on my mind, that he is a good and a wise man, and worthy to be the king of a virtuous people, the purest specimen of the Gothic race.

[a] 1st ed: a [b] 1st ed: Jacobitual

[1] Speech made at the opening of the extraordinary Storthing on 29 Apr 1828. After stating that "the existence of every constitutional state is founded upon the due balance of its constituent powers" the Swedish King, Charles XIV, who reigned 1818–44, went on to say: "My duty as a king does not allow me to assume that each successive Storthing shall be permitted to apply or interpret the fundamental law as they shall please." C copied this statement, from a report in *The Times*, in N F° f 74^{v}, prefacing the quotation: "Admirable throughout! History cannot boast of another such King since the Days of Alfred—and yet we scarcely hear his name mentioned by our H. of Commons, or Crown and Anchor Patriots or the Newspapers—." Cf C's praise of the King of Sweden in *TT* 15 Aug 1831. Charles XIV John was formerly Count Bernadotte, one of Napoleon's marshals, who had been accepted as crown prince years before he became king.

[2] In 1716 the Septennial Act enacted that Parliament should continue for seven years, thus repealing the Triennial Act, which had been in force since the reign of Charles I. C objected to the Act on the grounds that it was unconstitutional for Members elected for three years to prolong their power for another four—they could have continued to sit indefinitely, if they so decided, the Whigs then having a safe majority.

[3] In 1717 Convocation was prorogued and, except on important occasions, its powers remained in abeyance until 1852. The suppression was "one of the causes of lethargy and want of spirituality not unjustly imputed to the English church of the eighteenth century", according to Basil Williams *The Whig Supremacy 1714–1760* (Oxford 1939) 79–80. In an annotation on Baxter's *Reliquiae*, C called the suppression "a bitter disgrace & wrong": *C 17th C* 356. In 1819–20 he wrote: "I am inclined likewise to hold that in good policy not to say common Justice, the Clergy, as a Property *sui generis*, ought either to have their Convocation restored or to elect a ⟨Parliamentary⟩ Representative in each diocese or one from two or three Dioceses according to number &c...". N 28 f 51. In N 30 f 53^{v} he wrote (c 1824): "O! if even now, at the eleventh Hour, the Crown would permit and instruct the Convocation to sit."

ciple was ever invaded or trampled on, that did not sooner or later avenge itself on the country, and even on the governing classes themselves, by the consequences of the precedent. The statesman who has not learnt this from history, has missed its most valuable result, and might in my opinion as profitably, and far more delightfully have devoted his hours of study to Sir Walter Scott's Novels.*

But I must draw in my reins. Neither my limits permit, nor does my present purpose require that I should do more than exemplify the limitation resulting from that latent or *potential* Power, a due proportion of which to the actual powers I have stated as the second condition of the health and vigor of a body politic, by an instance bearing directly on the measure, which in the following section I am to aid in appreciating, and which was the occasion of the whole work. The principle itself, which, as not contained within the rule and compass of law, its practical manifestations being indeterminable and inappreciable *a priori*, and then only to be recorded as having manifested itself, when the predisposing causes and the enduring effects prove the unific mind and energy of the nation to have been in travail; when they have made audible to the historian that Voice of the People which is the Voice of God—[2] this Principle, I say, (or the Power, that is the subject of it) which by its very essence existing and working as an *Idea* only, except in the rare and predestined epochs of Growth and Reparation, might seem to many fitter

* This would not be the first time, that these fascinating volumes had been recommended as a substitute for History—a ground of recommendation, to which I could not conscientiously accede, though some half dozen of these Novels with a perfect recollection of the contents of every page, I read over more often in the course of a year, than I can honestly put down to my own credit.[1]

[1] C may have had in mind Hazlitt's essay on Scott in *The Spirit of the Age* (1825), in which Scott is called "the amanuensis of truth and history". *H Works* IX 63. According to the editor of *CM*, C annotated fifteen of the novels, which he read in three different sets, *Novels and Tales of the Author of Waverley* (12 vols Edinburgh 1823), *Historical Romances of the Author of Waverley* (6 vols Edinburgh 1824), and *Novels and Romances of the Author of Waverley* (7 vols Edinburgh 1825). In a letter to William Blackwood of 20 Oct 1829 C wrote that "Sir Walter's novels have been my comforters in many a sleepless night when I should but for them have been comfortless". *CL* VI 821. (In this same letter he offered an article for *Blackwood's* entitled "A Sequel to the Catholic Bill and the Free Trade measure, or What is to be done now?")

[2] Cf p 40 and n 2, above. John James Park referred in his *The Dogmas of the Constitution* (1832) 130 to "what Mr Coleridge obscurely intimates on this point" and suggested that C "means that it is what I should call a principle of extreme *application* in politics, i.e., a principle acting at extreme points, like the safety valve, for example". For details of Park, see Introduction, above, p lxi, and below, p 105 and n 1.

matter for verse than for sober argument, I will, by way of compromise, and for the amusement of the reader, sum up in the rhyming prose of an old Puritan Poet, consigned to contempt by Mr. Pope,[1] but whose writings, with all their barren flats and dribbling commonplace, contain nobler principles, profounder truths, and more that is properly and peculiarly *poetic* than are to be found in his *own works. The passage in question, however, I found occupying the last page on a flying-sheet of four leaves, entitled *England's Misery and Remedy, in a judicious Letter from an Utter-Barrister to his Special Friend, concerning Lieut.-Col. Lilburne's Imprisonment in Newgate, Sept.* 1745;[2] and I beg leave to borrow the introduction, together with the extract, or that part at least, which suited my purpose.

"Christian Reader, having a vacant place for some few Lines, I have made bold to use some of Major GEORGE WITHERS, his verses out of VOX PACIFICA, *page* 199.

> Let not your King and Parliament in *One*,
> Much less apart, mistake themselves for that
> Which is most worthy to be thought upon:
> Nor think they are, essentially, the STATE.
> Let them not fancy, that th' Authority
> And Priviledges upon them bestown,
> Conferr'd are to set up a MAJESTY,
> A POWER, or a GLORY of their own!
> But let them know, 'twas for a deeper life,
> Which they but *represent*—
> That there's on earth a yet auguster Thing,
> Veil'd tho' it be, than Parliament and King."[3]

* If it were asked whether the Author then considers the works of the one of equal value with those of the other, or that he holds George Withers as great a writer as Alexander Pope? his answer would be, that he is as little likely to do so, as the Querist would be to put no greater value on a highly wrought vase of pure silver from the hand of a master, than on an equal weight of Copper Ore that contained a small per centage of separable Gold scattered through it. The Reader will be pleased to observe, that in the stanza here cited, the "STATE" is used in the largest sense, and as synonimous with the Realm, or entire Body Politic, including Church and *State*, in the narrower and special sense of the latter term.
S. T. C.

1 George Wither (1588–1667), bracketed with Quarles by Pope as a type of feeble writer and called "wretched Wither": *Dunciad* Bk I line 126 (Twickenham ed) v 78–9.

2 *England's Miserie and Remedie... Sept: 1645.*

3 Ibid p 8. C quotes (var) the lines of Wither *Vox Pacifica* (published 1645; canto 4) as given in the pamphlet; in line 9 he substitutes "a deeper life" for "another thing", deletes the remainder of line 10, omits lines 11–26, and alters the last two lines:

> And, know, there is, on earth, a
> *greater-thing*,
> Then, an unrighteous *Parliament*,
> or *King*.

[a]CHAPTER XII

The preceding position exemplified. The origin and rationale of the Coronation Oath, in respect of the National Church. In what its moral obligation consists. Recapitulation[b]

AND here again the "Royalist's Defence" furnishes me with the introductory paragraph: and I am always glad to find in the words of an elder writer, what I must otherwise have said in my own person—*otium simul et autoritatem.*[1]

"All Englishmen grant, that Arbitrary power is destructive of the best purposes for which power is conferred: and in the preceding chapter it has been shown, that to give an unlimited authority over the fundamental Laws and Rights of the nation, even to the King and two Houses of Parliament jointly, though nothing so bad as to have this boundless power in the King alone, or in the Parliament alone, were nevertheless to deprive Englishmen of the Security from Arbitrary Power, which is their birth right.

"Upon perusal of former statutes it appears, that the Members of both Houses have been *frequently* drawn to consent, not only to things *prejudicial* to the Commonwealth, but, (even in matters of greatest weight) to alter and contradict what formerly themselves had agreed to, and that, as it happened to please the fancy of the present Prince, or to suit the passions and interests of a prevailing Faction. Witness the statute by which it was enacted that the Proclamation of King Henry VIII. should be equivalent to an Act of Parliament; another declaring both Mary and Elizabeth bastards; and a third statute empowering the King to dispose of the Crown of England by Will and Testament. Add to these the several statutes in the times of King Henry VIII. Edward VI. Queen Mary, and Queen Elizabeth, setting up and pulling down each other's religion, every one of them condemning even to death the profession of the one before established."—*Royalist's Defence*, p. 41.[2]

[a–b] 1st ed: *The preceding position exemplified.*

[1] "[It gives me] at the same time leisure and authority".

[2] *The Royalist's Defence* (see above, p 97 and n 1) 40–1 (var); the first paragraph is largely C's paraphrase, and in the second paragraph C supplies "or to suit...Faction".

So far my anonymous author, evidently an old Tory Lawyer of the genuine breed, too enlightened to obfuscate and incense-blacken the shrine, through which the kingly Idea should be translucent, into an Idol to be worshipped in its own right; but who, considering both the reigning Sovereign and the Houses, as limited and representative functionaries, thought they saw reason, in some few cases, to place more confidence in the former than in the latter: while there were points, which they wished as little as possible to trust to either. With this experience, however, as above stated, (and it would not be difficult to increase the catalogue,) can we wonder that the nation grew sick of parliamentary *Religions?* or that the Idea should at last awake and become operative, that what virtually concerned their humanity, and involved yet higher relations, than those of the citizen to the state, duties more awful, and more precious privileges, while yet it stood in closest connection with all their *civil* duties and rights, as their indispensable condition and only secure ground—that this was not a matter to be voted up or down, off or on, by fluctuating majorities! that it was too precious an inheritance to be left at the discretion of an Omnipotency, that had so little claim to Omniscience? No interest of a single generation, but an entailed Boon too sacred, too momentous, to be shaped and twisted, pared down or plumped up, by any assemblage of Lords, Knights, and Burgesses for the time being? Men perfectly competent, it may be, to the protection and management of those interests, in which, as having so large a stake they may be reasonably presumed to feel a sincere and lively concern, but who, the experience of ages might teach us, are not the class of persons most likely to study, or feel a deep concern in, the interests here spoken of, in either sense of the term CHURCH; *i.e.* whether the interests be of a kingdom "not of the World,"[1] or those of an Estate of the Realm, and a constituent part, therefore, of the same System with the State, though as the opposite Pole. The results at all events have been such, whenever the Representatives of the One Interest have assumed the direct control of the other, as gave occasion long ago to the rhyming couplet, quoted as proverbial by Luther:

Cum Mare siccatur, cum Daemon ad astra levatur,
Tunc Clero Laicus fidus Amicus erit.[2]

[1] John 18.36 (var), Rev 11.15 (var); see above, pp 51, 55, and below, 114.

[2] Luther *Colloquia Mensalia* ch 22 (1652) 288. Tr:

When the Sea dries up, when the
Devil is raised to the stars,
Then the Laity will be a
true friend to the Clergy.

Cf above, p 56, and below, p 112.

But if the nation willed to withdraw the religion of the realm from the changes and revolutions incident to whatever is subjected to the suffrages of the representative assemblies, whether of the state or of the church, the trustees of the proprietage or those of the nationalty, the first question is, how this reservation is to be declared, and by what means to be effected. These means, the security for the permanence of the established religion, must, it may be foreseen, be imperfect; for what can be otherwise, that depends on human will? but yet it may be abundantly sufficient to declare the aim and intention of the provision. Our ancestors did the best it was in their power to do. Knowing by recent experience that multitudes never blush, that numerous assemblies, however respectably composed, are not exempt from temporary hallucinations, and the influences of party passion; that there are things, for the conservation of which—

> Men safelier trust to heaven, than to themselves,
> When least themselves, in storms of loud debate
> Where folly is contagious, and too oft
> Even wise men leave their better sense at home
> To chide and wonder at them, when returned.
>
> ZAPOLYA[1]

Knowing this, our ancestors chose to place their reliance on the honour and conscience of an individual, whose comparative height, it was believed, would exempt him from the gusts and shifting currents, that agitate the lower region of the political atmosphere. Accordingly, on a change of dynasty they bound the person, who had accepted the crown in trust—bound him for himself and his successors by an oath, to refuse his consent (without which no change in the existing law can be effected), to any measure subverting or tending to subvert the safety and independence of the National Church, or which exposed the realm to the danger of a return of that foreign usurper, misnamed spiritual, from which it had with so many sacrifices emancipated itself. However unconstitutional therefore the royal veto on a Bill presented by the Lords and Commons may be deemed in all ordinary cases, this is clearly an exception. For it is no additional power conferred on the king; but a limit imposed on him by the constitution itself for its own safety. Previously to the ceremonial act, which announces him the only lawful and sovereign head of both the church and the state, the oath is

[1] Prelude Sc i lines 368–72 (var): *PW* (EHC) II 895. In the original the second line of the quotation reads:

> When least themselves in the mad whirl of crowds.

administered to him *religiously* as the representative person and crowned majesty of the nation. *Religiously*, I say, for the mind of the nation, existing only as an *Idea*, can act *distinguishably* on the ideal powers alone—that is, on the reason and conscience.

It only remains then to determine, what it is to which the Coronation Oath obliges the conscience of the king.[1] And this may be best determined by considering what in reason and in conscience the Nation had a right to impose. Now that the Nation had a right to decide for the King's conscience and reason, and for the reason and conscience of all his successors, and of his and their counsellors and ministers, laic and ecclesiastic, on questions of theology, and controversies of faith—*ex. gr.* that it is not allowable in directing our thoughts to a departed Saint, the Virgin Mary for instance, to say Or*a* pro nobis, Beata Virgo, though there would be no harm in saying, Or*et* pro nobis, precor, beata Virgo;[2] whether certain books are to be held canonical; whether the text, "They shall be saved as through fire," refers to a purgatorial process in the body, or during

[1] For the crucial clause in the Coronation Oath see Introduction, above, p xxxvi and n 1. The King and the Protestant High Tories believed that the Oath ensured the survival of the Protestant Reformed religion, that it offered a check to Parliament's sovereignty, and that it constituted an absolute barrier to Catholic Emancipation. C does not go so far as Dr Phillpotts, Bp of Exeter, who said that the King was not "a *branch* of the legislature, but rather is the legislator". G. F. A. Best remarks that the Protestant Tories "were in some danger of making him in effect a separate branch of the legislature". *Transactions of the Royal Historical Society* 5th ser VIII (1958) 116. An annotation on Johnson *Works* (1710) 309–10 makes C's objection clearer: he wrote that he detested "Lord Grey & his Gang" for nullifying the kingly office, by reducing the Coronation Oaths to Highgate Oaths [jesting oaths made by innkeepers, involving the forfeit of bottles of wine]. For a genuine English King is the greatest possible Security for Freedom...the King is bound by the most solemn Oaths before God & to the Nation, to make abortive every projected Law, destructive of Freedom". In an annotation on John James Park *The Dogmas of the Constitution* (1832) 11, C stated that the royal veto "is and remains an essential part of the constitution" but "that, in the spirit of compromise, characteristic of England, it acts virtually and by prevention, does not evacuate the power itself". *NTP* 228. Cf *TT* 12 Mar 1833.

[2] C suggests that it is not permissible to say "Pray for us, blessed Virgin", but that there is no harm in saying "Let the blessed Virgin pray for us, I beseech thee" (that is, direct address to God, not to the B.V.M.). The first phrase is from the Litany of the Saints (also the Litanies for Holy Saturday) in the Roman Missal. Cf an annotation on Johnson *Works* 157: "Oh! if at the Union we had had a Statesman of the Old English Breed/ a John of Gaunt, who would have nothing to do for or against Transsubst[ant]iation, or the Dispute between Or*a* pro nobis, Sanctissima Maria! and Or*et* pro nobis Maria, but waged war, body and soul, against the *Pope* & that diluted Pope, an anti-national Clergy!"

the interval between its dissolution and the day of judgment;[1] whether the words, "this is my body,"[2] are to be understood literally, and if so, whether it is by consubstantiation with, or transubstantiation of, bread and wine;[3] and that the members of both Houses of Parliament, together with the Privy Counsellors and all the Clergy shall abjure and denounce the theory last mentioned—this I utterly deny. And if this were the whole and sole object and intention of the Oath, however large the number might be of the persons who imposed or were notoriously favorable to the imposition, so far from recognising the Nation in their collective number, I should regard them as no other than an aggregate of intolerant mortals, from bigotry and presumption forgetful of their fallibility, and no less ignorant of their own rights, than callous to those of succeeding generations. If the articles of faith therein disclaimed and denounced were the substance and proper intention of the Oath, and not to be understood, as in all common sense they ought to be, as temporary marks because the known accompaniments of other and legitimate grounds of disqualification; and which only in reference to *these*, and only as long as they implied their existence, were fit objects of political interference; it would be as impossible for me, as for the late Mr. Canning,[4] to attach any such sanctity to the Coronation Oath, as should prevent it from being superannuated in times of clearer light and less heat. But that these theological articles, and the [a]open profession of the same by a portion of the king's subjects[b] as parts of their creed, are not the evils which it is the true and legitimate purpose of the oath to preclude, and which constitute and define its obligation on the royal conscience; and what the real evils are, that

[a–b] 1st ed: exclusion of all, who professed to receive them

[1] A reference to 1 Cor 3.15, still considered by Roman Catholics to mean purgatory.

[2] Matt 26.26.

[3] C himself did not take the sacrament after Cambridge until 1827, but gave much thought to theological problems relating to the Eucharist.

[4] On 26 May 1825 and 6 Mar 1827 Canning, who had consistently supported Catholic Emancipation, referred approvingly to Lord Liverpool's view of the Coronation Oath (Hansard NS XIII 893, XVI 1003). On 17 May 1825 Liverpool, the Prime Minister, had said: "He could not consider the coronation oath as an obstacle to the removal of the civil and political disabilities of the Catholics. The oath was an oath to protect the established church and clergy of the realm. The removal of the disabilities might possibly affect the church, but it could only do so consequentially. Many wise and good men were of opinion that it would strengthen the church; and if parliament presented a bill to the King for his acceptance grounded on this assumption, he did not see how the King could be advised to consider it at variance with the obligations of the oath that he had taken". Hansard NS XIII 750. See above, p 105 n 1.

do indeed disqualify for offices of national trust, and give the permanent obligatory character to the engagement—this, in which I include the exposition of the essential characters of the Christian or Catholic Church; and of a very different church, which assumes the name; and the application of the premises to an appreciation on principle of the late bill, and now the law of the land;[1] will occupy the remaining portion of the volume.

And now I may be permitted to look back on the road, we have past: in the course of which, I have placed before you, patient fellow-traveller! a small part indeed of what might, on a suitable occasion, be profitably said; but it is all, that for my present purpose, I deem it necessary to say respecting three out of the five themes that were to form the subjects of the first part of this—small volume, shall I call it? or large and dilated epistle? [a]But let me avail myself of the pause, to repeat my apology[b] to the reader for any *extra* trouble I may have imposed on him, by employing the same term (the State, namely) in two senses; though I flatter myself, I have in each instance so guarded it as to leave scarcely the possibility, that a moderately attentive reader should understand the word in one sense, when I had meant it in the other, or confound the STATE as a *whole*, and comprehending the Church, with the State as one of the two constituent parts, and in contra-distinction from the [c]Church.

BRIEF RECAPITULATION

First then,[d] I have given briefly but, I trust, with sufficient clearness the right idea of a STATE, or Body Politic; "State" being here synonimous with a *constituted* Realm, Kingdom, Commonwealth, or Nation, *i.e.* where the integral parts, classes, or orders are so balanced, or interdependent, as to constitute, more or less, a moral unit, an organic whole; and as arising out of the Idea of a State I have added the Idea of a Constitution, as the informing principle of its coherence and unity. But in applying the above to our own kingdom (and with this qualification the reader is requested to understand me as speaking in all the following remarks), it was necessary to observe, and I willingly avail myself of this opportunity to repeat the observation—that the Constitution, in its widest sense as the Constitution of the Realm, arose out of, and in fact consisted in, the co-existence of the Constitutional STATE (in the second

[a–b] 1st ed: —First, but here let me apologize [c–d] 1st ed: church—first,

[1] The royal signature was given 13 Apr 1829. See Introduction, above, p li. The Act is reproduced in full in App B, below, pp 203–9.

acceptation of the term) with the King as its head, and of the CHURCH (*i.e.* the *National* Church), likewise the King as its head; and lastly of the King, as the Head and Majesty of the whole Nation. The reader was cautioned therefore not to confound it with either of its constituent parts; that he must first master the true idea of each of these severally; and that in the synopsis or conjunction of the three, the Idea of the English Constitution, the Constitution of the Realm, will rise of itself before him. And in aid of this purpose and following this order, I have given according to my best judgment, first, the Idea of the State, [a](in the second or *special* sense of the term;) of[b] the State-legislature; and of the two constituent orders, the landed, with its two classes, the Major Barons, and the Franklins; and the Personal, consisting of the mercantile, or commercial, the manufacturing, the distributive and the professional; these two orders corresponding to the two great all-including INTERESTS of the State,—the landed, namely, to the PERMANENCE,—the Personal to the PROGRESSION. The Possessions of both orders, taken collectively, form the *PROPRIETAGE of the Realm. In contradistinction from this and as my second theme, I have explained (and as being the principal object of this work, more diffusely) the NATIONALTY, its nature and purposes, and the duties and qualifications of its Trustees and Functionaries. In the same sense as I at once oppose and conjoin the NATIONALTY to the PROPRIETAGE;[2] in the same antithesis and conjunction I use and understand the phrase, CHURCH and STATE. Lastly, I have essayed to determine the Constitutional Idea of the CROWN, and its relations to the Nation,

* To convey his meaning precisely is a *debt*, which an Author owes to his readers.[1] He therefore who to escape the charge of pedantry, will rather be misunderstood than startle a fastidious critic with an unusual term, may be compared to the man who should pay his creditor, in base or counterfeit coin, when he had gold or silver ingots in his possession, to the precise amount of the debt; and this under the pretence of their unshapeliness and want of the mint impression.

[a–b] 1st ed: and

[1] C did not always discharge this debt and confessed to Poole (9 Oct 1809; *CL* III 234) that there was "an *entortillage* in the sentences" in *The Friend*. But coinages, desynonymising, and accurate definition reflect his continuous search for greater clarity. For other discussions of the problems of communication, see *Lects 1795* (*CC*) 51–2; essays in the *M Post: EOT* (*CC*) I 114–17; *SM* (*CC*) 43, 46, and *LS* (*CC*) 152–5; *BL* (1817) I 157–61; *TL* (1848) 42; *CN* II 2629. See C's defence, in a note on Copy G, of "new words", below, p 118 n 2.

[2] *OED* notes that "proprietage", meaning the property of individuals collectively, the whole body of personal property, is a C coinage and cites this passage in *C&S*.

to which I have added a few sentences on the relations of the Nation to the State.

To the completion of this first part of my undertaking, two subjects still remain to be treated of—and to each of these I shall devote a small section, the title of the first being "On the Idea of the Christian Church;" that of the other, "On a third Church:" the name of which I withhold for the present, in the expectation of deducing it by contrast from the contra-distinguishing characters of the former.

IDEA OF THE
CHRISTIAN CHURCH

"WE, (said Luther), tell our Lord God plainly: If he will have his Church, then He must look how to maintain and defend it; for we can neither uphold nor protect it. And well for us, that it is so! For in case we could, or were able to defend it, we should become the proudest Asses under heaven. Who is the Church's Protector, that hath promised to be with her to the end, and the gates of Hell shall not prevail against her? Kings, Diets, Parliaments, Lawyers? Marry, no such cattle."—*Colloquia Mensalia*.[1]

[1] Luther *Colloquia Mensalia* ch 20 (1652) 265. "Who is...such cattle" is not in the original and contains allusions to Matt 28.20, 16.18. See above, p 56 n 1, p 103 and n 2, and below, p 177 and n 3.

IDEA OF THE CHRISTIAN CHURCH

THE practical conclusion from our enquiries respecting the origin[a] and Idea of the National Church, the paramount end and purpose of which is the continued and progressive civilization of the community (*emollit mores nec sinit esse feros*),[1] was this: that though many things may be conceived of a tendency to diminish the *fitness* of particular men, or of a particular class, to be chosen as trustees and functionaries of the same; though there may be many points more or less adverse to the perfection of the establishment; there are yet but two absolute disqualifications: namely, allegiance to a foreign power, or an acknowledgment of any other visible head of the Church, but our sovereign lord the king; and compulsory celibacy in connection with, and dependence on, a foreign and extra-national head.[2] We are now called to a different contemplation, to the Idea of the Christian Church.

Of the Christian *Church*, I say, not of Christianity. To the ascertainment and enucleation of the latter, of the great redemptive process which began in the separation of light from Chaos (*Hades, or the Indistinction*),[3] and has its end in the union of life with God, the whole summer and autumn, and now commenced winter of my life have been dedicated. HIC labor, HOC opus est,[4] on which alone the author rests his hope, that he shall be found not to have lived altogether in vain.[5] Of the Christian *Church* only, and of this no

[a] 1st ed: organ

[1] See above, p 81 and n 1, where C first quotes this passage from Ovid.

[2] See above, p 53 and n 2, pp 77–81.

[3] Gen 1 and John 1.1–9, which is the connexion in C's mind between the "redemptive process" and the separation of light from chaos; cf "...if Christ be that Logos or Word that was in the beginning, by whom all things *became*; if it was the same Christ who said, Let there be *Light*: who in and by the Creation commenced that great redemptive Process, the history of *Life* which begins in its detachment from Nature and is to end in its union with God...". Annotation on Henry More *Theological Works* (1708): *C 17th C* 317. C perhaps also alludes to Milton *Paradise Lost* VII 243–51. Chaos and Hades, though not originally the same, do coincide in meaning *Indistinction*. Chaos was the gaping void, the abyss beneath the world, or the confusion of unformed matter; Hades, the invisible, the god, or the place of the dead. Cf also *CN* III 4418 and n.

[4] Virgil *Aeneid* 6.129 (var). "This is the toil, this the task!" Tr H. R. Fairclough (LCL 1940) I 515.

[5] Years earlier, C had rested his faith that he had not lived in vain on

further than is necessary for the distinct understanding of the National Church, it is my purpose now to speak: and for this purpose it will be sufficient to enumerate the essential characters by which the Christian church is distinguished.

FIRST CHARACTER.—The Christian Church is not a KINGDOM, REALM, (*royaume*), or STATE, (*sensu latiori*)[1] of the WORLD, that is, of the aggregate, or total number of the kingdoms, states, realms,[a] or bodies politic, (these words being as far as our present argument is concerned, perfectly synonimous), into which civilized man is distributed; and which, collectively taken, constitute the civilized WORLD. The Christian Church, I say, is no state, kingdom, or realm of this world;[2] nor is it an Estate of any such realm, kingdom or state; but it is the appointed Opposite to them all *collectively*—the *sustaining*, *correcting*, *befriending* Opposite of the world! the compensating counterforce to the inherent* and inevitable

* It is not without pain that I have advanced this position, without the accompanying proofs and documents which it may be thought to require, and without the elucidations which I am sure it deserves; but which are precluded alike by the purpose and the limits of the present tract. I will, however, take this opportunity of earnestly recommending to such of my readers as understand German, Lessing's ERNST und FALK: Gespräche für Freymäurer. They will find it in Vol. vii. of the Leipsic edition of Lessing's Works. I am not aware of a translation.[3] Mr. Blackwood, or I should say Christopher North,[4] would add

[a] 1st ed: realms
2nd ed: realm

his political journalism, esp for *M Post: BL* ch 10 (1817) I 211–17. But in later life, when his studies turned more and more to religion, it was natural for him to see things differently.

[1] "In a wider sense".

[2] John 18.36, Rev 11.15; cf similar allusions above at pp 51, 55, and 103, and below, pp 174–5.

[3] In C's edition of Lessing's *Sämmtliche Schriften* (30 pts in 15 vols) pt VII has Berlin 1792 as the imprint on the title-page but Leipzig 1792 on the half-title, *Vermischte Schriften. Ernst und Falk* appears in vol IV pt VII 222–322, and C has made five marginal notes on it, one of which is given above, p 65 n 5. A translation was published by the Rev A. Cohen in 1927 (see below). What attracted C in Lessing's dialogues on freemasonry was the limitations seen in even the ideal state. Falk, one of the speakers, says in the second dialogue: "Assume the best political constitution that can possibly be conceived already devised; assume that all peoples throughout the whole world have adopted this ideal constitution; are you not of the opinion that even then out of this very ideal constitution, things must arise which are most injurious to human happiness, and of which man in his natural state knew absolutely nothing." Tr Cohen *Lessing's Masonic Dialogues* (1927) 44. C refers to "Lessing's exquisite Dialogues" in a note in "To Mr Justice Fletcher" II (29 Sept 1814): *EOT (CC)* II 382. See Introduction, above, p xlvi.

[4] Christopher North, pseudonym of John Wilson (1785–1854), a regular contributor to *Blackwood's Magazine*. A neighbour of C and WW in the Lake District, he wrote an essay with Alexander Blair for *The Friend* No 17

evils and defects of the STATE, *as* a State, and without reference to its better or worse construction as a particular state; while whatever is beneficent and humanizing in the aims, tendencies, and proper objects of the state, [a]the Christian Church[b] collects in itself as in a focus, to radiate them back in a higher quality: or to change the metaphor, it completes and strengthens the edifice of the state, without interference or commixture, in the mere act of laying and securing its own foundations. And for these services the Church of Christ asks of the state neither wages nor dignities. She asks only protection, and *to be let alone*. These indeed she demands; but

one to the very many obligations he has already conferred on his readers, (among whom he has few more constant or more thankful than myself) by suggesting the task to some of his contributors. For there are more than one, I doubt not, who possess taste to feel, and power to transfer the point, elegance, and exquisite, yet effortless precision and conciseness of Lessing's philosophic and controversial writings. I know nothing that is at once like them, and equal to them, but the Provincial Letters of Pascal.[1] The four Dialogues,[2] to which I have referred, would not occupy much more than a quarter of a sheet each, in his magazine, which, in a deliberate and conscientious adoption of a very common-place compliment, I profess to think, as a magazine, and considering the number of years it has *kept on the wing—incomparable*—but at the same time I crave the venerable Christopher's permission to avow myself a sturdy dissentient as on some other points, so especially from the *Anti-Huskissonian*[3] part of his Toryism.
S. T. C.

[a–b] 1st ed: it

(14 Dec 1809): *Friend* (*CC*) II 222–9, and later called C's tr of *Wallenstein* "the best translation of a foreign drama which our English literature possesses". C now repaid the compliment.

[1] C recorded his discovery of the *Provincial Letters* in a letter to Sir George Beaumont 22 Sept 1803: *CL* II 994; he praised the combination of "Wit, Irony, Humour, Sarcasm, Scholastic Subtilty, & profound Metaphysics". For C's use of a tetraglot ed of *Les Provinciales* (Cologne 1684) see *CN* II 2133–6 and nn. See below, p 134 n 2.

[2] There are five, not four dialogues.

[3] William Huskisson (1770–1830) provided the dominant influence on government economic policy. In his various government positions he reduced duties on goods and was for free trade. He represented the mercantile interests of the big commercial cities and was viewed with suspicion and hostility by the landed interest and by Wellington, from whose ministry he resigned on a minor issue of parliamentary reform in 1828. He was killed by a train at the opening of the Manchester and Liverpool Railway on 15 Sept 1830. An example of Wilson's anti-Huskissonianism is: "Has not Huskisson, the Complete Letter Writer, been ejected in the manner so graphically depicted in the print-shops, by the vigorous application of the toe of the Duke's [Wellington's] jackboot to his *os coccygis*? Does not Free Trade stink in the nostrils of the people?" *Noctes Ambrosianae* No 37, in *Blackwood's* Oct 1828. Wilson was also hostile to Huskisson's pro-Catholic views.

even these only on the ground, that there is nothing in her constitution, nor in her discipline, inconsistent with the interests of the state, nothing resistant or impedimental to the state in the exercise of its rightful powers, in the fulfilment of its appropriate duties, or in the effectuation of its legitimate objects. It is a fundamental principle of all legislation, that the state shall leave the largest portion of personal free agency to each of its citizens, that is compatible with the free agency of all, and not subversive of the ends of its own existence as a state.[1] And though a negative, it is a most important distinctive character of the Church of Christ, that she asks nothing for her members as Christians, which they are not already entitled to demand as citizens and subjects.

SECOND CHARACTER.—The Christian Church is not a secret community. In the once current (and well worthy to be re-issued) terminology of our elder divines, it is objective in its nature and purpose, not mystic or subjective,[2] *i.e.* not like reason or the court of conscience, existing only in and for the individual. Consequently the church here spoken of is not "the kingdom of God which is *within*, and which cometh not with observation (*Luke* xvii. 20, 21),[3] but most observable (*Luke* xxi. 28–31)."[4]—A city built on a hill, and not to be hid[5]—an institution consisting of visible and public communities. In one sentence, it is the Church visible and militant under Christ. And this visibility, this *publicity*, is its second distinctive character. The

THIRD CHARACTER—reconciles the two preceding, and gives the condition, under which[a] their co-existence in the same subject

[a] Copy G: which, and under which alone,

[1] Cf a long note written at the end of Aug 1823: "To secure to each the greatest sphere of freedom compatible with the safety, the security, & the unity of the whole, this (it has been often asserted) is the proper aim, & true object of a state, & therefore contains the definition of the word.—This is very plausible, it says much and there was a time, and that of many years continuance in which I thought that it means all; but of late years I have begun to fear that it means little. At all events more is conveyed to my mind & far more definitely in the affirmation that the true aim & object of a state & its implied definition is—by the restraint of all—to enlarge the outward spheres of the inly free, so as at the same time to increase the inward freedom of those, whose outward spheres it had contracted." N 20 ff 42–2[v].

[2] C had a special reason for wishing to see these terms revived, because they played a dominant part in his own and Schelling's philosophy (cf *BL* ch 12) and because they illustrated its deep roots in the seventeenth century. In an annotation on the front flyleaf of More *Theological Works* (1708), he complained of "a perpetual confusion of the Subjective with the objective, in the arguments of our [elder] Divines". *C 17th C* 317.

[3] Luke 17.20, 21, 20 (var).

[4] Luke 21.29–31, the parable of the fig-tree.

[5] Matt 5.14 (var).

My dear James! you cannot too often think of the great scheme or formula of all Logical Distribution of our Conceptions, which I have entitled the

150

that they are opposites. Inter res heterogeneas non datur oppositio, *i. e.* contraries cannot be opposites. Alike in the primary and the metaphorical use of the word, Rivals (Rivales) are those only who inhabit the opposite banks of *the same stream.*

Now, in conformity to character the first, the Christian Church dare not be considered as a counter-pole to any particular STATE, the word, State, here taken in the largest sense. Still less can it, like the national clerisy, be opposed to the STATE in the narrower sense. The *Christian* Church, as such, has no *nationalty* entrusted to its charge. It forms no counter-balance to the collective *heritage* of the realm. The phrase, Church and State, has a sense and a propriety in reference to the *National* Church alone. The Church of Christ cannot be placed in this conjunction and antithesis without forfeiting the very name of Christian. The true and only contra-position of the Christian Church is to the world. Her paramount aim and object, indeed, is *another* world, not a world *to come* exclusively, but likewise *another world that now is* (*See* APPENDIX, A), and to the concerns of which alone the epithet spiritual, can without a mischievous abuse of the word, be applied.

Nation.

Logical Pentad: viz. Prothesis, Thesis, Meso-thesis, Antithesis, and Synthesis: or Identity, (or super-relative Position, i.e. Preposition); relative Position; relative Counter-position; Mid-position, or the Indifference of the two; and Composition.– Having mastered this, or

3. A corrected page of *Church and State* containing the beginning of a letter to the Rev James Gillman. See p 117.

becomes possible. Antagonist forces are necessarily of the same kind. It is an old rule of logic, that only concerning two subjects of the same kind can it be properly said that they are opposites.[1] Inter res heterogeneas non datur oppositio,[2] *i.e.* contraries cannot be opposites. Alike in the primary and the metaphorical use of the word, Rivals (Rivales) are those only who inhabit the opposite banks of *the same stream.*[3]

Now, in conformity to character the first, the Christian Church dare not be considered as a counter-pole to any particular STATE, the word, State, here taken in the largest sense.[a] Still less can it, like the national clerisy, be opposed to the STATE in the narrower sense. The *Christian* Church, as such, has no *nationalty* entrusted to its charge.[4] It forms no counter-balance to the collective *heritage* of the realm. The phrase, Church and State, has a sense and a propriety in reference to the *National* Church alone. The Church of Christ cannot be placed in this conjunction and antithesis without forfeiting the very name of Christian. The true and only contra-position of the Christian Church is to the world. Her paramount aim and object, indeed, is *another* world, not a world *to come* exclusively, but likewise *another world that now is* (*See* APPENDIX, A),[5] and to the concerns of which alone the epithet spiritual, can without a mischievous abuse of the word, be applied. But as the necessary consequence and accompaniments of the means by which she seeks to attain this especial end; and as a collateral object, it is her office to counteract the evils that result by a common necessity from all Bodies Politic, the system or aggregate of which is the WORLD. And observe that

[a] Copy G: sense = NATION.

[1] In Copy G, C has written a long letter to James Gillman expounding the "logical Distribution of our Conceptions" in terms of "the logical Pentad: viz. Prothesis, Thesis, Mesothesis, Antithesis and Synthesis: or Identity". It begins at the top of p 150 and ends at 161. For the complete text of the letter, see App E, below, pp 233–4.

[2] "Between things that differ in kind there is no opposition".

[3] According to the *Digest* 43.20.1 § 26 etc, *rivales* means people sharing the water from the same stream running through their properties and therefore likely to quarrel about it. Cf also Robert Ainsworth *Latin Dictionary* (numerous editions) under *rivales:* "They are called *rivales* whose land boundaries are determined by some river, which by the uncertainty and constant changing of its course cause frequent disputes between them."

[4] In contradistinction to the National Church, to which is granted nationalty, that is, a portion of the nation's wealth in order to fulfil its religious, educational, and cultural ends.

[5] The Appendix (not lettered "A"), below, pp 165–85, is in the form of a letter, originally sent to the Rev Edward Coleridge, 21 Jul 1826: *CL* VI 593–601; see Introduction, above, pp lv–lvi.

the nisus, or counter-agency, of the Christian Church is against the evil *results* only, and not (directly, at least, or by primary intention) against the defective institutions that may have caused or aggravated them.

But on the other hand, by virtue of the second character, the Christian Church is to exist in every kingdom and state of the world, in the form of public communities, is to exist as a real and ostensible power. The consistency of the first and second depends on, and is fully effected by, the

THIRD CHARACTER

of the Church of Christ: namely, the absence of any visible head or sovereign—by the non-existence, nay the utter preclusion, of any local or personal centre of unity, of any single source of universal power. This fact may be thus illustrated. Kepler and Newton,[1] substituting the idea of the infinite for the[a] conception of a finite and determined world,[b] assumed in the Ptolemaic Astronomy,[c] superseded and drove out the notion of a one central point or body of the [d]Universe. Finding[e] a centre in every point of matter and an absolute[f] circumference no where, they[g] explained at once the unity and the distinction[h][2] that co-exist throughout the creation by focal

[a] Copy G: that [b] Copy G: world (which had been [c] Copy G: Astronomy),
[d–e] 1st ed: Universe: and finding [f] Copy G: actual
[g] Added in 2nd ed [h] Copy G: distinctity

[1] Cf C's use of Newton *Principia* bk I Definition 5 to satirise the Church of England in *Watchman* No 2 (*CC*) 67–8, "A Defence of the Church Establishment from its similitude to the grand and simple Laws of the Planetary System". An interesting linking of Kepler and Newton occurs in an annotation on Manuel Lacunza's *The Coming of Messiah in Glory and Majesty* (2 vols 1827): "...all Science is necessarily prophetic, so truly so, that the power of prophecy is the test, the infallible criterion, by which any presumed Science, is ascertained to be actually & verily science. The Ptolemaic Astronomy was barely able to prognosticate a lunar eclipse; with Kepler and Newton came Science and Prophecy." Note on I lxxxii (Edward Irving's preliminary discourse). See below, p 132 n 2. For further discussion of Johann Kepler (1571–1630), see *Friend* (*CC*) I 485–7; *P Lects* Lects XI, XII (1949) 331, 361, and *TT* 8 Oct 1830.

[2] C defends "distinctity" in a note written on a blank sheet at the end of Copy G of *C&S*: "Where the Thought requires a fixed, and appropriated Term; and the popular Language does not supply one, it is the worst of cowardly pedantries to eschew a new word, however pedantic it may sound to an unaccustomed & uninterested Ear. This privilege is cheerfully conceded, to the Anatomist, the Mineralogist, nay, even the licentious exercise of the privilege, to the Botanist &c. Why then is it to be denied to the Prima Scientia, the Scientia Scientiarum [the First Science, the Science of Sciences]. Hence, I have not hesitated to mint the term Distinc[t]ity—ex. gr. REASON is the Identity, or Co-inherence, of Unity and Distinctity. Unity without Distinctity is = SPACE:

instead of central bodies: the attractive and restraining power of the sun or focal orb, in each particular system, supposing and resulting from an actual power, present in all and over all, throughout an indeterminable multitude of systems. And this, demonstrated as it has been by science, and verified by observation, we rightly name the true system of the heavens. And even such is the scheme and true idea of the Christian Church. In the primitive times, and as long as the churches retained the form given them by the Apostles and Apostolic men, every community, or in the words of a father of the second century,[1] (for the pernicious fashion of assimilating the Christian to the Jewish, as afterwards to the Pagan, Ritual, by false analogies, was almost coeval with the church itself,) every altar had its own bishop, every flock its own pastor, who derived his authority immediately from Christ, the universal Shepherd, and acknowledged no other superior than the same Christ, speaking by his spirit in the unanimous decision of any number of bishops or elders, according to his promise, "*Where two or three are gathered together in my name, there am I in the midst of them.*"[2]*

Hence the unitive relation of the churches to each other, and of each

* Questions of dogmatic divinity do not enter into the purpose of this enquiry. I am even anxious not to give the work a theological character. It is, however, within the scope of my argument to observe, that, as may be incontrovertibly proved by other equivalent declarations of our Lord, this promise is not confined to houses of worship and prayer-meetings exclusively. And though I cannot offer the same justification for what follows, yet the interest and importance of the subject will, I trust, excuse me if I remark, that even in reference to meetings for divine worship, the true import of these gracious, soul-awing words, is too generally overlooked. It is not the comments or harangues of unlearned and fanatical preachers that I have in my mind, but sermons of great and deserved celebrity, and divines whose learning, well-regulated zeal, and sound scriptural views are as honourable to the established church, as their piety, beneficence, and blameless life, are to the Christian name, when I say that passages occur which might almost lead one to conjecture, that the authors had found the words, "*I will come and join you,*" instead of, "I am in the midst of you,"—(Compare I. *John*, iii. 24)—passages from which it is at least difficult not to infer, that they had interpreted the promise, as of a corporal co-presence, instead of a spiritual

Distinctity without Unity = TIME." *OED* credits C with this word, citing *LR* III 2 (in error dating material 1812 that HNC dated 1830) and III 129 (in error for 123, a note on Donne's *Sermons*). In the latter the same use as here—unity vs distinctity: "Donne had not attained to the reconciling of distinctity with unity,—ours, yet God's; God's, yet ours." Cf also a note in *SM* (1839): *SM* (*CC*) 68 n 3.

[1] Ignatius of Antioch (c 35–c 107) *Epistle to the Philadelphians* 4. "Be careful therefore to use one Eucharist (for there is one flesh of our Lord Jesus Christ, one cup for union with his blood, one altar, as there is one bishop...)". Tr Kirsopp Lake *The Apostolic Fathers* (2 vols LCL 1912–13) I 243.

[2] Matt 18.20.

to all, being equally *actual* indeed, but likewise equally IDEAL, *i.e.* mystic and supersensual, as the relation of the whole church to its

---

immanence (ὅτι μένει ἐν ἡμῖν)[1] as of an individual coming in or down, and taking *a place*, as soon as the required number of petitioners was completed! As if, in short, this presence, this actuation of the "I A M," [2](εἰμὶ ἐν μέσῳ αὐτῶν)[3] were an after-consequence, an accidental and separate result and reward of the contemporaneous and contiguous worshipping—and not the total act itself, of which the spiritual Christ, one and the same in all the faithful, is the originating and perfective focal unity. Even as the physical life *is* in each limb and organ of the body, "all in every part;" but is *manifested* as life, by being one in all and thus making all *one*: even so with Christ, our Spiritual Life! He *is* in each true believer, in his solitary prayer and during his silent communion in the watches of the night, no less than in the congregation of the faithful; but he *manifests* his indwelling presence more characteristically, with especial evidence, when many, convened in his name, whether for prayer or for council, do through him become ONE.

I would that these preceding observations were as little connected with the main subject of this volume, as to some they will appear to be! But as the mistaking of symbols and analogies for metaphors (See *Aids to Reflection*, pp. 198, 254 G. 398,)[4] has been a main occasion and support of the worst errors in Protestantism; so the understanding the same symbols in a literal *i.e. phaenomenal* sense, notwithstanding the most earnest warnings against it, the most express declarations of the folly and danger of interpreting *sensually* what was delivered of objects *super*-sensual—this was the rank wilding, on which "the prince of this world,"[5] the lust of power and worldly aggrandizement, was enabled to graft, one by one, the whole branchery of papal superstitition and imposture. A truth not less important might be conveyed by reversing the image—by representing the papal monarchy as the stem or trunk circulating a poison-sap through the branches successively grafted thereon, the previous and natural fruit of which was at worst only mawkish and innutritious. Yet among the dogmas or articles of belief that contra-distinguish the [a]Roman Catholic from the Reformed [b]Churches,[6]

[a–b] Copy G: *Roman* from the *Reformed* Catholic

1 "That he abideth in us". 1 John 3.24.

2 C often as here significantly linked Exod 3.14 with the verb "to be" used of Christ. See also below p 141 n 2, pp 168, 182.

3 "I am in the midst of them". Matt 18.20.

4 In *AR* (1825) 198, C stresses the necessity "of thoroughly understanding the distinction between *analogous* and *metaphorical* language. *Analogies* are used in aid of *Conviction: Metaphors*, as means of *Illustration*." At 254, C provides the definition: "*A Symbol is a sign included in the Idea, which it represents:* ex. gr. an actual *part* chosen to represent the *whole*, as a lip with a chin prominent is a Symbol of Man...". At 398, C attributes the failure to escape the slavery of the senses to the effects of the mechanico-corpuscular philosophy.

5 John 12.31.

6 In the margin of Copy G, five pages later, C explains his revision here. "Therefore instead of Roman Catholic and Reformed Churches, I have substituted (p. 155) the Roman and the Reformed Catholic Churches—admitting the former as a member of the Catholic CHURCH, tho' the Church in which the Antichrist is enthroned. England ceased not to be England, tho' it tolerated a USURPER." He continued on a blank sheet at the end:

"The Catholic Church, in all its outward *component* Churches, Greek,

one invisible Head,[4] the church with and under Christ, as a one kingdom or state, is hidden: while from all its several component monads, (the particular visible churches I mean,) Caesar receiving the things that are Caesar's,[5] and confronted by no rival Caesar,

the most important and, in their practical effects and consequences, the most pernicious, I cannot but regard as refracted and distorted truths, profound ideas sensualized into idols, or at the lowest rate lofty and affecting imaginations, safe while they remained general and indefinite, but debased and rendered noxious by their application in detail: *ex. gr.* the doctrine of the Communion of Saints, or the sympathy between all the members of the universal church, which death itself doth not interrupt, exemplified in St. Anthony and the cure of sore eyes,[1] St. Boniface and success in brewing,[2] &c. &c. &c. What the same doctrines now are, used as the pretexts and shaped into the means and implements of priestly power and revenue: or rather, what the whole scheme *is* of Romish rites, doctrines, institutions, and practices in their combined and full operation, where it exists in undisputed sovereignty, neither repressed by the prevalence, nor modified by the light of a purer faith, nor held in check by the consciousness of Protestant neighbours and lookers-on—this is a question, which cannot be kept too distinct from the former. And, as at the risk of passing for a secret favourer of superannuated superstitions, I have spoken out my thoughts of the Catholic theology, so, and at a far more serious risk of being denounced as an intolerant bigot, I will declare what, after a two years' residence in exclusively Catholic countries,[3] and in situations and under circumstances that afforded more than ordinary means of acquainting myself with the workings and the proceeds of the machinery,

or Roman, or Reformed; and the latter, whether the English, or Scotch, or ⟨the Churches⟩ of Sweden, Norway, Denmark, North and Mid Germany, who alike *protest* against the papal usurpations in the Roman, and *disown* the parthenolatrical & hagiolatrical Practices & Superstitions of the Greek—but without denying the *Catholicity* of either. In the true Church alone dare we *expect* to be saved: & God's grace prevent in us the evil doubt, that thousands and tens of thousands *are* saved thro' faith in Christ in *all* the Churches, who believe in the only-begotten Son of God incarnate in Christ Jesus, God and Man, God manifested in the Flesh for the Salvation of Sinners! If there be any communities, who reject this belief, I judge them not, but neither will I name them CHRISTIANS, but content with the open avowal, that I cannot admit them (⟨ex. gr.⟩ the so called Unitarians) to be *Christians*, without abjuring *my own* Claim to that blessed name, I judge them not; but leave them, as I leave the Deists, Mahometans, and Buddaists, to the uncovenanted Mercies of God. S. T. C."

[1] St Anthony of Egypt is usually credited with the cure of "sacred fire", i.e. erysipelas.

[2] Boniface, martyred 754, the patron saint of brewers; his feast-day is 5 Jun. Traditionally his birthplace was Crediton, Devon, well known to C as a boy.

[3] C lived in Malta from 18 May 1804 to 21 (or 23) Sept 1805, and in Italy until he returned to England in Jun 1806. Cf *CN* II 2420, in which he notes "the indefatigable ubiquitarian intrusion of the Catholic Superstition" in a hospital at Malta; cf also *CN* II 2571, 2738, 2760. A visit to Europe in 1828 confirmed these early impressions. "Every fresh opportunity of examining the Romish Catholic Religion *on the spot*—every fresh fact that presents itself convinces me, that its main and only independent Basis is the Wickedness, Ignorance and Misery of the Many—in short, the unfitness of men to be *Christians*." N 40 f 22v.

[4] Eph 5.22.

[5] Matt 22.21.

by no authority, which existing locally, temporally, and in the person of a fellow mortal, must be essentially of the same *kind* with

was the impression left on my mind as to the effects and influences of the Romish (most *un*-Catholic) religion,[1]—not as even according to its own canons and authorised decisions it *ought* to be; but, as it actually and practically exists.—(*See this distinction ably and eloquently enforced in a Catholic work, intitled* RIFORMA D'ITALIA).[2] This impression, and the convictions grounded thereon, which have assuredly not been weakened by the perusal of the Rev. Blanco White's most affecting statements,[3] and by the recent history of Spain and Portugal,[4] I cannot convey more satisfactorily to myself than by repeating the answer, which I long since returned to the same question put by a friend, viz.—

When I contemplate the whole system, as it affects the great fundamental principles of morality, the *terra firma*, as it were, of our humanity; then trace its operation on the sources and conditions of national strength and well-being; and lastly, consider its woeful influences on the innocence and sanctity of the female mind and imagination, on the faith and happiness, the gentle fragrancy and unnoticed ever-present verdure of domestic life—I can with difficulty avoid applying to it what the Rabbins fable of the fratricide CAIN, after the curse: that *the firm earth trembled wherever he strode, and the grass turned black beneath his feet*.[5]

Indeed, if my memory does not cheat me, some of the "mystic divines," in

1 Cf *TT* 29 Apr 1823.

2 Already referred to above, p 80. Pilati called for the subordination of the Church to the State and for the suppression of ecclesiastical privileges in the Catholic Church. Between 9 and 12 Dec 1826 C wrote: "What a frightful callus of the heart and hand, what a conscience-proof Reprobacy, in the Italian Clergy, especially of the Court of Rome, does not the placing of Riforma d'Italia instantly on its appearance in the Index Lib. prohib.—present to *my* mind. How alienated from all sense & feeling of Truth must the Soul of a Romish Priest of the least Learning & Intelligence be to peruse such notorious truths so free from all heretical dogmata even in their own code of Heresy, and feel only a lust to suppress the work & murder the Writer!—O it *is* antichrist: if there be meaning in words!" N F° f 59.

3 Joseph Blanco White described the evil effects of the Roman Catholic religious system on the innocence and sanctity of the female mind in *Practical and Internal Evidence Against Catholicism* ch 5 (1825). Under the pseudonym Don Leucadio Doblado, he attacked the system of perpetual vows in convents in *Letters from Spain* Letter VIII (1822), calling the convents "Bastilles of Superstition". C had read and annotated these and other works (see above, p 80 and n).

4 Spain and Portugal, after their liberalising revolutions in the 1820's, returned to absolutism. In Spain Ferdinand VII annulled the liberal decrees and ruled as an absolute monarch, but this was not sufficient for the extreme rightists, who revolted in 1827, among their other demands calling for the restoration of the Inquisition. In Portugal Don Miguel seized the throne in 1828 and with the help of the Church party began his absolutist reign with a "white terror" of executions and arrests to destroy all liberal resistance.

5 Cf "Some say that wherever he stopped, the earth shook and trembled about him." *An Universal History from the Earliest Account of Time to the Present* (1736–65) I i 75n. Bayle's *Dictionary* under "Cain" (1735 II 247n) quotes a similar passage. The second part of the rabbins' fable has not been traced. Louis Ginzberg *The Legends of the Jews* (7 vols Phila 1947) gives sources in rabbinical literature

his own, notwithstanding any attempt to belie its true nature under the perverted and contradictory name of *spiritual*,[a] sees only so many loyal groups, who, claiming no peculiar rights, make themselves known to him as Christians,[b] only by the more scrupulous and exemplary performance of their duties as [c]citizens and subjects. And[d] here let me add a few sentences on the use, abuse, and misuse of the phrase, *spiritual* Power. In the only appropriate sense of the words, *spiritual* power is a power that acts on the *spirits* of men. Now the spirit of a man, or the spiritual part of our being, is the intelligent Will:[3] or (to speak less abstractly) it is the capability, with which the Father of Spirits[4] hath endowed man of being determined to action by the *ultimate ends*, which the reason alone can present. (The Understanding, which derives all its materials from the Senses, can dictate *purposes* only, *i.e.* such ends as are in their turn *means* to other ends.) The ultimate ends, by which the will is to be determined, and by which alone the will, not corrupted, "*the spirit made perfect*," *would* be determined, are called, in relation to the Reason, moral *Ideas*.[5] Such are the Ideas of the Eternal, the Good, the True, the Holy, the Idea of God as the Absoluteness and Reality (or real ground) of all these, or as the Supreme Spirit in which all these substantially *are*, and are ONE. Lastly, the idea of

---

their fond humour of allegorizing, tell us, that in Gen. iv. 3–8.[1] is correctly narrated the history of the first apostate church, that began by sacrificing amiss, impropriating the fruit of *the ground* (*i.e.* temporal possessions) under spiritual pretexts; and ended in slaying the shepherd brother who brought "the firstlings of his fold," holy and without blemish, to the Great Shepherd, and presented them as "*new* creatures,"[2] before the Lord and Owner of the Flocks.—S. T. C.

[a] Copy G: spiritual—the Caesar, I ~~may~~ say, the rightful Sovereign of the State, in all these Churches
[b] Copy G: *Christians,* [c–d] Copy G: *citizens* and *subjects.* §. a fresh Paragraph. And

---

for Cain and the quaking earth and the cursed ground (I 110–12, V 141). C was interested in rabbinical lore, translated four rabbinical tales in *The Friend* (*CC*) II 154–6, 170–1, 308–9, and was a friend of Hyman Hurwitz (1770–1844), author of *Hebrew Tales* (1826), which included three of C's translations.

1 These verses relate the story of Cain and Abel.

2 Cf 2 Cor 5.17, Gal 6.15, etc.

3 Cf *AR* "Elements of Religious Philosophy" (1825) 131–40.

4 Heb 12.9; cf similar allusions below, pp 127 and 169.

5 C refers to Heb 12.23. For a discussion of the relation of will and reason in C, see J. R. Barth *Coleridge and Christian Doctrine* (Cambridge, Mass. 1969) ch 4. See also Owen Barfield *What Coleridge Thought* (Middletown, Conn. 1972) chs 9 (on "Reason"), 10 (on "Ideas, Method, Laws").

the responsible will itself; of duty, of guilt, or evil in itself without reference to its outward and separable consequences, &c. &c.

A power, therefore, that acts on the appetites and passions, which we possess in common with the beasts, by motives derived from the senses and sensations, has no pretence to the name; nor can it without the grossest abuse of the word be called a *spiritual* power. Whether the man expects the *auto de fè*, the fire and faggots, with which he is threatened, to take place at Lisbon or Smithfield, or in some dungeon in the centre of the earth, makes no difference in the *kind* of motive by which he is influenced; nor of course in the nature of the power, which acts on his passions by means of it. It would be strange indeed, if ignorance and superstition, the dense and rank fogs that most strangle and suffocate the light of the spirit in man, should constitute a spirituality in the power, which takes advantage of them!

This is a gross *abuse* of the term, spiritual. The following, sanctioned as it is by custom and statute, yet (speaking exclusively as a philologist and without questioning its legality) I venture to point out, as a *misuse* of the term. Our great Church dignitaries sit in the Upper House of the Convocation, as *Prelates* of the National Church: and as *Prelates*, may exercise *ecclesiastical* power. In the House of Lords they sit as *barons*, and by virtue of the baronies which, much against the will of those haughty prelates, our kings forced upon them: and as such, they exercise a *Parliamentary* power. As bishops of the Church of Christ only can they possess, or exercise (and God forbid! I should doubt, that as such, many of them do faithfully exercise) a *spiritual* power, which neither king can give, nor King and Parliament take away. As Christian *bishops*, they are spiritual *pastors*, by power of the spirit[a] ruling the flocks committed to their charge; but they are *temporal* peers and prelates. The

Fourth Character

of the Christian Church, and a necessary consequence of the first and third, is its Catholicity, *i.e.* universality. It is neither Anglican, Gallican, nor Roman, neither Latin nor Greek.[1] Even the Catholic and Apostolic Church *of* England is a less safe expression than the Churches of Christ in England: though the Catholic Church *in* England, or (what would be still better,) the Catholic Church under Christ throughout Great Britain and Ireland, is justifiable and

[a] Copy G: *spirit*

[1] See C's notes in Copy G, above, p 120 n 6.

appropriate: for through the presence of its only head and sovereign, entire in each and one in all, the Church universal is spiritually perfect in every true Church, and of course in any number of such Churches, which from circumstance of place, or the community of country or of language, we have occasion to speak of collectively. (I have already, here and elsewhere, observed, and scarcely a day passes without some occasion to repeat the observation, that an equivocal term, or a word with two or more different meanings, is never quite harmless.[1] Thus, it is at least an inconvenience in our language, that the term Church, instead of being confined to its proper sense, Kirk, Aedes Kyriacae, or the Lord's House, should likewise be the word by which our forefathers rendered the ecclesia, or the eccleti (ἔκκλητοι) i.e. evocati, the called out of the world, named collectively, and likewise our term for the clerical establishment.[2] To the Called at Rome—to the Church of Christ at Corinth—or in Philippi—such was the language of the apostolic age; and the change since then has been no improvement.) The true Church *of* England is the National Church, or Clerisy. There exists, God be thanked! a Catholic and Apostolic church *in* England: and I thank God also for the Constitutional and Ancestral Church *of* England.

These are the four distinctions, or peculiar and essential marks, by which the church with Christ as its head is distinguished from the National Church, and *separated* from every possible counterfeit, that has, or shall have, usurped its name. And as an important comment on the same, and in confirmation of the principle which I have attempted to establish, I earnestly recommend for the reader's perusal, the following transcript from DR. HENRY MORE'S *Modest Enquiry, or True Idea of Anti-christianism*.[3]

"We will suppose some one prelate, who had got the start of the

[1] Hence C's frequent practice of desynonymising; cf above, p 108 n 1.

[2] "Aedes Kyriacae" means, as C tr, "the Lord's House"; the derivation of "church" from the Greek adjective κυριακ- seems very probable and is made by Hooker *Ecclesiastical Polity* v 13: *Works* (1682) 202. In AR "Aphorisms on Spiritual Religion" II, C notes that "the *kyriak*, Aedes *Dominicae*, Lord's House, *Kirk*; and *Ecclesia*, the sum total of the Eccalūmeni, *evocati*, *Called-out*; are both rendered by the same word Church". *AR* (1825) 166. Cf "A sphere for the mischief had been gradually prepared by the narrowing of the Church into the Clergy, and the confusion of *Ecclesia* with *Aedes Kyriacae*—i.e. the Kirk and its Indwellers." Ms note in N F° f 61. On C's use of the word *ecclesia*, see above, p 45.

[3] Henry More (1614–87) *A Modest Inquiry into the Mystery of Iniquity* II ix: *Theological Works* (1708) 486–7 (var with omissions). C's copy of this book, in the BM, has no marginal comment on this passage.

rest, to put in for the title and authority of Universal Bishop: and for the obtaining of this sovereignty, he will first pretend, that it is unfit that the visible Catholic Church, being one, should not be united under one visible head, which reasoning, though it makes a pretty shew at first sight, will yet, being closely looked into, vanish into smoke. For this is but a quaint concinnity urged in behalf of an impossibility. For the erecting such an office for one man, which no one *man* in the world is able to perform, implies that to be possible which is indeed impossible. Whence it is plain that the *head* will be *too little for the body;* which therefore will be a piece of mischievous assymmetry or inconcinnity also. No one mortal can be a competent head for that church which has a right to be *Catholic*, and to overspread the face of the whole earth. There can be no such head but Christ, who is not mere man, but God in the Divine humanity, and therefore present with every part of the church, and every member thereof, at what distance soever. But to set some one mortal bishop over the whole church, were to suppose that great bishop of our spirit absent from it, who has promised that he *will be with her to the end of the world.* Nor does the Church Catholic on earth lose her unity thereby. For[a] rather hereby only is or can she be one.["][1] "As rationally might it be pretended, that it is not the Life, the *Rector Spiritus praesens per totum et in omni parte*,[2] but the Crown of the skull, or some one Convolute of the brain, that causes and preserves the unity of the Body Natural."—*Inserted by the transcriber*.[3]

Such and so futile is the first pretence. But if this will not serve the turn, there is another in reserve. And notwithstanding the demonstrated impossibility of the thing, still there must be one visible head of the church universal, the successor and vicar of Christ, *for the slaking of controversies*, for the determination of disputed points! We will not stop here to expose the weakness of the argument (not alas! peculiar to the sophists of Rome, nor employed in support of *papal* infallibility only), that this or that *must be*, and consequently *is*, because sundry inconveniences would result from the want of it!

[a] 1st ed: Far

[1] The passage from More ends here, with the last sentence a very loose paraphrase; the remainder was added by C.

[2] Source untraced. Tr: "The ruling Spirit, present throughout the whole and in every part".

[3] The whole sentence "inserted by the transcriber" was included in the 1st and 2nd eds, but was appropriately relegated to a note by HNC in *C&S* (1839).

and this without considering whether these inconveniences *have been* prevented or removed by its (pretended) presence; whether they do not continue in spite of this pretended remedy or antidote; whether these inconveniences were *intended* by providence to be precluded, and not rather for wise purposes permitted to continue; and lastly, whether the remedy may not be worse than the disease, like the sugar of lead administered by the Empiric, who cured a fever fit by exchanging it for the dead palsy.[1] Passing by this sophism, therefore, it is sufficient to reply, that all points necessary are so plain and so widely known, that it is impossible that a Christian, who seeks those aids which the true head of the church has promised shall never be sought in vain, should err therein from lack of knowing better. And those who, from defects of head or heart, are blind to this widely diffused light, and who neither seek nor wish those aids, are still less likely to be influenced by a minor and derivative authority. But for other things, whether ceremonies or conceits, whether matters of discipline or of opinion, their diversity does not at all break the unity of the outward and visible church, as long as they do not subvert the fundamental laws of Christ's kingdom, nor contradict the terms of admission into his church, nor contravene the essential characters, by which it subsists, and is distinguished as the Christian Catholic Church.

To these sentiments, borrowed from one of the most philosophical of our learned elder Divines,[2] I have only to add an observation as suggested by them—that as many and fearful mischiefs have ensued from the confusion of the Christian with the National Church, so have many and grievous practical errors, and much unchristian intolerance, arisen from confounding the outward and visible church of Christ, with the spiritual and invisible church, known only to the Father of all Spirits.[3] The perfection of the former is to afford every opportunity, and to present no obstacle, to a gradual advancement in the latter. The different degrees of progress, the imperfections, errors and accidents of false perspective, which lessen indeed with

[1] Acetate of lead, a poison. Cf "Almost all the modern physicians, I know, scruple not to administer it [*Saccharum Saturni*] in intermitting fevers, and other distempers....And tho it may cure the fever, it is apt to leave a worse disorder behind it." Hermann Boerhaave *A New Method of Chemistry* tr P. Shaw and E. Chambers (2 pts 1727) ii 277 (Process CLVIII), a copy of which belonging to James Gillman C annotated; the notes are printed in *NTP* 231–7. C used "sugar" and "sugar of lead" as examples of the need for desynonymising; see e.g. *P Lects* Lect IV (1949) 151.

[2] Henry More.

[3] Heb 12.9; cf similar allusions, above, p 123, and below, p 169.

our[a] advance—spiritual *advance*—but to a greater or lesser amount are inseparable from all progression: these, the interpolated half-truths of the twilight,[1] through which every soul must pass from darkness to the spiritual sunrise, belong to the visible church as objects of Hope, Patience, and Charity alone.

[a] 1st ed: your

[1] See above, p 7 and n 2.

ON THE
THIRD POSSIBLE CHURCH,
OR THE

CHURCH OF ANTICHRIST[1]

> Ecclesia Catholica non, ma il Papismo denunciamo, perchè suggerito dal Interesse, perchè fortificato dalla menzogna, perchè radicato dal piu abbominevole despotismo, perchè contrario al diritto e ai titoli incommunicabili di Cristo, ed alla tranquillità d'ogni Chiesa e d'ogni Stato.—SPANZOTTI[2]

1 The idea of Antichrist was common to Jewish and Christian traditions and signified either a false Messiah or an opponent of the true Messiah, alternative meanings present in the Greek prefix *anti*. In the early Christian Church the belief in an archetypal opponent of Christ and his Church, expected to appear before the end of the world, was bound up with the belief in Christ's Second Coming. The word appears in the New Testament in 1 John 2.18, 22; 4.3; 2 John 7; the idea is linked with the Second Coming in 2 Thess 2.1–10. The Protestant Reformers identified Antichrist with the Pope, as C points out below, p 133. His own definition combines the ideas of pretence, usurpation, and subversion and is applied to the papacy.

2 Girolamo Vincenzo Spanzotti *Disordini morali e politici della Corte di Roma* (2nd ed Turin 1801) II 197 (var; words before the first *perchè* supplied by C, who also substitutes "al diritto ... Cristo" for "alla giustizia al buon ordine"). Tr: "It is not the Catholic Church, but the Papacy that I denounce, because it springs from Self-interest, because it gathers strength from falsehood, because it takes root from the most hateful despotism, because it is contrary to the inalienable rights and titles of Christ, and to the peace of every Church and of every State." See also below, pp 136–8 and nn. In N 40 f 20[v], overleaf from a long transcription from Spanzotti vol II, C has written: "Hear the language in which a Zealous Catholic describes the *existing* constitution and system of the ~~Romish~~ Poperly Church in contrast with that of the ancient Catholic Church/ he denounces the former, and calls aloud for its subversion, perchè suggerito..." continuing in similar wording to the passage above.

THUS, on the depluming of THE POPE, every bird had his own feather: in the partage whereof, what he had gotten by *Sacrilege*, was restored to Christ; what by *Usurpation*, was given to the king, the (National) Church and the State; what by *Oppression*, was remitted to each particular Christian.

Fuller's Church History of Britain, Book v[1]

[1] Bk v sec iii § 63 (var); among minor changes, C alters Fuller's "*God*" to "Christ" and adds the word "National". C's copy of Thomas Fuller *The Church-History of Britain* (1655), in the BM (the passage quoted above appears at I 199), contains marginal comments, some of which are reproduced in *NED* I 124–7; for his praise of Fuller as next to Shakespeare and his wish to meet him in heaven, see I 127.

ON THE CHURCH, NEITHER NATIONAL NOR UNIVERSAL

If our forefathers were annoyed with the *cant* of over-boiling zeal, arising out of the belief, that the Pope is Antichrist, and likewise (*sexu mutato*) the Harlot of Babylon:[1] we are more endangered by the *twaddle* of humid charity, which (some years ago at least) used to drizzle, a something between mist and small rain, from the higher region of our church atmosphere. It was sanctioned, I mean, both in the pulpit and the senate by sundry dignitaries, whose horror of Jacobinism during the then panic of Property[2] led them to adopt the principles and language of Laud and his faction.[3] And once more the Church of Rome, in contrast with the Protestant Dissenters, became "a right dear, though erring Sister." And the heaviest charge against the Romish Pontificate was, that the Italian politics and Nepotism of a series of Popes had converted so great a good into an intolerable grievance. We were reminded, that GROTIUS and LEIBNITZ had regarded a visible head of the Catholic church as most desirable:[4] that they, and with them more than one Primate of our own church,

1 "With a change of sex". For the "harlot of Babylon", see Rev 17.

2 Cf *Conciones: Lects 1795* (*CC*) 30–1 and n 1, and *Friend* (*CC*) I 218; cf also "But when will Partizans be cool enough to bear in mind, [that] of two hostile Parties the probability is, that both are in the wrong. The inadvertence to this truth was the occasion of Mr Fox's blundering speeches at the commencement of the Anti-Jacobin War, by which he alienated all sober people, reduced his own followers to a hand-full & enabled Pitt to raise that Panic of Property which rendered him irresistible." Annotation on Johnson *Works* 22.

3 Although William Laud (1573–1645), who became Archbishop of Canterbury in 1633, defended the Anglican Church as a national institution and resisted the claims of the Church of Rome to infallibility and universality, C frequently criticised Laud's use of state power to stamp out religious dissent and was suspicious of his policies towards Rome. For C's interest in Laud's works see *CL* V 294–5 and nn, and for hostile comments, *C 17th C* 34, 223–30.

4 Grotius (see also below, p 135 and n 1) in e.g. *Annotata ad Consultationem Cassandri* Article 7 and *Votum pro pace ecclesiastica* Article 7: *Opera theologica* (4 vols Basel 1732) IV 617, 659, and Leibniz (see also below, p 165 and n 4) in *Systema theologicum* (first pub Paris 1819) 302 (English tr London 1850 pp 143–4) and Letter VIII to Johann Fabricius: *Opera omnia* (6 vols Geneva 1768) ed L. Dutens V 228–30.

yearned for a conciliating settlement of the differences between the Romish and Protestant churches; and mainly in order that there might exist *really*, as well as *nominally*, a visible head of the church universal, a fixt centre of unity. Of course the tenet, that the Pope was in any sense the Antichrist predicted by Paul,[1] was decried as fanatical and puritanical cant.

Now it is a duty of Christian charity to presume, that the men, who in the present day employ this language, are, or believe themselves to be, Christians: and that they do not privately think that St. Paul, in the two celebrated passages of his First and Second Epistles to the Church of Thessalonica, (I. iv., 13–18; II ii. 1–12),[2] practised a *ruse de guerre*, and meant only by throwing the fulfilment beyond the life of the present generation, and by a terrific detail of the horrors and calamities that were to precede it, to damp the impatience, and silence the objections, excited by the expectation and the delay of our Lord's personal re-appearance. Again: as the persons, of whom we have been speaking, are well educated men, and men of sober minds, we may safely take for granted, that they do not understand by Antichrist any nondescript monster, or suppose it to be the proper name or designation of some one individual man or devil exclusively. The Christians of the second century, sharing in a delusion that prevailed over the whole Roman Empire, believed that Nero would come to life again, and be Antichrist:[3] and I have been informed, that a learned clergyman of our own times, endowed

[1] Paul did not use the word Antichrist. C is conflating 1 John 2.18 and 2 Thess 2.1–10.

[2] Both passages deal with Paul's prophecy of the Second Coming of Christ. C interprets the second, 2 Thess 2.1–10, as "a well-knit and highly poetical evolution of a part of this and our Lord's more comprehensive prediction, *Luke* xvii", in an annotation to *The Coming of Messiah in Glory and Majesty* (2 vols 1827), a work translated by Edward Irving from the Spanish of Manuel Lacunza, a converted Jew who wrote under the pseudonym of Juan Josafat Ben-Ezra. In the same note, he rebuked Irving for allowing his "spirit [to] be drawn away from passages" such as 2 Thess 2.1–10 "to guess and dream over the rhapsodies of the Apocalypse". *NTP* 347. For Edward Irving see below, p 133 and n 1.

[3] It was widely believed after Nero's death in 64 that he was not dead or would return to life (Tacitus *Histories* 2.8, Suetonius *Lives of the Caesars*: Nero 57), and this belief is thought to lie behind the references to the Beast in Revelation 13, 17. The belief reappears as late as the second century in the Sibylline Oracles 4, 5, but C may have in mind Irenaeus (c 130–c 200) with his interpretation of the number of the Beast (Rev 13.18) as Lateinos (*Adversus omnes haereses* 5.30.3). See the marginal notes on J. C. Wolf quoted in *CN* III 3793n, on Henry More in *LR* III 166–7, and on *Apocalypsis Graece* ed J. H. Heinrichs (2 vols Göttingen 1818–21) in *LR* III 167.

with the gift of prophecy by assiduous study of Daniel, and the Apocalypse, asserts the same thing of Napoleon Bonaparte.[1]

But, as before said, it would be calumnious to attribute such pitiable fanaticism to the parties here in question. And to *them* I venture to affirm, that if by Antichrist be meant—what alone can rationally be meant—a power in the Christian church, which in the name of Christ, and at once pretending and usurping his authority, is systematically subversive of the essential and distinguishing characters and purposes of the Christian church: that *then*, if the papacy, and the Romish Hierarchy as far as it is papal, be *not* Antichrist, the guilt of schism, in its most aggravated form, lies on the authors of the Reformation. For nothing less than this could have justified so tremendous a rent in the Catholic church, with all its foreseen most calamitous consequences. And so Luther himself thought; and so thought Wickliffe before him. Only in the conviction that Christianity itself was at stake; that the cause was that of Christ in conflict with Antichrist: could, or did even the lion-hearted Luther with unquailed spirit avow to himself: I bring not peace, but a sword into the world.[2]

[1] The "learned clergyman" was probably Edward Irving (1792–1834), who came to London from Glasgow in 1822 and rapidly won fame as a popular preacher at the chapels at Hatton Garden and later Regent Square. He met C in 1823 and visited him frequently, but after 1826 C became highly critical of his "*interpretations* of the Apocalypse and the Book of Daniel". In 1830 Irving was charged with heresy, in 1832 he was dismissed by the Regent Square trustees, and in the same year he and his followers founded the "Holy Catholic Apostolic Church". Irving identifies Bonaparte with Antichrist in *Babylon and Infidelity Foredoomed of God: a Discourse on the Prophecies of Daniel and the Apocalypse* (2 vols Glasgow 1826). James Hatley Frere, to whom the work was dedicated, had earlier written of Bonaparte as a personal Antichrist in *A Combined View of the Prophecies of Daniel, Esdras and S. John* (1815). In a letter to Edward Coleridge on 8 Feb 1826, C records that Irving had been seeing too much of Hatley Frere (brother of C's patron and friend, J. H. Frere) and ridicules the absurdities of "the Revd. G. S. Faber School" (Faber wrote voluminously of the prophetic implications of the Bible, linking these with the restoration of Napoleon in 1815). C sees Irving's mistake as lying in the false assumption that the Apocalypse contains "a series of events in an historico-chronological Arrangement...not as the Prophets predicted but as the Annalist in the Books of Samuel, Kings, or Chronicles *narrated*—nay, with an exactness not attempted even by the latter, but to be parallelled only in modern Chronicles". *CL* VI 557.

[2] The Contemporary Records of the Proceedings at Worms, 16–26 Apr 1521, report Luther as saying "from my point of view, it would be a most happy turn of events if the word of God were to become the subject of inquiry and argument. That is but the way and work and consequence of the word of God, for we read: I have not come to bring peace, but a

It is my full conviction, a conviction formed after a long and patient study of the subject in detail; and if the author in support of this competence only added that he has read, and with care, the Summa Theologiae of Aquinas,[1] and compared the system with the statements of Arnold[2] and Bossuet,[3] the number of those who in the present much-reading, but not very hard-reading age, would feel themselves entitled to dispute his claim, will not, perhaps, be very formidable—

It is, I repeat, my full conviction that the rites and doctrines, the *agenda et credenda*,[4] of the Catholics, could we separate them from the adulterating ingredients combined with, and the use made of them, by the sacerdotal Mamelukes of the Romish monarchy, for the support of the Papacy and papal hierarchy, would neither have brought about, nor have sufficed to justify, the convulsive separation under Leo X.[5] Nay, that if they were fairly, and in the light of a sound philosophy, compared with either of the two main divisions of Protestantism, as it now exists in this country, *i.e.* with the

sword". *Reformation Writings of Martin Luther* ed Bertram Lee Woolf (2 vols 1953–6) II 149. Luther refers to Matt 10.34.

[1] Cf "...when I hear a Theologian speak of the emptiness, and poverty of Thought, of all the School-men, I shall venture to tell him, that he has never read the Summa Theologia of Thomas Aquinas...". An annotation on Tennemann *Geschichte der Philosophie* vol IX: *C 17th C* 438. In a letter to Josiah Wedgwood 18 Feb 1801 (*CL* II 681) C, discussing innate ideas, says he has not read Aquinas, but by 1803 his name appears in a notebook entry for a projected work: "Revolutionary Minds, Thomas Aquinas, Scotus, Luther, Baxter as represent. of the English Presbyterians & as affording a place for the Church of England—Socinus, G. Fox." *CN* I 1646. In the ninth of the Philosophical Lectures (1819), he said: "But I happen to have read a considerable portion of the works of Thomas Aquinas". *P Lects* (1949) 280; n 37 (pp 437–8) neatly summarises C's knowledge and reading of Aquinas. In Oct 1829, probably about the time the passage in *C&S* was written, Lamb sent "honest Tom" to C when he was ill. *LL* III 230.

[2] Antoine Arnauld (1612–94) was a Jansenist. His outspoken attacks on Jesuitical methods and the resulting decision of the Sorbonne to expel him led Pascal to write *Lettres provinciales*. C would have met his views when he first read Pascal's work in 1803; see above, p 115 n 1. In the Conclusion of *AR* (1825) 380, C speaks of Arnauld's "great Work on Transubstantiation, (not without reason the Boast of Catholicism)", i.e. *La Perpétuité de la foi de l'église catholique touchant l'Eucharistie*.

[3] Jacques Bénigne Bossuet (1627–1704), bp of Meaux, defended the rights and liberties of the Gallican Church in *Discours sur l'histoire universelle* (1681), *Exposition sur la doctrine catholique* (1671), and *L'Histoire des variations des églises protestantes* (1688).

[4] "Things to be done and things to be believed".

[5] The grants of indulgences by Leo X (Giovanni de' Medici: Pope 1513–21) helped to arouse the spirit of revolt against the abuses of the Church that culminated in the Reformation. He excommunicated Luther in 1520.

fashionable doctrines and interpretations of the Arminian[a] and Grotian school on the one hand, and with the tenets and language of the modern Calvinists on the other,[1] an enlightened disciple of John and of Paul would be perplexed, which of the three to prefer as the least unlike the profound and sublime system, he had learnt from his great masters. And in this comparison I leave out of view the extreme sects of Protestantism, whether of the Frigid or of the Torrid Zone,[2] Socinian or fanatic.[3]

[a] 1st ed: Armenian

[1] C attributes the origin of the first class of doctrines to the Dutch theologian Jacobus Arminius (1560–1609) and to the Dutch jurist and theologian, Hugo Grotius (1583–1645); see above, p 131 and n 4. By fashionable doctrines of the Arminian and Grotian school C means those of the Wesleyan Methodists, who were anti-Calvinist, and the expounders of the rational explanations of Christianity, with proofs and evidences, which C scorned. As for "the modern Calvinists", C has in mind the Calvinist Methodists, with their emphasis on the distinction between the visible and the invisible Church. C was tempted, he wrote, "to write a brief Essay under the title of 'Christianity defended against its Defenders'" and complained of such times and countries as his "where He who will not swear by Grotius must expect to be considered as under bonds to Calvin—or, worse still, as an Upholder of that 'Modern Calvinism', which with all due respect to the late D[r] Williams [Edward Williams (1750–1813), Dissenting minister, author of *Equity of Divine Government*, the work that set forth the doctrines of modern Calvinism], its Archaspistes, I am persuaded that Calvin himself would have welcomed with an Anathema Maranatha". Annotation on Robert Leighton *Whole Works* (4 vols 1820) I 88–94; C's copy is in the BM.

[2] Cf "Socinianism moonlight—Methodism a Stove! O for some Sun to unite heat & Light!" *CN* I 1233. C associated "coldness" with atheism and believed Unitarianism (Socinianism) to approach atheism. On coldness see LRR I in *Lects 1795* (*CC*) 92 and n 1, 96 and n 1. And cf the Allegoric Vision in *SM*, in that work an attack on rationalism rather than on the Established Church, as in LRR, in C's Unitarian days: *SM* (*CC*) 137.

[3] The dismissive reference to Socinianism is of special interest in view of C's early attachment to Unitarianism; see Introduction, above, p xli and n 4, and cf C's account of his religious development in the "Brief Dialogue—between B. A. and S. T. C." in N Q, in which he noted that "at the period of commencing Manhood" he adhered "to the Priestleian Infra-Socinianism: and during little less than two years was, I think (God forgive my errors of Ignorance, and the immaturities of a growing Mind!) was sufficiently loud and open in my avowals of dissent from, and hostility to, the *Faith*, all the *fundamental* Articles of the Faith, of the Established Church: and this to the known, and distinctly foreseen, abandonment of all my worldly prospects—and the alienation of all my nearest and natural Connections. At the close of this period I became unsatisfied with my Unitarian Scheme, as a Creed of Negatives; and having collected in this what I did *not* believe, applied myself seriously to find out, what I *did* believe, to make a Creed of Positives—The result was, a final and decisive Return to the doctrines of the Catechism, I had learnt as a child; to a full and avowed Conviction of the Faith of Luther, Melancthon, and the Fathers and Founders of the Church, in which I was baptized & bred, the Established Protestant Church of England." N Q ff 47[v]–8.

During the summer of last year, I made the tour of Holland, Flanders, and up the Rhine as far as Bergen,[1] and among the few notes then taken, I find the following:—"Every fresh opportunity of examining the Roman Catholic religion on the spot, every new fact that presents itself to my notice, increases my conviction, that its immediate basis, and the true grounds of its continuance, are to be found in the wickedness, ignorance, and wretchedness of the many; and that the producing and continuing cause of this deplorable state is, that it is the interest of the Romish Priesthood, that so it should remain, as the surest, and in fact, only support of the Papal Sovereignty and influence against the civil powers, and the reforms wished for by the more enlightened governments, as well as by all the better informed and wealthier class of Catholics generally. And as parts of the same policy, and equally indispensable to the interests of the Triple Crown, are the ignorance, grossness, excessive number and poverty of the lower Ecclesiastics themselves, including the religious orders. N.B.—When I say the Pope, I understand the papal hierarchy, which is, in truth, the *dilated Pope:* and in this sense only, and not of the individual Priest or Friar at Rome, can a wise man be supposed to use the word."—COLOGNE, *July* 2, 1828.[2]

I feel it as no small comfort and confirmation, to know that the same view of the subject is taken, the same conviction entertained, by a large and increasing number in the Catholic communion itself, in Germany, France, Italy, and even in Spain; and that no inconsiderable portion of this number consists of men who are not only pious as Christians, but zealous as Catholics; and who would contemplate with as much horror a Reform *from* their Church, as they look with earnest aspirations and desires towards a Reform *in* the Church. Proof of this may be found in the learned work, intitled "Disordini morali et politici della Corte di Roma,"—evidently the work of a zealous Catholic, and from the ecclesiastical erudition displayed in the volumes, probably a Catholic priest.[3] Nay, from the

[1] In company with WW and his daughter Dora, C visited Holland, Flanders, and Germany in the summer of 1828; for details see *W Life* (M) II 434–6. "Bergen" is an error for Bingen, correctly named in *CL* VI 749, 751.

[2] The first part of the passage to "wretchedness of the many" copied (var) from N 40 f 22^{v}.

[3] The author, Girolamo Vincenzo Spanzotti (1741–1812), from whom C has already quoted the epigraph to this section of *C&S*, was indeed a priest; he was also a Jacobin, a lawyer, and secretary to the National University at Turin. His *Disordini morali e politici* was first published in 1798, when his native Piedmont had become a French satellite republic, and his name appears on the title-page as "Citizen" Spanzotti. C used the 2nd ed, expanded and revised (Turin 1801).

angry aversion with which the foul heresies of those sons of perdition,[1] Luther and Calvin, are mentioned, and his very faint and qualified censure of the persecution of the Albigenses and Waldenses,[2] I am obliged to infer, that the writer's attachment to his communion was zealous even to bigotry!

The disorders denounced by him are:—[3]

1. The pretension of the Papacy to temporal power and sovereignty, directly or as the pretended consequence of spiritual dominion; and as furnishing occasion to this, even the retention of the primacy *in honour* over all other bishops, after Rome had ceased to be the metropolis of Christendom, is noticed as a subject of regret.

2. The boast of papal infallibility.

3. *The derivation of the Episcopal Power from the Papal, and the dependence of Bishops on the Pope, rightly named the evil of a false centre.*

4. The right of exercising authority in other dioceses besides that of Rome.

5. The privilege of reserving to himself the *greater causes—le cause maggiori.*

6, 7, 8, 9, 10. Of conferring any and every benefice in the territory of other bishops; of exacting the Annates, or First Fruits; of receiving appeals; with the power of subjecting all churches in all parts, to the ecclesiastical discipline of the church of Rome; and lastly, the dispensing Power of the Pope.

11. The Pope's pretended superiority to an Ecumenical Council.

12. The exclusive power of canonizing Saints.

Now, of the twelve abuses here enumerated, it is remarkable that ten, if not eleven, are but expansions of the one grievance—the Papal Power as the centre, and the Pope as the one visible head and sovereign of the Christian church.

[1] John 17.12 and 2 Thess 2.3.

[2] Spanzotti II 150–5; esp 151, to the effect that had the Pope dealt more gently with heresy, we should not have had the inconvenience of deploring the damage to the Catholic Church that resulted from the pertinacity of the heretics. This mildness is surely ironical, as is the fact that the whole work is addressed to Pope Pius VI (a prisoner of the French at the time of the 1st ed, succeeded by Pius VII in 1800), and adopts the tone of policy and persuasion throughout. The inhumanity of the Inquisition is condemned in the most forthright terms later in this chapter.

[3] This summary consists mainly of fairly close translations of Spanzotti's chapter headings, with a few additional comments on the contents. There is a similar but slightly briefer summary in N 40 (ff 16–17), followed (ff 19^v–20) by the transcription of a passage from II 428–30; see also above, p 129 n 2.

The writer next enumerates the personal Instruments, &c. of these abuses: viz.—1. The Cardinals. 2. The excessive number of the Priests and other Ecclesiastics. 3. The Regulars, Mendicant Orders, Jesuits, &c.

Lastly: the means employed by the Papacy to found and preserve its usurped power, namely:—

1. The institution of a Chair of Canon Law, in the university of Bologna, the introduction of Gratian's Canons, and the forged decisions, &c.[1] 2. The prohibition of books, wherever published. 3. The Inquisition. 4. The tremendous power of Excommunication. The two last in their temporal inflictions and consequences equalling, or rather greatly exceeding, the utmost extent of the punitive power exercised by the temporal sovereign and the civil magistrate, armed with the sword of the criminal law.

It is observable, that the most efficient of all the means adopted by the Roman Pontiffs, viz.—THE CELIBACY OF THE CLERGY, is omitted by this writer: a sufficient proof that he was neither a Protestant nor a *Philosopher*, which in the Italian states, and, indeed, in most Catholic Countries, is the name of Courtesy for an Infidel.

One other remark in justification of the tenet avowed in this chapter, and I shall have said all I deem it necessary to say, on the third form of a Church. That erection of a temporal monarch under the pretence of a spiritual authority, which was not possible in Christendom but by the extinction or entrancement of the spirit of Christianity, and which has therefore been only partially attained by the Papacy—this was effected in full by Mahomet, to the establishment of the most extensive and complete despotism, that ever warred against civilization and the interests of humanity. And had Mahomet retained the name of Christianity, had he deduced his authority from Christ, as his *Principal*, and described his own Caliphate and that of his successors as *vicarious*, there can be no doubt, that to the Mussulman Theocracy, embodied in the different Mahometan dynasties, would belong the name and attributes of Antichrist. But the Prophet of Arabia started out of Paganism an unbaptized Pagan. He was no traitor in the church, but an enemy from without, who levied war against its outward and formal existence, and is, therefore,

[1] Gratian (d not later than 1179) compiled the *Concordantia discordantium canonum*, or the *Decretum*, and thereby laid the foundation of canon law. Gratian innocently included some of the "False Decretals", which had been forged to provide early authority for papal supremacy. Their spuriousness was not generally recognised until the early seventeenth century.

Power in the Church itself which in the name of Christ and pretending his Authority systematically subverts or counteraction of the peculiar aims and purposes of Christ's Mission, and vesting in a mortal his incommunicable Headship destroys (and exchanges for the contrary) the essential contra-distinguishing Marks or Characters of his Kingdom on Earth. But apply it, as Wickliff, Luther,* and indeed all the first Reformers did to the Papacy, and Papal Hierarchy, and we understand at once the grounds of the great Apostle's premonition, that this Anti-christ could not appear till after the dissolution of the Roman Empire and the extinction of the Imperial Power in Rome—and the cause, why the Bishops of Constantinople, with all imaginable good wishes and disposition to do the same, could never raise the Patriarchate of the Greek Empire into a Papacy.—The Bishops of the other Rome became the Slaves of the Ottoman, the moment they ceased to be the Subjects of the Emperor.

---

* And (be it observed) without any reference to the Apocalypse, the canonical character of which Luther at first rejected and never cordially received. And without

(turn over)

4. A leaf (f 204) of the manuscript draft of *Church and State*, BM MS Egerton 2801. See p 139.

not chargeable with *apostacy* from a faith, he had never acknowledged, or from a church to which he had never appertained. Neither in the Prophet nor in his system, therefore, can we find the predicted *Anti-Christ*, *i.e.* a usurped power[1] *in* the church itself, which, in the name of Christ, and pretending his authority, systematically subverts or counteracts the peculiar aims and purposes of Christ's mission; and which, vesting in a mortal his incommunicable headship, destroys (and exchanges for the contrary) the essential contra-distinguishing marks or characters of his kingdom on earth.[2] But apply it, as Wickliffe, Luther,* and indeed all the first Reformers

* And (be it observed) without any reference to the Apocalypse, the canonical character of which Luther at first rejected, and never cordially received.[3] And without the least sympathy with Luther's suspicions on this head, but on the contrary receiving this sublime poem as the undoubted work of the Apostolic age, and admiring in it the most perfect specimen of symbolic poetry, I am as little disposed to cite it on the present occasion—convinced as I am and hope shortly to convince others, that in the whole series of its magnificent imagery there is not a single symbol, that can be even plausibly interpreted of either the

[1] BM MS Egerton 2801 ff 204–7v contains a ms draft in C's hand of the text from here to the end of the paragraph, together with the whole footnote. It is reproduced below, App C, pp 222–4. For a reproduction of f 204, showing text and beginning of footnote, see the illustration facing p 138.

[2] Cf the "Brief Dialogue—between B. A. and S. T. C." in N Q:

> B. A.... You seem to make three Churches, first, the National.
> S. T. C. Right.
> B. A. Then the Catholic or Church of Christ.
> S. T. C. Right! But the third?
> B. A. The Church of Antichrist.
> S. T. C. Christ forbid! I thought, I had shewn that Mahomet or the Mahometan Caliphate & Imanry could not be the Antichrist, even because Mahomet neither was or pretended to be of, or in the Catholic Church—acted in his own name, and by an authority directly given to him and not derived from Christ, nor in Christ's name. No! I admit but of two possible *Churches*, speaking of Churches *according* to the *Idea*: viz. the National, and the Catholic or Christian Church. But speaking *historically* and in respect of the Realization of the Idea, I subdivide the Catholic Church into the two unequal, and at different aeras varying, proportions: that in which Antichrist continued to reign, and continued to be acknowleged; and that, the Members of which had emancipated themselves, and protesting against the Usurpation had placed themselves under Christ, as the *Alone* Head, under a Spiritual, as the only possible, Head of the Church Universal.
> B. A. What then? You hold the Roman Catholic for a true Church?
> S. T. C. With John Milton I hold the *Roman Catholic* for one of the Pope's Bulls—a round triangle—a square Circle—a particular Universal—a Roman (ergo, not Catholic, ergo, Uncatholic Catholic Church...).

N Q ff 46–46v.

[3] Luther writes in "Preface to the Revelation of St John" (1522): "I miss so many things in this book that I cannot hold it to be either apostolic or prophetic...it is not the way of the apostles to recount visions, but to prophesy in clear and simple words." *Reformation Writings of Martin Luther* II 309.

did to the Papacy, and Papal Hierarchy; and we understand at once the grounds of the great apostle's premonition, that this Antichrist could not appear till after the dissolution of the Latin empire, and the

Pope, the Turks, or Napoleon Buonaparte. Of charges not attaching to the moral character, there are few, if any, that I should be more anxious to avoid than that of being an affecter of paradoxes. But the dread of other men's thoughts shall not tempt me to withhold a truth, which the strange errors grounded on the contrary assumption render important. And in the thorough assurance of its truth I make the assertion, that the perspicuity, and (with singularly few exceptions even for *us*) the uniform intelligibility, and close consecutive meaning, verse by verse, with the simplicity and grandeur of the plan, and the admirable *ordonnance* of the parts, are among the prominent beauties of the Apocalypse.[1] Nor do I doubt that the substance and main argument of this sacred oratorio, or drama *sui generis* (the Prometheus of Eschylus comes the nearest to *the kind*)[2] were supplied by John the Evangelist: though I incline with Eusebius[3] to find the poet himself in John, an Elder and Contemporary of the Church of Ephesus.

P.S.—It may remove, or at least mitigate the objections to the palliative language in which I have spoken of the doctrines of the Catholic Church, if I remind the Reader that the *Roman* Catholic Church dates its true origin from the Council of Trent.[4] Widely differing from my valued and affectionately

[1] Characteristically C applies literary criteria (organic form exhibited through *ordonnance*) to this Biblical question; cf *CIS* passim. For C on the relation of parts to whole in a poem, see *BL* ch 14 (1907) II 10. In an annotation on the half-title of Lacunza *The Coming of Messiah* vol II C called the Apocalypse "a Symbolic Drama.... I know indeed no Poem ancient or modern, unless it be the Paradise Lost, that can be compared with it either in the felicity of its structure or the Sublimity of the parts." In an annotation on II 91–3 C writes of the "false assumption, that the Apocalyptic Vision contains a series of particular Predictions no where else to be found in the Scripture, by the decyphering of which they [the interpreters] expect to prognosticate" and of the second fault of such interpreters, "their utter want of all poetic Genius, and all Eye, Taste and Tact for Poetry generally, with a total ignorance of the character and canons of Symbolic Poesy and Species. Hence, they forget—if men can be said to forget what they had never learnt, that the Apocalypse is a POEM, and a Poem composed by a Hebrew Poet, after the peculiar type of Hebrew Poetry." Cf also C's plan, given in a footnote to *LS*, "to have translated the Apocalypse into verse, as a Poem...and to have annexed a Commentary in Prose". See *LS* (*CC*) 147n and nn 2, 3.

[2] On the Apocalypse as a sacred drama—and as C puts it, a drama "in a class of its own"—see J. G. Eichhorn *Commentarius in Apocalypsin Joannis* (Göttingen 1791) and *Einleitung in das Neue Testament* II 334ff. See also *LS* (*CC*) 147. Cf "On the *Prometheus* of Aeschylus", read at the Royal Society of Literature 18 May 1825: *Misc* 55–83.

[3] Cf "It is likely that the second [i.e. John the Presbyter, of Ephesus]—if we cannot accept the first—saw the Revelation that bears the name of John." Eusebius (c 260–c 340) *Ecclesiastical History* 3.39. This and other passages are discussed by Eichhorn *Einleitung in das Neue Testament* II 385, 387.

[4] The Council of Trent (1545–63) defined the essentials of the Roman Catholic faith and explicitly repudiated Protestant doctrines. It did not mark the beginning of the Roman Catholic Church, but of a clearly formulated doctrinal system.

extinction of the Imperial Power in Rome—and the cause why the Bishop of Constantinople, with all imaginable good wishes and disposition to do the same, could never raise the Patriarchate of the

---

respected friend, the Rev. Edward Irving, in his *interpretations* of the Apocalypse and the Book of Daniel,[1] and no less in his *estimation* of the latter, and while I honour his courage, as a Christian minister, almost as much as I admire his eloquence as a writer, yet protesting against his somewhat too adventurous speculations on the Persons of the Trinity and the Body of our Lord[2]—I have great delight in extracting (*from his "Sermons, Lectures, and Discourses,"* vol. iii. p. 870)[3] and declaring my cordial assent to the following just observations: viz.—"that *after* the Reformation had taken firmer root, and when God had provided a purer Church, the Council of Trent did corroborate and decree into unalterable laws and constitutions of the Church all those impostures and innovations of the Roman See, which had been in a state of uncertainty, perhaps of permission or even of custom; but which every man till then had been free to testify against, and against which, in fact, there never wanted those in each successive generation who did testify. The Council of Trent *ossified* all those ulcers and blotches which had deformed the Church, and stamped the hitherto much doubted and controverted prerogative of the Pope with the highest authority recognized in the Church." Then first was the Catholic converted and particularized into the Romish Church, the Church of the Papacy.

No less cordially do I concur with Mr. Irving in his remark in the following page. For I too, "am free to confess and avow moreover, that I believe the soil of the Catholic Church, when Luther arose, was of a stronger mould, fitted to bear forest trees and cedars of God, than the soil of the Protestant Church in the times of Whitfield and Wesley,[4] which (*though sown with the same word—? qu.*)[5]

---

[1] The guarded reference to Edward Irving is an attempt to pay tribute to the man C expected much from after he first heard him preach at the Chapel at Hatton Garden while at the same time dissociating himself from Irving's later fanaticism. In *Babylon and Infidelity Foredoomed of God* (2 vols Glasgow 1828) and in *Church and State Responsible to Christ and to One Another* (Glasgow 1829), Irving produced the wildest interpretation of Daniel and Revelation. For C's protests see *NED* II 336 and *TT* 15 May 1830, in which he distinguishes between Irving's "purest eloquence" and outbreaks of "almost madman's babble". A. L. Drummond *Edward Irving and His Circle* (1937) traces Irving's career and changing relations with C. See also C's marginalia on Irving in *LR* IV 399–415. See above, p 133 and n 1.

[2] It was mainly these "adventurous speculations" that gained Irving notoriety and ultimately dismissal. C writes of Irving's "ignorance respecting the Absolute, the abysmal Ground of the Trinity—his consequent utter misapprehension of the Trinity itself, neither apprehending aright the unity or the distinctities—hence his ignorance of the subsistences in the only begotten *Word* as the pleroma—and of the Father, as the I AM correlative to the Ὢν or HE IS, the Son εν τῳ κολπῳ τοῦ πατρος [John 1.18], hence his fantastic notions respecting an all powerful Personage or Individual whom he calls the Holy Ghost". Annotation on Irving *Sermons*... (3 vols 1828) II 351.

[3] Ibid III 869–70 (var), C supplying the first two clauses.

[4] C had a low opinion of the Church in the eighteenth century, when George Whitefield (1714–70) and Charles Wesley (1707–88) sought its reformation; cf below, p 177 and n 2. C substitutes Whitefield for "Romaine"—i.e. William Romaine (1714–95), Whitefield's disciple—in Irving's passage.

[5] Irving wrote: "which, though sown with the same word and impregnated by the same quickening Spirit,". HNC in *C&S* (1839) omits "—? *qu.*".

Greek empire into a Papacy. The Bishops of the other Rome became the slaves of the Ottoman, the moment they ceased to be the subjects of the Emperor.

hath brought forth only stunted undergrowths, and creeping brushwood." I too, "believe, that the faith of the Protestant Church in Britain had come to a lower ebb, and that it is even now at a lower ebb,[1] than was the faith of the Papal Church when the Spirit of the Lord was able to quicken in it and draw forth of it, such men as Luther, and Melancthon, and Bullinger, Calvin, Bucer, and Latimer, and Ridley, and a score others whom I might name."[2]

And now, as the conclusion of this long note, let me be permitted to add a word or two of Edward Irving himself. That he possesses my unqualified esteem as a man, is only saying, that I know him, and am neither blinded by envy nor bigotry. But my name has been brought into connexion with his, on points that regard his public ministry; and he himself has publicly distinguished me as his friend on public grounds;[3] and in proof of my confidence in his regard, I have not the least apprehension of forfeiting it by a frank declaration of what I think. Well, then! I have no faith in his prophesyings;[4] small sympathy with his

[1] C's endorsement of this low estimate of the Church "even now" is surprising, but it expresses his deep dissatisfaction and also his determination to shock his readers out of their complacency.

[2] Irving *Sermons* III 871 (var), C adding Bucer and omitting John Knox. The list includes the main Continental and English reformers. Philipp Melanchthon (1497–1560), a fellow-worker with Luther and author of the great Protestant work of dogmatic theology, *Loci communes rerum theologicarum*; Johann Heinrich Bullinger (1504–75), a Swiss reformer and Protestant theologian who was influential in England and became Regius Professor of Divinity at Cambridge; for C's views on Calvin (1509–64) see *C 17th C* 185 and passim; Martin Butzer or Bucer (1491–1551) was a German reformer; Hugh Latimer (1485–1555), bp of Worcester, preached sermons advocating reformation; Nicholas Ridley (c 1500–55), bp of London, another reformer. Together with Latimer and Cranmer, Ridley was burned for his supposedly heretical views.

[3] C refers to Irving's long and affectionate dedication to *For Missionaries after the Apostolical School* (1825), in which Irving notes that C has been misunderstood. Irving expressed "the gratitude of a disciple to a wise and generous teacher". Cf Lamb to Leigh Hunt: "Irving...is a humble disciple at the foot of Gamaliel S. T. C. Judge how his own sectarists must stare when I tell you he has dedicated a book to S. T. C., acknowledging to have learnt more of the nature of Faith, Christianity, and Christian Church, from him than from all men he ever conversed with." *LL* II 457. In a later letter Lamb reports: "Some friend told [Irving], 'This dedication will do you no Good,' *i.e.* not in the world's repute or with your own people. 'That is a reason for doing it,' quoth Irving." To Bernard Barton 23 Mar 1825. *LL* II 464. For one of C's marginal comments on *For Missionaries* see *IS* 297–8.

[4] On 8 Feb 1826, C wrote: "To... the study of the Apocalypse I was impelled solely by the rumours, that had reached me, of my friend, Edward Irving's, Aberrations (for such, I fear, they are) into the Cloud-land of Prophecies". C goes on to say: "But these studies were against my inclinations & cravings. I needed Prayer...". N F° f 28v. In 1828 John Sterling reported that C said that Irving failed when he relied on Daniel and Revelation, but was on sounder ground when he relied on "passages in the Gospels and in St. Paul, that the Apostles interpreted the ancient prophecies as foreshowing a second advent of Christ

We will now proceed to the Second Part, intended as a humble aid to a just appreciation of the measure, which under the auspices

fulminations; and in certain peculiarities of his *theological* system, as distinct from his religious principles, I cannot see my way.[1] But I hold withal, and not the less firmly for these discrepancies in our moods and judgments, that EDWARD IRVING possesses more of the spirit and purpose of the first Reformers, that he has more of the Head and Heart, the Life, the Unction, and the genial power of MARTIN LUTHER, than any man now alive; yea, than any man of this and the last century.[2] I see in EDWARD IRVING a minister of Christ after the order of Paul; and if the points, in which I think him either erroneous, or excessive and *out of bounds*, have been at any time a subject of serious regret with me, this regret has arisen principally or altogether from the apprehension of their narrowing the sphere of his influence, from the too great probability that they may furnish occasion or pretext for withholding or withdrawing many from those momentous truths, which the age especially needs, and for the enforcement of which he hath been so highly and especially gifted! Finally, my friend's intellect is too instinct with life, too *potential* to remain stationary; and assuming, as every satisfied believer must be supposed to do, the truth of my own views, I look forward with confident hope to a time when his soul shall have perfected her victory over the dead letter of the senses and its apparitions in the sensuous understanding; when the Halycon[3] IDEAS shall have alit on the surging sea of his conceptions,[4]

in the body upon earth. It is for Mr Irving's opponents to show reason for dissenting from the Apostles on this point." But at a breakfast party with WW and Aders on 18 Jun 1828, HCR reported that C said that he had silenced Irving by showing "how completely he had mistaken the sense of the revelations and prophecies" and concluded "I think him *mad*—literally mad". *C Talker* 335, 344.

1 Cf C's annotation on Irving *Sermons* II 351 (end of the same note in which he writes of Irving's misconceptions of the Trinity): "I begin to fear that I ought to regret my intercourse with Mr I. on his own account. For if he had never been tempted out of the popular way of thinking, & guided wholly & exclusively by his honest feelings & the letter of Scripture, treating each subject as an integer, standing on its own grounds, and exerting its appropriate influences within its own sphere, disregarding its connections with other truths, otherwise than as *one* among many others, and thus regarding Theology as a bag of Coins, each of which had a value for itself & might be put out to interest on its own account—he might by his Zeal and exalted disinterestedness and extraordinary eloquence have been the Benefactor of thousands & ten thousands—giving them the medicines, to each what the disease needest, without troubling either the Patients or himself with any *System* of rational Pathology grounded on more general principles of Physiology, and at all events would have avoided his offensive Errors into which a supposed System has seduced him."

2 In an annotation on Lacunza *Coming of Messiah* I cxxvi, C calls him "my Luther-hearted Friend".

3 A favourite image; cf *To William Wordsworth* line 90: *PW* (EHC) I 408.

4 Implicit is C's familiar distinction between reason and understanding and his belief that "Reason and Religion differ only as a two-fold application of the same power". *SM* (*CC*) 59. If Irving were enslaved to the understanding he could have religious conceptions but not true religious ideas. Cf also an annotation on Irving *Sermons* I (140) xxxiv–xxxviii: "...my Friend...has plunged into the saddest error of the Romish

of Mr. Peel and the Duke of Wellington is now the Law of the land.[10] This portion of the volume was written while the measure was yet *in prospectu;* before even the particular clauses of the Bill were made public. It was written to explain and vindicate the author's refusal to

Which then shall quite forget to rave,
While Birds of Calm sit brooding on the charmed wave.
MILTON[1]

But to return from the *Personal*, for which I have little taste at any time, and the contrary when it stands in any connection with myself—in order to the removal of one main impediment to the spiritual resuscitation of Protestantism, it seems to me indispensable, that in freedom and unfearing faith, with that courage which cannot but flow from the inward and life-like assurance, "that neither death, nor things present nor things to come, nor heighth, nor depth,nor any other creature, shall be able to separate us from the love of God, which is in Christ Jesus our Lord"—(Rom. viii. 38, 39)[2]—the rulers of our Churches and our teachers of theology should meditate and draw the obvious, though perhaps unpalatable, inferences from the following two or three plain truths:—First, that Christ, "the Spirit of Truth,"[3] has promised to be with his Church even to the end.[4] Secondly: that Christianity was described as a Tree to be raised from the Seed, so described by Him who brought the Seed from Heaven and first sowed it.[5] Lastly: that in the process of Evolution,[6] there are in every plant growths of transitory use and duration. "The integuments of the seed, having fulfilled their destined office of protection, burst and decay. After the leaves have unfolded, the Cotyledons, that had performed their functions, wither and drop off."* The husk is a genuine growth of "The Staff of Life;" yet we must separate it from the grain. It is, therefore, the cowardice of faithless[8] superstition, if we stand in greater awe of the palpable interpolations of vermin; if we shrink from the removal of excrescences that contain nothing of nobler parentage than maggots of moth or chafer. Let us cease to confound oak-apples with acorns; still less, though gilded by the fashion of the day, let us mistake them for Golden Pippins or Renates.†

* Smith's Introduction to Botany.[7]

† The fruit from a Pippin grafted on a Pippin, is called a Rennet, *i.e.*, Renate (re-natus) or twice born.[9]

Church...condensing the great *Ideas*, the living Spiritual Verities, of the Gospel into Idols— = Things, i.e. phaenomena or appearances defined either for sight or for the fancy by outlines...". Note dated 1 Jan 1829.

[1] *On the Morning of Christ's Nativity* lines 67–8 (var). At this point, and after the quotation from Rom 8.38, 39 (below), MS Egerton 2801 refers the printer to another page (which has not survived); see App C, below, p 224.

[2] The two versions are conflated.

[3] John 16.13.

[4] Matt 28.20.

[5] Matt 7.17–24.

[6] Cf above, p 66 and n 2.

[7] James Edward Smith *An Introduction to Physiological and Systematical Botany* (1807) 94.

[8] The ms ends here: BM MS Egerton 2801 f 207^{v}.

[9] C copied this detail from the brief biographical preface to Sidney's *Arcadia* (1674) into his notebook in 1801 (*CN* I 1012; see 1011n). *OED* gives the derivation from *reine*, *reinette*, instead, and Skeat *Etymological Dictionary* calls the *re-natus* derivation a mistake.

[10] The Bill was introduced into the Commons by Sir Robert Peel and into the Lords by the Duke of Wellington in Mar 1829. See Introduction, above, p li.

sign a Petition[1] against any change in the scheme of Law and Policy established at the Revolution. But as the arguments are in no respect affected by this circumstance; nay, as their constant reference to, and dependence on, one fixed General Principle, which will at once explain both why the author finds the actual Bill so much less objectionable than he had feared, and yet so much less complete and satisfactory than he had wished, will be rendered more striking by the reader's consciousness that the arguments were suggested by no wish or purpose either of attacking or supporting any particular measure: it has not been thought necessary or advisable to alter the form. Nay, if the author be right in his judgment, that the Bill lately passed,[2] if characterized by its own contents and capabilities, really *is*—with or without any such intention on the part of its framers—a STEPPING-STONE, and nothing more; whether to the subversion[3] or to the more perfect establishment of the Constitution in Church and State, must be determined by other causes; the Bill in itself is equally fit for either—*Tros Tyriusve*,[4] it offers the same facilities of transit to both, though with a foreclosure to the first comer.—If this be a right, as it is the author's sincere judgment and belief, there is a propriety in retaining the language of anticipation. Mons adhuc parturit: the "ridiculus Mus" was but an omen.[5]

[1] At the beginning of 1829 meetings were held throughout the country to petition Parliament not to change the laws relating to Catholics. The dubious means used to collect signatures were questioned in Parliament. In sentiment many of the petitions re-echoed Lord Eldon's views "that if ever a Roman Catholic was permitted to form part of the legislature of this country, or to hold any of the great executive offices in the country, from that moment the Sun of Great Britain would set". Hansard NS XX (Feb–Mar 1829) 17; Machin 144, 148–9.

[2] This passage must have been written after 13 Apr 1829, when the Bill was passed.

[3] Later utterances express fear of subversion; see *TT* 14 Jun 1834.

[4] Virgil *Aeneid* 1.574 (var). "Trojan or Tyrian [I shall treat with no distinction]".

[5] "Parturient montes, nascetur ridiculus mus". Horace *Ars Poetica* 139. "Mountains will labour, to birth will come a laughter-rousing mouse". Tr H. R. Fairclough (LCL 1926) 463; cf House 166.

SECOND PART:
OR, AIDS TO
A RIGHT APPRECIATION OF

THE BILL

ADMITTING CATHOLICS
TO SIT IN BOTH HOUSES
OF PARLIAMENT, &c. &c.

'Αμέλει, μὰ τὸν Δί' οὐκ ἐνασπιδώσομαι·
Λέξω δ' ὑπὲρ 'Ετερογνωμόνων, ἅ μοι δοκεῖ·
Καίτοι δέδοικα πολλά· τούς τε γὰρ τρόπους
Τοὺς ξυμπολίτων οἶδα χαίροντας σφόδρα,
'Εάν τις αὐτοὺς εὐλογῇ καὶ τὴν πόλιν,
'Ανὴρ ἀλαζὼν, καὶ δίκαια κἄδικα·
Κἀνταῦθα λανθάνουσ' ἀπεμπολώμενοι.
'ΑΡΙΣΤΟΦ. Αχαρνῆς. 367.[1]

[1] Aristophanes *The Acharnians* 368–74 (var). In line 369 C has altered Λακεδαιμονίων ("Spartans") to 'Ετερογνωμονων ("those holding heterodox views"); in line 371 he has altered τῶν ἀγροίκων ("of rustic natures") to ξυμπολίτων ("of [our] fellow citizens").
Tr:

I'll never hug myself within my shield;
I'll speak my mind, moreover, about the Spartans,
And yet forsooth a secret anxious fear
Appals me; for I know the turn and temper
Of rustic natures, then delighted most
When from some bold declaimer, right or wrong,
They hear their country's praises and their own;
Delighted but deluded all the while,
Unconsciously bamboozled and befool'd.

Tr John Hookham Frere (1840) 22–3. On Frere and his translations of Aristophanes see below, p 149 n 1.

TO A FRIEND[1]

YES, Sir, I estimate the beauty and benefit of what you have called "A harmony in fundamentals, and a conspiration in[a] the constituent parts of the Body Politic," as highly as the sturdiest zealot for the petition, which I have declined to subscribe. If I met a man, who should deny that an imperium in imperio was in itself an evil,[2] I would not attempt to reason with him: he is too ignorant. Or if, conceding this, he should deny that the Romish Priesthood in Ireland does in fact constitute an *imperium in imperio*, I yet would not argue the matter with him: for he must be a Bigot. But my objection to the argument is, that it is nothing to the purpose. And even so, with regard to the arguments grounded on the dangerous errors and superstititions of the Romish Church. They may be all very true; but they are nothing to the purpose. Without any loss they might *pair off* with "the Heroes of Trafalgar and Waterloo," and "our Catholic ancestors, to whom we owe our Magna Charta," on the other side. If the *prevention* of an evil were the point in question, *then* indeed! But the day of prevention has long past by. The evil exists: and neither rope, sword, nor sermon, neither suppression nor conversion, can remove it. Not that I think slightingly of the last; but even those who hope more sanguinely, than I can pretend to do respecting the effects ultimately to result from the labours of missionaries, the dispersion of controversial tracts, and whatever other lawful means and implements it may be in our power to employ—even these must admit that if the remedy could cope with the magnitude and inveteracy of the disease, it is wholly inadequate to the urgency of the symptoms. In this instance it would be no easy

[a] 1st ed: of

[1] Since *C&S* partly originated in remarks addressed to J. H. Frere, the friend may be Frere. It may, however, be a stylistic device; cf *BL* ch 13 and above, p 5 and n. *The Acharnians*, from which C selected his epigraph to this pt II, was one of the plays Frere translated, which makes the "Friend" referred to throughout *C&S* even likelier to be Frere. C at this time had Frere's ms of the translation; see C's will, dated 17 Sept 1829; *CL* VI 999.

[2] For C's consistent opposition to any *imperium in imperio* (an empire within an empire, or an authority within the jurisdiction of another authority), see Introduction, above, p xli and n 2; cf also *LS* (*CC*) 170 and n 2.

matter to take the horse to the water; and the rest of the proverb you know. But why do I waste words? There is and can be but one question: and there is and can be but one way of stating it.[1] A great numerical majority of the inhabitants of one integral *part* of the realm profess a religion hostile to that professed by the majority of the whole realm: and a religion, too, which the latter regard, and have had good reason to regard, as equally hostile to liberty, and the sacred rights of conscience generally. In fewer words, three-fourths of His Majesty's Irish subjects are Roman Catholics, with a papal priesthood, while three-fourths of the sum total of his Majesty's subjects are Protestants. This with its causes and consequences is the evil. It is not in our power, by any immediate or direct means, to effect its removal. The point, therefore, to be determined is: Will the measures now in contemplation be likely to diminish or to aggravate it? And to the determination of this point on the probabilities suggested by reason and experience, I would gladly be aidant, as far as my poor mite of judgment will enable me.

Let us, however, first discharge what may well be deemed a debt of justice from every well educated Protestant to his Catholic fellow-subjects of the Sister Island. At least, let us ourselves understand the true cause of the evil as it now exists. To what, and to whom is the present state of Ireland mainly to be attributed? This should be the question: and to this I answer aloud, that it is mainly attributable to those, who during a period of little less than a whole century used as a *Substitute* what Providence had given into their hand as an *Opportunity;* who chose to consider as *superseding* the most sacred duty a code of law, that [a]could have been[b] excused only on the plea, that it enabled them to perform it! To the sloth and improvidence, the weakness and wickedness, of the gentry, clergy, and governors of Ireland, who persevered in preferring intrigue, violence, and selfish expatriation to a system of preventive and remedial measures, the efficacy of which had been warranted for them by the whole provincial history of ancient Rome, cui *pacare* subactos summa erat

[a–b] 1st ed: can be

[1] C criticised Lord Grenville's speech of 17 Apr 1821 for his failing to see the essential question and accused him of spouting away "like a Lead-gutter in a Thaw"; see Introduction, above, p xlix and n 2. In the third of the projected "Letters to C. A. Tulk", C planned to deal with "The ⟨true⟩ *Root* of the Question: i.e. the actual Ground of the Danger on each side". N 20 f 9v. The definition of the essential question (BM MS Egerton 2800 ff 109–9v), quoted in the Introduction, above, p l n 1, may have been intended for one of the "Letters to C. A. Tulk" in 1821. The ms note is given in full in App D 1, below, pp 227–8.

sapientia;[1] warranted for them by the happy results of the few exceptions to the contrary scheme unhappily pursued by their and our ancestors.

I can imagine no work of genius that would more appropriately decorate the dome or wall of a Senate house, than an abstract of Irish history from the landing of Strongbow to the battle of the Boyne,[2] or a yet later period, embodied in intelligible emblems—an allegorical history-piece designed in the spirit of a Rubens or a Buonarroti, and with the wild lights, portentous shades, and saturated colours of a Rembrandt, Caravaggio, and Spagnoletti.[3] To complete the great moral and political lesson by the historic contrast, nothing more would be required, than by some equally effective means to possess the mind of the spectator with the state and condition of ancient Spain, at less than half a century from the final conclusion of an obstinate and almost unremitting conflict of two hundred years by Agrippa's subjugation of the Cantabrians, omnibus Hispaniae populis devictis et *pacatis*.[4] At the breaking up of the empire, the

[1] "Whose highest wisdom was to *pacify* the defeated". Probably C's own Latin. The conclusion of this paragraph of *C&S* and most of the subsequent one are a revision of a rough draft of an essay entitled "Paragraphs on the Catholic Question", BM MS Egerton 2800 (watermarked 1826) ff 110–10ᵛ. In the ms C writes (f 110ᵛ, after a prior attempt f 110): "The answer must be in the knowlege in detail of the Colonial Policy & Principles of the Romans, istiusque *Romanissimae* Scientiae de artibus et mediis devictas *pacandi* regiones et populos", i.e. "and of that most *Roman* Science of the arts and methods of *pacifying* defeated regions and populations".

[2] That is, from the landing of Richard de Clare, 2nd Earl of Pembroke and Strigul, in May 1170 until July 1690, when the victory of William III over the former King James II inaugurated the Protestant ascendancy in Ireland.

[3] In the ms fragment (see note above), C writes of "a crowded History-piece", with "all the portentous shades, savage Lights and saturated Colours of a Caravaggio or a Spagnoletto". MS Egerton 2800 f 110. In published and unpublished works, C reveals acute sensitivity to pictorial art; see comments on Sir George Beaumont's works (*CN* II 1899 and n), one of which he likened to the work of the Flemish painter Peter Paul Rubens (1577–1640). C probably first saw works by Michelangelo Buonarotti (1475–1564) in July 1799 (*CL* I 522 and VI 1012), and saw Michelangelo Merisi da Caravaggio's (c 1569–1609) famous *Beheading of St John* in Valletta in 1805. A painting of Cain killing Abel, at Valletta, ascribed to Jusepe or José de Ribera, called lo Spagnoletto (c 1590–1652), was in fact by his pupil Bartolommeo Passante. *CN* II 2101n. C refers to Rembrandt (1606–69) in Dec 1803 (*CN* I 1755).

[4] "All the peoples of Spain being subdued and *pacified*". Cf Florus *Epitome* 2.33.1: "Omnibus ad occasum et meridiem pacatis gentibus". Augustus sent Agrippa to Spain to quell the Cantabrians. After he had overcome all resistance in 19 B.C., he divided the country into three regions, ordered the building of good roads, founded new cities, and persuaded even semi-nomadic people to adopt a settled urban existence.

West Goths conquered the country and made division of the lands. Then came eight centuries of Moorish domination. Yet so deeply had Roman wisdom impressed the fairest characters of the Roman mind, that at this very hour, if we except a comparatively insignificant portion of Arabic Derivatives, the natives throughout the whole peninsula speak a language less differing from the Romana Rustica, or Provincial Latin, of the times of Lucan and Seneca,[1] than any two of its dialects from each other. The time approaches, I trust, when our political economists may study the science of the *provincial* policy of the ancients in detail, under the auspices of hope, for immediate and practical purposes.[2]

In my own mind I am persuaded, that the necessity of the penal and precautionary statutes passed under Elizabeth and the three succeeding reigns, is to be found as much in the passions and prejudices of the one party, as in the dangerous dispositions of the other. The best excuse for this cruel code[3] is the imperfect knowledge and mistaken maxims common to both parties. It is only to a limited extent, that laws can be wiser than the nation for which they are enacted. The annals of the first five or six centuries of the Hebrew nation in Palestine present an almost continued history of disobedience, of laws broken or utterly lost sight of, of maxims violated, and schemes of consummate wisdom left unfulfilled. Even a yet diviner seed must be buried and undergo an apparent corruption before—at a late period—it shot up and could appear in its own kind.[4] In our judgments respecting *actions* we must be guided by the idea, but in applying the rule to the *agents*, by comparison.[5] To

[1] C suggests that the Vulgar Latin of c A.D. 60 is closer to Spanish than, say, Spanish is to Rumanian. Cf the ms: "...the Natives...speak a Language far less ~~unlike~~ dissimilar from the Latin actually spoken by the ~~Mass of the~~ People at large during the four first Centuries of the Christian Aera, than this ⟨*Lingua Romana Rustica*⟩ from the ~~Latin of~~ artefact Latin of Literature & *Patrician* Rome". MS Egerton 2800 ff 110–10^{v}. Lucan the poet (Marcus Annaeus Lucanus, A.D. 39–65) and Seneca the philosopher (Lucius Annaeus Seneca, c 4 B.C.–A.D. 65), both born in Spain, were outstanding writers of Latin of their period.

[2] For the importance C assigned to this branch of study, see his notes prepared for a review of *An Inquiry into the Colonial Policy of the European Powers* (2 vols Edinburgh 1803) by Henry Peter Brougham (BM MS Egerton 2800 ff 106–8) and "Observations on Egypt" (Egerton 2800 ff 118–26), the second published in *EOT* (*CC*) III 188–99.

[3] After the defeat of James II at the Battle of the Boyne in July 1690 by William III, the Treaty of Limerick inflicted a new penal code on the Roman Catholics: they were excluded from Parliament, were not allowed to vote or sit on juries, to serve as soldiers and sailors, their lands did not descend intact but were divided among all the sons, and they could not buy land or inherit it from Protestants.

[4] Cf John 12.24, also Matt 13.

[5] Cf *Friend* (*CC*) I 324–5, 425.

speak gently of our forefathers is at once piety and policy. Nor let it be forgotten, that only by making the detection of their errors the occasion of our own wisdom, do we acquire a right to censure them at all.

Whatever may be thought of the settlement that followed the battle of the Boyne and the extinction of the war in Ireland, yet when this had been made and submitted to, it would have been the far wiser policy, I doubt not, to have provided for the safety of the Constitution by improving the quality of the elective franchise, leaving the eligibility open, or like the former limited only by considerations of property. Still, however, the scheme of exclusion and disqualification had its plausible side. The ink was scarcely dry on the parchment-rolls and proscription-lists of the Popish parliament.[1] The crimes of the man were generalized into attributes of his faith; and the Irish Catholics collectively were held accomplices in the perfidy and baseness of the king. Alas! his immediate adherents had afforded too great colour to the charge. The Irish massacre was in the mouth of every Protestant, not as an event to be remembered, but as a thing of recent expectation, fear still blending with the sense of deliverance.[2] At no time, therefore, could the disqualifying system have been enforced with so little reclamation of the conquered party, or with so little outrage on the general feeling of the country. There was no time, when it was so capable of being indirectly useful as a *sedative* in order to the application of the remedies directly indicated, or as a counter-power reducing to inactivity whatever disturbing forces might have interfered with their operation. And *had* this use been made of these exclusive laws, and had they been enforced as the precursors and negative conditions, but above all as *bonâ fide* accompaniments of a process of *emancipation*, properly and worthily so named, the code would at this day have been remembered in Ireland only as when recalling a dangerous fever of our boyhood we

[1] The Irish "Patriot Parliament" of 1689 called by James II, with its large Catholic majority, repealed the Acts of Settlement and Explanation, restoring the lands to those who possessed them on 22 Oct 1641, the day before the Irish Rebellion had begun, and passed the Act of Attainder, which subjected the 2400 persons (mainly landholders) who had left Ireland and were attainted of high treason to return, surrender, and stand trial or have their property confiscated.

[2] Not only in the mouth of every Protestant: James II himself, at the Patriot Parliament, when more severe penalties had been proposed in dealing with the "rebels", asked: "What, gentlemen, are you for another '41?" In the Irish Massacre (at the beginning of the Rebellion of 1641) thousands of English and Scottish Protestants were killed—exaggerated accounts in England claimed the figure to be in the hundreds of thousands, with priests as the ringleaders of the massacre.

think of the nauseous drugs and drenching-horn, and congratulate ourselves that our doctors now-a-days know how to manage these things less coarsely. But this angry code was neglected as an opportunity, and mistaken for a *substitute*: et hinc illae lacrymae![1]

And at this point I find myself placed again in connection with the main question, and which I contend to be the pertinent question, *viz.*, The evil being admitted, and its immediate removal impossible, is the admission of Catholics into both Houses of Legislature likely to mitigate or to aggravate it? And here the problem is greatly narrowed by the fact, that no man pretends to regard this admissibility as a *direct* remedy, or specific antidote for the diseases, under which Ireland labours. No! it is to act, we are told, as introductory to the direct remedies. In short, this Emancipation is to be, like the penal code which it repeals, a *sedative*, though in the opposite form of an anodyne cordial, that will itself be entitled to the name of a remedial measure in proportion as it shall be found to render the body susceptible of the more direct remedies that are to follow. Its object is to tranquillize Ireland. Safety, peace, and good neighbourhood, influx of capital, diminution of absenteeism, industrious habits, and a long train of blessings will follow. But the indispensable condition, the *causa causarum et causatorum*,[2] is general tranquillity. Such is the language held by all the more intelligent advocates and encomiasts[a] of Emancipation. The sense of the question therefore is, will the measure tend to produce tranquillity?

Now it is evident, that there are two parties to be satisfied, and that the measure is likely to effect this purpose according as it is calculated to satisfy reasonable men of both. Reasonable men are easily satisfied: would they were as numerous as they are pacable![3] We must, however, understand the word comparatively, as including all those on both sides, who by their superior information, talents, or property, are least likely to be under the dominion of vulgar antipathies, and who may be rationally expected to influence (and in certain cases, and in alliance with a vigorous government, to over-rule) the feelings and sentiments of the rest.

Now the two indispensable conditions under which alone the measure can permanently satify the reasonable, that is, the *satis-*

[a] 1st ed: economists

[1] "And hence these tears", a phrase used by Terence in *Andria* (line 125), became proverbial in Latin literature (e.g. Horace *Epistles* 1.19.41); cf *Lects 1795* (*CC*) 288 and n.

[2] "The cause of causes and effects".

[3] *OED* quotes this (misdating it 1834) for the earliest use of "pacable" (meaning capable of being pacified). A misprint for "placable"?

fiable, of both parties, supposing that in both parties such men exist, and that they form the influencive class in both, are these. First, that the Bill for the repeal of the exclusive statutes, and the admission of Catholics to the full privileges of British subjects, shall be grounded on some determinate PRINCIPLE, which involving interests and duties common to both parties as British subjects, both parties may be expected to recognize, and required to maintain inviolable. Second, that this principle shall contain in itself an evident definite and unchangeable *boundary*, a line of demarcation, a *ne plus ultra*, which in all reasonable men and lovers of their country shall preclude the *wish* to pass beyond it, and extinguish the hope of so doing in such as are neither.

But though the measure should be such as to satisfy all reasonable men, still it is possible that the number and influence of these may not be sufficient to leaven the mass,[1] or to over-rule the agitators. I admit this; but instead of weakening what I have here said, it affords an additional argument in its favour. For if an argument satisfactory to the reasonable part should nevertheless fail in securing tranquillity, still less can the result be expected from an arbitrary adjustment that can satisfy no part. If a measure grounded on principle, and possessing the character of an ultimatum should still, through the prejudices and passions of one or of both parties, fail of success, it would be folly to expect it from a measure that left full scope and sphere to those passions; which kept alive the fears of the one party, while it sharpened the cupidity of the other. With confidence, therefore, I re-assert, that only by reference to a principle, possessing the characters above enumerated, can any satisfactory measure be framed, and that if this should fail in producing the tranquillity aimed at, it will be in vain sought in any other.

Again, it is evident that no principle can be appropriate to such a measure, which does not bear directly on the evil to be removed or mitigated. Consequently, it should be our first business to discover in what this evil truly and essentially consists. It is, we know, a compound of many ingredients. But we want to ascertain what the *base* is, that communicates the quality of evil, of *political* evil, of evil which it is the duty of a *statesman* to guard against, to various other ingredients, which without the base would have been innoxious: or though evils in themselves, yet evils of such a kind, as to be counted by all wise statesmen among the tares, which must be suffered to

[1] Cf Matt 13.33.

grow up with the wheat to the close of the harvest,[1] and left for the Lord of the Harvest[2] to separate.

Further: the principle, the grounding and directing principle of an effectual enactment, must be one, on which a Catholic might consistently vindicate and recommend the measure to Catholics. It must therefore be independent of all differences purely theological. And the facts and documents, by which the truth and practical importance of the principle are to be proved or illustrated, should be taken by preference from periods anterior to the division of the Latin Church into Romish and Protestant. It should be such, in short, that an orator might with strict historical propriety introduce the Framers and Extorters of Magna Charta pleading to their Catholic descendants in behalf of the measure grounded on such a Principle, and invoking them in the name of the Constitution, over whose growth *they* had kept armed watch, and by the sacred obligation to maintain it which they had entailed on their posterity.

This is the condition under which alone I could conscientiously vote, and which being fulfilled, I should most zealously vote for the admission of Lay Catholics, not only to both houses of the Legislature, but to all other offices below the Crown, without any exception. Moreover, in the fulfilment of this condition, in the solemn recognition and establishment of a Principle having the characters here specified, I find the only necessary security—convinced, that this, if acceded to by the Catholic Body, would in effect be such, and that any other security will either be hollow, or frustrate the purpose of the Bill.

Now this condition would be fulfilled, the required Principle would be given, provided that the law for the repeal of the sundry statutes affecting the Catholics were introduced by, and grounded on, a declaration, to which every possible character of solemnity should be given, that at no time and under no circumstances has it ever been, not can it ever be, compatible with the spirit or consistent with the[a] safety of the British Constitution, to recognize in the Roman Catholic Priesthood, as now constituted, a component Estate of the realm, or persons capable, individually or collectively, of becoming the Trustees and usufructuary Proprietors of that elective and circulative property, originally reserved for the permanent maintenance of the

[a] Added in 2nd ed

[1] Cf Matt 13.24–30.

[2] Matt 9.38, Luke 10.2.

National Church.[1] And further, it is expedient that the Preamble of the Bill should expressly declare and set forth, that this exclusion of the Members of the Romish Priesthood (comprehending all under oaths of canonical obedience to the Pope as their ecclesiastical sovereign) from the trusts and offices of the National Church, and from all participation in the proceeds of the Nationalty, is enacted and established on grounds wholly irrelative to any doctrines received and taught by the Romish Church as Articles of Faith, and protested against as such by the Churches of the Reformation; but that it is enacted on grounds derived and inherited from our ancestors before the Reformation, and by them maintained and enforced to the fullest extent that the circumstances of the times permitted, with no other exceptions and interruptions than those effected by fraud, or usurpation, or foreign force, or the temporary fanaticism of the meaner sort.

In what manner the enactment of this principle shall be effected, is of comparatively small importance, provided it be distinctly set forth as that great constitutional *security*, the known existence of which is the ground and condition of the *right* of the Legislature to dispense with other less essential safe-guards of the constitution, not unnecessary, perhaps, at the time of their enactment, but of temporary and accidental necessity. The form, I repeat, the particular mode in which the principle shall be recognized, the security established, is comparatively indifferent. Let it only be understood first, as the provision, by the retention of which the Legislature possess a moral and constitutional right to make the change in question; as that, the known existence of which permits the law to *ignore* the Roman Catholics under any other name than that of British subjects; and secondly, as the express condition, the basis of a virtual compact between the claimants and the nation, which condition cannot be broken or evaded without subverting (morally) the articles and clauses founded thereon.

N.B.—I do not assert that the provision here stated *is* an absolute security. My positions are,—first, that it may with better reason and more probability be proposed as such, than any other hitherto devised; secondly, that no other securities can supersede the expe-

[1] Wellington's cautious plan for Emancipation in the summer of 1828 included the "securities" that the Catholic clergy should be compelled to obtain a royal licence and be paid by the State. Peel dissuaded him from continuing with either. Payment by the State seemed to C an improper use of the Nationalty, or wealth entrusted to the National Church; see also Introduction, above, p l, and above, pp 11–12 and n 1.

diency and necessity of this, but that this will greatly diminish or altogether remove the necessity of any other: further, that without this the present measure cannot be rationally expected to produce that tranquillity, which it is the aim and object of the framers to bring about; and lastly, that the necessity of the declaration, as above given, formally and solemnly to be made and recorded, is not evacuated by this pretext, that no one intends to transfer the Church Establishment to the Romish priesthood, or to divide it with them.

One thing, however, is of importance, that I should premise—namely, that the existing state of the Elective Franchise* in Ireland, in reference to the fatal present of the Union Ministry to the Landed Interest, that the true Deianira Shirt of the Irish Hercules,[2] is altogether excluded from the theme and purpose of this disquisition. It ought to be considered by the Legislature, abstracted from the creed professed by the great majority of these nominal Freeholders. The recent abuse of the influence resulting from this profession should be regarded as an accidental aggravation of the mischief, that displayed rather than constituted its malignity. It is even desirable, that it should be preserved separate from the Catholic Question, and in no necessary dependence on the fate of the Bill now on the eve of presentation to Parliament.[3] Whether this be carried or be lost, it will still remain a momentous question, urgently calling for the decision of the Legislature—whether the said extension of the elective franchise has not introduced an uncombining and wholly incongruous ingredient into the representative system, irreconcilable with the true principle of election, and virtually disfranchising the class,

* Though by the Bill which is now Law, the Forty Shilling Freeholders no longer possess the elective franchise, yet as this particular clause of the Bill already has been, and may hereafter be, made a pretext for agitation, the following paragraph has been retained, in the belief, that its moral uses have not been altogether superseded by the retraction[a] of this most unhappy boon.[1]

[a] 1st ed: retractation

[1] In 1829 three Bills were introduced: one to suppress the Catholic Association, another to remove disabilities from Roman Catholics, and a third to raise the franchise qualification in the Irish counties from 40s to £10.

[2] An allusion to Deianira's innocent gift to the unfaithful Hercules of the poisoned shirt of Nessus that killed him.

[3] This suggests that this part of *C&S* was written in Jan or Feb 1829, before the Act was passed raising the franchise qualification from 40s to £10. Pt II "Aids to a Right Appreciation of the Bill" appears to have been written before the preceding section, "The Third Possible Church", which ends with a reference to the Act for the Relief of Roman Catholics "lately passed"; cf above, p 145 and n 2.

to whom, on every ground of justice and of policy, the right unquestionably belongs—under *any* circumstances overwhelming the voices of the rest of the community; in *ordinary* times concentering in the great Land-owners a virtual monopoly of the elective power; and in times of factious excitement depriving them even of their natural and rightful influence.

These few suggestions on the expediency of revising the state of the representation in Ireland are, I am aware, but a digression from the main subject of the Chapter. But this in fact is already completed, as far as my purpose is concerned. The reasons on which the necessity of the proposed declaration is grounded, have been given at large in the former part of the volume. Here, therefore, I should end; but that I anticipate two objections, of sufficient force to deserve a comment, and form the matter of a concluding paragraph.

First, it may be objected, that after abstracting the portion of evil, that may be plausibly attributed to the peculiar state of landed property in Ireland, there are evils directly resulting from the Romanism of the most numerous class of the Inhabitants, besides that of an extra-national priesthood, and against the political consequences of which the above declaration provides no security. To this I reply, that as no bridge ever did or can possess the demonstrable perfections of the mathematical arch,[1] so can no existing state adequately correspond to the *idea* of a state. In nations and governments the most happily constituted, there will be deformities and obstructions, peccant humours and irregular actions, which affect indeed the *perfection* of the state, but not its essential forms; which retard, but do not necessarily prevent its progress: casual disorders, which though they aggravate the *growing pains* of a nation, may yet, by the vigorous counteraction which they excite, even promote its *growth*. Inflammations in the extremities, and unseemly boils on the surface, dare not be confounded with exhaustive misgrowths, or the poison of a false life in the vital organs. Nay, and this remark is of special pertinency to our present purpose—even where the former derive a malignant character from their co-existence with the latter, yet the wise physician will direct his whole attention to the *constitutional* ailments, knowing that when the source, the fons et fomes veneni,[2] is sealed up, the accessories will either dry up of themselves, or, returning to their natural character rank among the infirmities, which flesh is heir to; and either admit of a gradual

[1] For the use of the "arch" and "bridge" example cf *Friend* (*CC*) I 497.

[2] "The source and the seat of the infection".

remedy, or where this is impracticable, or when the medicine would be worse than the disease, are to be endured, as *tolerabiles* ineptiae,[1] trials of patience, and occasions of charity. We have here had the state chiefly in view; but the Protestant will to little purpose have availed himself of his free access to the Scriptures, will have read at least the Epistles of St. Paul, with a very unthinking spirit, who does not apply the same maxims to the church of Christ, who has yet to learn, that the church militant is "a floor whereon wheat and chaff are mingled together;"[2] that even grievous evils and errors may exist that do not concern the nature or being of a church, and that they[a] may even prevail in the particular church, to which we belong, without justifying a separation from the same, and without invalidating its claims on our affection as a true and living part of the Church Universal. And with regard to such evils we must adopt the advice that Augustine (a man not apt to offend by any excess of charity) gave to the complainers of his day—ut misericorditer corripiant quod possunt, quod non possunt patienter ferant, et cum delectione lugeant, donec aut emendet Deus aut in messe eradicet zizania et paleas ventilet.[3]

Secondly, it may be objected that the declaration, so peremptorily by me required is altogether unnecessary, that no one thinks of alienating the church property, directly or indirectly, that there is no intention of recognising the Romish Priests in law, by entitling them as such, to national maintenance, or in the language of the

[a] Added in 2nd ed

[1] Cf Jeremy Taylor: "...for when certain zealous persons fled to *Frankford*...the quarrel was about the Common-Prayer-Book, and some of them made their appeal to the judgment of Mr. *Calvin*...and yet the worst he said upon the provocation of those prejudices was that even its vanities were tolerable. *Tolerabiles ineptias* was the unhandsome Epithete he gave...". *Apology for Authorized and Set Forms of Liturgy* Preface § 12: *Polemicall Discourses* (1674) b5. In his copy C has written a note on this passage on "who began the Quarrel", and in a note on § 13 repeats Calvin's Latin phrase. Calvin's letter, of 18 Jan 1555, is in *Opera* xv (Brunswick 1876) 394 in *Corpus Reformatorum.*

[2] Cf Matt 3.12.

[3] Tr: "...that they should compassionately chastise what they can, but should bear patiently with what they cannot chastise and should lovingly [reading *dilectione*] grieve over it until God either corrects it himself or, in the time of harvest, roots up the tares and scatters the chaff". Cf St Augustine: "Misericorditer igitur corripiat homo quod potest: quod autem non potest, patienter ferat; et dilectione gemat atque lugeat, donec aut ille desuper emendet et corrigat, aut usque ad messem differat eradicare zizania, et paleam ventilare". *Contra epistolam Parmeniani* 3.2.5: Migne *PL* XLIII 94.

day, by taking them into the pay of the state. In short, that the National Church is no more in danger than the Christian. And is this the opinion, the settled judgment, of one who has studied the signs of the times? Can the person who makes these assertions, have ever read a pamphlet by Mr. Secretary Croker?[1] Or the surveys of the Counties, published under the authority of the now extinct Board of Agriculture?[2] Or has he heard, or attentively perused the successive debates in both Houses during the late agitation of the Catholic Question? If he have—why then, relatively to the objector, and to as many as entertain the same opinions, my reply is:—the objection is unanswerable.

[1] C refers to *A Sketch of the State of Ireland, Past and Present* (1808), which ran through twenty editions and established John Wilson Croker (1780–1857) as an expert on Irish affairs. Secretary to the Admiralty from 1809 until 1830, he was an advocate of Emancipation, but believed that his party's conversion had come too late. His views on the prudence of conciliating "so large a portion of our community as the Roman Catholics" are stated in *Substance of the Speech of John Wilson Croker Esq* (1819), but he had advocated Emancipation with five safeguards from as early as 1808 in *A Sketch*. John Lawless in *An Address to the Catholics of Ireland* (1825) held Croker responsible for suggesting the endowment of the Catholic clergy and the abolition of the 40s householders, which became the "Wings" of Burdett's Bill of 1825. In a letter to HNC 7 May 1832, C expressed his feeling in relation to Croker of "the mutually exclusive Contrariety of his principles to mine, respecting the National Clerisy—whom he, in one of his pamphlets, has declared to be neither more or less than Government Cooks in office, to be kept, or dismissed, by the Ministers & Majority of the Houses for the time being, whereas, it will be one of my principal Objects to expose the hollowness & bull-froggery of our (I could almost say, blasphemously called) Legislature...". *CL* VI 903.

[2] The Board set up by Pitt in 1793 had as its first president Sir John Sinclair (1754–1835), one of the earliest statisticians. At first he planned parish-by-parish surveys but later settled on a county-by-county basis. These "General Views" provide much useful information about the state of agriculture, though Arthur Young (1741–1820) described them as a "wretched mass of erroneous and insufficient information". The Board expired in 1821, not to be replaced until 1838, when the Royal Agricultural Society was founded. For C on the Board's survey of 1816 see *LS* (*CC*) 212n–13 and n 1 (C objected then as now to commutation of tithes), 219, 221–2, 226–7, and nn.

AUTHOR'S APPENDIX

GLOSSARY TO THE APPENDED LETTER[1]

As all my readers are not bound to understand Greek, and yet, according to *my* deepest convictions, the truths set forth in the following Combat of Wit, between the Man of Reason and the Man of the Senses have an interest for all, I have been induced to prefix the explanations of the few Greek words, and words minted from the Greek:

COSMOS—world. TOUTOS[2] cosmos—*this* world. HETEROS—the other, in the sense of opposition to, or discrepancy with some former; as Heterodoxy, in opposition to Orthodoxy. ALLOS—an other, simply and without precluding or superseding the one before mentioned. ALLOCOSMITE—a Denizen of another world.

MYSTES, from the Greek μύω—one who *muses* with closed lips,[3] as meditating on *Ideas* which may indeed be suggested and awakened, but cannot, like the images of sense and the conceptions of the understanding, be adequately *expressed* by words.

N.B.—Where a person mistakes the anomalous misgrowths of his own individuality for ideas, or truths of universal reason, he may, without impropriety, be called a *Mystic*, in the abusive sense of the term; though pseudo-mystic, or phantast, would be the more proper designation. Heraclitus, Plato, Bacon, Leibnitz, were Mystics, in the primary sense of the term: Iamblichus, and his successors, Phantasts.[4]

1 The letter appears below, pp 173–85.

2 Correct Greek would be Houtos. HNC notes in *C&S* (1839) that C uses Toutos for the sake of euphony.

3 The connexion between μύω, to close or to be shut, especially of eyes or mouth; μυέω, to initiate, teach; and μύστης, an initiate, or a mystic, is generally accepted. C adds to it the meaning of the English verb "muse", which is probably unrelated etymologically, though he may be connecting it with Muse, which, according to Eusebius, was also said by some to be derived from μυέω. Both derivations are in Scapula *Lexicon Graeco-Latinum*, of which C owned the Lyons 1663 ed.

4 Cf "Conclusion" of *AR* (1825), which includes a section on "Mystics and Mysticism" 377–86. C admired Heraclitus as an early exponent of the Logos and of the philosophy of the opposites; see *SM* (*CC*), *CN* III, and *P Lects* (1949) indexes. He consistently stressed the importance of the idea and truth of universal reason in Plato and Bacon ("the English Plato"). Curiously, C makes little of the Platonic mystical side of Leibniz in *P Lects* Lect XIII (1949) 388; see ibid 463 n 23 and Thomas McFarland

Ἔπεα ζώοντα—living words.[1]—The following words from Plato may be Englished: "the commune and the dialect of Gods with, or toward men;"[2] and those attributed to Pythagoras: "the verily subsistent numbers or powers, the most prescient (or provident) principles of the Earth and the Heavens."[3]

And here, though not falling under the leading title, Glossary, yet, as tending to the same object that of fore-arming the reader for the following dialogue, I transcribe two or three annotations which I had *penciled*, (for the book was lent to me by a friend who had himself borrowed it) on the margins of a volume, recently published, and entitled, "The Natural History of Enthusiasm."[4] They will, at least, remind some of my old school-fellows of the habit for which I was even then noted: and for others they may serve, as a specimen of the Marginalia, which, if brought together from the various books, my own and those of a score others, would go near to form as bulky a volume as most of those old folios, through which the larger portion of them are dispersed.[5]

Coleridge and the Pantheist Tradition (Oxford 1969) 297–300. Lamb records C's admiration for Iamblichus at Christ's Hospital School. C's lasting enthusiasm for the Neoplatonists (see e.g. *CN* III 3935) was probably never unmixed with criticism. For further comment on the wildness of the later Neoplatonists, among them Iamblichus (c 250–c 325) and "Dionysius the Areopagite", see *CN* III 3824 (in which he calls them "the Alexandrians"), 3869, 3934, and below, p 170.

[1] See below, p 184 and n 2.

[2] Plato *Symposium* 203A. See below, p 184 and n 3.

[3] Iamblichus *De vita Pythagorae* 146; for the Greek see below, p 184 and n 1.

[4] *Natural History of Enthusiasm*, a historical-philosophical account of the perversions of religious imagination, was published anonymously in May 1829. Its author was Isaac Taylor (1787–1865), a draftsman and engraver who spent his life trying to combine Christian belief and Baconian inductive methods, a preoccupation with special appeal to C. Ronald Knox *Enthusiasm* (Oxford 1950) calls it "the most uniformly dull book ever written", but it soon ran through nine editions, the third appearing as early as Apr 1830. Taylor probably wrote the review of *C&S* in the *Eclectic Review*, with which he was closely connected: VI (July 1831) 1–28. See Introduction, above, p lxvi, and below, p 171 and n 6.

[5] C's copy of *Natural History of Enthusiasm* has not been traced. This reference to his early habit of writing marginalia is of special interest, as the marginalia that survive belong mainly to his later adult life. The already published material occupies several volumes (*LR*, *NED*, *NTP*, *C 17th C*) and thus justifies C's claim, which will be even further substantiated with the publication of *CM* ed G. Whalley, which will run to four or five volumes of annotations on some 500 works.

HISTORY OF ENTHUSIASM

I

"Whatever is practically important on religion or morals, may at all times be advanced and argued in the simplest terms of colloquial expression."—p. 21.

NOTE

I do not believe this. Be it so, however. But why? Simply, because, the terms and phrases of the Theological Schools have, by their continual iteration from the pulpit, *become* colloquial. The science of one age becomes the common sense of a succeeding.—(See Aids to Reflection, pp. 7–11; but especially at the note at p. 252.)[1] The author adds—"from the pulpit, perhaps, no other style should at any time be heard." Now I can conceive no more direct means of depriving Christianity of one of its peculiar attributes, that of enriching and enlarging the mind, *while* it purifies, and in the very *act* of purifying, the will and affections, than the maxim here prescribed by the historian of Enthusiasm. From the intensity of commercial life in this country, and from some other less creditable causes, there is found even among our better educated men, a vagueness in the use of words, which presents, indeed, no obstacle to the intercourse of the market, but is absolutely incompatible with the attainment or communication of distinct and precise conceptions. Hence in every department of exact knowledge, a peculiar nomenclature is indispensable. The Anatomist, Chemist, Botanist, Mineralogist, yea, even the common artizan, and the rude Sailor, discover that "the terms of colloquial expression," are too general and too lax to answer *their* purposes: and on what grounds can the science of self-knowledge, and of our relations to God and our own spirits, be presumed to form an exception? Every new term expressing a fact, or a difference, not precisely and adequately expressed by any other word in the same language, is a new organ of thought for the mind that has learnt it.[2]

[1] *AR* (1825) 7–11 contains general observations on language. In stressing the importance of etymology C writes: "There are cases, in which more knowledge of more value may be conveyed by the history of a *word*, than by the history of a campaign." *AR* (1825) 6n. The passage at p 252 runs: "The creed of true Common Sense is composed of the *Results* of Scientific Meditation, Observation, and Experiment, as far as they are *generally* intelligible.... The Common Sense of a People is the moveable *index* of its average judgment and information. Without Metaphysics Science could have no language, and Common Sense no materials."

[2] Cf above, p 13 n 2, pp 24, 108, 123–4.

II

"The region of abstract conceptions, of lofty reasonings, has an atmosphere too subtle to support the health of true piety.—In accordance with this, the Supreme *in his word* reveals barely a glimpse of his essential glories. By some naked affirmations we are, indeed, secured against grovelling notions of the divine nature; but *these hints are incidental, and so scanty, that every excursive mind goes far beyond them in its conception of the Infinite Attributes.*"—p. 26.[1]

NOTE

By abstract conceptions the author means what I should call *Ideas*, [a]which as such I[b] contradistinguish from conceptions, whether abstracted or generalized.[2] But it is with his *meaning*, not with his terms, that I am at present concerned. Now that the *personëity*[3] of God, the idea of God as the I AM,[4] is presented more prominently in Scripture, than the (so called) physical attributes, is most true; and forms one of the distinctive characters of its superior worth and value.[5] It was by dwelling too exclusively on the Infinites,[c] that the ancient Greek Philosophers, Plato excepted, fell into Pantheism, as in later times did Spinosa. *I forbid you*, says Plato, *to call God the Infinite! If you dare name him at all, say rather the Measure of Infinity.*[6]

[a–b] 1st ed: and as such [c] 1st ed: Infinities

[1] Taylor *Natural History of Enthusiasm* 26 (var, with omissions: C's italics).

[2] Cf above, pp 12–13 and n 1.

[3] *OED* notes that "personeity" is a C coinage, dating it 1822 from a letter to Allsop, i.e. *CL* v 252.

[4] Exod 3.14.

[5] For the distinction between worth and value, see *Friend* (*CC*) I 440, 556 and n, and *P Lects* Lect XII (1949) 364.

[6] In fact Plato did not use these words. C's ultimate source appears to be F. H. Jacobi, who summarises Plato in two paragraphs in *Ueber eine Weissagung Lichtenbergs* (1801), afterwards prefixed to Jacobi's *Von den göttlichen Dingen* (1811) and finally published in Jacobi *Werke* III (Leipzig 1816). The paragraphs are on pp 211–12 of the last, which C annotated. Schelling, in *Denkmal der Schrift von den göttlichen Dingen etc. des Herrn Friedrich Heinrich Jacobi* (Tübingen 1812) 96–7 (a book also annotated by C), quotes the beginning of Jacobi's two paragraphs, as follows, in inverted commas, so that he might be understood by a hasty reader to be translating from Plato rather than quoting Jacobi: "Nennt Gott nicht das unendliche Wesen, sagt Platon, denn dem Unendlichen widerstehet das Daseyn; es ist wesentlich wesenlos.—Nennet ihn den, der das Mass gibt, in dem ursprunglich das Mass ist, saget: Er ist selbst das Mass." Tr: "Do not call God infinite Being, says Plato, for Infinity is the opposite to Existence; it is essentially non-existent. Call him that which gives measure, in whom measure is from the beginning. Say that he himself is measure." C's last sentence also echoes Protagoras in Plato, "Man is the measure of all things". *Theaetetus* 152A. For another possible use of Jacobi see below, p 184 and n 3.

Nevertheless, it would be easy to place *in synopsi*[1] before the author such a series of Scripture passages, as would incline him to retract his assertion. The Eternal, the Omnipresent, the Omniscient, the one absolute Good, the Holy, the Living, the Creator as well as Former of the Universe, the Father of Spirits—can the author's mind go *far* beyond these?[2] Yet these are all clearly affirmed of the Supreme ONE in the Scriptures.

III

The following pages from p. 26 to p. 36 contain a succession of eloquent and splendid paragraphs on the celestial orders, and the expediency or necessity of their being concealed from us, least we should receive such overwhelming conceptions of the divine greatness as to render us incapable of devotion and prayer on the Scripture model. "Were it," says the eloquent writer, "indeed permitted to man to gaze upwards from step to step, and from range to range of these celestial hierarchies, to the lowest steps of the Eternal Throne, what liberty of heart would afterwards be left him in drawing near to the Father of Spirits?"[3] But the substance of these pages will be found implied in the following reply to them.

NOTE

More weight with me than all this Pelion upon Ossa of imaginary Hierarchies has the single remark of Augustine, there neither are nor can be but three essential differences of Being, viz. the Absolute, the Rational Finite, and the Finite irrational; i.e. God, Man, and Brute![4] Besides, the whole scheme is unscriptural, if not contra-

[1] "In synopsis".

[2] Among the references, "The Eternal" (Deut 33.27, 1 Tim 1.17), "The Omnipresent, the Omniscient" (Ps 139, Heb 4.13), "the one absolute Good" (Matt 19.17), "the Holy" (Isa 6.3, Rev 4.8), "the Living" (Deut 5.26, Joshua 3.10), "the Creator as well as the Former of the Universe" (Gen 1), "the Father of Spirits" (Heb 12.9).

[3] *History of Enthusiasm* 28 (var with omissions); for "Father of Spirits", see Heb 12.9.

[4] Cf a marginal comment on Hooker *Ecclesiastical Polity* Bk I § 4: "St Augustine well remarks that only three distinct Genera of ⟨Living⟩ Beings are conceivable—1. The Infinite Rational: 2. The finite rational: 3. The finite irrational—i.e. God: Man: Animal." *Works* (1682) 76: *C 17th C* 147. Cf marginal comments on Hacket and Oxlee: *LR* III 178, IV 316. No such remark by St Augustine has been traced, though it might be deduced from such passages as e.g. *Confessions* 10.6–7 and *De vera religione* 113. St Augustine certainly believed in angels. C later expressed a joyful but modified acceptance of the belief, and a dread of "even the appearance of an approximation to the Neo-platonic Proclo-plotinian Scheme & Process.—" *CL* VI 961. See also below, App E, p 234.

scriptural. Pile up winged Hierarchies on Hierarchies, and outblaze the Cabalists, and Dionysius the Areopagite;[1] yet what a gaudy vapor for a healthful mind is the whole conception (or rather Phantasm) compared with the awful Hope held forth in the Gospel, to be one with God[2] in and through the Mediator Christ,[3] even the living, co-eternal Word and Son of God![4]

But through the whole of this eloquent Declamation, I find two errors predominate, and both, it appears to me, dangerous errors. First, that the rational and consequently the only true Ideas of the Supreme Being, *are* incompatible with the spirit of prayer and petitionary pleading taught and exemplified in the Scriptures. Second, that this *being* the case, and "supplication with arguments and importunate requests" *being* irrational and *known* by the Supplicant to be such, it is nevertheless a duty to pray in this fashion.[5] In other words, it is asserted that the Supreme Being requires of his rational creatures, as the condition of their offering acceptable worship to him, that they should wilfully blind themselves to the light, which he had himself given them, as the contradistinguishing character of their Humanity,[6] without which they could not pray to him at all; and that drugging their sense of the truth into a temporary *doze*, they should *make believe*, that they knew no better! As if the God of Truth[7] and Father of all lights[8] resembled an Oriental or African Despot, whose courtiers, even those whom he had himself enriched and placed in the highest rank, are commanded to approach him only in beggars' rags and with a beggarly whine.

[1] The winged hierarchies were the result of the application of the multiple emanations of the Neoplatonic system to Jewish and Christian beliefs. The Cabbala is a combination of Jewish tradition with Neoplatonic myth, magic, and mysticism. C used its imagery and read works on it from his youth onwards; see *P Lects* Lect x (1949) 299–300 for his historical account. The pseudo-Dionysius (flc 500), in mediaeval times thought to have been a contemporary of St Paul and therefore an unimpeachable authority, likewise combined Christianity and Neoplatonism and described the nine celestial hierarchies in detail. C read and commented on *De divisione naturae* by John Scotus Erigena (c 810–c 877) and his translations of Maximus the Confessor, both of which often quote "Dionysius the Areopagite". See *CN* I 1369, 1382; also below, p 182 and n 4.

[2] John 17.11.

[3] 1 Tim 2.5.

[4] John 1.1, 2, 34.

[5] C refers to: "And though reason and Scripture assure us that He neither needs to be informed of our wants, nor waits to be moved by our supplications, yet will He be approached with the eloquence of importunate desire. He is to be supplicated with arguments as one who needs to be swayed and moved...". *Natural History of Enthusiasm* 30.

[6] John 1.9; cf below, p 176.

[7] Deut 32.4.

[8] James 1.17.

I on the contrary find "the Scripture model of devotion,"[1] the prayers and thanksgiving of the Psalmist, and in the main of our own Church Liturgy, perfectly conformable to the highest and clearest convictions of my *Reason*. (I use the word in its most comprehensive sense, as comprising both the *practical* and the intellective, not only as the Light but likewise as the Life which *is* the Light of Man. John i. 3.)[2] And I do not hesitate to attribute the contrary persuasion principally to the three following oversights. First (and this is the Queen Bee in the Hive of error),[3] the identification of the universal Reason with each man's individual Understanding,[4] subjects not only different but diverse, not only *allo*geneous but *hetero*geneous. Second, the substitution of the idea of the Infinite for that of the Absolute. Third and lastly, the habit of using the former as a sort of Superlative Synonime of the vast or indefinitely great. Now the practical difference between my scheme and that of the Essayist, for whose talents and intentions I feel sincere respect, may perhaps be stated thus.

The essayist would bring down his understanding to his Religion: I would raise up my understanding to my reason, and find my Religion in the focus resulting from their convergence. We both alike use the same penitential, deprecative and petitionary prayers; I in the full assurance of their congruity with my Reason, he in a factitious oblivion of their being the contrary.

The name of the Author of the Natural History of Enthusiasm is unknown to me and unconjectured.[5] It is evidently the work of a mind at once observant and meditative. And should these notes meet the Author's eye,[6] let him be assured that I willingly give to his genius that respect which his intentions without it would secure for him,

[1] "The Scripture models of devotion, far from encouraging vague and inarticulate contemplations, consist of such utterances of desire, or hope, or love, as seem to suppose the existence of correlative feelings, and indeed of every *human* sympathy." *Natural History of Enthusiasm* 30.

[2] More appropriately John 1.4.

[3] Cf above, p 59 and n 1.

[4] Cf "On the Grounds of Government as Laid Exclusively in the Pure Reason": *Friend* (*CC*) I 186–202. See also above, p 58 and n 5.

[5] The author was Isaac Taylor; see above, p 166 n 4.

[6] C's notes were seen by Taylor; in the 4th ed of the *Natural History of Enthusiasm* (1830) he added a substantial note, pp 21–4, saying: "Who would not wish to employ language always with the utmost precision of which it is capable?...But alas! unless the mass of mankind could be induced to *think* always with philosophical precision...the new terms...will acquire manifold incrustations of error". A reviewer (probably Taylor) later took up the point in relation to C's *C&S* in the *Eclectic Review* July 1831; see above, p 166 n 4.

in the breast of every good man. But in the present state of things, infidelity having fallen into disrepute, even on the score of intellect, yet the obligation to shew a *reason* for our faith having become more generally recognized, as reading and the taste for serious conversation have increased, there is a large class of my countrymen disposed to receive, with especial favour, any opinions that will enable them to make a compromise between their new knowledge and their old belief.[1] And with these men, the author's evident abilities will probably render the work a high authority. Now it is the very purpose of my life to impress the contrary sentiments. Hence these notes.

S. T. COLERIDGE

[1] In *LS* C had argued that the neglect of philosophy in religious faith and the misleading emphasis on the "simplicity" of the Christian religion had left men's minds free to spend their energies on worldly matters, thus increasing the undesirable over-balance of the commercial spirit in the nation. *LS* (*CC*) 194–5. Cf above, p 47.

APPENDIX

(*Referred to in page* 117)

MY DEAR ——,[1]

IN emptying a drawer of under-stockings, rose-leaf bags, old (but, too many of them) unopened letters,[2] and paper scraps, or brain fritters, I had my attention directed to a sere and ragged half-sheet by a gust of wind, which had separated it from its companions, and whisked it out of the window into the garden.[3]—Not that I went after it. I have too much respect for the numerous tribe, to which it belonged, to lay any restraint on their movements, or to put the Vagrant Act[4] in force against them. But it so chanced that some after-breeze had stuck it on a standard rose-tree, and there I found it, as I was pacing my evening walk alongside the lower ivy-wall, the bristled runners from which threaten to entrap the top branch of the cherry tree in our neighbour's kitchen garden. I had been meditating a letter to you, and as I ran[a] my eye over this fly-away tag-rag and bob-tail,[5] and bethought me that it was a bye-blow of my own, I felt a sort of fatherly remorse, and yearning towards it, and exclaimed—"If I had a frank for — —,[6] this should help to make up the ounce." It was far too decrepit to travel per se—besides that the seal would have looked like a single pin on a beggar's coat of tatters—and yet one does not like to be stopt in a kind feeling, which my conscience interpreted as a sort of promise to the said scrap, and therefore, (frank or no frank), I will transcribe it. *A dog's leaf at the top worn off, which must have contained I presume, the syllable*

VE

[a] 1st ed: run

[1] Originally sent as a letter to Edward Coleridge 27 Jul 1826: *CL* VI 593–601. It is given here var with omissions.

[2] For C's reluctance to open letters, see *C Life* (JDC) 28, 177, 182, 186.

[3] Gillman's garden at Highgate; see a pencil sketch in *C at H* 52.

[4] The laws relating to idle and disorderly persons had recently been consolidated, temporarily in 1822 and more permanently by the Vagrancy Act of 1824; hence C's ironic allusion to not wishing to restrain his disorderly papers by the new Act.

[5] There is a ms volume in the V&A containing mss by Lamb, WW, and C entitled "Rag-Tag and Bobtail"; see *LS* (*CC*) 235.

[6] Eton: *CL* VI 594. Edward Coleridge was an assistant master at Eton College.

—RILY, quoth Demosius of Toutoscosmos, Gentleman, to Mystes the Allocosmite,[1] thou seemest to me like an out-of-door's patient of St. Luke's[2] wandering about in the rain without cap, hat, or bonnet, poring on the elevation of a palace, not the House that Jack built, but the House that is to be built for Jack, in the suburbs of the City, which his cousin-german, the lynx-eyed Dr. Gruithuisen has lately discovered in the moon.[3] But through[a] a foolish kindness for that Phyz of thine, which whilome belonged to an old school-fellow of the same name with thee, I would get thee shipped off under the Alien Act, as a Non Ens,[4] or Pre-existent of the other World to come!—To whom Mystes retorted—Verily, Friend Demos, thou art too fantastic for a genuine Toutoscosmos man! and it needs only a fit of dyspepsy, or a cross in love to make an Heterocosmite of thee; this same Heteroscosmos being in fact the endless shadow which the Toutoscosmos casts at sun-set! But not to alarm or affront thee, as if I insinuated that thou wert in danger of becoming an Allocosmite, I let the whole of thy courteous address to me pass without comment or objection, save only the two concluding monosyllables and the preposition (Pre) which anticipates them. The world in which I exist is another world indeed, but not to come. It is as present as (if *that* be at all) the magnetic planet, of which, according to the Astronomer HALLEY,[5] the visible globe, that we inverminate, is

[a] 1st ed: for

[1] See above, p 165. In an annotation on his copy of Jakob Böhme *Works*, now in the BM, C contrasts those like himself who "hold and teach, that... the only real and effective Convictions are the working of the spirit" with the "*toutoukosmou* Professors" of Christianity who reduce Biblical truths to "the common sense and the acquired convictions of the Understanding". Note on Böhme *Works* (4 vols 1764–81) III i 4–6.

[2] St Luke's Hospital for lunatics, instituted in London in 1751 to care for patients who could not pay for a private asylum.

[3] C notes in the version sent as a letter to Edward Coleridge: "The Dr tells us that he can see distinctly with his Frauenhofer Telescope of the power 90 what the best living observers can barely see with one of 270. Entdeckung &c p 33". *CL* VI 594n. E. L. Griggs supplies the title, *Entdeckung vieler deutlichen Spuren der Mondbewohner, besonders eines colossalen Kunstgebäudes derselben* (1824). Franz von Paula Gruithuisen (1774–1852), professor of medicine and then of astronomy at Munich, from the appearances of artificial alterations in the surface of the moon inferred that there were artificial roads and great buildings. See a report in *G Mag* XCIV pt 2 (Aug 1824) 163.

[4] "Non-entity".

[5] Edmund Halley (1656–1742), the English astronomer who discovered the comet of 1682, now called after him, posited the existence of a magnetic inner globe as a solution to the variations in the magnetic needle. "An Account of the Cause of the Change of the Variation of the Magnetic Needle; with an Hypothesis of the Structure of the Internal Parts of the Earth" *Phil Trans* XVII (1692). Halley justifies his theory to those who might enquire as

the case or travelling-trunk—a neat little world where light still exists *in statu perfuso*,[1] as on the third day of the Creation,[2] before it was polarised into outward and inward, *i.e.* while light and life were one and the same, NEITHER existing *formally*, yet BOTH *eminenter:*[3] and when herb, flower, and forest, rose as a vision, in proprio lucido,[4] the ancestor and unseen yesterday of the sun and moon. Now, whether there really is such an elysian *mundus mundulus*[5] incased in the Macrocosm, or Great World, below the Adamantine Vault that supports the Mother Waters, that support the coating crust of that mundus immundus[6] on which we, and others less scantily furnished from nature's *Leggery*, crawl, delve, and nestle—(or, shall I say The Liceum, οὗ περιπατοῦν οἱ τούτου κόσμου φιλόσοφοι)[7]—the said Dr. Halley may, perhaps, by this time, have ascertained: and to him and the philosophic ghosts, his compeers, I leave it. But that another world is inshrined in the Microcosm I not only believe, but at certain depths of my Being, during the solemner Sabbaths of the Spirit, I have held commune therewith, in the power of that Faith, which is "the substance of the things hoped for,"[8] the living stem that will itself expand into the flower, which it now foreshews.[9]

---

to the Creator's purpose. The inner globe might be habitable; it might be lit by ways of which we are wholly ignorant; "the Medium it self may be always luminous after the manner of our *Ignes fatui*...". He goes on to quote Virgil and Claudian "inlightning their *Elysian Fields* with Sun and Stars proper to those infernal, or rather internal, Regions". Ibid XVII 575–6.

1 "In a diffused state".

2 Gen 1.9–18.

3 "Eminently" or "on a higher level of reality". C repeatedly uses the word in this sense. Cf the word in a similar context in *TL* (1848) 42.

4 "In the light in the proper sense" or "in their own light".

5 "Clean little world". Cf *TT* 10 Apr 1833.

6 "Unclean world". St Augustine played on the double meaning of *mundus* and *immundus* in *City of God* 7.26 and elsewhere.

7 "Where walk [disputing] the philosophers of this world". The letter to Edward Coleridge reads (*CL* VI 595) "περιπατοῦμεν...ψιλόσοφοι" ("where we, the psilosophers of this world, walk"). Περιπατοῦν is incorrect and has been variously emended by later editors, but περιπατοῦσιν ("[they] walk") seems best to fit the context. On "psilosophers" and "psilosophy" see *CN* II 3158, *CN* III 3244 and n, and *CL* IV 922. The verb stem περιπατ- alludes to the Peripatetics, the school of Aristotle, who used to walk about in the Lyceum, as earlier philosophers of this world, whereas the Platonists are philosophers of the next. The spelling "Liceum" stresses the pun on lice.

8 Heb 11.1 (var).

9 Cf C's annotation on a copy of *SM* that "the metaphors for our noblest and tenderest relations, for all the Affections and Duties that arise out of the Reason, the Ground of our proper Humanity, are almost wholly taken from Plants, Trees, Flowers, and their functions and accidents". *SM* (*CC*) 72 n 2.

How should it not be so, even on grounds of natural reason, and the analogy of inferior life? Is not nature prophetic up the whole vast pyramid of organic being? And in which of her numberless predictions has nature been convicted of a lie? Is not every organ announced by a previous instinct or act? The Larva of the Stag-beetle lies in its Chrysalis like an infant in the coffin of an adult, having left an empty space half the length it occupies—and this space is the exact length of the horn which distinguishes the perfect animal, but which, when it constructed its temporary Sarcophagus, was not yet in existence. Do not the eyes, ears, lungs of the unborn babe, give notice and furnish proof of a transuterine, visible, audible atmospheric world? We have eyes, ears, touch, taste, smell; and have we not an answering world of shapes, colours, sounds, and sapid and odorous bodies? But likewise—alas for the man for whom the one has not the same evidence of fact as the other—the Creator has given us spiritual senses, and sense-organs—ideas I mean—the idea of the good, the idea of the beautiful, ideas of eternity, immortality, freedom, and of that which contemplated relatively to WILL is Holiness, in relation to LIFE is Bliss. And must not these too infer the existence of a world correspondent to them? There is a Light, said the Hebrew Sage,[1] compared with which the Glory of the Sun is but a cloudy veil: and is it an ignis fatuus[2] given to mock us and lead us astray? And from a yet higher authority we know, that it is a light that lighteth every man that cometh into the world.[3] And are there no objects to reflect it? Or must we seek its analogon in the light of the glow-worm, that simply serves to distinguish one reptile from all the rest, and lighting, inch by inch, its mazy path through weeds and grass, leaves all else before, and behind, and around it in darkness?[4] No! Another and answerable world there is; and if any man discern it not, let him not, whether sincerely or in contemptuous irony, pretend a defect of faculty as the cause. The sense, the light,

[1] Cf Isa 60.19, Wisd 7.29.

[2] "Fatuous fire", i.e. will-o'-the-wisp. Cf "fatuous fires of FANCY": *LS* (*CC*) 146n.

[3] John 1.9.

[4] Cf an annotation on Marcus Aurelius *Meditations* 3.10: "I have compared a human Soul to a Glow-worm creeping on in the night a little, pleasing inch of Light before and behind and on either side, and a World of Darkness all around. Yea, even the vast Sun & Systems of Heavenly Truth partake, to us, of our own littleness, & are but Glow-worms, & Sparkles, in the black Ether—Reason enlarges them indeed somewhat by her Telescope; but their true dimensions are deduced by Faith availing herself of the Instruments of Reason." *The Emperor Marcus Aurelius Antoninus His Conversation with Himself* tr Jeremy Collier (2 pts 1701) i 36–7; C's copy in PML.

and the conformed objects are all there and for all men. The difference between man and man in relation thereto, results from no difference in their several gifts and powers of *intellect*, but in the will. As certainly as the individual is a man, so certainly *should* this other world be present to him: yea, it is his proper home. But he is an absentee and *chooses* to live abroad. His freedom and whatever else he possesses which the dog and the ape do not possess, yea, the whole revenue of his humanity, is derived from this—but with the Irish Land-owner in the Theatres, Gaming-houses, and Maitresseries of Paris, so with *him*. He is a voluntary ABSENTEE! I repeat it again and again—the cause is altogether in the WILL: and the defect of intellectual power, and "the having no turn or taste for subjects of this sort," are effects and consequences of the alienation of the WILL—*i.e.* of the man himself. There may be a defect, but there was not a deficiency, of the intellect. I appeal to facts for the proof. Take the science of Political Economy[1]—no two Professors understand each other—and often have I been present where the subject has been discussed in a room full of merchants and manufacturers, sensible and well-informed men: and the conversation has ended in a confession, that the matter was beyond their comprehension. And yet the science professes to give light on Rents, Taxes, Income, Capital, the Principles of Trade, Commerce, Agriculture, on Wealth, and the ways of acquiring and increasing it, in short on all that most passionately excites and interests the Toutoscosmos men. But it was avowed, that to arrive at any understanding of these matters requires a mind gigantic in its comprehension, and microscopic in its accuracy of detail. Now compare this with the effect produced on promiscuous crowds by a Whitfield, or a Wesley[2]—or rather compare with it the shaking of every leaf of the vast forest to the first blast of Luther's trumpet. Was it only of the world to come that Luther and his compeers preached? Turn to Luther's table talk,[3] and see if the

[1] Cf an entry in *TT* for 17 Mar 1833, in which C calls political economy "solemn humbug", asserts that it "can never be a pure science", that "there are no theorems in political economy—but problems only", and attacks the folly of reducing prices of goods at the expense of the well-being of "your fellow-countrymen". He offered further comments on 17 May 1833, 20 and 23 Jun 1834.

[2] By concentrating on the essentials of Christian faith in their preaching, George Whitefield and John Wesley (1703–91) converted large numbers of people. See above, p 141 n and n 4. When C gave his political lectures in Bristol in 1795, he praised the practical effects of Methodism. *Lects 1795* (*CC*) 43–4.

[3] "Next to the Scriptures my main book of meditation"; see above, p 56 and n 1, p 103 and n 2, p 112 and n 1.

larger part be not of that other world which now is, and without the being and working of which the world to come would be either as unintelligible as Abracadabra, or a mere reflection and elongation of the world of sense—Jack Robinson between two looking-glasses, with a series of Jack Robinsons in secula seculorum.[1]

Well, but what *is* this *new* and yet other world? The Brain of a man that is *out of his senses?*[2] A world fraught "with Castles in the air, well worthy the attention of any gentleman inclined to *idealize* a large property?"

The sneer on that lip, and the arch shine of that eye, Friend Demosius, would almost justify me, though I should answer that question by retorting it in a parody. What, quoth the owlet, peeping out of his ivy-bush at noon, with his blue fringed eye-curtains dropt,[3] what is this LIGHT which is said to exist together with this *warmth*, we feel, and yet is something else? But I read likewise in that same face, as if thou wert beginning to prepare that question, a sort of mis-giving from within, as if thou wert more positive than sure that the reply, with which you would accommodate me, is as wise, as it is witty. Therefore, though I cannot answer your question, I will give you a hint how you may answer it for yourself.—1st. Learn the art and acquire the habit of contemplating things abstractedly from their *relations*. I will explain myself by an instance. Suppose a body floating at a certain height in the air, and receiving the light so equally on all sides as not to occasion the eye to conjecture any solid contents. And now let six or seven persons see it at different distances and from different points of view. For A it will be a square! for B a triangle; for C two right-angled triangles attached to each other; for D two unequal triangles; for E it will be a triangle with a Trapezium hung on to it; for F it will be a square with a cross in it

[1] "For ever and ever". Vulgate NT passim, OT occasionally.

[2] This sentence and the next are an addition to the letter to Edward Coleridge. The man apparently "out of his senses" is almost a commonplace with C, who sometimes connects himself with Giordano Bruno as such; see *Omniana* I 242–3, quoted in *SM* (*CC*) 4 n 2; cf ibid 21.

[3] Cf:

and, bold with joy,
Forth from his dark and lonely hiding-place,
(Portentous sight!) the owlet Atheism,
Sailing on obscene wings athwart the noon,
Drops his blue-fringéd lids, and holds them close,
And hooting at the glorious sun in Heaven,
Cries out, "Where is it?"

Fears in Solitude lines 80–6: *PW* (EHC) I 259.

⊠; for G it will be an oblong quadrangle with three triangles in it ⊠ ; and for H three unequal triangles.

Now it is evident that neither of all these is the figure itself, (which in this instance is a four-sided pyramid), but the contingent *relations* of the figure. Now transfer this from Geometry to the subjects of the real (*i.e.* not merely formal or abstract) sciences—to substances and bodies, the materia subjecta[1] of the Chemist, Physiologist and Naturalist, and you will gradually (that is, if you choose and sincerely *will* it) acquire the power and the disposition of contemplating your own imaginations, wants, appetites, passions, opinions, &c., on the same principles, and distinguish that, which alone is and abides, from the accidental and impermanent relations arising out of its co-existence with other things or beings.

My second rule or maxim requires its prolegomena. In the several classes and orders that mark the scale of organic nature, from the plant to the highest order of animals, each higher implies a lower, as the condition of its actual *existence*—and the same position holds good equally of the vital and organic powers. Thus, without the first power, that of growth, or what Bichat and others name the vegetive life,[2] or productivity, the second power, that of total[3] and locomotion (commonly but most infelicitously called irritability), could not exist—*i.e. manifest* its being. Productivity is the necessary antecedent of irritability, and in like manner, irritability of sensibility. But it is no less true, that in the *idea* of each power the lower derives its *intelligibility* from the higher: and the highest must be presumed to inhere latently or potentially in the lowest, or this latter will be wholly unintelligible, inconceivable—you can have *no conception* of it. Thus in sensibility we see a power that in every instant *goes out* of itself, and in the same instant retracts and falls back on itself: which

[1] "Subject/underlying matter".

[2] Marie François Xavier Bichat (1771–1802), French physiologist, does not use the word "vegetive" (or *vegétif*) in *Recherches physiologiques sur la vie et la mort* (1800) in the sense C gives, but *organique*. *OED* records "vegetive" as an earlier word revived by C. There is another reference to Bichat in N 29 f 150: "Mr Gillman's View of the Absorbents, as found... generally in the lower vegetoid (= Bichat's *Organic* & what the later German philosophizing Physiologists (Natur-philosophen) more happily term the Reproductive) System". C drew on Bichat in *P Lects* Lect XII (1949) 355; cf *TL* 22.

[3] HNC emends to "totality" in *C&S* (1839), but neither this reading nor that of the 1st and 2nd eds ("total") makes very good sense. Nevertheless, the fact that "total" is the reading in the letter to Edward Coleridge (*CL* VI 598) suggests that "total", however unlikely, may be the correct reading, and that by the whole phrase C means motion of the whole body and motion from place to place ("loco-").

the great fountains of pure Mathesis, the Pythagorean and Platonic Geometricians, illustrated in the production, or self-evolution, of the point into the circle. Imagine the going-forth and the retraction as two successive acts, the result would be an infinity of angles, a growth of zig-zag. In order to the imaginability of a circular line, the extrõitive and the retrõitive[1] must co-exist in one and the same act and moment, the curve line being the product. Now what is *ideally* true in the generations or productive acts of the intuitive faculty (of the *pure* sense, I mean, or Inward Vision—the *reine Anschauung* of the German Philosophers)[2] must be assumed as truth of fact in all living growth, or wherein would the growth of a plant differ from a chrystal? The latter is formed wholly by apposition ab extra:[3] in the former the movement ab extra is, in order of thought, consequent on, and yet coinstan[tan]eous with, the movement ab intra.[4] Thus, the *specific* character of Sensibility, the highest of the three powers, is found to be the *general* character of Life, and supplies the only way of *conceiving*, supplies the only insight into the *possibility* of, the first and lowest power. And yet even thus, growth taken as separate from and exclusive of sensibility, would be unintelligible, nay, contradictory. For it would be an act of the life, or productive *form* (vide Aids to Reflection, p. 68.)[5] of the plant, having the life itself as its *source*, (since it is a going forth from the life), and likewise having the life itself as its *object*, for in the same instant it is *retracted:* and yet the product (*i.e.* the plant), exists not for *itself*, by the hypothesis that has excluded sensibility. For all sensibility is a self-finding; whence the German word for sensation or feeling is Empfindung, *i.e.* an *inward finding*.[6] *Therefore* sensibility cannot be excluded: and as it does not exist *actually*, it must be involved *potentially*. Life does not yet manifest itself in its highest *dignity*, as a self-*finding;* but in an evident tendency thereto, or a

[1] *OED* cites C for "extroitive", dating it 1834 (in *CN* III 4272 dated Dec 1815); "retroitive" is not in *OED*. Cf "Growth, Life = the identity of co-instantaneity of the extrõitive and retrõitive, in itself a circle or cycloid?" N F° f 77.

[2] Cf C's use of this phrase from German philosophy in a letter to J. H. Green 28 Jun 1824: *CL* V 371.

[3] "From outside".

[4] "From inside".

[5] C refers to "Moral and Religious Aphorisms" VI, in which he comments on unity in relation to the crocus: "That the root, stem, leaves, petals &c. cohere to one plant, is owing to an antecedent Power or Principle in the Seed, which existed before a single particle of the matters that constitute the *size* and visibility of the Crocus, had been attracted from the surrounding Soil, Air, and Moisture." *AR* (1825) 68.

[6] C again attempts to illuminate the meaning of a word by calling attention to its derivation; cf above, p 13 and n 2. On *Empfindung* cf *CN* III 3605 and n.

self-*seeking*—and this has two epochs, or intensities. Potential sensibility in its first epoch, or lowest intensity, appears as growth: in its second epoch, it shews itself as irritability, or vital instinct. In both, however, the sensibility must have pre-existed, (or rather pre-inhered) though as latent: or how could the irritability have been evolved out of the growth? (*ex. gr.* in the stamina of the plant during the act of impregnating the germen). Or the sensibility out of the irritability? (*ex. gr.* in the first appearance of nerves and nervous bulbs, in the lower orders of the insect realm.) But, indeed, evolution as contradistinguished from *apposition*, or superinduction *ab aliunde*,[1] is implied in the conception of *life:* and is that which essentially differences a living fibre from a thread of Asbestos, the Floscule or any other of the moving fairy shapes of animalcular life from the frost-plumes on a window pane.

Again: what has been said of the lowest power of life relatively to its highest power—growth to sensibility, the plant to the animal—applies equally to *life* itself relatively to *mind.* Without the latter the former would be unintelligible, and the idea would contradict itself. If there had been no self-*retaining* power, a self-finding would be a perpetual self-*losing*. Divide a second into a thousand, or if you please, a million of parts, yet if there be an absolute chasm separating one moment of self-finding from another, the chasm of a millionth of a second would be equal to all time. A being that existed for itself only in moments, each infinitely small and yet absolutely divided from the preceding and following, would not exist *for itself* at all. And if all beings were the same, or yet lower, it could not be said to *exist* in any sense, any more than *light* would exist as *light*, if there were no eyes or visual power: and the whole conception would break up into contradictory positions—an intestine conflict more destructive than even that between the two cats, where one tail alone is said to have survived the battle.[2] The conflicting factors of our conception would eat each other up, tails and all. *Ergo:* the mind, as a self-retaining power, is no less indispensable to the intelligibility of life as a self-finding power, than a self-finding power, *i.e.* sensibility, to a self-seeking power, *i.e.* growth. Again: a self-retaining mind—(*i.e.*

[1] "From elsewhere".

[2] An allusion to the fable of the Kilkenny cats. The story runs that during the rebellion of Ireland Kilkenny was garrisoned by a troop of Hessian soldiers who to amuse themselves tied two cats together by their tails. The officers determined to stop this practice. But a look-out man who saw an officer approaching cut the tails and the cats made their escape. He explained coolly to the officer that the cats had been fighting, had devoured each other, and left only the tails behind.

memory, which is the primary sense of mind, and the common people in several of our provinces still use the word in this sense)[1]—a self-*re*taining power supposes a self-*con*taining power, a self-conscious being. And this is the definition of *mind* in its proper and distinctive sense, a subject that is its own object[2]—or where A contem*plant* is one and the same subject with A contem*plated*. Lastly, (that I may complete the ascent of powers for my own satisfaction, and not as expecting, or in the present habit of your thoughts even wishing you to follow me to a height, dizzy for the strongest spirit, it being the apex of all human, perhaps of angelic knowledge to know, that *it must be:* since absolute *ultimates* can only be seen by a light thrown backward from the Penultimate,—John's Gosp. i. 18.)[3] Lastly, I say, the self-*containing* power supposes a self-*causing* power. *Causa sui*, αἰτία ὑπερούσιος.[4] Here alone we find a problem which in its very statement contains its own solution—the one self-solving power, beyond which no question *is possible*. Yet short of this we dare not rest; for even the 'Ο ῎ΩΝ,[5] the Supreme *Being*,[6] if it were contemplated abstractly from the Absolute WILL, whose essence it is to be causitive of *all* Being, would sink into a Spinozistic Deity. That this is not evident to us arises from the false notion, of Reason (Ὁ Λόγος)[7] as a quality, property, or faculty of the Real: whereas reason *is* the supreme reality, the only true *being* in all things visible and invisible! the Pleroma, in whom alone God loveth the world! Even in man *will* is deeper than *mind*: for mind does not cease to be *mind* by having an antecedent; but Will is either the first (τὸ ἀεὶ πρόπρωτον, τὸ nunquam *positum*, semper *sup*ponendum)[8] or it is not WILL at all.

[1] C expands in the letter to Edward Coleridge: "ex. gr. Don't you *mind* him? i.e. remember him?—*Mind* you call on Mr —— when you get to Ottery...". *CL* VI 600.

[2] Cf the statement and solution of the problem of the identity of subject and object in *BL* ch 12 (1907) I 174–9.

[3] "No man hath seen God at any time; the only begotten Son, which is [ὁ ὤν] in the bosom of the Father, he hath declared *him*." See also n 5, below.

[4] "Cause of itself, a cause above Being". The Greek ὑπερούσιος is found in Proclus and afterwards much used, by e.g. Dionysius the Areopagite and by Erigena in the book that C was reading in 1803, *De divisione naturae* I § 16 (1681) 10; cf above, p 170 and n 1.

[5] This is from the Septuagint. In this context: "HE WHO IS"; in the Old Testament: "[I am] THAT I AM". Exod 3.14 etc.

[6] In the letter to Edward Coleridge "*Being*" is "Reality", and the subsequent "Being" is "*Reality*". *CL* VI 600.

[7] "The Logos", "The Reason", or "The Word".

[8] "Which is always first of all, which is never *posited* [laid down], must always be *sup*posed [laid underneath, as a foundation]". C plays on the meaning of *ponere* and *supponere*; cf *CN* III 3587 and *Friend* (*CC*) I 477 n 3.

And now, friend! for the practical rules which I promised, or the means by which you may *educate* in yourself that state of mind which is most favourable to a true knowledge of both the worlds that *now are*, and to a right faith in the *world to come*.[1]

I. Remember, that whatever *is*, *lives*. A thing absolutely lifeless is inconceivable, except as a thought, image, or fancy, in some other being.

II. In every living form, the conditions of its *existence* are to be sought for in that which is *below* it; the grounds of its *intelligibility* in that which is *above* it.

III. Accustom your mind to distinguish the relations of things from the things themselves. Think often of the latter, independent of the former, in order that you may never think of the former apart from the latter, *i.e.* mistake mere relations for true and enduring realities: and with regard to *these* seek the solution of each in some higher reality. The contrary process leads demonstrably to Atheism, and though you may not get quite so far, it is not well to be seen travelling on the road with your face towards it.

I might add a fourth rule: Learn to distinguish permanent from accidental relations. But I am willing that you should for a time take permanent *relations* as real things—confident that you will soon feel the necessity of reducing what you now call *things* into relations, which immediately arising out of a somewhat else may properly be contemplated as the *products* of that somewhat *else*, and as the means by which its existence is made known to you. But known as what? not as a *product:* for it is the somewhat *else*, to which the product stands in the same relation as the words, you are now hearing, bear to my living soul. But if not as products, then as productive *powers:* and the result will be that what you have hitherto called *things* will be regarded as only more or less permanent *relations* of things, having their derivative reality greater or less in proportion as they are regular or accidental relations; determined by the pre-established fitness of the true thing to the organ and faculty of the percipient, or resulting from some defect or anomaly in the latter.

With these convictions matured into a habit of mind, the man no longer seeks, or believes himself to find, true reality except in the

[1] This and the following two paragraphs do not appear in the letter to Edward Coleridge, which continues: "Now then for the second Rule: in all things accustom yourself to seek the solution of the lower in the higher.—And the first Rule was—? I will comprize both in one sentence." The subsequent paragraph in *C&S* continues the letter: "Accustom your mind..." etc. *CL* VI 600.

powers of nature; which living and actuating POWERS are made known to him, and their *kinds* determined, and their *forces* measured, by their proper products. In other words, he thinks of the products in reference to the productive [a]*powers*, τοῖς[b] ὄντως ὑπάρχουσιν Ἀριθμοῖς ἢ Δυνάμεσι, ὡς ταῖς προμαθεστάταις ἀρχαῖς τοῦ πάντος οὐρανοῦ καὶ γῆς,[1] and[c] thus gives to the former (to the *products*, I mean) a true reality, a life, a beauty, and a physiognomic expression. For *him* they are the ἜΠΕΑ Ζ'ΩΟΝΤΑ,[2] ἡ ὁμιλία καὶ ἡ διάλεκτος Θεοῖς πρὸς Ἀνθρώπους.[3] The Allokosmite, therefore (though he does not bark at the image in the glass, because he knows what it is), possesses the same world with the Toutoscosmites; and has, besides, in *present* possession *another* and *better* world, to which he can transport himself by a swifter vehicle than Fortunatus's Wishing Cap.[4]

Finally, what is Reason? You have often asked me; and this is my answer;

> Whene'er the mist, that stands 'twixt God and thee
> Defecates to a pure transparency,
> That intercepts no light and adds no stain—
> There Reason is, and there[d] begins her rein![5]

[a–b] 1st ed: *powers*, the [c] 1st ed: of the Samian sage: and [d] 1st ed: then

[1] Already tr by C in the Glossary (above, p 166) and attributed to Pythagoras. C adapts the second part of the phrase from Iamblichus *De vita Pythagorae* 146. The following quotation from Thomas Taylor's tr (1818, repr 1926 cited) 79 gives the context: "[Pythagoras said:] Orpheus the son of Calliope said that the eternal essence of number is the most providential principle of the universe, of heaven and earth and the intermediate nature; and further still, that it is the root of the permanency of divine nature, of Gods and daemons." The source of the preceding Greek word has not been traced.

[2] "LIVING WORDS", already tr by C in the Glossary (above, p 166); cf *AR* Preface, in which he refers to Horne Tooke's "celebrated work, Ἔπεα πτερόεντα, Winged Words: or Language, not only the *Vehicle* of Thought but the *Wheels*. With my convictions and views, for ἔπεα I should substitute λόγοι, *i.e.* Words *select* and *determinate*, and for πτερόεντα, ζώοντες, *i.e.* *living* Words." *AR* (1825) vii. Cf *Sh C* II 104. For C's opinion of this work of John Horne Tooke (1736–1812), Ἔπεα πτερόεντα, *or the Diversions of Purley* (2 vols 1798, 1805), see *TT* 7 May 1830.

[3] Plato *Symposium* 203A (var). Tr by C in the Glossary (above, p 166). C quoted the sentence from the *Symposium* in N 29 f 55. The attribution to Diotima, the character speaking, instead of Plato in N 29 and in Jacobi, and the omission of words, suggest that C's immediate source was Jacobi *Allwills Briefsammlung* XXI: *Werke* I (Leipzig 1812) 226; cf above, p 168 n 6.

[4] Fortunatus was a mediaeval folk hero who secured the marvellous hat from the Sultan of Turkey; it transported the wearer wherever he wished to go. At this point the letter to Edward Coleridge concludes (the ms breaks off): "Wishing-Cap, whenever he is tired of doing nothing, & passively *done up*.—" *CL* VI 601.

[5] These lines by C were first published in *C&S*.

But, alas!

————tu stesso ti fai grosso
Col falso immaginar, si che non vedi
Cio che vedresti, se l'avessi scosso.

DANTE; *Paradiso, Canto I*[1]

[1] Dante *Paradiso* I 88–90:

With false imagination thou thyself
Makest dull; so that thou seest not the thing
Which thou hadst seen, had that been shaken off.

Tr Henry Francis Cary, who published a translation of the *Inferno* in 1805 and the complete *Divina commedia* in 1814. C met him in 1817, praised his translation in a lecture of Feb 1818, and became a close friend and admirer. In this passage from the *Paradiso* Beatrice is telling Dante that he is not still on earth as he believes, after he has gazed at the sun, but has ascended and is surrounded by a vast sea of light and flame.

EDITOR'S APPENDIXES

APPENDIX A

PREFACE TO CHURCH AND STATE (1839)

BY HENRY NELSON COLERIDGE

PREFACE
TO THE CHURCH AND STATE

A RECOLLECTION of the value set upon the following little work by its Author,* combined with a deep sense of the wisdom and importance of the positions laid down in it, will, it is hoped, be thought to justify the publication of a few preliminary remarks, designed principally to remove formal difficulties out of the path of a reader not previously acquainted with Mr. Coleridge's writings, nor conversant with the principles of his philosophy. The truth is that, although the Author's plan is well defined and the treatment strictly progressive, there is in some parts a want of detailed illustration and express connexion, which weakens the impression of the entire work on the generality of readers. "If," says Mr. Maurice, "I were addressing a student who was seeking to make up his mind on the question, without being previously biassed by the views of any particular party, I could save myself this trouble by merely referring him to the work of Mr. Coleridge, on the Idea of Church and State, published shortly after the passing of the Roman Catholic Bill. The hints respecting the nature of the Christian Church which are thrown out in that work are only sufficient to make us wish that the Author had developed his views more fully; but the portion of it which refers to the State seems to me in the highest degree satisfactory. When I use the word satisfactory, I do not mean that it will satisfy the wishes of any person who thinks that the epithets *teres atque rotundus*[1] are the highest that can be applied to a scientific work; who expects an author to furnish him with a complete system which he can carry away in his memory, and, after it has received a few improvements from himself, can hawk it about to the public or to a set of admiring disciples. Men of this description would regard Mr. Coleridge's book as disorderly and fragmentary; but those who have some notion of what Butler meant when he said, that the best writer would be he who merely stated his premisses, and left his readers to work out the conclusions for themselves;—those who feel that they want just the assistance which Socrates offered to his scholars—assistance, not in providing them with thoughts, but in bringing forth into the light thoughts which they had within them before;—these will acknowledge that Mr. Coleridge has only deserted the common high way of exposition, that he might follow more closely the turnings and windings which the mind of an earnest thinker makes when it is groping after the truth to which he wishes to conduct it.

* See *Table Talk*, 2nd edit. p. 5, note.

1 Horace *Satires* 2.7.86. "Smooth and rounded". Tr Fairclough (LCL 1926) 231.

To them, therefore, the book is satisfactory by reason of those very qualities which make it alike unpleasant to the formal schoolman and to the man of the world. And, accordingly, scarcely any book, published so recently and producing so little apparent effect, has really exercised a more decided influence over the thoughts and feelings of men who ultimately rule the mass of their countrymen."*

Under these circumstances, the following argument or summary of the fundamental and more complicated portion of the work may be serviceable to the ingenuous but less experienced reader.

I. The constitution of the State and the Church is treated according to the Idea of each. By the Idea of the State or Church is here meant that conception, which is not abstracted from any particular form or mode in which either may happen to exist at any given time, nor yet generalized from any number or succession of such forms or modes, but which is produced by a knowledge or sense of the ultimate aim of each. This idea, or sense of the ultimate aim, may exist, and powerfully influence a man's thoughts and actions, without his being able to express it in definite words, and even without his being distinctly conscious of its indwelling. A few may possess ideas in this meaning;—the generality of mankind are possessed by them. In either case an idea, so understood, is in order of thought always and of necessity contemplated as antecedent,—a mere conception, strictly defined as an abstraction or generalization from one or more particular forms or modes, is necessarily posterior,—in order of thought to the thing thus conceived. And though the idea is in its nature a prophecy, yet it must be carefully remembered that the particular form, construction, or model, best fitted to render the idea intelligible to a third person, is not necessarily—perhaps, not most commonly—the mode or form in which it actually arrives at realization. For in consequence of the imperfection of means and materials in all the works of man, a law of compensation and a principle of compromise are perpetually active; and it is the first condition of a sound philosophy of State to recognize the wide extent of the one, the necessity of the other, and the frequent occurrence of both.

II. The word State is used in two senses,—a larger, in which it comprises, and a narrower, in which it is opposed to, the National Church. A Constitution is the ideal attribute of a State in the larger sense, as a body politic having the principle of its unity within itself; and it is the law or principle which prescribes the means and conditions by and under which that unity is established and preserved. The Constitution, therefore, of this Nation comprises the idea of a Church and a State in the narrower sense, placed in simple antithesis one to another. The unity of the State, in this latter sense, results from the equipoise and interdependence of the two great opposite interests of every such State, its Permanence and its Progression. The permanence of a State is connected with the land; its progression with the mercantile, manufacturing, distributive, and professional classes. The first class is subdivided into what our law books have called Major and Minor Barons;—both of these subdivisions, as such, being

* *Kingdom of Christ*, vol. iii. p. 2. A work of singular originality and power.

opposed to the representatives of the progressive interest of the nation, yet the latter of them drawing more nearly to the antagonist order than the former. Upon these facts the principle of the Constitution of the State, in its narrower sense, was established. The balance of permanence and progression was secured by a legislature of two Houses; the first, consisting wholly of the Major Barons or landholders; the second, of the Minor Barons or knights, as the representatives of the remaining landed community, together with the Burgesses, as representing the commercial, manufacturing, distributive, and professional classes—the latter constituting the effectual majority in number. The King, in whom the executive power was vested, was in regard to the interests of the State, in its antithetic sense, the beam of the scales.

This is the Idea of that State, not its history; it has been the standard or aim, the *Lex Legum*,[1] which, in the very first law of State ever promulgated in the land, was pre-supposed as the ground of that first law.

III. But the English Constitution results from the harmonious opposition of two institutions, the State, in the narrower sense, and the Church. For as by the composition of the one provision was alike made for permanence, and progression in wealth and personal freedom; to the other was committed the only remaining interest of the State in its larger sense, that of maintaining and advancing the moral cultivation of the people themselves, without which neither of the former could continue to exist.

IV. It was common, at least to the Scandinavian, Keltic, and Gothic, with the Semitic tribes, if not universal in all the primitive races, that in taking possession of a new country, and in the division of the land into heritable estates among the individual warriors or heads of families, a Reserve should be made for the Nation itself. The sum total of these heritable portions is called the Propriety, the Reserve the Nationalty. These were constituent factors of the commonwealth; the existence of the one being the condition of the rightfulness of the other. But the wealth appropriated was not so entirely a property as not to remain, to a certain extent, national; nor was the wealth reserved so exclusively national as not to admit an individual tenure. The settlement of the Nationalty in one tribe only of the Hebrew confederacy, subservient as it was to a higher purpose, was in itself a deviation from the idea, and a main cause of the comparatively little effect which the Levitical establishment produced on the moral and intellectual character of the Jewish people during the whole period of their existence as an independent state.

V. The Nationalty was reserved for the maintenance of a permanent class or order, the Clerisy, Clerks, Clergy, or Church of the Nation. This class comprised the learned of all denominations, the professors of all those arts and sciences, the possession and application of which constitute the civilization of a country. Theology formed only a part of the objects of the National Church. The theologians took the lead, indeed, and deservedly so;—not because they were priests, but because under the name of theology were contained the study of languages, history, logic,

[1] "Law of Laws"; see above, pp 21, 31.

ethics, and a philosophy of ideas; because the science of theology itself was the root of the knowledges that civilize man, and gave unity and the circulating sap of life to all other sciences; and because, under the same name were comprised all the main aids, instruments, and materials of National Education. Accordingly, a certain smaller portion of the functionaries of the Clerisy were to remain at the fountain heads of the humanities, cultivating and enlarging the knowledge already possessed, watching over the interests of physical and moral science, and the instructors of all the remaining more numerous classes of the order. These last were to be distributed throughout the country, so as not to leave even the smallest integral division without a resident guide, guardian, and teacher, diffusing through the whole community the knowledge indispensable for the understanding of its rights, and for the performance of the correspondent duties. But neither Christianity, nor *a fortiori*, any particular scheme of theology supposed to be deduced from it, forms any essential part of the being of a National Church, however conducive it may be to its well being. A National Church may exist, and has existed, without, because before, the institution of the Christian Church, as the Levitical Church in the Hebrew, and the Druidical in the Keltic, constitutions may prove.

VI. But two distinct functions do not necessarily imply or require two different functionaries: on the contrary, the perfection of each may require the union of both in the same person. And in the instance now in question, as great and grievous errors have arisen from confounding the functions of the National Church with those of the Church of Christ, so fearfully great and grievous will be the evils from the success of an attempt to separate them.

VII. In process of time, however, and as a natural consequence of the expansion of the mercantile and commercial order, the students and professors of those sciences and sorts of learning, the use and necessity of which were perpetual to the Nation, but only occasional to the Individuals, gradually detached themselves from the National Clerisy, and passed over, as it were, to that order, with the growth and thriving condition of which their particular emoluments were found to increase in equal proportion. And hence by slow degrees the learned in the several departments of law, medicine, architecture and the like, contributed to form under the common name of Professional, an intermediate link between the national clerisy and the simple burgesses.

VIII. But this circumstance cannot alter the tenure, or annul the rights, of those who remained, and who, as members of the permanent learned class, were planted throughout the realm as the immediate agents and instruments in the work of increasing and perpetuating the civilization of the nation; and who, thus fulfilling the purposes for which the Nationalty was reserved, are entitled to remain its usufructuary trustees. The proceeds of the Nationalty might, indeed, in strictness, if it could ever be expedient, be rightfully transferred to functionaries other than such as are also ministers of the Church of Christ. But the Nationalty itself cannot, without foul wrong to the nation, be alienated from its original purposes; and those who being duly appointed thereto, exercise the functions and perform the duties attached to the Nationalty, possess a right to the same by a title to which the thunders from Mount Sinai might give greater authority, but not additional evidence.

IX. Previously to the sixteenth century, large masses were alienated from the heritable proprieties of the realm, and confounded with the Nationalty under the common name of Church property. At the period of the Reformation a re-transfer of these took place, and rightfully so: but together with, and under pretext of, this restoration to the State of what properly belonged to it, a wholesale usurpation took place of a very large portion of that which belonged to the Church. This was a sacrilegious robbery on the Nation, and a deadly wound on the constitution of the State at large. The balance of the reserved and appropriated wealth of the Nation was deranged, and thus the former became unequal to the support of the entire burthen of popular civilization originally intended to be borne by it.* Barely enough—indeed, less than enough—was left for the effectual maintenance of that primary class of the Clerisy, which had not fallen off into separate professions, but continued to be the proper servants of the public in producing and reproducing, in preserving, promoting and perfecting all the necessary sources and conditions of the civilization of the Nation itself.†

X. Though many things may detract from the comparative fitness of individuals, or of particular classes, for the trust and functions of the Nationalty, there are only two absolute disqualifications;—allegiance to a foreign power, or the acknowledgment of any other visible head of the National Church but the King;—and compulsory celibacy, in connection with, and dependence on, a foreign and extra-national head.

XI. The legitimate objects of the power of the King and the two Houses of Parliament, as constituting the State, in its special and antithetic sense, comprise, according to the idea, all the interests and concerns of the Propriety, and rightfully those alone.

* "Give back to the Church what the Nation originally consecrated to its use, and it ought then to be charged with the education of the people; but half of the original revenue has been already taken by force from her, or lost to her through desuetude, legal decision, or public opinion: and are those whose very houses and parks are part and parcel of what the Nation designed for the general purposes of the Clergy, to be heard, when they argue for making the Church support, out of her diminished revenues, institutions, the intended means for maintaining which they themselves hold under the sanction of legal robbery?" *Table Talk*, Pref. p. xvi. 2nd edit.

† See an approach to an expression of the Author's idea of the National Church thus regarded, in the Bishop of London's late Charge, Oct. 1838, p. 2, &c.[1]

[1] In his *Charge* of 1838, Blomfield stressed the Church's duty to provide "for the spiritual instruction and pastoral superintendence of a vast population, which had immeasurably outgrown the teaching and discipline of the established Church", and appealed for support of the National Society for the Education of the Poor, saying that on its success "will mainly depend the decision of the question, whether the education of the country is to be a religious education, and a church education, conducted, as it has hitherto been, by the parochial Clergy". For C's marginal comments on Blomfield's *Charge* of 1830, see above, p 62 n 5.

XII. The King, again, is the Head of the National Clerisy, and the supreme trustee of the Nationalty; the power of which in relation to its proper objects is rightfully exercised, according to the idea, by the King and the two Houses of Convocation, and by them alone. The proper objects of this power are mentioned in No. V.

XIII. The Coronation Oath neither does, nor can, bind the conscience of the King in matters of faith. But it binds him to refuse his consent (without which no change in the existing law can be effected) to any measure subverting or tending to subvert the safety and independence of the National Church, or which may expose the realm to the danger of a return of that foreign Usurper, misnamed spiritual, from which it has with so many sacrifices emancipated itself. And previously to the ceremonial act which announces the King the only lawful and sovereign head of both the Church and the State, this oath is administered to him religiously as the representative person and crowned majesty of the Nation;—religiously; —for the mind of the Nation, existing only as an idea, can act distinguishably on the ideal powers alone,—that is, on the reason and conscience.

The several other points comprised in the remainder of this work, though of great interest and importance, require neither analysis nor comment for their perfect comprehension. But it will naturally occur to the reader to consider how far the idea of the Church and of its relation to the State presented in these pages coincides with either of the two celebrated systems, those of Hooker and Warburton, which, under one shape or another, have divided the opinions of thinking persons up to the present day.

According to Hooker, the Church is one body,—the essential unity of which consists in, and is known by, an external profession of Christianity, without regard in any respect had to the moral virtues or spiritual graces of any member of that body. "If by external profession they be Christians, then are they of the visible Church of Christ: and Christians by external profession they are all, whose mark of recognizance hath in it those things which we have mentioned, yea, although they be impious idolaters, wicked heretics, persons excommunicable, yea, and cast out for notorious improbity. Such withal we deny not to be the imps and limbs of Satan, even as long as they continue such." (E. P. III. c. i. s. 7. *Keble's* edit. vol. i. p. 431.)

With this Warburton and Coleridge in general terms agree. (*Alliance*, &c. II. c. ii. s. 2.—*Church and State*, p. 127.)[1] And the words of the nineteenth Article,[2] though apparently of a more restricted import, may be presumed not to mean less.

[1] The grouping of Warburton and C might mislead the reader into thinking that there is a greater similarity than really exists in their views on Church and State. It is only in this limited area (the signs of the outward and visible church) that they agree.

[2] Article XIX "Of the Church" states: "The visible Church of Christ is a congregation of faithful men, in which the pure Word of God is preached, and the Sacraments be duly ministered according to Christ's ordinance in all those things that of necessity are requisite to the same. As the Church of Jerusalem, Alexandria, and Antioch, have erred; so also the Church of Rome hath erred, not only in their living and manner of Ceremonies, but also in matters of Faith."

But, further, Hooker insists that the Church, existing in any particular country, and the State are one and the same society, contemplated in two different relations, "A Commonwealth we name it simply in regard of some regiment or policy under which men live; a Church for the truth of that religion which they profess. * * * When we oppose the Church, therefore, and the Commonwealth in a Christian society, we mean by the Commonwealth that society with relation unto all the public affairs thereof, only the matter of true religion excepted; by the Church, the same society with only reference unto the matter of true religion, without any other affairs besides: when that society, which is both a Church and a Commonwealth, doth flourish in those things which belong unto it as a Commonwealth, we then say, 'the Commonwealth doth flourish;' when in those things which concern it as a Church, 'the Church doth flourish;' when in both, then 'the Church and Commonwealth flourish together.'" (E. P. VIII. c. i. s. 5. vol. iii. p. 420–1.)

To this view Warburton, as is well known, is directly opposed. He argues that, although two societies may be so closely related to each other as to have one common *suppositum*,—that is, the same natural persons being exclusively members of each,—the societies themselves, as such, are factitious bodies, and each of them must therefore of necessity be distinct in personality and will from the other. "The artificial man, society, is much unlike the natural; who being created for several ends hath several interests to pursue, and several relations to consult, and may therefore be considered under several capacities, as a religious, a civil, and a rational animal; and yet they all make but one and the same man. But one and the same political society cannot be considered in one view, as a religious—in another, as a civil—and in another, as a literary—community. One society can be precisely but one of these communities." (*Alliance*, &c. ii. c. v.) Accordingly Warburton insists, in opposition to Hooker, that the Puritan premiss,—that the Church and the State are distinct and originally independent societies,—was and is the truth; but he denies the Puritan inference, that such independency must therefore be perpetual;—affirming the existence of an alliance between these two societies upon certain terms; and a resulting mutual inter-dependency of one on the other; whereby the consequence from the position of the Puritans—an *imperium in imperio*, or subjugation of the State to the Church,—and the consequence from the position of Hooker—the enslavement of the Church by the State—are equally precluded. The Church subordinates itself to the State upon faith of certain stipulations for support by the latter; and if the State violates, or withdraws from the fulfillment of, those stipulations, the Church is thereby remitted to her original independence.*

Now so far as the distinct inter-dependency of the State and the Church

* It is worthy of remark that, if Warburton had lived in these days, and had adhered to the principles advocated by him in this treatise, he must several years ago have declared the terms of convention between the Church and State in this country violated by the latter, and the alliance of the two at an end. See his third book, and especially the second chapter. It is to be observed, also, that Warburton confounds the Christian with the Established Church as much as Hooker. See B. II. c. iii. 3.

is in question, Coleridge agrees with Warburton.[1] But the peculiarity of his system, as expressly laid down in this work and incidentally mentioned in many of his other writings,—a peculiarity fruitful in the most important consequences—is grounded on a distinction taken between the visible Church of Christ, as localized in any Christian country, and the National or Established Church of that country. *Distinction*, be it observed, not separation,—for the two ideas

—bene conveniunt, et in una sede morantur;[2]

they not only may co-exist in the same *suppositum*, but may require an identity of subject in order to the complete development of the perfections of either. According to Coleridge, then, the Christian Church is not a kingdom or realm of this world, nor a member of any such kingdom or realm; it is not opposed to any particular State in the large or narrow sense of the word; it is in no land national, and the national Reserve is not entrusted to its charge. It is, on the contrary, the opposite to the World only; the counterforce to the evils and defects of States, as such, in the abstract,—asking of any particular State neither wages nor dignities, but demanding protection, that is, to be let alone.

With so much therefore of the preceding and all other theories as considers any branch of the Church of Christ, *as such*, in the character of a National Establishment, and arrogates to it, *as such*, upon any ground, worldly riches, rank or power—Coleridge is directly at variance. But we have already seen (v. vi. vii. viii.) that there is, nevertheless, in this and in almost every other country raised above the level of barbarism a Church, which is strictly and indefeasibly National; and in the ideal history herein presented of its origin and primary elements, its endowment, its uses, duties, ends, and objects, its relation to the State, and its present representatives, a solemn warning is recorded of the fatal consequences of either confounding it with, or separating it from, the visible Church of Christ.

The Christian Church is a public and visible community, having ministers of its own, whom the State can neither constitute nor degrade, and whose maintenance amongst Christians is as secure as the command of Christ can make it: for *so hath the Lord ordained that they which preach the Gospel should live of the Gospel.* (1. Cor. ix. 14.) The National Church is a public and visible community, having ministers whom the Nation, through the agency of a Constitution, hath created trustees of a reserved national fund, upon fixed terms and with defined duties, and whom, in case of breach of those terms or dereliction of those duties, the Nation, through the same agency, may discharge. "If the former be *Ecclesia*, the communion of such as are called out of the World, that is, in reference to the especial ends and purposes of that communion; the latter might more expressively have been

[1] Again HNC's linking of the two writers is misleading and obscures C's radical objection to Warburton's treatment of Church and State as factitious interdependent societies that engage in a pseudo-legal "alliance"; see above, p 196.

[2] Ovid *Metamorphoses* 2.846 (var). "...go well together, and tarry long in the same dwelling-place". Tr adapted from Frank Justus Miller (LCL 1921) I 119.

called *Enclesia*, or an order of men chosen in and of the realm, and constituting an estate of the realm."[1]

Now there is no reason why the ministers of the one Church may not also be ministers of the other: there are many reasons why they should be.

When therefore it is objected that Christ's *kingdom is not of this world*, it is admitted to be true; but the text is shown to have no application in the way of impeachment of the titles, emoluments or authorities, of an institution which rightfully *is* of this world, and would not answer the end of its constitution if it ceased to belong to, and in a certain sense to sympathize with, the world. When again it is alleged that "the best service which men of power can do to Christ is without any more ceremony to sweep all and leave the Church as bare as in the day it was first born"—"that if we give God our hearts and affections, our goods are better bestowed otherwise,"* the spirit and reason of that allegation are humbly submitted to God's own judgment; but it is at the same time confidently charged in reply, that the notion of the Church, as the established instructress of the people, being improved in efficiency by the reduction of its ministers to a state bordering on mendicancy—can in its flagrant folly be alone attributed to that meanness of thought, which is at once the fruit and the punishment of minds enslaved to party and the world, and rendered indifferent to all truth by an affected toleration of every form of error. When further it is said that the Bishops of the Church of Christ have no vocation to interfere in the legislation of the country, it is granted; but with this parallel assertion, that the Prelates of a National Establishment, charged with the vast and awful task of preserving, increasing and perpetuating the moral culture of the people, have a call to be present, advise, and vote in the National Council, which can only cease to be a right when the representatives of the dearest national interest are denied a voice in the national assembly; and which is no more impaired by the fact of those Prelates sustaining in their individual persons another and still more sacred character than by their being members of a literary club or a botanical society. When, finally, it is insisted to be contrary to justice to compel those who dissent from a religious system either as to its doctrines or its forms of worship, to contribute to the maintenance of its priests and ministers, it is not denied; but it is withal maintained, that a national dedication of funds for the support of a determinate class of men, with the duty of national civilization to perform, can no more be vacated or qualified by reason of the voluntary secession of such dissenters from that religious system, because the seceders understand the character and obligation of that duty in a way of their own, than the rights of Parliament to levy taxes for the protection of our independence from foreign aggression can be affected by the dogma of rich philanthropists that war is unlawful, and to pay a shilling towards its support an offence against God.

But after all, it is urged, the funds set apart by the Nation for the support of the National Church are now in fact received by the ministers of the Church of Christ in this country! True; but, according to the idea,—and

* Hooker, B. V. lxxiv. 17.

[1] HNC quotes from *C&S* above, p 45.

that idea involves a history and a prophecy of the truth—it is not because they are *such* ministers that they receive those funds, but because, being now the only representatives, as formerly the principal constituents, of the National Clerisy or Church, they alone have a commission to carry on the work of national cultivation on national grounds—transmuting and integrating all that the separate professions have achieved in science or art—but, with a range transcending the limits of professional views, or local or temporary interests, applying the product simple and defecated, to the strengthening and subliming of the moral life of the Nation itself.

Such a Church is a principal instrument of the divine providence in the institution and government of human society. But it is not that Church against which we know that Hell shall not prevail.

For when the Nation, fatigued with the weight of dear and glorious recollections, shall resolve to repudiate its corporate existence and character, and to resolve its mystic unity into the breathing atoms that crowd the surface of the land,—then the national and ancestral Church of England will have an end. But it cannot be destroyed before. It lies within the folds of that marvellous Constitution, which patriots have out-watched the stars to develope and to protect, and is not separable from it. The time may come when it may seem fit to God that both shall perish, for ever, or for a season;—and the sure token of that time will be, when the divorce of scientific from religious education shall have had its full work throughout the length and the breadth of the land. Then although the Church *of* England may fall, the Church of Christ *in* England will stand erect; and the distinction, lost now in a common splendour, will be better seen and more poignantly felt by that darkening World to which the Christian Church must become a more conspicuous opposite.

—— οὐ γάρ νιν θνατὰ
φύσις ἀνέρων ἔτικτεν, οὐδὲ
μήν ποτε λάθα κατακοιμάσει·
μέγας ἐν ταύτῃ Θεὸς,
οὐδὲ γηράσκει.[1]

LINCOLN'S INN,
Nov. 29, 1838

[1] Sophocles *Oedipus tyrannus* 868–72 (var).

No mortal birth she owns;
N'er shall she slumber in oblivion cold,
For God in her is strong and grows not old.

Tr F. Storr (adapted) *Sophocles* (LCL 1912) I 79, 81. HNC adapts the pronouns of the original.

APPENDIX B

THE CATHOLIC EMANCIPATION ACT 1829

THE CATHOLIC EMANCIPATION ACT 1829

WHEREAS by various Acts of Parliament certain Restraints and Disabilities are imposed on the Roman Catholic Subjects of His Majesty, to which other Subjects of His Majesty are not liable: And whereas it is expedient that such Restraints and Disabilities shall be from henceforth discontinued: And whereas by various Acts certain Oaths and certain Declarations, commonly called the Declaration against Transubstantiation, and the Declaration against Transubstantiation and the Invocation of Saints and the Sacrifice of the Mass, as practised in the Church of *Rome* are or may be required to be taken, made, and subscribed by the Subjects of His Majesty, as Qualifications for sitting and voting in Parliament, and for the Enjoyment of certain Offices, Franchises, and Civil Rights: Be it enacted by the King's most Excellent Majesty, by and with the Advice and Consent of the Lords Spiritual and Temporal, and Commons, in this present Parliament assembled, and by the Authority of the same, That from and after the Commencement of this Act all such Parts of the said Acts as require the said Declarations, or either of them, to be made or subscribed by any of His Majesty's Subjects, as a Qualification for sitting and voting in Parliament or for the Exercise or Enjoyment of any Office, Franchise, or Civil Right, be and the same are (save as hereinafter provided and excepted) hereby repealed.

II. And be it enacted, That from and after the Commencement of this Act it shall be lawful for any Person professing the Roman Catholic Religion, being a Peer, or who shall after the Commencement of this Act be returned as a Member of the House of Commons, to sit and vote in either House of Parliament respectively, being in all other respects duly qualified to sit and vote therein, upon taking and subscribing the following Oath, instead of the Oaths of Allegiance, Supremacy and Abjuration:

I, *A.B.*, do sincerely promise and swear, That I will be faithful and bear true Allegiance to His Majesty King *George* the Fourth, and will defend him to the utmost of my Power against all Conspiracies and Attempts whatever, which shall be made against his Person, Crown, or Dignity; and I will do my utmost Endeavour to disclose and make known to His Majesty, His Heirs and Successors, all Treasons and traitorous Conspiracies which may be formed against him or them: And I do faithfully promise to maintain, support, and defend, to the utmost of my Power, the Succession of the Crown, which Succession, by an Act intituled *An Act for the further Limitation of the Crown, and better securing the Rights and Liberties of the Subject*, is and stands limited to the Princess *Sophia*, Electress of *Hanover*, and the Heirs of her Body being Protestants; hereby utterly renouncing and abjuring any Obedience or Allegiance unto any other Person claiming or pretending a Right to the Crown of this Realm: And I do further declare, That it is not an Article of my Faith, and that I do renounce, reject, and abjure the Opinion, that Princes excommunicated or deprived by the Pope, or any other Authority of the See of *Rome*, may be deposed or murdered by their Subjects, or by any Person whatsoever: And I do declare, That I do not believe that the Pope of *Rome*, or any other Foreign Prince, Prelate, Person, State, or Potentate, hath or ought to have any Temporal or Civil Jurisdiction, Power, Superiority, or Pre-eminence, directly or indirectly, within this Realm: I do swear, That I will defend to the utmost of my Power the Settlement of Property within this Realm, as established by the Laws: And I do hereby disclaim, disavow and solemnly abjure Any Intention to subvert the present Church Establishment as settled by Law within this Realm: And I do solemnly swear, That I never will exercise any Privilege to which I am or may become entitled, to disturb or weaken the Protestant Religion or Protestant Government, in the United Kingdom: And I do solemnly, in the Presence of God, profess, testify, and declare, That I do make this Declaration, and every Part thereof, in the plain ordinary Sense of the Words of this Oath, without any Evasion, Equivocation, or mental Reservation whatsoever. So help me GOD."

IV. Provided always, and be it further enacted, That no Peer professing the Roman Catholic Religion, and no Person professing the Roman Catholic Religion, who shall be returned a Member of the House of Commons after the Commencement of this Act, shall be capable of sitting or voting in either House of Parliament respectively, unless he shall first take and subscribe the Oath herein-before appointed and set forth, before the same Persons, at the same Times and Places, and in the same Manner as the Oaths and the Declaration now required by Law are respectively directed to be taken, made, and subscribed; and that any such Person professing the Roman Catholic Religion who shall sit or vote in either House of Parliament, without having first taken and subscribed, in the Manner aforesaid, the Oath in this Act appointed and set forth, shall be subject to the same Penalties, Forfeitures, and Disabilities, and the Offence of so sitting or voting shall be followed and attended by and with the same Consequences, as are by Law enacted and provided in the Case of Persons sitting or voting in either House of Parliament respectively, without the taking, making, and subscribing the Oaths and the Declaration now required by Law.

V. And be it further enacted, That it shall be lawful for Persons professing the Roman Catholic Religion to vote at Elections of Members to serve in Parliament for *England* and for *Ireland*, and also to vote at the Elections of Representative Peers of *Scotland* and of *Ireland*, and to be elected such Representative Peers, being in all other respects duly qualified, upon taking and subscribing the Oath herein-before appointed and set forth, instead of the Oaths of Allegiance, Supremacy, and Abjuration, and instead of the Declaration now by Law required, and instead also of such other Oath or Oaths as are now by Law required to be taken by any of His Majesty's Subjects professing the Roman Catholic Religion, and upon taking also such other Oath or Oaths as may now be lawfully tendered to any Persons offering to vote at such Elections.

IX. And be it further enacted. That no Person in Holy Orders in the Church of *Rome* shall be capable of being elected to serve in Parliament as a Member of the House of Commons; and if any such Person shall be elected to serve in Parliament as aforesaid, such Election shall be void; and if any Person, being elected to serve in Parliament as a Member of the House of Commons shall, after his Election, take or receive Holy Orders in the Church of *Rome*, the Seat of such Person shall immediately become void; and if any such Person shall, in any of the Cases aforesaid, presume to sit or vote as a Member of the House of Commons, he shall be subject to the same Penalties, Forfeitures, and Disabilities as are enacted by an Act passed in the Forty-first Year of the Reign of King *George* the Third, intituled *An Act to remove Doubts respecting the Eligibility of Persons in Holy Orders to sit in the House of Commons*; and Proof of the Celebration of any Religious Service by such Person, according to the Rites of the Church of *Rome*, shall be deemed and taken to be *prima facie* Evidence of the Fact of such Person being in Holy Orders, within the Intent and Meaning of this Act.

X. And be it enacted, That it shall be lawful for any of His Majesty's Subjects professing the Roman Catholic Religion to hold, exercise, and enjoy all Civil and Military Offices and Places of Trust or Profit under His Majesty, His Heirs or Successors, and to exercise any other Franchise or Civil Right, except as herein-after expected, upon taking and subscribing, at the Times and in the Manner herein-after mentioned, the Oath herein-before appointed and set forth, instead of the Oaths of Allegiance, Supremacy, and Abjuration, and instead of such other Oath or Oaths as are or may be now by Law required to be taken for the Purpose aforesaid by any of His Majesty's Subjects professing the Roman Catholic Religion.

XI. Provided always, and be it enacted, That nothing herein contained shall be construed to exempt any Person professing the Roman Catholic Religion from the Necessity of taking any Oath or Oaths, or making any Declaration, not herein-before mentioned, which are or may be by Law required to be taken or subscribed by any Person on his Admission into any such Office or Place of Trust or Profit as aforesaid.

XII. Provided also, and be it further enacted, That nothing herein contained shall extend or be construed to extend to enable any Person or Persons professing the Roman Catholic Religion to hold or exercise the Office of Guardians and Justices of the United Kingdom, or of Regent of the United Kingdom, under whatever Name, Style, or Title such Office may be constituted nor to enable any Person otherwise than as he is now by Law enabled, to hold or enjoy the Office of Lord High Chancellor, Lord Keeper or Lord Commissioner of the Great Seal of *Great Britain or Ireland*; or the office of Lord Lieutenant, or Lord Deputy, or other Chief Governor or Governors of *Ireland*; or His Majesty's High Commissioner to the General Assembly of the Church of *Scotland*.

XIV. And be it enacted, That it shall be lawful for any of His Majesty's Subjects professing the Roman Catholic Religion to be a Member of any Lay Body Corporate, and to hold any Civil Office or Place of Trust or Profit therein, and to do any Corporate Act, or vote in any Corporate Election or other Proceeding, upon taking and subscribing the Oath hereby appointed and set forth, instead of the Oaths of Allegiance, Supremacy, and Abjuration; and upon taking also such other Oath or Oaths as may now by Law be required to be taken by any Persons becoming Members of such Lay Body Corporate, or being admitted to hold any Office or Place of Trust or Profit within the same.

XV. Provided nevertheless, and be it further enacted, That nothing herein contained shall extend to authorize or empower any of His Majesty's Subjects professing the Roman Catholic Religion, and being a Member of any Lay Body Corporate, to give any Vote at, or in any Manner to join in the Election, Presentation, or Appointment of any Person to any Ecclesiastical Benefice whatsoever, or any Office or Place belonging to or connected with the United Church of *England* and *Ireland*, or the Church of *Scotland*, being in the Gift, Patronage, or Disposal of such Lay Corporate Body.

XVI. Provided also, and be it enacted, That nothing in this Act contained shall be construed to enable any Persons, otherwise than as they are now by Law enabled, to hold, enjoy, or exercise any Office, Place, or Dignity of, in, or belonging to the United Church of *England* and *Ireland*, or the Church of *Scotland*, or any Place or Office whatever of, in, or belonging to any of the Ecclesiastical Courts of Judicature of *England* and *Ireland* respectively, or any Court of Appeal from or Review of the Sentences of such Courts, or of, in, or belonging to the Commissary Court of *Edinburgh* or of, in, or belonging to any Cathedral or Collegiate or Ecclesiastical Establishment or Foundation; or any Office or Place whatever of, in, or belonging to any of the Universities of this Realm; or any Office or Place whatever, and by whatever Name the same may be called, of, in, or belonging to any of the Colleges or Halls of the said Universities, or the Colleges of *Eton*, *Westminster*, or *Winchester*, or any College or School within this Realm; or to repeal, abrogate, or in any Manner to interfere with any local Statute, Ordinance, or Rule, which is or shall be established by competent Authority within any University, College, Hall, or School, by which Roman Catholics shall be prevented from being admitted thereto, or from residing or taking Degrees therein: Provided also, that nothing herein contained shall extend or be construed to extend to enable any Person otherwise than as he is now by Law enabled, to exercise any Right of Presentation to any Ecclesiastical Benefice whatsoever; or to repeal, vary, or alter in any Manner the Laws now in force in respect to the Right of Presentation to any Ecclesiastical Benefice.

XXI. And be it enacted, That if any Person professing the Roman Catholic Religion shall enter upon the Exercise or Enjoyment of any Office or Place of Trust or Profit under His Majesty, or of any other Office or Franchise, not having in the Manner and at the Times aforesaid taken and subscribed the Oath herein-before appointed and set forth, then and in every such Case such Person shall forfeit to His Majesty the Sum of Two hundred Pounds; and the Appointment of such Person to the Office, Place, or Franchise so by him held shall become altogether void, and the Office, Place, or Franchise shall be deemed and taken to be vacant to all Intents and Purposes whatsoever.

XXIII. And be it further enacted, That from and after the passing of this Act no Oath or Oaths shall be tendered to or required to be taken by His Majesty's Subjects professing the Roman Catholic Religion, for enabling them to hold or enjoy any Real or Personal Property, other than such as may by Law be tendered to and required to be taken by His Majesty's other Subjects; and that the Oath herein appointed and set forth, being taken and subscribed in any of the Courts, or before any of the Persons above mentioned shall be of the same Force and Effect, to all Intents and Purposes, as, and shall stand in the Place of, all Oaths and Declarations required or prescribed by any Law now in force for the Relief of His Majesty's Roman Catholic Subjects from any Disabilities, Incapacities, or Penalties; and the proper Officer of any of the Courts above mentioned, in which any Person professing the Roman Catholic Religion shall demand to take and subscribe the Oath herein appointed and set forth, is hereby authorised and required to administer the said Oath to such Person, and such Officer shall make, sign, and deliver a Certificate of such Oath having been duly taken and subscribed, as often as the same shall be demanded of him, upon Payment of One Shilling; and such Certificate shall be sufficient Evidence of the Person therein named having duly taken and subscribed such Oath.

XXIV. And whereas the Protestant Episcopal Church of *England* and *Ireland*, and the Doctrine, Discipline and Government thereof, and likewise the Protestant Presbyterian Church of *Scotland*, and the Doctrine, Discipline and Government thereof, are by the respective Acts of Union of *England* and *Scotland*, and of *Great Britain* and *Ireland*, established permanently and inviolably: And whereas the Right and Title of Archbishops to their respective Provinces, of Bishops to their Sees, and of Deans to their Deaneries, as well in *England* as in *Ireland*, have been settled and established by Law; be it therefore enacted, That if any Person, after the Commencement of this Act, other than the Person thereunto authorized by Law, shall assume or use the Name, Style, or Title of Archbishop of any Province, Bishop of any Bishoprick, or Dean of any Deanery, in *England* or *Ireland*, he shall for every such Offence forfeit and pay the Sum of One hundred Pounds.

XXV. And be it further enacted, That if any Person holding any Judicial or Civil Office, or any Mayor, Provost, Jurat, Bailiff, or other Corporate Officer, shall, after the Commencement of this Act, resort to or be present at any Place or public Meeting for Religious Worship in *England* or in *Ireland*, other than that of the United Church of *England* and *Ireland*, or in *Scotland*, other than that of the Church of *Scotland*, as by Law established, in the Robe, Gown, or other peculiar Habit of his Office, or attend with the Ensign or Insignia, or any Part thereof, of or belonging to such his Office, such Person shall, being thereof convicted by due Course of Law, forfeit such Office, and pay for every such Offence the Sum of One hundred Pounds.

XXVI. And be it further enacted, That if any Roman Catholic Ecclesiastic, or any Member of any of the Orders, Communities, or Societies herein-after mentioned shall after the Commencement of this Act, exercise any of the Rites or Ceremonies of the Roman Catholic Religion, or wear the Habits of his Order, save within the usual Places of Worship of the Roman Catholic Religion, or in private Houses, such Ecclesiastic or other Person shall, being thereof convicted by due Course of Law, forfeit for every such Offence the Sum of Fifty Pounds.

XXVIII. And whereas Jesuits, and members of other Religious Orders, Communities, or Societies of the Church of *Rome*, bound by Monastic or Religious Vows, are resident within the United Kingdom; and it is expedient to make Provision for the gradual Suppression and final Prohibition of the same therein; be it therefore enacted, That every Jesuit and every Member of any other Religious Order, Community, or Society of the Church of *Rome*, bound by Monastic or Religious Vows, who at the Time of the Commencement of this Act shall be within the United Kingdom, shall, within Six Calendar Months after the Commencement of this Act, deliver to the Clerk of the Peace of the County or Place where such Person shall reside, or to his Deputy, a Notice or Statement, in the Form and containing the Particulars required to be set forth in the Schedule to this Act annexed; which Notice or Statement such Clerk of the Peace, or his Deputy, shall preserve and register amongst the Records of such County or Place, without any Fee, and shall forthwith transmit a Copy of such Notice or Statement to the Chief Secretary of the Lord Lieutenant, or other Chief Governor or Governors of *Ireland*, if such Person shall reside in *Ireland*, or if in *Great Britain*, to One of His Majesty's Principal Secretaries of State; and in case any Person shall offend in the Premises, he shall forfeit and pay to His Majesty, for every Calendar Month during which he shall remain in the United Kingdom without having delivered such Notice or Statement as is herein-before required, the Sum of Fifty Pounds.

XXIX. And be it further enacted, That if any Jesuit, or Member of any such Religious Order, Community, or Society as aforesaid, shall, after the Commencement of this Act, come into this Realm, he shall be deemed and taken to be guilty of a Misdemeanor, and being thereof lawfully convicted, shall be sentenced and ordered to be banished from the United Kingdom for the Term of his natural Life.

XXXIII. And be it further enacted, That in case any Jesuit, or Member of any such Religious Order, Community, or Society as aforesaid, shall after the Commencement of this Act, within any Part of the United Kingdom, admit any Person to become a Regular Ecclesiastic, or Brother or Member of any such Religious Order, Community, or Society, or be aiding or consenting thereto, or shall administer or cause to be administered, or be aiding or assisting in the administering or taking, any Oath, Vow, or Engagement purporting or intended to bind the Person taking the same to the Rules, Ordinances, or Ceremonies of such Religious Order, Community, or Society, every Person offending in the Premises in *England* or *Ireland* shall be deemed guilty of a Misdemeanor, and in *Scotland* shall be punished by Fine and Imprisonment.

XXXIV. And be it further enacted, That in case any Person shall, after the Commencement of this Act within any Part of this United Kingdom, be admitted or become a Jesuit, or Brother or Member of any other such Religious Order, Community, or Society as aforesaid, such Person shall be deemed and taken to be guilty of a Misdemeanor, and being thereof lawfully convicted shall be sentenced and ordered to be banished from the United Kingdom for the Term of his natural Life.

XXXVII. Provided always, and be it enacted, That nothing herein contained shall extend or be construed to extend in any Manner to affect any Religious Order, Community, or Establishment consisting of Females bound by Religious or Monastic Vows.

APPENDIX C

MANUSCRIPT DRAFTS OF *CHURCH AND STATE*

MANUSCRIPT DRAFTS OF *CHURCH AND STATE*

BM ADD MS 34225 ff 115–27v

Watermark 1828; mainly in Coleridge's hand, those pages in Joseph Henry Green's hand indicated in the textual notes; for the printed text, see above, pp 53–75.

re-producing,[a] in preserving, continuing and perfecting the necessary sources and conditions of National Civilization, this being itself an indispensable condition of ~~the~~ National ~~Po~~ Safety, Power and Welfare, ~~of the Nation~~, the strongest Security and the surest Provision ~~fo~~ both for the Permanence and the progressive advance of whatever (~~Act~~ Laws, Institutions, Tenures, Rights, Privileges, Freedoms, Obligations, &c &c) ~~are the~~ constitute the Public Weal. These ~~the~~ parochial ~~Clergy~~ Clerks (Clerici) ~~not only would form~~ being the great majority of the National Clergy, ~~but~~ and the ⟨comparatively⟩ small remain~~ing~~der ~~number must be contemplationed as far as their as are in their~~ ~~*national*ly characters~~, being principally* *in* ~~reference~~ *ordine ad hos*, [. . .] ~~in strengthening the minds of the Instructors or preparing the materials of instruction~~ Cleri doctores ut [. . .] Clerus Populi ~~seu Laici~~—

I may be allowed to ~~define the office and purpose of the whole by~~ express the final cause of the whole by the Office and Purpose of the greater part—~~that~~ and this is, to form and train up the People of the Country to obedient, free, useful, organizable Subjects, Citizens, and Patriots, living to the benefit of the State, and prepared to die for its defence. The proper *Object* ~~of~~ and End of the National Church is Civilization with Freedom—: and the ~~proper aim~~ duty of its Ministers, could they be contemplated ~~as~~ merely and exclusively as Offic~~ers~~iaries of the *National* Church, would be fulfilled, in the communication of that ~~quantity~~ degree and kind of Knowlege ⟨to all,⟩ the possession of which is ~~either~~ necessary ~~or~~ for All in order to their CIVILITY, meaning by this term all the qualities essential to a Citizen, and devoid of which ~~neith~~ no People or Class of the People can be calculated on by the Rulers and Leaders of the State ~~as~~ for the ~~Services~~ conservation or promotion of its essential Interests;

* Considered, I mean, in their national relations, and in that which forms their *ordinary*, ~~and most purpose~~ their most conspicuous purpose & utility: for ~~from~~ Heaven forbid, I should deny or ~~overlook~~ forget, that the Sciences, and not only the Sciences both abstract and experi~~ent~~mental, but the Literae Humaniores, ~~Literary Excellence~~ e[illegible] the Products of Genial Power of whatever name, have an immediate and positive value, even in their bearings on the National Interests—

[a] f 115; ms foliated 30–42 by C

and in regard of the grounds and principles of Action and Conduct ~~by the~~ the State has a right to[a] demand of the National Church, that its Instructions should be fitted to ~~secure~~ diffuse throughout the people *Legality*, the obligations of a well calculated Self-interest, enlivened by the affections and the warrantable prejudices of ~~*Patriotism*~~ Nationality—~~or at least~~, or at least, that whatever of ~~prior~~ higher Origin and nobler & wider Aim the Ministers of the National Church, in some other capacity, and in the performance of other duties, might labor to implant and cultivate in the minds and hearts of their Congregations and Seminaries, should include the practical consequences of the *Legality* above ~~stated—that their moral teaching~~ mentioned. The State requires that the Basin should be kept full, and the Stream that supplies the Hamlet and ~~waters the field~~ turns the Mill and waters the meadow-fields, should be fed and kept flowing. If this be done, the State is content, indifferent for the rest, whether the Basin be filled by the Spring in its first ascent, and rising but a ~~few inches~~ hand's-breadth above the bed, or whether drawn from ~~far loftier ⟨high⟩ sources it rises at aloft in~~ a more elevated Source ~~or rises~~ shooting aloft in a stately column, ~~with~~ that reflect~~ings~~ the Light of Heaven ~~streamin~~ from its Shafft, and ~~with~~ bears the Iris, ~~*Coeli decus atque J at promissa fides,*~~[1] Coeli decus, promissumque Jovis lucidum, on its spray, it fills the Basin in its descent.

In what relation then do you place Christianity to the National Church? Tho' ~~it is an anticipation of a to answer this question I must in some measure~~ unwilling to anticipate what belongs to ~~another~~ a part of my Subject yet to come, namely, the Idea of the Catholic or Christian Church, ~~yet~~ I am still more averse to leave this question even for a moment unanswered. And this is my Answer.

In relation to the *National* Church, Christianity, or the Church of Christ, is a blessed Accident, ⟨a providential Boon,⟩ a Grace of God, a mighty and faithful ~~Ally~~ Friend, ~~which having for its ultimate end in administering the Laws, and promoting the interests of a State, which is not of this World, which~~ the Envoy indeed and Liege Subject of another State, ~~of a State which is not of this World~~, but which can~~not~~ neither administer the laws ~~or~~ nor promote the ends of this State, which is not of this World, without advantages and direct[b] and indirect to the true interests of the States, the Aggregate of which is ~~meant~~ what we mean by the World—i.e. the Civilized World. (What we ought to mean at least: for I blush to think, ~~commonc~~urrent as the term is ~~in the mouths of men~~ among the religious public in consequence of its frequent occurrence in the New [Testament] how many ~~Preachers~~ Discourses I have heard in which the Preacher has made it only too evident that he understood in the term the Earth which turns round us, the Planet TELLUS, of the Astronomers!) As the Olive Tree is said in its growth to fertilize the ~~soil in its neighborhood and~~ surrounding Soil, and to invigorate the ~~vine~~ Roots of the Vines in its immediate neighborhood, and improve the strength and flavor of ~~of~~ the

[a] f 116 [b] f 117

[1] Virgil *Aeneid* 6.346. Tr: "promised faith". Cancelled because in the context a rebuke for a broken promise?

Wines, such is the relation of the Christian to the National Church. But as the Olive is not the same plant with the Vines, ~~nor~~ or with the Elm or Poplar (= the State) with which it is wedded; and as the Vine with its Prop may exist, tho' in less perfection, without the Olive, or prior to its implantation—even so is Christianity, ~~much~~ and a fortiori any particular scheme of Theology derived and supposed (by its partizans) to be *deduced* from Christianity, no essential ~~plan~~ part of the *Being* of the *National* Church, however conducive or even indispensable it may be to its *well*-being. And even so a National Church ~~might—ch~~: might exist, and has existed, without, because before the institution of the *Christian* Church—as [. . .] the Levitical Church in the Hebrew Constitution, & the Druidical in the Celtic, would suffice to prove. Only, I earnestly intreat, let two things be remembered—first, that it is my Object to present the *Idea* of a National Church, as the only safe Criterion, by which the Judgement can decide on the existing state of things: for when we are in full and clear possession of the ultimate Aim of an Institution, it is comparatively easy to ascertain, in what respects this aim has been attained in other ways, arising out of the growth of the Nation and the gradual & successive expansion of its Germs; in what respects the aim has been frustrated ~~or~~ by Errors & Diseases in[a] the Body Politic; and in what respects the Existing Institution still answers the original purpose, and ~~or remains~~ continues to be a Means to ~~mo~~ necessary or ~~mos~~ most important ends, for which no adequate substitute can be found. First, I say, let me borne in mind, that my object has been to present the *Idea* of a National Church, not the history of *the* ~~English National~~ Church established in this Nation. Secondly, that two distinct Functions do not necessarily imply or require two different Functionaries. Nay, the perfection of each may require the union of both in the same person. And in the instance now in question, great and grievous errors have arisen from confounding the ~~two~~ functions; and fearfully great and grievous will be the Evils from the success of ~~an~~ the Attempt ⟨to separate them—an attempt ~~to~~⟩ long and passionately pursued, in many forms & thro' many various channels, by a numerous Party, that, ~~now, I fear~~, has already the Ascendancy in the State, and ~~if~~ unless far other Minds and far other Principles than the Opponents of this Party have hitherto allied with their cause are ~~not~~ called into action, *will* obtain the ascendancy in the Nation.

I have already said that the Subjects, which lie right and left of my road, ~~and even fl~~ or even jut into it, are so many & so important, that ~~tho~~' I ~~am not~~ offer this ⟨epistolary⟩ pamphlet but as a catalogue *raisonnè* of Texts and Theses, that will have answered their purpose if they excite a certain class of Readers to desire or to supply the commentary. ~~For you, To you, Sir! these few unjointed Sentences will suffice to shew To~~ But you, Sir! are no stranger to the ways, in which my Mind travels. To you ~~even it~~ my words ἑρμηνέως οὐ χατίζει[1]—scarcely need an interpreter: and the following few and jointless sentences will suffice to shew "the Burden of

[a] f 118

[1] Pindar *Olympian Odes* 2.86 (var). Cf *LS* (*CC*) 126n and n 2.

the Valley of Vision, even the Burden upon the ⟨crowned⟩ Isle, whose Merchants are Princes, whose Traffickers the honorable of the Earth; who stretcheth out her hand over the Sea, and She is the Mart of Nations!" (Isai: XXIII.)

The[a] National Church, in the *dark Age* of Queen Elizabeth, in the unenlightened times of Burleigh, Hooker, Spenser, Shakespear and Lord Bacon, A GREAT VENERABLE ESTATE OF THE REALM; but now by "*All* the Intellect of the Kingdom," ~~it~~ determined to be ~~a~~ one of the ~~very~~ many theological Sect⟨s⟩, ~~transferred from among in~~ Churches or Communities, ~~existing~~ established ~~in the Britis England~~, in the realm; but distinguished from the rest by ~~its being endowed~~, having its Priesthood *endowed*, durante bene placito, by favor of the Legislature—that is, ~~the~~ of the M~~inister~~ajority ~~and~~ for the time being of the two Houses of Parliament.—The Church reduced to *a* Religion~~,~~. ~~and b~~By ⟨virtue of⟩ this ~~reduction~~ Religion separated from the Church, and made a subject of Parliamentary Determination, independent of the Church. ~~The nation separated from Religion~~ The Poor withdrawn from the Discipline of the Church—. The Education of the People detached from the Ministry of the Church. Religion, *a noun of multitude*, or nomen collectivum, ~~of~~ expressing the Aggregate of all the different Groups of Notions and Ceremonies connected with the Invisible and Supernatural. On the plausible (and in *this* sense of the word, unanswerable) Pretext of the multitude and variety of *Religions*, and for the suppression of Bigotry and Negative Persecution, National Education to be finally sundered from all Religion, but speedily and decisively emancipated from the Superintendence of the National Clergy.—~~But~~ SCHEDULE. ~~in the~~ It is ~~preceding Article~~ Thereis ~~exists however~~ article not to be understood or inferred from the preceding Article, that there is any Objection to its being transferred to Jesuits, Benedictines, Franciscans, or Unitarians. Education reformed. Defined as synonimous with Instruction. ~~*Groundwork*~~ *Axiom of Education so defined.* Knowlege being Power, ~~this at a~~ those Attainments ~~only~~, which give a man the power of doing what he wishes to obtain what he desires, are alone to be consider~~ing~~ed as Knowlege, or ~~to allowed~~ to be admitted into the Scheme of National Education.—Subjects to be taught ⟨in the National Schools⟩ Reading, Writing, Arithmetic, the Mechanic Arts, ~~all~~ the ⟨Elements & Results of⟩ Physical ~~and Experimental~~ Sciences, but to be taught, as much as possible, empirically. Experimentalism.[b]—Morality: ~~this last to consist~~ to wit, a Digest of the Penal or Criminal Code, ⟨together with a course⟩ of Lectures on Diet, Digestion, Infection, and the ⟨nature and⟩ effects of the specific Virus communicable by Living Bodies: Experimental[c] Philosophy. (How otherwise could men be Philosophers?)—Morality.—The course to consist of a Digest of the Criminal Laws, and the Evidence requisite for conviction under the same: Lectures on Diet, on Digestion, on Infection and the nature and effects of a specific virus incidental to and communicable by Living Bodies in the intercourse of society. N.B. In order to balance the Interests of ~~the~~ Individuals and the Interests of the State, the Dietetic and Peptic Text-books to be under the Censorship of the Board of Excise.—

[a] f 119 [b] f 121v [c] f 120

Shall I proceed with my Chapter of Hints? Game Laws, Corn-laws, Cotton Factories, Spitalfields, the[a] Tillers of the Land paid by poor-rates and the remainder of the population arranged into engines and machines for the manufactory of new rich men,—yea, ~~the whole scarcely better~~ the machinery of the wealth of the nation ~~now a~~ made up of the wretchedness disease and depravity of those who should constitute the strength of the nation—disease, I say, vice & neediness ~~during the progress~~ while the machine is in full motion but at the first stop to become converted into an intolerable weight of pauperism. Spoliation of the Nationalty, half of which to be distributed among the landowners, and the other half among the stockbrokers and stock-owners, who are to receive it in lieu of the interest formerly due to them. But enough.—I will ask only one question. ~~Have the results, as far as they are hitherto known~~, Has the national welfare ~~advanced equally~~ have the worth & happiness of the people advanced with the increase of ~~our~~ its circumstantial prosperity? ~~Have the Many~~ Is the increasing number of wealthy men in a State that which ought to be understood by the wealth of the nation? In answer to this permit me to ~~transcribe~~ annex ~~and~~ the following brief history* of the last 130 years by a lover of Old England, ~~published by me some twelve years ago~~, ~~Friend Vol 3 p 130/~~

A.[c] Declarati~~on~~ve—Acti~~on~~ respecting certain parts of the Constitution with provisions against the further violation of the same, erroneously entitled, THE REVOLUTION of 1688.

B. The mechanico-corpuscular Theory raised to the Title of the Mechanic Philosophy, and espoused as a Revolution in Philosophy by the ~~dwarf~~ Actors and Partizans of the (so called) Revolution in the State.

C. Result illustrated ~~and exemplified~~ in the remarkable Contrast between the ~~use~~ acceptation of the word, Idea, *before* the Restoration, ~~its use~~ and the *present* use of the same word. *Before* ~~then~~ *1660*: the Magnificent SON OF COSMO was wont to discourse with FICINO, POLITIAN and the princely MIRANDULA on the IDEAS of Will, God, Freedom: SIR PHILIP SIDNEY, the Star of serenest brilliance in the glorious Constellation of Elizabeth's Court, communed with Spenser on the IDEA of The Beautiful: and the younger ALGERNON, Soldier, Patriot and Statesman, with HARRINGTON, MILTON and NEVIL, on the IDEA of the STATE: and in what sense it may be ~~wisely~~ more truly affirmed, that the People (i.e. the component particles of the Body Politic at any one moment existing as such) are ~~made for~~ in order to the State, ~~not~~ than that the State ~~for~~ exists for the sake of the People.—

Present use of the word:

DR HOLOFERNES, in a Lecture on Metaphysics delivered at one of the Mechanics' Institutions, explodes all *ideas* but those of sensation; and his friend, DEPUTY COSTARD, has no *idea* of a better flavored Haunch of

* ~~Written i~~ With exception of the last sentence, which is extracted from my "AIDS TO REFLECTION," p. 293, this "brief History" was written about the year 1808, and republished in the FRIEND, Vol. III. p. 130.[b]

[a] remainder of leaf in Green's hand [b] footnote in C's hand [c] f 121

Venison, than he dined off at the London Tavern last week. He admits, (~~that~~ for the Deputy has travelled) that the French have an excellent *idea* of Cooking in general; but holds that their most accomplished *Maitres du Cuisine* have no more *idea* of dressing a turtle than the Parisian Gourmands themselves have any *real* idea of the true *taste* and *color* of the Fat.

D. Consequences exemplified. State of Nature, or the Ouran outang theory of the origin of the Human Race substituted for the Book of Genesis, Ch. I–X. Rights of Nature for the Duties and Privileges of Citizens. Idealess Facts, misnamed proofs from History, grounds of Experience, &c for[a] Principles and the Insight derived from them: State-policy, a Cyclops with one eye, and that in the back of the head; measures of policy a series of anachronisms, ~~a constant~~ or a truckling to events substituted for the science, that should command them: for all true Insight is Foresight. (Documents. The measures ~~which~~ of the British Cabinet from the Boston Port-bill, March 1774; ~~to the Peace of Amiens~~ but particularly from 1789 to the Union of Ireland and the Peace of Amiens.) Mean time, the true historical Feeling, the ~~dignity~~ immortal life of an historical Nation, Generation linked to generation by faith, freedom, heraldry, ⟨and ancestral fame,⟩ languishing and giving place to the Superstitions of Wealth, and Newspaper Reputations.

E. Talents without Genius: a swarm of clever, well-informed Men; ~~or~~ Anarchy of minds, despotism of Maxims. Despotism of Finance in Government and Legislation—of Vanity and Sciolism in the intercourse of life—of presumption, ~~an~~ temerity and hardness of heart in Political Economy.

F. The Guess-work of General Consequences substituted for Moral & Political Philosophy—adopted as a Text-book in one of the Universities, and cited, as Authority, in the Legislature. Plebs pro Senatu Populoque: the Wealth of Nations (i.e. of the Wealthy Individuals the~~mselr~~eof and the Magnitude of the Revenue) for the Well-being of the People.

G. Gin consumed by Paupers to the ~~Amount~~ value of about Eighteen Millions ~~year~~ yearly. Government by Journeymen Clubs; by Saint and Sinner Societies, Committees, Institutions; by Reviews, Magazines, and above all by Newspapers. Lastly, Crimes quadrupled for the whole Country, and in some Counties decupled.

Concluding Address to the ⟨Parliamentary⟩ Leaders of the Liberalists and Utilitarians ~~in Parliament~~.

I respect the Talents ~~and~~ of many, ~~among your number~~ and the motives ~~of~~ and character of some among you too sincerely to court ~~your~~ the Scorn/, ~~But nei~~ which I anticipation. But neither shall the fear of it prevent[b] me from declaring aloud, ~~any truth~~ and as a truth which I hold it the disgrace and calamity of a professed Statesman not to know and acknowlege, that a permanent, nationalized, Learned Order, a National Clerisy or Church, is an essential Element of a rightly Constituted Nation, ⟨without which ~~there~~ it wants the best security alike for its permanence & its progression; and⟩ for which neither Tract Societies, nor Conventicles, nor Lancastrian Schools, nor Mechanics' Institutions, not Lecture-bazaars under the absurd name of Universities, not all these collectively, can be a Substitutes ~~and without which a national~~, ~~in regard to its real interests~~

[a] f 122 [b] f 123

~~can neither be permanent nor progressive~~. For they ~~h~~ are all marked with the same asterisk of spuriousness, shew the same distemper-spot on the front, that they are ~~all attempts to counteract empirical~~[a] ~~Specifics for the evils morbid several symptoms that indicate the disturbed of constitutional Disease~~ so ~~many~~ all ~~specifics~~ empirical Specifics for morbid *symptoms* that help to feed and continue the disease.

But[b] you wish for *general* illumination: you would spur-arm the Toes ~~of the Body Politic~~ of Society, and enlighten the higher ranks per ascensum ab imis. You begin, therefore, with the attempt to *popularize* science: but you will only effect its *plebification.* It ~~al~~ is folly ~~ever~~ to think of making all or the Many Philosophers, or even Men of Science, or of systematic Knowlege; but it is duty and wisdom to ~~promote~~ aim at making as Many as possible [. . .] & ~~absolutely~~ soberly and steadily religious;—inasmuch as ~~the moral habits and Prudence qualities~~ Morality, i.e. the practical maxims ⟨and habits,⟩ which abstracted from the interests of another and future World ~~in individuals that are all and without reference to the well being of that concern~~ that especially respect ~~the~~ Individuals; ⟨and these,⟩ not as fractions ~~of~~ or components parts of an Organic Unit, but each ~~as~~ integrally as an imperishable Person ⟨—inasmuch, I say, as the Morality which⟩ the State requires in its citizens for its own well-being and ideal immortality, can only exist for ~~a Nation~~ the People in the form of Religion. But ~~as this~~ the existence of a true Philosophy, or the power and habit of contemplating Particulars in the unity and fontal mirror of the Ideas, is indispensable to a sound state of religion in all Classes. In fine, Religion, true or false, is and ever has been the centre of Gravity, in a ~~State~~ Realm, to which all other things must and will accomodate themselves.

The[c] deep interest, which during the far larger portion of my life since early manhood I have attached to these convictions have I perceive hurried me onwards as by the rush from the letting forth of accumulated waters by the sudden opening of the sluice gates. I must intreat of your patience that I ~~may commence anew~~ may say over again, that our 8th Henry would have ~~realized~~ acted in correspondence to the great principles of our constitution if having restored the original balance on both sides he had determined the nationalty to the following objects 1st To the maintenance of the Universities and the great liberal Schools 2dly To the maintenance of a pastor and Schoolmaster in every parish. 3dly To the raising & keeping in repair of the Churches Schools &c and Lastly: ⟨To the maintenance⟩ of the proper that is the infirm poor whether from age or sickness—in other words for this too was included in the original purpose of the national reserve for the alleviation of those evils, which in the best forms of worldly states must arise and must have been foreseen as arising from the institutions of individual properties and primogeniture. If these duties were efficiently performed and these purposes adequately fulfilled the very increase of the population which would by these very means have been prevented from a vicious population would have more than counterbalanced those savings in the expenditure of the nationalty occasioned by the practising part of law, medicine &c detaching themselves from the national clergy[.] That this transfer of this national ~~revenue~~-

[a] f 122v [b] f 123 [c] f 124, in Green's hand

serve from what had become ~~public~~ national evils to its original & inherent purpose of national benefits, instead of the sacrilegious alienation which actually took place—that this was impracticable is[a] historically true; but no less true is it philosophically that this impracticability, arising wholly from moral causes, that is from loose manners & corrupt principles does not rescue this wholesome Sacrilege from deserving the character of the first & deadliest wound inflicted on the constitution of the Kingdom: which term constitution in the body politic, as in bodies natural, expresses not only what is & what has been evolved, but likewise whatever is potentially contained in the seminal principle of the particular body, and would in its due time have appeared but for emasculation or ~~the infusion of a false & alien life~~ disease[.] Other wounds, by which indeed the constitution of the nation has suffered, but which ⟨much more⟩ immediately concern the constitution of the Church we shall perhaps find another place to mention.

§. 3. The Mercantile and Commercial Class or to comprize all the classes, which I have opposed to the landed order, as ~~having~~ more characteristically conspiring to the interests of progression, the improvement & general freedom of the country, did, as I have already remarked, in the earlier states of the constitution exist but as in the bud. But during ⟨all⟩ this ~~time~~ period ~~which might be called~~ of potential existence or what we may call the minority of the burgess order, the National Church was the substitute for the most important national benefits resulting from the same. The National Church presented the only ~~opening~~ breathing hole of hope. ~~It alo~~ The Church alone relaxed the iron fate by which feudal dependency primogeniture and entail ~~had pr~~ would otherwise have predestined every native of the realm to Lord or Vassal. To the Church alone could the Nation look for the benefits of the existing Knowledge and for the means of future civilization. Lastly let it never be forgotten that under the fostering wings of the Church the class of free citizens and[b] burghers were reared. To the feudal system we owe the *forms*, to the Church the *substance* of our liberty. ~~As comment~~ We mention only two of many facts that would form the proof & comment of the above first the origin of towns & cities in the privileges attached to the vicinity of churches & monasteries, and which preparing an asylum for the fugitive vassal & oppressed franklin thus laid the first foundations of a class of freemen detached from the land[.] Secondly, the holy war, which the national clergy in this instance faithful to their national duties waged against slavery & villenage & with such success that in the reign of Charles 2^{d} the law which declared every native of the realm free by birth had merely ~~too~~ to sanction an opus jam consummatum. Our Maker has distinguished man from the brute that perishes by making hope, first an instinct of his nature, & secondly, an indispensable condition of his moral & intellectual progression:

> For every Gift of noble Origin
> Is breathed upon by Hope's perpetual breath.
>
> WORDSWORTH.

[a] f 125, in Green's hand

[b] f 126, in Green's hand, except for the verses, which are in C's; C's hand again from "§. IV."

But a natural instinct constitutes a ~~natural~~ right as far as its gratification is compatible with the equal rights of others—~~hence our ancestors classed all who were incapable of altering their condition from that of their parents as bondsmen~~.

§. IV. Recapitulation of the preceding, in respect of the Idea of the National Church.

Among the primary ends of a STATE (in that highest sense of the word, in which it is equivalent to the Nation, considered as one Body Politic, and therefore includes the National Church) there are two, of which the National Church (according to its idea) is the especial and constitutional Organ and Means. The one is, to secure to the Subjects of the Realm generally the Hope, the Chance, of bettering their own or their Children's Condition. And tho' ~~this this~~[a] ~~great Purpose within the three last centuries~~ during the last three or four Centuries the National Church has found a~~n~~ ~~effective~~ most powerful Surrogate and Ally ~~in Trade, and Commerce, and~~ for the effectuation of this great purpose in ~~the powers~~ her former Wards and Foster-children, Trade, Commerce, Free Industry and the Arts; yet still the Nationalty under all defalcations continues to act, as a vast horizontal wheel drawing up from the Mass below ~~whatever is~~ a ~~portion~~ regular Supply for the middle Class, and ~~this not only without~~ thus providing Hope for Individual Families while it secures tranquillity and subordination for the whole Realm.—This is one of the two ends.

The other is, ~~the~~ to develope~~ment~~, in every Native of the Country, those faculties, and to ~~qu~~ provide for every Native that knowledge and those attainments, which are ~~necessary required and supposed in~~ necessary to qualify him for a Member of the State, the free Subject of a Civilized Realm. We do not mean those degrees of moral and intellectual Cultivation which distinguish man from man in the same civilized society, much less those that separate the Christian from the This-worldian; but those only that constitute the civilized man in contra-distinction from the Barbarian, the Savage, and the Animal.

~~While~~ I ~~have shall~~ have ⟨now⟩ brought ~~before the Reader all that I think necessary is requisite for the explanation~~ together all that ~~is~~ seemed requi~~red~~site to put the intelligent Reader in full possession of (what I believe to be) the right Idea of the National Clergy, as an Estate of the Realm, ~~and~~. But I cannot think my task finished without an attempt to rec~~ollect~~tify the ~~most~~ too frequent false *Feeling* on this subject, and to remove ~~the more prominent of the~~ certain Vulgar Errors, errors, alas! not confined to those whom the World call the Vulgar. Ma nel Mondo non è se no volgo, says Machiavel. I shall make no apology ⟨therefore⟩ for ~~concluding this, the most important division of my Subject, by with~~ interposing between the preceding Statements, and the practical conclusion from them, the following Paragraph, ⟨extracted⟩ from a Work long out of Print, and of ~~which~~ such very limited[b] Circulation, that ~~my~~ I might have stolen from myself with little risk of detection, had it not been my wish to shew that the Convictions expressed in the preceding pages are not the ~~growth~~ work of the moment, formed for the present occasion; but that the ~~Principles avowed Sentiments ass professed in 1829 are but~~

[a] f 127 [b] f 127v

~~an expansion of the Principles publicly asserted~~ Reflections now submitted to the Public are but an expansion of Sentiments & Principles publicly avowed in the year 1817.

(~~Then print from the Biographia Literaria~~, ~~Vol~~. ~~I~~, ~~p~~. ~~226~~. ~~l~~. ~~5~~.)

<Proceed with p. 43–46.>

§. V Among the numerous Blessings of the ~~An~~ Constitution inherited from our remote Ancestors, the introduction of an
(*printed from Biographia Literaria, Vol. I. p. 226 1. 7——to p. 228. last line but three—ending with the words* "*expected to withhold five.*")

BM MS EGERTON 2801 ff 204–7v

(No watermark date; in C's hand; for the printed text, see above, pp 139–44)

Power[a] *in* the Church itself which in the name of Christ and pretending his Authority [?works] systematically ~~to the~~ subvert~~ions~~ or counteract~~ions~~ ~~of~~ the ~~essential~~ peculiar ~~Objects~~ aims and purposes of Christ's Mission, and ~~placing~~ vesting in a mortal his incommunicable Headship, destroys (and exchanges for the contrary) the essential contra-distinguishing Marks or Characters of his Kingdom on Earth. But apply it, as Wickliff, ~~and all~~ Luther* and indeed all the first Reformers did to the Papacy, and Papal Hierarchy; and we understand at once the grounds of the great Apostle's premonition, that this Anti-christ could not appear till after the dissolution of the ~~Roman~~ Latin Empire and the extinction of the Imperial Power in Rome—and the cause, why the ~~Greek Patriarchate~~, ~~at with~~ the Bishops of Constantinople, with all imaginable good wishes and disposition to do the same, could never raise the Patriarchate of the Greek Empire into a Papacy.—The Bishops of the other Rome became the Slaves of the Ottoman, ~~as~~ the moment they ceased to be the Subjects of the Emperor.

* And (be it observed) without any reference to the Apocalypse, the canonical character of which Luther at first rejected and never cordially received. ~~And neither to the Apocalypse nor to Daniel does the present writer refer—of Daniel~~ And without the[b] least sympathy with Luther's Suspicions on this head, but on the contrary receiv~~ed~~ing ~~it in~~ thi[s] sublime Poem as the undoubted work of the apostolic Age, and admiring in it the most perfect Specimen of Symbolic Poetry, I am as little disposed to cite it on the present occasion—convinced as I am, and hope shortly to convince others, that in the whole series of its magnificent Imagery there is not a single Symbol, that can be even plausibly interpreted of either the Pope, the Turks, or Napoleon Bonaparte. Of charges ~~that do not affect~~ not attaching to the moral character, there ~~is not one~~ are few, if any, that I should be more ~~grieved~~ anxious to avoid tha~~t~~n that of being an Affecter of Paradoxes. But the dread of ~~this~~ other men's Thoughts shall not ~~allow~~ tempt me ~~from~~ to ~~av~~withhold a truth, which the strange Errors grounded on the contrary assumption render important.—And ~~I do not hesitate~~ in the thorough assurance of its truth I ~~avow~~ make the assertion, that the perspicuity, and (with singularly few exceptions, even for *us*) the uniform intelligibility, and close consecutive Meaning, verse by verse, with the simplicity and grandeur of the Plan and the admirable ordonnance of the parts, are among the prominent Beauties of the Apocalypse.

[a] f 204; ms foliated 12–18 by C [b] f 204v

Nor do I doubt, that[a] the substance and main Argument of this sacred Oratorio, or Drama *sui generis* (the Prometheus of Eschylus comes the nearest to *the kind*) were supplied by John the Evangelist: tho' I incline with Eusebius to find the Poet himself in John, an Elder and Contemporary of the Church of Ephesus.

P.S. It may remove or at least mitigate the objections, to the palliative language, in which I have spoken of the doctrines of the Catholic Church, if I remind the Reader, that the *Roman* Catholic Church dates its true origin from the Council of Tr~~uth~~ent. Widely differing from my valued and affectionately respected Friend, the Revd Edward Irving, in his *interpretations* of the Apocalypse and the Book of Daniel, and I no less in his *estimation* of the latter; and while I honour his courage, ⟨as a Christian ~~Preacher~~ minister,⟩ almost as much as I admire his Eloquence as a ~~Preacher~~ Writer, yet protesting against his somewhat too adventurous speculations on the Persons of the Trinity and the Body of our Lord—I have great delight in extracting (*from ~~the~~ his "Sermons, Lectures, and Discourses," Vol. III. p. 870*) and[b] declaring my cordial assent to the following ~~passages, i.e.~~ just observations:—viz. that *after* the Reformation had taken firm root, and when God had provided a purer Church, "the Council of Trent did corroborate and decree into unalterable laws and constitutions of the Church all those impostures and innovations of the Roman See which had been in a state of uncertainty, perhaps of permission or even of custom, but which every man had till then been free to testify against, and against which in fact, ~~many there had never failed in each successive a succession of or~~ there never wanted those in each successive generation who did testify. The Council of Trent *ossified* all those ulcers and blotches which had ~~overspread~~ deformed the Church, and stamped the thitherto much doubted and controverted prerogatives of the Pope with the highest Authority recognized in the Church."—Then first was the Catholic converted & particularized into the Romish Church, the Church of the Papacy.

No less cordially do I concur with Mr Irving in his remark in[c] the following page. For I too "am free to confess and avow moreover, that I believe the Soil of the Catholic Church, when Luther arose, was of a stronger mold, fitter to bear forest trees and cedars of God, than the soil of the Protestant Church in the times of Whitfield and Wesley, which (*tho' sown with the same word—? qu.*) hath brought forth ~~not one~~ only stunted undergrowths and creeping brush-wood." I too "believe, that the faith of the Protestant Church in Britain had come to a lower ebb, and that it is even now at a lower ebb, than was the faith of the Papal Church when the Spirit of the Lord was able to quicken in it and draw forth of it, such men as Luther, and Melancthon, and Bullinger, Calvin, Bucer, and Latimer, and Ridley and a score others whom I might name." ~~each of them a host~~

And now, as the conclusion of this long note, let me be permitted to ~~say~~ add a[d] word or two of Edward Irving himself. That he possesses my unqualified Esteem as a Man, is only saying, that I know him, and am neither blinded by envy nor bigotry. But my name has been brought into connection with his, on points that regard his public ministry: and he himself has publicly ~~honored~~ distinguished me, as his friend, on public grounds: and in proof of my confidence in hi~~m~~s regard, I have not the least apprehension of ~~offending him~~ forfeiting it by a frank declaration of what I think ~~of him~~—. Well, then! I have no faith in his Pr~~edictions~~ophesyings; ~~and applications of the Prophecies~~; small sympathy with his fulminations; and in certain peculiarities of his *theological* system, as distinct from his religious principles, I cannot see my way. But I hold withal, and not the less firmly for these *discrepances* in our moods and Judgements, that EDWARD IRVING possesses more of the spirit and purposes of the first Reformers,

[a] f 205 [b] f 205v [c] f 206 [d] f 206v

that he has more of the Head and Heart, the Life, the Unction and the genial Power of MARTIN LUTHER, than any[a] man now alive ~~or who has lived~~; yea, than any Man of this and the last Century. I see in EDWARD IRVING a Minister of Christ after the order of Paul: and if the points, in which I think him ⟨either⟩ erroneous, or excessive and *out of bounds*, have been at any time a subject of serious regret with me, this regret has arisen principally or altogether from the apprehension of their narrowing the sphere of his influence, from the ~~dread~~ too great probability that they may furnish occasion or pretext for withholding or withdrawing ~~or~~ many from those momentous truths, ~~of~~ which the Age ~~is~~ especially needs, and for the enforcement ⟨of⟩ which ~~Heaven~~ He hath ⟨been⟩ so highly and especially gifted ~~him~~! Finally, ~~assuming, as every satisfied Believer must be supposed to do, that my own views of the Christian Dispensation are the true views, as long as they retain this attribute of truth for my mind, so long to obtain the compleat I look forward with fearful hope~~ my friend's Intellect is too instinct with life, too *potential*, to remain stationary: and assuming, as every satisfied Believer must be supposed to do, the truth of my own views, I look forward with ~~a~~ confident hope to a time, when ~~it~~ his Soul shall have perfected ~~its emancipation~~ ⟨~~detachment~~⟩ ~~from~~ her victory over the dead Letter of[b] the Senses and its Apparitions in the sensuous Understanding; ~~and~~ when the Halcyon IDEAS shall ⟨have⟩ alig~~ht~~t on the surging Sea of his Conception~~r~~,

> "Which then shall quite forget to rave
> ~~And~~ While Birds of Calm sit brooding on the charmed wave~~s.~~"
>
> MILTON.

see[c] *p. 19*

~~In order to this, little more is needed than~~ that in freedom and unfearing faith, with that courage which ~~has~~ cannot but flow from the inward and life-like assurance, "that neither death, nor life, nor things present nor things to come, nor height, nor depth, nor any other creature, shall be able to separate us from the Love of God, which is in Christ Jesus our Lord" (Rom. VIII. 38.39) ⟨*see p. 19*⟩ ~~to reflect on this two or three indisputable truths~~. First: that Christ, ~~has~~ "the Spirit of Truth," has promised to be with his Church even to the end. Secondly: that Christianity ~~was to be~~ was ~~by him declared~~ described, as a Tree ⟨to be ~~ra~~⟩ raised from the Seed: ⟨*see p. 20*⟩ Lastly: that in the process of ~~growth~~ Evolution, there are in every Plant Growths of transitory use and duration. "The integuments of the Seed, having fulfilled their destined office of protection, burst and decay. After the Leaves have unfolded, the Cotyledons, that had performed their functions, wither and drop of."* The Husk is a genuine growth of "The Staff of Life": yet we must separate it from the grain. It is, ⟨therefore,⟩ the cowardice of faithless

* Smith's Introd. to Botany.

[a] f 207 [b] f 207v [c] C inserted two carets before "see"

APPENDIX D

1. MANUSCRIPT FRAGMENT ON THE CATHOLIC QUESTION

2. MANUSCRIPT FRAGMENT ON THE ORIGIN OF THE PRIESTHOOD

MANUSCRIPT FRAGMENT ON THE CATHOLIC QUESTION

BM MS Egerton 2800 ff 109–9v

The fragment reproduced below (the ms has no watermark date) may have been written as early as 1811, but it is more likely that it was written in 1821 for one of the projected "Letters to C. A. Tulk" on the Catholic Question; see Editor's Introduction, above, p l.

During the last 15 years I have studied with deep interest and proportional attention the Catholic Question, as it is called—a name less objectionable, indeed, than that of Catholic Emancipation, but still not *the* truth if it even convey truth at all. The problem, which Parliament is actually called on to solve, the true legislatorial Question ~~is this~~ may be stated thus: Does there now exist aught in the ⟨average⟩ moral, intellectual, concorporative, and circumstantial condition of the ~~Ques~~ Irish Population, which ~~should~~ makes it incumbent on the Legislature of the British Empire to withhold from the ~~Irish~~ Non-protestant Population of Ireland the full exercise of ~~all these~~ the political Rights and Privileges~~?~~, which,—supposing no such obstacle to exist, would give them collectively the share of legislative power, direct and indirect, proportional to their comparative Number, as a component part of the united Common-weal?—The answer would commence by narrowing the question to be answered: viz. There is a known and *separable* Part of the Irish Population, ~~concerning~~ to which no such impediment applies, or exists: and this part, distinguishable and actually contra-distinguished by open avowal of Protestantism, is asserted to be, by some as 1 in 5, by others and with more confidence as 1 in 6.—This ⟨5th or sixth Part⟩ then being subtracted, the Question recurs with no other change, than that of adding the term "Non-protestant" to the words Irish Population. Does there exist in the———[1]condition of the *Non-Protestant Irish* aught, which &c?—This may appear a mere trifling with names; but it is far from being so. On the contrary, it is a most important Preventive of a dangerous error in the very statement of the Problem. For it does not follow, of necessity, that this Non-protestantism does in and for itself constitute ~~the~~ an impediment, ~~nor less that~~ or that all and each of the various Positives comprehended in this Negative must [. . .] do so . . . Catholicism, as it exists in Normandy for instance, might not, and yet Romanism might—or that might not, and yet Papistry might. Much less follows it, that the Non-protestantism, in whatever form

[1] The long dash apparently indicates that the words from the second sentence are to be supplied; i.e. "average moral, intellectual, concorporative, and circumstantial".

it exists, *is* THE impediment. It may be merely the *mark*, a signum significans. There is nothing poisonous in the seeds of the Poppy; and yet the *White* seed is the diagnostic of the Opium Species. The Poison-Hemlock is distinguishable from Plants that greatly resemble it in shape, size &c by the *Non*-pithness, by the absence of Pith, in the stem. A negation cannot *be*, but yet it may *occasion*, evil: (ex. gr. the negation of oxygen in the atmosphere of a Room) or it may neither be, nor occasion, but yet may *shew*.—And if we pass from this Negation to the specific Positive, in combination with which it is realized—say, Romanism, for instance—& allowing it to be more than a signum merè significans,[1] it may still be only a *part of* the impediment, nay, it may derive its impedimental quality from the other ingredients, and be dangerous only in that particular Mixture: and yet, on the other hand, *in* that combination may *give* ~~an evil~~ a malignity to the others, or awaken or aggravate the same.—Now had the Question been stated, ~~under this~~ from the point of view, in which a distinct contemplation of the ~~Subject~~ Terms would have placed the Reasoner. viz.—What obstacle to plenary Electiveness and Eligibility is there in Non-protestant *Irishism*, under the existing state and circumstances of the British Empire collectively we should not, I think, have heard so much declamation about theological tenets, the importance or insignificance of the points in dispute between Catholics and Protestants, or *foreign* influences in consequence of the Bishop acknowleged as their Primas Ecclesiae[2] by the former happening to live in Italy. Yet even this over-threshed Straw, haec mera et vera *Calamitas* Oratorum,[3] the Blaze and Bluster of the moment, ~~is more endurable~~ were but the easy Suffering of the moment; but not without an abiding pain can I listen to a British Senate quarreling, like girls, about what the Roman Catholics will or will not wish, will ~~not~~ or will not try, to do, if the Bill passes—

[1] "A sign that merely signifies".

[2] "Primate of the Church".

[3] "This unadulterated and genuine *Calamity* of Orators".

MANUSCRIPT FRAGMENT ON THE ORIGIN OF THE PRIESTHOOD

PML MS MA 2033G

In C's hand; no watermark date; see above, p 53 and n 2.

On the origin of the Priesthood or priestly caste

The power of a Priesthood, how ⟨it is⟩ beneficial—In the first place, it could not exist but by a splitting of the Savage [?Conqueror/Conjurer] into three parts, the warrior, the physician, and the priest—2. it could not exist, without a certain appropriation of Property, and must of necessity interest a very powerful Class in encouraging more certain modes of production than those of Hunting, or Fishing—3.—Conjuring abstracted or refined, the Priesthood must support their influence by external order & splendor which could not but forward arts, & the division of Labor—the introduction of abstract ideas and general terms—

4 the most important fact, that a Priesthood forming a separate Class provides a great bulwark against the Despotism of a military Chief or Aristocracy—Hence Rome fell at once from corrupt Republicanism into mere Despotism—but Christianity came—and its prodigious effect in checking & counterbalancing the Imperial Power, & afterwards in rendering it less revolutionary, on the side of the Soldiers at least, is admitted by Gibbon himself—and his History swarms with instances & proofs.—It is even now felt as a blessing in Turkey—and what a blessing—the dark ages, during the feudal Polyarchy, you know still better or at least by a greater number of apt instances than I.—Whatever checks the Government of brute force must *indirectly* protect the people/ but it ~~was~~ is the perpetual Interest of a powerful Priesthood to protect the People directly, at least against all others but themselves. 5. It would be difficult to imagine any other repository of Experience in a people or numerous Tribe emerging from ~~Barb~~ Savagery into Barbarism, & so on into civilization, than a Priesthood—but whatever preserves must accumulate, & whatever accumulates experience must increase reflection, invention &c—

6. We should not be too much scared by the bloody rites of the Mexican Superstition/ These could not have been introduced but in a Tribe of bloody Customs—& in all probability, substituted decimation for massacre—Nor should we be misled by the History of the Grecian Republics, the rise and existence of which we may fairly deem in many respects a splendid anomaly—deriving the advantages of a Priesthood from Egypt & the East.

7. The maintenance of a large Body of Priests distinct from that of the military Chiefs could not exist without regulations that must arrange & so form *Laws* for Property in general—nor could the ceremonial Laws exist without extending to a general tho' perhaps imperfect Code of criminal Law.

I have said, that the [?Conqueror/Conjurer] must split himself into the Warrior, Physician, Priest—It may be objected that the Priests of Egypt were at once Priests, & Physicians—& those of Palestine, Priests, Physicians, & Lawyers—This is however merely nominal—the *Priest* was the Class name/ but it ~~was~~ could not but happen, & did happen, that a certain order of the Priests applied themselves more particularly to healing, others, to the Ceremonies, others to public Teaching—i.e. Legislation.—

APPENDIX E

A LETTER FROM COLERIDGE TO THE REV JAMES GILLMAN WRITTEN IN A COPY OF *CHURCH AND STATE*

A LETTER FROM COLERIDGE TO THE REV JAMES GILLMAN

(Written in the margins of a copy of *Church and State*—2nd ed 1830—150–61, now in the Beinecke Library, Yale University; not in *CL*)

My dear James! You cannot too often think of the great scheme or formula of all logical *Distribution* of our Conceptions, which I have entitled the Logical Pentad: viz. Prothesis, Thesis, Mesothesis, Antithesis, and Synthesis: or Identity, (~~or~~ *super*-relative Position, i.e. Praeposition); relative Position; relative Counter-position; Mid-position, or the *Indifference* of the two; and *Com*position.—Having mastered this, or rather the Idea, of which the Formula is the Exponent, you will then direct your attention to a—necessity? or defect? or (shall I say?) a necessary Defect, of Language, by which the Term which expresses the Prothesis, is repeated in a modified sense as the Term of the Thesis. Thus, for instance, Metaphysics in the prothetic sense, includes all the sciences, the evidence of which transcends, or is beyond, the evidence of the Senses. τα μετα τα φυσικα.[1] Now these are either Truths of the pure REASON, i.e. Ideas; or Truths of the pure UNDERSTANDING, i.e. Universal *Conceptions*, or *Laws* of necessary Thinking; or Truths of the Pure Sense, i.e. Theorems; or lastly, the first in application the latter, or Ideas manifested as POWERS. Now here the Thesis assumes the name of the Prothesis: and the term, Metaphysics, is now inclusive of all the other three; and now opposed, as Thesis, to Mathematics, or its Antithesis, and the Formula will be

a Metaphysics
b Metaphysics c Logic d Mathematics
e Dynamics.

a.= Prothesis: b. Thesis. c Mesothesis. d. Antithesis.
e. Synthesis. So again

a. State
b. State. c. the Press. d. the Church.
e. the Crown.

The State (i.e. the *Nation*—n.b. NOT the People) is the Prothesis: *including* ⟨both⟩ the *State* in its *thetic* sense, *and* the Church, the antithesis of the latter; while the Crown, or ideal King, is the *Syn*thesis of the *b.* and *d.*= State and Church; and the ideal Press the mesothesis. Doubtless, it would be better to adopt the word, NATION, as the Prothesis.

Nation
State Church—, but alas!

how few, even among the highly educated who must ever be the Few,

[1] "The [things that come] after the physical" or "metaphysics".

have learnt to distinguish the PEOPLE, which is a *real* living THING, from the Nation, which is an *actual* living IDEA! S. T. C.—So again—and *this*, my dear James! is a most momentous Instance and Illustration of the Principle—the double Sense of the term, *Real*, *Reality*. In the ~~prothetic~~ (~~pro or pre positive~~ transcendent application of the Word) God is the Supreme REALITY: and the Identity of the Real and Actual. In reference to him there is no distinction between the two words. They are absolutely synonimous: for God is well-defined by Boetius & afterwards by the School Divines, ens realissimum, Actus purissimus sine ullâ POTENTIALI-[TA]TE.[1] What ever is *real* in God is likewise ACTUAL and this is the true Idea of the Eternal: of whatever truly IS, and can truly BE, the simultaneous Act, Fruition, and *very* Being! But for the Non-absolute, even the Host of Heaven, Angels & Archangels—need I say then, for the Offspring of the Chaos under the impregnation of the Almighty LOVE, then first manifested in the form of MERCY—for the fallen Creature? for *Man*? For ~~us~~ all non-absolute, even Angels, the formula is

	Identity or Prothesis,	
Thesis	REAL.	Antithesis
ACTUAL		POTENTIAL—

I now *sit* and the power of *writing* is *actual*. The power of *talking*, or of *running*, is equally REAL, but it is at this moment not *actual*, but potential: non in *actu* nihilominus verò in *potentiâ*.[2]—But hence results for *us* creatures who understand thro' the *Senses*, another sense of the Words: and for *us* that, which manifests its existence to us thro' our *Senses*, we call REAL, in distinction from, & at length in opposition to, that which makes itself known to us in and by our Reason, as *ideal*! tho' the latter be *eminently*, at all events equally, *actual*; and therefore in the highest sense of the term, equally and often pre-eminently REAL. Attend to this treble sense of one and the same word. First Real = Actual, and Actual = Real. The ~~prothetic~~ transcendent, theosophical Sense. Secondly, the Prothetic or Logical Sense, in which the Real as the Prothesis *contains* the ACTUAL and the Potential, as its Thesis and Antithesis, or as its positive & negative Poles. Thirdly, the popular and metaphorical Sense, in which the Real is opposed to the Ideal, as the phaenomenal or sensuous to the spiritual or supersensuous. O how many plausible Sophisms will this enable you to detect & expose!—

[1] "Most real being, most pure Actuality without any POTENTIALITY'.

[2] "Not in *actuality*, but nevertheless in *potentiality*".

APPENDIX F

ANNOTATED COPIES OF *CHURCH AND STATE*

ANNOTATED COPIES

SECOND EDITION

1. The Rev James Gillman's copy. (Copy G in the textual notes.)
Beinecke Library, Yale University, C678,830b.

It contains James Gillman's autograph on the title-page, and the book-plate of Alexander William Gillman, who was his son and the grandson of Dr James Gillman, Coleridge's medical attendant and benefactor at Highgate. This copy contains in all about 1600 words of manuscript comment by the author in ink, together with a few pencil comments probably by the Rev James Gillman. Coleridge's marginalia include a long letter to the recipient, outlining the importance of the "pentad" in Coleridge's philosophical system and relating it to the argument of *Church and State*. The letter is printed as Appendix E, above, pp 233–4.

2. Jonathan Green's copy.
Berg Collection, NYPL.

Inscribed by the author: "To Jonathan Green Esqre respectfully from S. T. Coleridge 8 March 1831."

Jonathan Green (c 1788–1864), a surgeon, wrote several books on fumigating baths and on skin diseases.

This copy contains a note by the author on both sides of the front end-leaf. The note, which states that the essay presents the idea, not the history, of the Constitution and defines the essential argument, is reproduced in a footnote, above, p 31 n 2.

3. Lord Lyndhurst's copy.
Huntington Library, San Marino, Cal., HEHL 110737.

Inscribed by the author: "To Lord Lyndhurst &c &c this work is respectfully submitted by the Author, S. T. Coleridge."

This copy bears Lord Lyndhurst's book-plate, contains no annotations of the text by the author, but once included an ALS originally bound in the front (since removed). It is a note (HM 2175) to John Abraham Heraud, editor of the *Monthly Magazine*, from Henry Nelson Coleridge, dated 13 Jan (probably 1839). The note thanks Heraud for the "first Number" of the magazine and reminds him that HNC had "the Church & State & Lay Sermons" some time ago. This clearly refers to HNC's 1839 edition, but whoever bound the letter into Lyndhurst's copy must have thought it had some reference to the 2nd ed of 1830.

4. Wordsworth's copy. (Copy W in the textual notes.)
Houghton Library, Harvard University, EC8/C 6795/8300b.

Inscribed by the author: "W. Wordsworth from S. T. Coleridge 27 Decr 1830."

Title-page inscribed by the owner: "Wm Wordsworth".

This copy contains corrections and additions by Coleridge on several pages (14, 15, 25, 27). It also contains light pencil scorings (presumably by Wordsworth) and a note by him. He objects to Coleridge's statement that borough rights were not made conditional (see above, p 29 n 1).

INDEX

* = Coleridge's footnotes
n = editorial footnotes
a = textual notes
q = quoted
tr = translated

Textual misspellings, often Coleridge's peculiarities, are indicated within parentheses and quoted, following the correct spelling; e.g. Wycliffe ("Wickliffe").

All works appear under the author's name; anonymous works, newspapers, periodicals, etc are listed under titles.

Subentries are arranged alphabetically, sometimes in two parts, the first containing general references, the second particular works. For example, under Bacon, "on ideas", "and Plato" precede *Novum Organum*. Subentries, where possible, are given in Coleridge's own words.

Birth dates of persons now living are not given.